Discovering
ALEX RUSSELL

The Man and His Legacy

4 June 1892 – 22 November 1961

NEIL CRAFTER & JOHN GREEN

RYAN PUBLISHING

ii

Discovering Alex Russell

First published 2017 by Ryan Publishing
Second edition 2024
PO Box 7680, Melbourne, 3004
Victoria, Australia

Ph: 61 3 9505 6820

Email: books@ryanpub.com
Website: www.ryanpub.com

RYAN PUBLISHING

National Library of Australia Cataloguing-in-Publication entry

Creator: Crafter, Neil, author.

Title: Discovering Alex Russell : the man and his legacy / Neil
Crafter and John Green ; Graeme Ryan (editor) ; Luke Harris (designer).

ISBN: 9781876498689 (hardback)

ISBN: 9781876498665 (paperback)

Notes: Includes bibliographical references and index.

Subjects: Russell, Alex.

Golf course architects--Australia--Biography.

Athletes--Australia--Biography.

Australia--Officials and employees--Biography.

Other Creators/Contributors:

Crafter, Neil and Green, John - authors.

Ryan, Graeme, editor.

Harris, Luke, book designer.

Typesetting by Luke Harris, Working Type Studio, Victoria, Australia.
www.workingtype.com.au

DEDICATION

This book is dedicated to the memory of **Hedley Ham** (1939 – 2007), a long-standing member of the Yarra Yarra Golf Club, without whose invaluable research into the life and golf design works of Alex Russell this book would not have been possible.

Neil Crafter / John Green

Alex and Jess Russell c.1944, with Alex in his uniform as Chief Commissioner of the Australian Red Cross Field Force. Alex and Jess were married for 44 years

Contents

Foreword

Peter Thomson AO, CBE

An Australian Open Champion playing as an amateur, Mr Alex Russell was a country squire with a wool property at Beaufort on Victoria's Western Plains. He was one of Australia's best golfers during the time of the 1926 visit of the Scot, Dr Alister MacKenzie, who was contracted to the Royal Melbourne Golf Club to produce plans for a new course at Sandringham.

It is a matter of history that Russell joined in partnership with MacKenzie as the famous man left for California, alas never to return. Russell it was that put together the Yarra Yarra course on the sandbelt of Warrigal Road under the name of MacKenzie and Russell. Whatever he learned from the association certainly went into Yarra Yarra, principally the vast and many bunkers that MacKenzie made fashionable. His par 3 holes on that course are magnificently unique, the 11th and 15th being, even today, the most difficult propositions around. How the golfers of 1930 coped with them I can only wonder.

Fields further away beckoned his services, since if MacKenzie could not come, Russell was there nearer to represent him. Western Australia called and so did New Zealand. Russell took up the challenge.

The West was something else. Perth is an entire city built on sand. Beautiful white stuff that cries out for golf holes. Lake Karrinyup is nowadays more or less central, but when Russell visited Perth, it was rural. Why the property was chosen or adopted for a golf club is not clear, for apart from its white sand and beautiful birdlake, it is a rather unusual and hilly piece of land.

This made Russell's task more difficult. No Royal Melbourne flowing undulations here, but a number of steep climbs and descents to be dealt with. The clubhouse was sited for the best access and views, which meant a nice friendly descending first and tenth holes, but come the end of the nines, there had to be climbs. Nothing wrong with that indeed for stout hearts, but a far cry from Royal Melbourne and later, Paraparaumu Beach. Russell laid down the makings of a beautiful course of variety and strength, which over recent years has seen additional length and features added, until today, when Lake Karrinyup stands as one of Australia's most powerful championship courses when it is stretched, ever faithful to Russell's routing.

New Zealand dealt him a fine hand in the territory of Paraparaumu Beach, a coastal linksland then an hour's hilly drive north of the capital, Wellington. It was the dream of just a few enthusiasts who could spot a natural golf course when they saw one in the "rough". Paraparaumu was a dunesland of grey sand, full of ridges and hollows of no great magnitude, thus requiring an absolute minimum of earthworks to create an outstanding playing arena at small cost.

Russell trudged the acreage no doubt in the manner of MacKenzie himself, sniffing the air, whilst mentally envisaging the holes. He would start out from here, until he reached a high ridge, tucking away a par 4 to start with. Then there appeared before his eyes a marvellous par 3 nestled in a depression, requiring for practicality just a day or two of earthworks to lift the green to where it could be seen. Not all of it. No! This is a links and a touch of blindness is an ingredient.

Then he would have followed north with a longer hole, and then turned back adjacent before crossing the main "Apennines" through a small "Khyber Pass". There presented itself another mighty par 3, this one a little short shot to a flat top mound surrounded on three sides by deep, wet hollows.

And so it went. Until he got back to the clubhouse site with a quiver empty of stakes and a warm feeling that this course might be seen to be better than anything Australia had to offer! Well, if he thought that, he kept it to himself. He had done his best and he left it to the enthusiasts to build and complete. They in turn were faithful to his plan. Paraparaumu Beach Golf Club took several years to pull together, with a paucity of funds, so that some of the precious land had to be sold off to pay for things.

And there was only just enough left for comfort. A tiny practice area for one thing, and a hole that passed too close to the hook-side of a fence, beyond which was a high house that got fed up with golf balls breaking tiles. The house owners eventually won an injunction to stop the pounding, and Russell's wonderful 9th was no more.

Even so, in structure and content, Paraparaumu Beach grew to be respected widely, and stood at the top of New Zealand golf for the rest of the century. The modern golf ball has alas made the course almost pathetically short, and there is nowhere to expand. But if ever the authorities of the game bite the bullet and do something about ball aerodynamics, Paraparaumu will come back into its own, and Russell will be hailed again.

In a notable coincidence, two consecutive events on the Australasian Tour of the summer of 2001 – 2002 were played over courses that were the planning brainchild of Alex Russell. The Johnny Walker Classic that season was played at Lake Karrinyup while the venue for the Heineken Classic was Royal Melbourne's famed Composite Course. In the same season the New Zealand Open was held at Paraparaumu Beach and the Australian Ladies Open was decided at Yarra Yarra, a remarkable achievement for one architect.

Alex Russell was the first home-grown Australian golf architect to achieve fame. It is a pity he was not able to create more. Whether his work was really MacKenzie by another name is debatable. For mine, he was his own man and indeed who knows – MacKenzie may have picked up a thing or two from Alex Russell.

Melbourne, 2016

Introduction

It could be said that this book has three parents: the two authors and the late Hedley Ham of Yarra Yarra Golf Club, to whom this book is dedicated. As a golf course architect and past Australian Eisenhower Trophy representative, Neil Crafter became interested in Alex Russell as Australia's first home-grown amateur golf course architect and Dr MacKenzie's Australian partner, together with his interest in Russell's design strategies and the playability of his courses. John Green, a three-time club champion at Royal Melbourne, became involved in cataloguing the minutes of the club's Council meetings as a member of the History and Archives Committee, where he discovered how significant Alex Russell's contribution to the club had been, and how little this had been recognised. Hedley Ham had begun researching early club golf in Melbourne, particularly that of Yarra Yarra, where he was a member, and whose course had been designed by Russell. Hedley was working in an era prior to digitisation of newspapers where one can readily search a particular topic on the National Library of Australia's newspaper archive website and his research was undertaken by the tedious method of going through microfilms by hand at the State Library of Victoria. Hedley willingly shared his findings with many clubs, but his emphasis was naturally on Yarra Yarra, and in the process he amassed a large body of information about Alex Russell, which not long before his death in 2009, he kindly passed over to Neil Crafter.

From what the two authors already knew, and from the material collected by Hedley Ham, it became abundantly clear that Alex Russell was far more than a wealthy pastoralist who just played golf and designed a few golf courses. Here was an interesting and complex man, who had notable achievements in many fields.

In any biography there are always questions that have not, and clearly cannot be answered 125 years after the birth of the subject person. The authors have researched every question as carefully as they could, only to find they were often faced with more questions. After all, *'The beginning of knowledge is the realisation that one does not know.'*

While Alex Russell is central to this book, it also relates the story of a set of brothers and cousins from one Scottish family that emigrated to Australia nearly two centuries ago. They were to play a major role in the development of the eastern part of the large pastoral plains in Victoria, known as the Western District. These were men of humble beginnings, who became successful

and prosperous, were highly respected in the district and in Melbourne, and who made considerable contributions to the wider community. This is a part of Victorian history, and Alex Russell was an integral part of that history.

This is a story that both authors wished to tell, and as they researched deeper and deeper into Alex Russell's life, they assembled a large body of knowledge that built upon Hedley Ham's earlier work. Thus, it became a story that needed to be recorded and, in memory of Hedley and his research, the authors felt that this responsibility was theirs to ensure that the story was told.

Neil Crafter   /   John Green

A cartoon by Wells depicting Alex Russell as "The Sweeper," taking all before him in the 1924 Australian Championships. He commented on Russell's recent wearing of glasses, suggesting that all the leading players would be inspired to wear them.

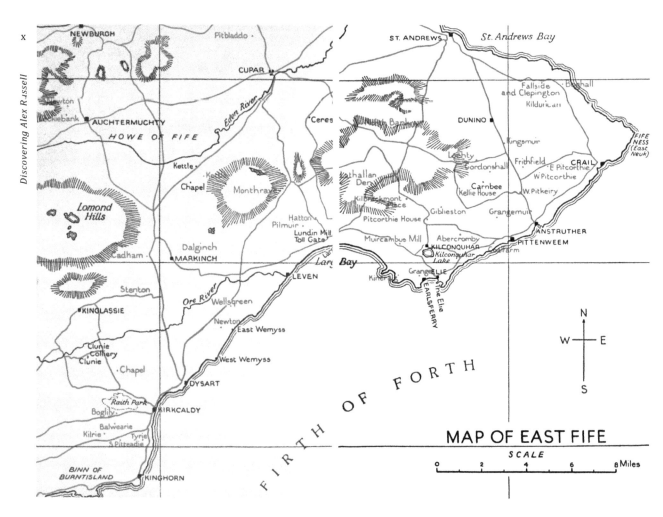

x

Map of the East Fife district of Scotland, showing locations (in red) that were relevant to the story of George Russell and his family, and from where Philip, George and Alexander Russell emigrated to Australia

FAMILY ORIGINS

In the 18th century the Russell family were Scottish farmers from East Fife. The years between 1690 and 1820 were the times of the Highland and Lowland clearances where many farmers lost their rights to farm the land they had worked for generations before. While the infamous Highland Clearances of the late 18th and early 19th centuries are better known, the Lowland Clearance, while much less brutal, involved tens of thousands of people, a much greater number than from the Highlands. These clearances forced people into the cities where there was over-crowding, with tuberculosis rife throughout Scotland at that time. While the industrial revolution provided employment, especially in the linen and cotton mills, for most the conditions and wages were poor. Consequently, many Scots chose to emigrate, taking their skills and culture to many diverse parts of the world, in particular to America, Canada, Australia and New Zealand. A decision to travel to Australia was a major one, given that the trip by sea took many months, with high risk of shipwreck and disease along the way.

'The Narrative of George Russell of Golf Hill' was published in 1935 and relates the recollections of George Russell as told to his son John. In it, the editor, P. L. Brown, noted that:

> "The Russells of Golf Hill and Mawallock, their cousins of Carngham and the Plains, the Simsons of Trawalla, and Mr William Lewis of Stoneleigh, all were descended from 'Old Gibliston'. Each came from one or other of certain farms on the north shore of the Firth of Forth, near Elie and Kirkcaldy: Banchory, Clunie, Balwearie, Boglily, and others. Their fathers were not prominent, and few held land by right of purchase or inheritance....Most of them rented the farms they occupied, conducted the labour themselves, and had neither claim nor wish to be ranked with the landed proprietors. Their education was simple but sufficient; their minds were vigorous and progressive; their religion was Presbyterian of a covenanting strain. They were often on terms of real friendship with the lairds of their neighbourhood. The class they represented seems to have vanished from Scotland."

Born in 1797, Philip Russell came out to Tasmania with Captain Patrick Wood and his family on the *'Castle Forbes'*, arriving in March 1822, and acting as Wood's secretary-tutor. He

subsequently took on the role of manager of properties for Captain Wood, whose son, John Dennistoun Wood, born in 1829, became a distinguished barrister and politician. In 1831, while Philip was managing 'Dennistoun', he was joined in Tasmania by his younger half-brother George, who had arrived in Hobart on the *'Drummore'*, after a nine-month long voyage from Leith.

PHILIP RUSSELL

After farming in Tasmania for five years, George was attracted by reports of the newly-opened settlement at Port Phillip on the mainland and went to investigate the area in 1836. Finding the land favourable, he left Tasmania for the new colony of Victoria in the latter part of that year. The Clyde Company of Glasgow was formed in October 1836 to establish a sheep station and George Russell was appointed manager in January 1837, with Captain Wood and Philip Russell as two of the original partners in the new company.

George Russell's house at 'Golf Hill' ca1890

Map of the Western District of Victoria showing the location of various properties with connections to the Russell family. Alexander Russell's 'Mawallok' lies at the top left, to the south-west of the town of Beaufort, with cousin Philip Russell's 'Carngham' to the south-east. George Russell's 'Golf Hill' is at the centre of the map, while Mt Elephant, the property later acquired by Jim Fairbairn, lies to the south of 'Mawallok.'

George Russell (left), his wife Euphemia Russell (middle), and their daughter Janet Russell (right)

The company prospered, and in 1841, George's younger brother Alexander sailed from Scotland, arriving in Hobart in August 1842. He then joined his brother, who by then was established at the property in the Leigh River Valley, some 25 miles (40 km) west of Geelong, which had been named 'Golf Hill', probably the first occasion that the word 'golf' had been used in a name in Australia. After working for some time with George, Alexander was appointed to another of the Clyde Company estates, 'Hopkins Hill'. He managed this property until 1847, when 'Mawallok', near Beaufort, was purchased from Thomas Steel, one of the two original owners of 'St. Enoch' estate, of which 'Mawallok' was half.

There is a family cemetery at 'Golf Hill' station containing seven Russell burials. Philip Russell died of tuberculosis, aged 47 years, at 'Golf Hill' in 1844 while visiting the property. He had earlier married Sophia Louisa Jennings but they had no children. William Russell died at sea in 1854 aged 59 years, while Alexander died in 1869, aged 54 years. The Reverend Robert Russell, who established the Presbyterian Church at Evandale, Tasmania, died in 1877 aged 69, and George Russell died in 1888 at 'Golf Hill,' aged 76. From an early date, George had become a respected magistrate in the district.

Philip Russell's cousin, James Russell, also emigrated from Scotland, first to Tasmania and then to the Western District. Perhaps the best known of these was another Philip Russell, a cousin of George and Alexander, and whose story was very

similar. Philip went on to become a Justice of the Peace and a Member of the Legislative Council.

Philip first went to Tasmania and then travelled to Melbourne in 1843 with his cousin, Robert Simpson, where at an insolvency auction they purchased the estate of 'Carngham', not far from 'Mawallok', at a very reasonable price, and which included a flock of sheep and lambs. This proved very profitable and Simpson returned to Britain for a year before returning with his younger brother and Philip's brother, Thomas, who was also to become prominent, becoming a Justice of the Peace and a Member of Parliament in the colony of Victoria.

Collectively, they bought further properties in the Western District. Eventually Philip Russell became the sole owner of 'Carngham', where he bred high quality merino sheep. In the merino section at the Ballarat Show, 'Carngham' wool was top or near top over many years, similar to the position of 'Mawallok' under Alexander's son, Philip, Alex Russell's father.

Back in Scotland, the family brothers who had remained at home, but had helped finance those going to the Colony of Victoria, were also reaping the benefits. From this it can be seen that the Russell clan, many of them by the name of Philip, were important pioneers in the development of the eastern part of the Western District.

It is against this background that the story of Alex Russell's life must be viewed.

Christian Names in the Russell Family

The giving of Christian names in the Russell family has long followed the Scottish tradition of the eldest son being named for the paternal grandfather and frequently the second son is given the name of the maternal grandfather. Thus there is Philip Russell, father of George and Alexander, the first immigrant from the Russell clan to Australia. The eldest sons of both George and Alexander were named Philip. Alexander's son Philip, in due course named his son Alex, pronounced 'Alec' with a hard c, and while he was certainly named for his grandfather Alexander, the name was simply reduced to Alex.

The pronunciation of Alex Russell's name was to prove of great difficulty for newspaper reporters and editors over the years with some writing his name correctly as it was spelt, while others spelt it as 'Alec' as it was pronounced. Others even spelt his name more phonetically as 'Alick' or even 'Aleck.' Many newspapers and magazines thought that his name was an abbreviation of Alexander so quite often his name was listed his name as 'Alex.' with a full stop. His only son was in turn named Philip, with his eldest son in turn named Alexander, and so the tradition has continued down through the Russell family.

MAWALLOK, VICTORIA

THE OLD MAWALLOK HOUSE

PART OF THE ORIGINAL HOMESTEAD

Above, map of the 'Mawallok' Estate from 1907 showing the various paddocks

Left, photographs from 1930 of the original 'Mawallok' homestead and old house from 1930

Alex Russell's Family Tree

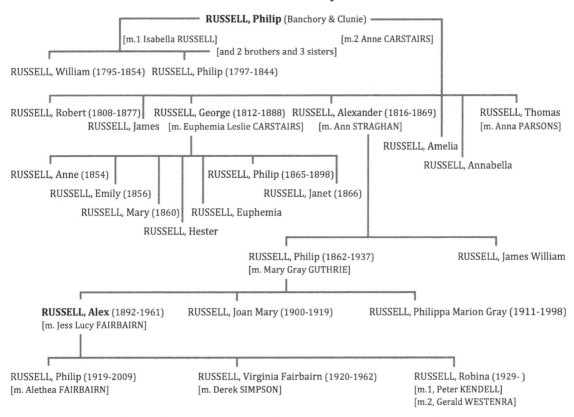

RUSSELL, Philip (Banchory & Clunie)

[m.1 Isabella RUSSELL]   [m.2 Anne CARSTAIRS]

[and 2 brothers and 3 sisters]

RUSSELL, William (1795-1854) RUSSELL, Philip (1797-1844)

RUSSELL, Robert (1808-1877) RUSSELL, George (1812-1888) RUSSELL, Alexander (1816-1869) RUSSELL, Thomas
RUSSELL, James [m. Euphemia Leslie CARSTAIRS] [m. Ann STRAGHAN] [m. Anna PARSONS]

RUSSELL, Amelia

RUSSELL, Annabella

RUSSELL, Anne (1854)

RUSSELL, Emily (1856)

RUSSELL, Mary (1860)   RUSSELL, Euphemia

RUSSELL, Philip (1865-1898)

RUSSELL, Janet (1866)

RUSSELL, Hester

RUSSELL, Philip (1862-1937)   RUSSELL, James William
[m. Mary Gray GUTHRIE]

RUSSELL, Alex (1892-1961)   RUSSELL, Joan Mary (1900-1919)   RUSSELL, Philippa Marion Gray (1911-1998)
[m. Jess Lucy FAIRBAIRN]

RUSSELL, Philip (1919-2009)   RUSSELL, Virginia Fairbairn (1920-1962)   RUSSELL, Robina (1929-)
[m. Alethea FAIRBAIRN]   [m. Derek SIMPSON]   [m.1, Peter KENDELL]
[m.2, Gerald WESTENRA]

Alex Russell's parents Philip Russell (left) and Mary 'Cissie' Russell (centre)
with their good friends Fred Fairbairn (right) and his wife Rhoda (seated).
The Fairbairns were the parents of Alex's best friend 'Bo' and his wife-to-be, Jess.

Chapter 2

EARLY LIFE

Alex Russell, the first child of Philip Russell and Mary Gray Guthrie, was born in Geelong on 4 June 1892. He was simply christened 'Alex' a shortened form of his grandfather's name, and unusually, was not given a middle name.

Philip Russell 1866 – 1937

Alex's father Philip Russell was born on 3 December 1866 in Geelong and attended Geelong Grammar School around 1879 before continuing his schooling in England. As well as owning the family property 'Mawallok' in Victoria's Western District that he had inherited from his father Alexander who had died when he was only three, Philip Russell purchased Osborne House in 1888. This was a large house and property in West Geelong overlooking Corio Bay and Limeburners Lagoon that had been built in 1858 by Robert Muirhead, a local squatter.

Philip suffered from consumption and was told by his doctor to live by the sea, and so Osborne House must have seemed like an ideal place to live. The young Alex Russell attended school in Geelong, and later wrote of his childhood experiences living at Osborne House, which was the family's main residence during the early years of his childhood in Australia. In 1892, Philip was one of the founding members of the Geelong Golf Club and later joined the Royal Melbourne Golf Club. While he was a keen and competent golfer, horses were his lifelong passion.

A good polo player, and a *"brilliant horseman"* according to his grandson, Philip Russell was considered the mainstay of the Geelong Polo Club, while his love of horses led him to become involved in importing, breeding and racing his own horses. He was first elected onto the committee of the Victoria Racing Club in 1896 before resigning in 1903 when he left for Britain. He was once more elected to the committee following his return from France and England in 1917, serving until 1937. In all he served some 27 years on the VRC Committee and it was later noted that *"he did much for the benefit and prestige of Victorian racing."*

Philip was also a keen cricketer and put together an Osborne House team of local players, known as 'The Nondescripts', that toured the Western District of Victoria as well as Tasmania to play matches against a range of opposition teams. In the Osborne House grounds was a cricket ground with a racetrack around its perimeter, a croquet lawn, a polo field and a private

Alex Russell as a young baby (top right) and his father Philip, a skilled horseman (right)

zoo with animals and birds, including pheasants. He erected stables and a coach-house in 1890 and in 1894 extended the house, adding a billiard room, conservatory, bedrooms, bathrooms, and offices, all with hot water, along with a dairy. He also grazed his own specially selected herd of Jersey dairy cows at Osborne, which unfortunately he was forced to sell in 1903 when he had to move to Britain for his health, entering a number of sanitariums in England and Scotland. The cows sold at an average price of £13, with one prize-winning cow realising the princely sum of £38.

Philip wrote back to a friend in Geelong in late 1903 to say that he had been sojourning near Balmoral for the benefit of his health, and that he had *"his first experience of fishing in a Scottish stream. It seems that Mr Russell landed two salmon – one weighing 25lb. and the other 6lb. He played with the former for 50 minutes, and Mr Russell added "That is not bad for a first go. I feel none the worse for it."'* The Russell family later took houses in other parts of Scotland, enabling Alex to attend Trinity College in Glenalmond, near Perth.

Philip served in France during World War I in a voluntary capacity in an ambulance that he had purchased and donated to the privately funded Lady Dudley Hospital that had been established in France on the golf course at Wimereux. Lady Dudley was the wife of the former Governor-General of Australia, William Ward, the 2nd Earl of Dudley. Philip, having studied to be a veterinarian in Scotland, would have been well-qualified as a first aid attendant, and he also employed a nurse to accompany him in the vehicle. It was reported that *"as soon as the war broke out Mr Russell had taken 'Scotch leave', and 'mizzled off' to the front.....driving a motor ambulance that he had donated himself."* His Peugeot vehicle was brought back to Australia after the war and later became the farm truck and fire truck at 'Mawallok' and was still in use around the property when Philip's great grandson William Keddell was a child, recalling that it was kept in the stables.

Philip was held in high esteem by his grandchildren, who called him 'Big Gran', with his grandson Philip noting that his grandfather *"was an animal lover who loved horses, raced horses and taught me to ride around the mulberry paddock. He was extraordinary with children and with dogs."*

Philip had some significant successes as a racehorse owner, breeder and trainer, winning the 1896 Australian Cup with Idolator and the 1917 event with Harriet Graham, while Maid of the Mist and Newberry were both successful for him in numerous races. In 1916, following his return from France to England, he purchased a number of young horses there, all fillies, and had them sent out to Australia and his stud at 'Mawallok'. The week prior to his death, Philip had just paid the highest price for a yearling at the Melbourne sales.

Philip died in Melbourne on 20 April 1937, leaving an estate of £180,337. He left his jewelry, books and other personal effects to his daughter Philippa, along with the right to select whatever horses she wanted from his stables. He gave some bequests to the Salvation Army and a Presbyterian Hospital, along with a bequest to Richard O'Neill, his former property manager at 'Mawallok'. To his son Alex he left two-thirds of his estate and the income from the remaining one-third to Philippa. Alex had taken over the running of 'Mawallok' from his father in 1932. His funeral was held the day after his death and he was buried in the Brighton Cemetery.

Philip was described in a death notice as:

"A racehorse owner of the best type. A modest bettor, he raced horses solely for his love of the sport, and at various times first-class performers carried his colours. For many years Mr Russell had been subject to heart attacks. He recently resigned from the Committee of the Victoria Racing Club owing to ill-health. Mr Russell was a member of the Russell family which owned the Carngham estate near Beaufort, and on his Mawallok estate he established a select stud. Major Alex Russell (son) and Miss Mary Russell (daughter) [note, this should be Philippa not Mary] survive Mr Philip Russell."

MAWALLOK, VICTORIA

THOROUGHBRED MARES AND FOALS

Philip Russell established a thoroughbred stud on his 'Mawallok' property

Mary Gray Russell nee Guthrie (1865 – 1928)

Alex's mother Mary was known as 'Cissie', and like Philip, was also of Scottish descent. She was born on 29 August 1865, the eldest of three sisters and she had three brothers. Her father Thomas Guthrie had been born in Berwickshire in 1833 and died in Melbourne in October 1928, living to the ripe old age of 95. 'Cissie' and Philip were married in 1888 at St George's Church in Geelong. Like her husband, 'Cissie' took up golf and was an associate member at both the Geelong and Royal Melbourne clubs, taking on the role as the inaugural ladies president at Geelong. Her father outlived his eldest daughter as 'Cissie' passed away nine months before him at the age of 62 on 31 January 1928 in Melbourne. Alex's daughter Robina recalls that, *"My grandmother Cissie was dead before I was born. After Dibsies' birth she never really recovered,"* with 'Dibsie' being the family's pet name for Alex's sister Philippa. Following her death in 1928 it was noted in 'The Argus' that 'Cissie' Russell had been *"an enthusiastic supporter of the Beaufort Girl Guides and the Women's Institute,"* and that upon her death she had held the role of District Commissioner for the Girl Guides.

Alex had two younger sisters, Joan and Philippa.

Joan Mary Russell (1896 – 1919)

Joan was born on 23 August 1896, some four years after her elder brother Alex. At the age of 12 she wrote to 'Patience' of 'The Australasian' newspaper's children's page describing her pets, three lambs and a dog called 'Tinkerbell'. She also had a pony, *"he is only a yard high. I used to ride him; but I am too big for him now, and he is very old."* It is very likely the pony was the same Shetland pony named 'Puddy' that Alex used to ride as a child. In October 1909 she wrote again to 'Patience', this time describing her family's holiday in Switzerland:

> *"From "Joan Russell" (Mawallok, Beaufort) – My dear 'Patience,' – I am going to tell you what I remember about my visit to Switzerland. I think St Moritz is one of the nicest places to spend the winter at; it is so pretty to see all the snow on the ground. I am very fond of tobogganing, but I cannot skate at all. I think it must be very difficult. The St Bernard dogs are very wonderful; how they go out and find people who have got lost in snowdrifts. The Swiss peasants dress very picturesquely, don't you think so 'Patience.' One thing that I noticed was the peculiar harness on the horses, and such a lot of bells, that it sounds very like the hansom cabs in London. I must stop now."*

Joan Russell (left) and with her elder brother Alex (below)

The following year Joan wrote a short story entitled "Autobiography of a Horse" and submitted it to 'The Australasian' and this was printed in their 5 February 1910 edition. Clearly horses were one of her main passions, just like her father. In 1918 Joan had her tonsils removed in a private hospital in Melbourne, which was considered newsworthy by one of the Melbourne papers that followed the social activities of the well-to-do. Joan and her mother were in the middle of a twelve-week stay in a flat at Toorak at the time.

In June 1919 Joan was struck down with influenza and she sadly passed away at South Yarra on 8 June at the young age of 22 due to complications from the disease. 'Table Talk' reported that:

> *"One of the most pathetic things that has happened through the influenza epidemic is the sad death of Mr and Mrs Philip Russell's young daughter, Joan. Few deaths have aroused more sympathy; she was one of the unaffected, charming girls who win affection everywhere. To her mother the blow will be overwhelming, for they were such close companions. While Mr Russell was away in England it was beautiful to see them together through the sad war days. Now, just as brighter times are here, and Mrs Russell was planning dances and other functions – to give her some of the girlish pleasures she had missed through the war – she was stricken down suddenly with the influenza, and from the first there was little hope, as her heart was so seriously affected. Only as recently as boatrace night Miss Russell was one of a bright young party in a box with her chum, Miss Jean Fairbairn."*

Another newspaper noted that she had contracted influenza after the Vice-Regal dance and died eight days later. It commented that she *"was only 22 and one of the handsomest girls in moneyed circles."* Alex was not long back from England himself with his new bride Jess following the trauma of his own service in the war, and the loss of his sister so soon after his return must have seemed like a cruel blow.

Philippa Marion Gray Russell (1911 – 1998)

Philippa was born on 23 October 1911, some 15 years after Joan, and her mother was 45 when she was born. She was known as 'Dibsie' to the family, and little is known of her life apart from the fact that she was a spinster and bred dogs. In 1938 she travelled to Canada and the United States, and lived for a number of years at Woodend in Victoria, before moving to Gisborne. When her father Philip passed away in 1937, two-thirds of his substantial estate totalling some £180,000 was left to Alex and one-third to Philippa. In 1953 she was one of 2,300 Victorians who received the Queen's Coronation Medal, which was awarded at the discretion of the Victorian Government. When she passed away on 18 April 1998, aged 86, she was living in the Lion's Club Hostel at Sunbury, and prior to that she had been living at Trentham.

Joan Russell, in hat, with her best friend Jean Fairbairn, the younger sister of 'Bo' and Jess

Alex Russell's Geelong Childhood

In his later years, Alex commenced to record reminiscences about his life with a working title of *"From 6 – 60,"* which suggested that he had begun writing it when he had turned 60 in 1952. Unfortunately, he did not progress very far, only completing some 13 handwritten note pages. When he started on this project, he would already have suffered some of the strokes that afflicted him in his later years. His characteristic handwriting at times makes deciphering a challenge, and there are spelling mistakes, neither of which equate with the scholarly man of earlier times. The impression gained is of a man trying to leave a record of his life before it was too late and putting his recollections down on paper to perhaps edit later. Whilst it would have been a great historical insight into his life had he been able to progress further, what he did write gives a wonderful glimpse into his childhood, without which there would have otherwise been no record.

Alex described Osborne House, overlooking Corio Bay, which now has a Heritage Listing, as a wonderful place for children. There was a large overgrown garden in which to play that spread over the cliff down to the waters of the bay, stables with a hay-loft above them and a private zoo that was out-of-bounds except when accompanied by his father. Clearly this was not the home of an average child in Victoria in the late 19th century, but that of the landed gentry. As already mentioned, there was also a polo ground as his father was a skilled horseman, and a cricket ground with a racetrack around it. The house contained a billiard table, although it is unknown at what age Alex was allowed to begin playing on it. By the time he reached Cambridge University he had become a very accomplished billiards player, an interest he kept his entire life.

Alex also described a time at his school, St Salvator's in Geelong, when his father came to collect him in a steam motor-car that he was trialling, and took him for a run. He recalled, *"There was a fair breeze blowing and the fire went out every cross street we came to & was lit again with a very satisfactory bang. Speed between streets about 6mph, including stops about 2mph, but it had rubber tyres and they looked enormous."*

To the young Alex, his father always seemed busy with his horses and was a strict disciplinarian who used his riding whip to punish misdoings. So Alex and his boyhood friend Gordon 'Bo' Fairbairn, the son of Russell family friends Fred and Rhoda Fairbairn, and who later became his brother-in-law, did their best to keep out of his way. Alex remembered his mother as cool, calm and gracious. The underlying impression is that Alex did not receive a great deal of warmth from either of his parents,

A young Alex Russell in knickerbockers, bow tie and jaunty cap

although the relationship was certainly cordial at the start of World War I when they were all in London together.

Alex, unlike his father, was not a horseman, although he ended up having a great deal to do with horses while serving in France and Belgium with the Royal Garrison Artillery during World War I. He had a Shetland pony at Osborne, a breed well-known for sometimes being capricious. 'Puddy', as the pony was called, would swipe Alex off on a branch, or manage to tip him and his friends out of the cart in some way or another. He found it was impossible to turn Puddy's head. This experience, combined with his father's determination to see him ride, and

possibly coupled with some jealousy over the amount of his father's time spent with his horses, left the young boy with a strong dislike of the animals.

He described himself as a larrikin and the group of his early friends, mostly sons of his father's friends living in the area, as *"a bunch of hooligans"*. This was probably an overstatement, which people looking back at their childhood, are perhaps apt to make. Philip Russell, with his quick temper, believed in physical punishment for misdeeds, making frequent use of his riding whip. When Alex was caught in the wrong, punishment did not vary, it was not delayed, there was no lecturing. It

The first two pages of Alex Russell's reminiscences "From 6 to 60" (above) that he began writing around 1952

Osborne House on the shores of Corio Bay in Geelong was Alex Russell's childhood home. The property had nearly one mile of frontage to the bay and featured a cricket ground, polo field, racetrack, stables and a private zoo

Extract from a 1909 map of Geelong showing the location of Osborne House (1) on the shores of Corio Bay. It was in close proximity to the links of the Geelong Golf Club (2) where the Russells and Fairbairns were members

certainly hurt, but was forgotten reasonably quickly by both sides. He wrote of three particular chastisements. The first was for Alex and 'Bo' being up on the glass roof over the billiard table at Osborne, one of the apples of his father's eye. The second was when his father discovered two young "pathfinders" standing horrified with "shanghais" in their hands and the body of a very rare pheasant lying dead on top of a nest of half-incubated chicks. Philip had hurried back from town, especially to see how the hen and family were getting on. Alex later recounted that although the stalking had been well done and the shot a magnificent one, these commendable aspects were not appreciated by his father at the time. The third episode again related to the firing of missiles, providing an insight into the child he was and the man he was to become:

"We had found an old clay pigeon trap in the loft. A very old trap which fired glass balls. Of course, we soon ran out of these, but by mounting the catapult on the castle towers – it's on the edge of the cliff – and by screwing it up to the hilt we could throw a faired sized stone well out into the bay and we got quite good at it.

Imagine our delight one evening to find a lone fisherman standing up going slowly past just under the cliff within range.

We had just fired a few practice shots, the range was perfect and we couldn't miss. We didn't miss! We put a shot just past the rower's ear and neatly through the bottom of the boat.

We listened to the words of the fisherman and the most enfeabling (sic) argument that went on. We learned a lot. We got our hiding in front of the fisherman but I always felt that deep admiration for a superb bit of shooting softened the blow."

The family left Osborne House in early 1903, so Alex would likely have been about 10 years of age at the time of the boat escapade. The house is set some distance back from the clifftop and so a shot from the roof to reach a boat out on the bay would have required a carry of at least 120 yards (110 metres) or more. Perhaps with this talent for judging projectile trajectories, Alex was a youth destined to become an artillery officer and a skilled golfer.

View of Osborne House (right) showing the glass skylight roof over the Billiard Room. Young Alex and 'Bo' Fairbairn were caught climbing on this roof by Philip Russell and duly suffered the consequences

The Lawn

The Stables.

Osborne House.

Views of Osborne House (above) that appeared in 'The Leader' newspaper on 3rd June 1899. The lawn is shown being mown at top left, possibly by Philip Russell, while the photograph of the stables shows two pony traps, with the smaller of the pair being drawn by the Shetland pony 'Puddy' and almost certainly Alex driving it with two young passengers. The bottom image shows a gardener at work with a young girl walking with what appears to be a cockatoo.

England and Scotland

When Philip Russell became very ill with tuberculosis, the family moved to Scotland in early 1903 so Philip could recover in a sanitarium. According to Alex, this was due to his father trying to ride polo ponies about a stone lighter than was reasonable. Philip later sold Osborne House in 1905 to the State of Victoria for £17,000. Alethea Russell, Alex's daughter-in-law, suggested that an earlier bout with tuberculosis was the reason Philip had purchased Osborne House in the first instance, so perhaps this was a re-occurrence of an earlier battle with the disease.

Alex recalled that *"the family wandered in England and Scotland for some years,"* and when Philip's health improved a little, he was allowed visits with the family and they eventually took a house in Aberdeenshire where there was *"fishing and rough shooting"*. In a letter from Philip to a friend in Geelong in late 1903, the family was described as *"sojourning near Balmoral ....for the benefit of his health. Mr Russell writes in a hopeful strain, and it will be learned with much satisfaction that he is progressing satisfactorily. In the letter, Mr Russell describes his first experience in fishing for salmon in a Scottish stream."* Here Alex *"naturally ran wild"* and was put in care of a 'ghillie', a Scottish term for a fishing and hunting attendant, by the name of Bathgate. Brief though it must have been, this was likely an important relationship in the life of the young Alex Russell.

Bathgate taught him to fish and to shoot. Alex had already learnt to fish at Geelong, so fishing in this context was undoubtedly fly-fishing. Bathgate also taught him less orthodox methods, and with the levels of the Don River low that year, these were far more productive. Alex claimed by the end of summer to be about as good a poacher as Bathgate. *"We took some salmon out of the pools by placing a triangle over their back, and had a lot more fish than anyone else did with orthodox methods and best of all we did not get caught."* The Don was also full of freshwater pearl mussels, of which about one in fifty would contain a small pink pearl, and one in a hundred a larger one. Alex found it easy to collect these using a tin with a glass base to look into the clear water from the boat, and then either lean over the side or wade in to collect them. He collected 'thousands' of shells and initially opened them, before simply leaving them to open as they rotted. This practice was *"not popular at home"*, Alex's use of the word 'home' is interesting in this context. He was able to exchange his pearls for £8 in Aberdeen, the equivalent of some £880 today, and a very significant sum in those days for a young lad.

Bathgate also took Alex around the woods and taught him to shoot, and this likely included the art of stalking. When shooting with elders, Alex found there was far too much

anxiety about what to do and what not to do, what to shoot and what not to shoot, while fishing with Bathgate was much more fun and his mistakes far less public. Alex had certainly learnt how to hold a gun and *"not to blow your neighbours ear off"*. He became an accomplished shot in later life, as was his father, and later, his own son.

The family tree lists a much earlier Philip Russell, Alex's great-grandfather, as being from the farms of Clunie Mains and Banchory in East Fife. While the Banchory Farm shares its name with the town of Banchory which lies on the Don River only 18 miles west of Aberdeen, the two locations are quite different. One report in the 'Geelong Advertiser' in August 1904 noted that Philip Russell was residing at Nordrach-on-Dee, which was a specialist tuberculosis sanitarium located near Banchory, and that he was *"gradually building up his health."*

His recollections stop at this point and the strong impression gained is that Bathgate, while aware of his position, was teaching young Alex, then aged around twelve to fourteen, the skills he would have taught his own son. Alex in turn found in Bathgate someone who was interested in teaching him, one he could relate to as a father figure, and he consequently matured.

A group of Scottish ghillies (top right) and the Banchory Sanitarium (right) where Philip Russell convalesced in 1904

Education

Osborne House, Geelong (1898 – 1900)

Alex Russell's schooling, together with his friend 'Bo' Fairbairn, began with a governess named Dorothea when he was aged six. He became a pupil at St Salvator's Preparatory School in 1900, so his time under Dorothea's charge would probably have been around two years. Alex looked back on this time with pleasure but also an element of reproach for the practical jokes they used to play on Dorothea who arrived in the mornings on her bicycle to teach them. Dorothea seemed an attractive and charming young lady, but Alex and 'Bo' were insensitive to this, and he later wrote that if they had been a few years older they would have attempted instead to have her stay longer rather than the reverse.

St Salvator's Preparatory School, Geelong (1900 – 1902)

St Salvator's Preparatory School in Geelong was opened in 1900 by Peter Corsar Anderson, who had been teaching for the four previous years at the nearby Geelong Grammar School. His new school was located on the corner of Pakington and Austin Streets in Newtown, Geelong, where he also lived with his wife Agnes. Anderson was born in Forfarshire in Scotland in 1871, had studied theology at Madras College, St Andrews University and chose the name of the university chapel there for his new school in Geelong. He was ordained a Presbyterian Minister but never took up an appointment because of an illness. An outstanding golfer, winning the British Amateur Championship in 1893 at Prestwick, Anderson held the record score for the Old Course at St Andrews for six months.

In 1896, he undertook a recuperative trip to Australia to visit his brother Mark in Albany, Western Australia, and ended up staying in Australia, eventually settling in Victoria for a period before returning to Western Australia. Whilst in Victoria, Anderson was a member of both the Royal Melbourne and Geelong golf clubs, with the latter his primary club. In 1904, Anderson was appointed Headmaster of Scotch College in Perth, a position he would hold for 41 years before retiring at the age of 75, a highly respected man and educator.

Alex did not write much of his time at St Salvator's, only that Anderson would take the boys for a walk in Queens Park, often taking a golf club with him. Alex later described Anderson's swing as being like poetry, and perhaps "P.C." introduced the young Alex to the game that would become his lifelong passion.

The new school's first annual sports meeting and prize distribution was held at Osborne House on Saturday 21 December 1901, and the *"cricket ground, which was kindly lent for the occasion*

ST. SALVATOR'S, GEELONG, 1902.—P. C. Anderson (principal), Stan Armytage, Bo Fairbairn, Clive Newman, F. Lascelles, Eric Russell. Sitting: N. L. Campbell, Esmie Govett, Rex Bell, Les. Hodges, Erskine Collins, Lawrence Shaw, Alex. Russell. Ten of the above have gone to the front.

A 1915 newspaper clipping (top) of the 1902 class at P.C. Anderson's St Salvator's School in Geelong that noted that ten of the students were serving at the front. Anderson posing with his trophy for the 1893 British Amateur Championship (right).

P.C. Anderson (seated) at the famous Ginger Beer stall on the 4th hole at St Andrews run by Old Daw Anderson. Note P.C.'s initials stencilled on his golf bag.

by Mr Philip Russell, presented quite a gay appearance, and there was a full muster of parents and friends." Philip Russell acted as the starter, while Fred Fairbairn was one of the judges. Alex Russell was listed as one of the boys who received a prize. St Salvator's Preparatory School's second annual sports meeting was held in December 1902, this time at Kardinia Park in Geelong. It was declared that the meeting had a real Western District ring to it, with Philip Russell and Fred Fairbairn acting as two of the judges. 'Bo' Fairbairn, who also attended the school with his friend Alex, won the junior championship, while Alex was recorded as one of the successful competitors who were awarded their prizes by the Mayoress of Geelong.

In August 1903, 'The Australasian' reported that P.C. Anderson had taken to playing golf *"with his boys at Queen's-park, Geelong. He is of course, careful not to let it interfere either with their cricket or lessons,"* so they generally played on a Saturday, and had recently competed for prizes. While Alex Russell was not mentioned by name, it is quite possible that both Alex and 'Bo' Fairbairn had played golf in Queen's Park under Anderson's tutelage before leaving the school in 1902. After Anderson left for Perth, the schoolhouse was taken over by Miss Meta Moore who opened the Woomargama Ladies' School.

Hindhead, Surrey, England (1903 – 1904)

Alex's memories of his schooling in Hindhead are brief, and the actual school he attended is not known. He later recalled:

> *"I remember a prep school near Hindhead where there was a great upset because it was rumoured that the missing waiter from the local hotel had been thrown down the well. It certainly did smell very funny. We played soccer. It seemed to rain a lot. There seems (sic) to be a lot of matrons and looker afters about. I was too young to realise if it was a nice school or not."*

A studio portrait of Alex taken in London c.1904 when he was about 12 years of age

18 **Trinity College, Glenalmond, Perthshire, Scotland**
(1905 – 1907)

In May 1905, Alex Russell was enrolled at Trinity College, Glenalmond, situated some 8 miles (13 km) west of Perth, commencing in Junior School Form III. By November that year he had been promoted to a higher class based on merit not age. In October 1906, he won the Science Prize for the Middle School and had work in Science and Geography "sent up" to the Warden/Headmaster. He took second place in a swimming race held in the Almond River and played in the Under 14 Cricket Team. The College had its own seven-hole golf course laid out by one of the masters, Mr Goodacre, who often took pupils to play as guests at clubs around Perthshire and St Andrews. The Headmaster, Canon Hyslop, was also a keen golfer. While there is no record of young Alex playing golf at Glenalmond, there is a photograph of two Trinity schoolboy golfers on a green taken at the course some two years before Alex arrived, with the young golfers' putting stances near identical to the one used by Alex Russell in his golfing career.

Alex also had an ongoing love affair with St Andrews and played there whenever he visited Great Britain, and later in 1951, became one of the few Australians elected as a member of the Royal and Ancient Golf Club. In the absence of evidence to the contrary, it is a reasonable assumption that Glenalmond is where Alex Russell first learnt to play golf, although he may have had some tuition from P.C. Anderson in Geelong a few years earlier. He had certainly begun to play some time before leaving Australia for Cambridge in 1912, being listed in the Royal Melbourne Golf Club's 1915 Annual Report as a member on active service. His handicap had to be 2 or better to be a member at that age.

During the time Alex was being schooled at Glenalmond, his family rented an estate near the village of Methven, not far from the school. A newspaper report in 'The Australasian' of 6 January 1906 on Australians Abroad noted that, *"Mr and Mrs Philip Russell spent a thoroughly enjoyable summer, shooting and fishing on the estate which they rented in Perthshire where they intend to remain through the winter. They have done a good deal of motoring in the neighbourhood of Methven, which is an ideal part of the country for the purpose. Many Australian friends have been their visitors...."* Alex Russell left Trinity College in the middle of 1907. It was later renamed Glenalmond College.

TRINITY COLLEGE, GLENALMOND, PERTHSHIRE.

Trinity College at Glenalmond (top) and college students (above) playing golf on the college golf course c.1903

Glenalmond College

Alex Russell's cap (above) from the Officer Training Corps (OTC) at Trinity College, showing the Double Eagle cap badge (right) and the signed label inside (left)

Geelong Grammar School, Geelong (1908-1911)

The Russell family returned to Australia in late December 1907 and Alex, like his father before him, commenced the next school year at Geelong Grammar School at the age of 15 years and 8 months. On 14 February 1908, Alex joined the Cadet Corps and by 1911 he had risen to the rank of Sergeant. Only three students were Lieutenants, one being Charles F. Drought, the School Captain.

In 1908 Russell is mentioned in the school magazine '*Corio – Geelong Grammar School Quarterly*' as having made 29 runs in a cricket match against Geelong College while playing in the Second XI. For the next three years Russell played for the First XI. In 1909 he was third in the batting averages with a highest score of 70 and fifth in the bowling averages. In 1910, it appears that he played only four matches, missing several because of illness. He was ninth in the batting averages and fifth in the bowling, with his best bowling figures being 5 for 71 against Geelong College.

In 1911, he was appointed Vice-Captain to Charles Drought, and when Drought became ineligible because of age, Russell assumed the role as First XI Captain. In the magazine there is a comment about the poor fielding by the cricket team. Both Drought and Russell, however, are noted for their efforts and enthusiasm in trying to inspire the team in this area. It is perhaps not surprising that Alex Russell was awarded the Cuthbertson Prize for Fielding. In the Associated Public School matches, Russell was third in the school's batting averages and fifth in the bowling figures. In the practice matches at the end of the year, Russell made a score of 153, out of a total of nine for 313. In another practice match against South Geelong he took 3 wickets for 41.

Russell's sporting successes were not only in cricket. In 1910, Russell played in the Second XVIII Australian Rules football team, gaining mentions amongst the best players, and in 1911, he gained selection in the First XVIII. He also represented the school in its Shooting Team and placed third in the school's shooting championship, after losing a shoot-out for second place. In tennis he had reached the final with decisive wins but was forced to give a walk-over, possibly because of illness. In the handicap event, he and two others were given the mark of "owe 30", a big start to concede in each game and he was knocked-out in the first round of the singles, but won the handicap doubles. In athletics, he finished third in the shot-putt, while in the 1909 swimming carnival he finished third in the 100 yards handicap off 7 seconds.

Alex Russell's contribution to his school was, however, far more than just as a sportsman. In 1911, he was on the General

Geelong Grammar School was located at Maud Street, Geelong, at the time of Russell's attendance

Geelong Grammar School Archives – Geelong Grammar School Quarterly, October 1912, photograph by H. Fysh of the Camera Club

Alex Russell in his school blazer

Athletics Committee, with "Athletics" in this case meaning all sports. Of the Associated Sub-Committees, Russell was on those for Cricket and Tennis. He became one of seven prefects in the second half of the year. This, in view of the fact that he had only been at the school three and a half years, demonstrated high achievement and was evidence of how highly he must have been regarded by the Headmaster as a person and a leader. Charles Drought, the School Captain, Captain of Cricket, on the General Athletics and Cricket Committees, and who played in both the First and Second XVIII football teams with Russell, is mentioned in Russell's diary that he kept during World War I. Drought was sadly killed in France on 31 December 1915 at Ypres, shortly after Russell recorded meeting him in France on 18 September, *"Left billet at 2pm and drove to Bailleau* (Bailleul) *where I met Drought last seen at school he is in trenches just in front of me."*

As a scholar, Russell excelled, being top in Mathematics in Upper VI grade, an indication of his competence in this subject. This, along with his further mathematics taken at Cambridge, would prove invaluable during his war service. Alex left Geelong Grammar in December 1911 at the age of 19 years and 6 months, much older than today's students are when finishing their secondary education.

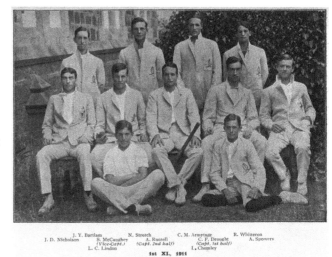

J. Y. Bartlam   N. Stretch   C. M. Armytage   R. Whitteron
J. D. Nicholson   S. McCaughey   A. Russell   C. F. Drought   A. Spowers
(Vice-Capt.)   (Capt. 2nd half)   (Capt. 1st half)
L. C. Lindon   L. Chomley

1st XI., 1911

The First XI Cricket Team for 1911 (top) with Alex Russell as captain. In the first half of 1911 Russell was 18 years old, and turned 19 in mid-year. Students in Russell's day were at least three years older than they are today in comparable grades.

The First XVIII Football Team for 1911 (left), with Russell third from left in the top row, and enlargement (above)

Opposite page, photographs of the Head Master and Prefects for 1911 and that year's college Shooting Team

Geelong Grammar School Archives

E. H. Britten   J. D. Nicholson   S. McCaughey   A. Spowers   A. Russell   C. O. Fairbairn
L. H. Lindon, M.A. *(Head Master)*   C. F. Drought

Head Master and Prefects, 1911

L. Cpl. J. Jackson   Cadet G. Hosking   Cpl. S. McCaughey   Sgt. A. Russell   L. Cpl. G. Burston
Sgt. C. O. Fairbairn   Sgt. A. Spowers   Lieut. J. D. Nicholson

Shooting Team, 1911.

Cambridge University, Jesus College, Cambridge, England (1912 – 1914)

Alex Russell returned to England to enter Cambridge University to study engineering, joining Jesus College on 22 October 1912, having been recommended to the college by the Headmaster of Geelong Grammar, L. H. Linden, Esq. He passed the usual first year examinations, including the Qualifying Examination in Mathematics and Mechanics for the Mechanical Sciences Tripos in June 1913, but did not graduate. He would have sat for the Mechanical Sciences Tripos in June 1915 if World War I had not intervened. While at Cambridge, Russell competed in tennis, golf and billiards for the university. His son Philip, thought his father had earned a Half Blue for golf, but he did not play in the golf team in their match against Oxford and therefore did not receive a Full Blue that the sport of golf was entitled to. However, he did receive a Half Blue for billiards, playing matches against Oxford in March 1914. The difference between earning a Full Blue or a Half Blue did not represent the contribution of the player, but the level of regard at which the particular sport was held within the university.

He also competed in the Freshmen's Lawn Tennis Tournament in April 1913, with play over three days to whittle down the 53 entrants. Russell was successful, winning all his matches and the final against P. G. Mayer of Trinity 6-4, 10-8. A newspaper account of the tournament noted that, *"the winner turned up in Russell, who is a freshman from Geelong, Australia. At present he hits rather softly, but will probably develop into a good tennis player after he has had more practice. The games were played on the University courts at Fenner's."*

When war broke out, Russell immediately left Cambridge to enlist and abandoned his degree. He was later awarded an honorary degree according to son Philip. After World War I, it was customary practice at Cambridge and other British universities to award BA degrees to those who had served during the war and had completed a significant part of their course prior to enlisting.

A studio portrait of Alex Russell (top) taken in Melbourne c.1912 prior to his departure for Cambridge, where he joined Jesus College (right) on the recommendation of the principal of Geelong Grammar School

A 1919 letter (opposite page) from Edwin Abbott, Russell's tutor in Jesus College, outlining his achievements.

Jesus College
Cambridge

20 September 1919

I beg to certify that Major Alex Russell came into residence at Jesus College in October ~~DOIH.~~ 1912.

After passing the Previous Examination of Cambridge University , Parts 1 and 2 and the Additional Subjects (Mechanics) for Honours Candidates, he passed in June 1913 the Qualifying Examination in Mathematics and Mechanics for the Mechanical Sciences Tripos.

He would have sat for the Mechanical Sciences Tripos in the ordinary course in June 1915, but was prevented by the War from so doing.

Edwin Abbott, M.A.

Tutor of Jesus College
Cambridge

L 307

Caterpillar tractor hauling a 6-inch Mark XIX gun of the 484th Siege Battery, Royal Garrison Artillery, during a retreat along the Bapaume-Albert road in France on 23 March 1918. Captain Alex Russell was an artillery officer with this battery at the time the photograph was taken. Note the camouflage netting over the gun barrel.

Imperial War Museum

Chapter 3

THE GREAT WAR

With the onset of World War I, Alex Russell immediately volunteered as a dispatch rider in London, riding down from Cambridge on his own motor-cycle the day that war was declared, according to his son Philip. Some three months later, on 9 October 1914, he was appointed an officer in the Land Forces with the rank of 2nd Lieutenant. The very next day he joined the Royal Garrison Artillery (RGA) in the British Expeditionary Force and was to serve in some of the bloodiest battles of the war in France and Belgium.

Why Alex chose the artillery is not known. His son Philip later recalled that it was one thing he never asked his father, even though he himself went on to serve in the artillery in World War II, after Alex pulled some strings to get his son transferred across from the infantry.

Engineers and those with higher levels of mathematics were vitally important to artillery batteries, since accurately aiming the guns was largely a matter of mathematics, in particular trigonometry. The ability to undertake the necessary calculations quickly and accurately by use of a slide-rule was invaluable. The Royal Field Artillery disparagingly referred to the RGA as "the slide-rule soldiers," however, they had a well-earned reputation as the most efficient and scientific gunners in the army.

Field gun batteries comprised the smaller, lighter field guns and light howitzers that could be quickly transported with horses. The British Army's heavy artillery was organised into heavy batteries and siege batteries. Heavy batteries comprised bigger, heavier guns, such as the 60 pounder, which typically could fire a shell a long way, but not high into the air. This meant they were not as effective at reaching targets that were behind steep hills or deep inside bunkers.

Siege batteries also utilised heavy guns but these were large howitzers which fired large diameter shells high into the air, which could then plunge down onto forts or behind hills. Heavy artillery often needed heavy vehicles, such as caterpillar tractors, to pull them around. They were far less mobile, and it took time to gather these big guns together to support a major attack.

Typically a battery was commanded by a Major, assisted by a Battery Captain and three or more Lieutenants. The senior enlisted man was referred to as a Battery Sergeant Major and there was also a Battery Quartermaster Sergeant. Each gun section (usually two guns) was commanded by one of the Lieutenants and a Sergeant was in charge of each gun. The No. 1

2nd Lieutenant Alex Russell, RGA, photographed in London shortly after the start of the war. At the time Russell was serving with the 12th (New) Heavy Battery.

for each gun was usually a Corporal or Bombardier and the rest of the crew for the gun were known simply as Gunners. The horses (or tractors) that pulled the guns were kept at the horse lines somewhat behind the guns under the direction of an officer. These officers were usually rotated from the guns for a period of rest. The Battery Sergeant Major and the Drivers rode (drove) and cared for the horses.

12th Heavy Battery RGA

On 31 May 1915, 2nd Lieutenant Alex Russell embarked at Southampton on the 'S.S. Inventor' bound for Le Havre as an officer of the 12th (New) Heavy Battery R.G.A. under the command of Major C.E. Rolland. The unit's first position was taken up in Brulooze, Belgium but after almost two months there, they moved to Dickerbusch and Kemmel, closer to Ypres. The fighting at Ypres had been fierce just before the 12th H.B. was sent there, and this had been the area where the Germans first released poison gas on 22 April, and again on 24 April. The British and French had lost considerable ground in the German attacks that followed, and the strategic salient at Ypres was endangered.

In an attempt to recover some of the lost ground to help make Ypres more secure, the British and French counter-attacked, but made little headway. The Germans with heavy bombardments made further advances but by 27 May they found they could progress no further either. This was known as the Second Battle of Ypres, and during that month of intense fighting the British casualties were 2,150 officers and 57,125 other ranks injured, with 10,519 killed. The German losses were reported to be 816 officers and 34,073 other ranks. The Third Battle of Ypres took place in 1917 and included the Battle for Passchendaele, where once again there were huge losses. The troops had to advance over duckboards and, if they were wounded and fell off the duckboards, risked drowning in the soft mud that had been created by the shellfire and very heavy rain.

The renowned Australian General (Sir) John Monash in his pre-war diaries had expressed the view that the British had not fully embraced the scientific and mechanical approach to warfare, and that the British generals that he had been in contact with still believed in cavalry charges and the overwhelming of the enemy by sheer numbers. It is clear that in the areas where Russell's unit was involved, logistics lacked the detailed planning that Monash would have demanded. Although his unit was transferred to the Somme, the carnage

Colorised photograph of a 6-inch gun battery at Gallipoli in 1915.

of Flanders was the general scene into which Alex Russell was thrust. While Russell's unit had exchanged their obsolete 4.7" guns for 60 pound guns before leaving England, unlike many units who had to continue with the 4.7", the heavy 60 pounders regularly broke down.

Of the four guns that each battery contained, at least one appeared to be out of action much of the time. Often two guns would be out of commission and parts would be cannibalised from one gun to keep the other gun operational. The maintenance workshops worked hard to make modifications that might extend the period between breakdowns. Those at the battery also took steps to extend the life of some parts. It can be said that no-one had ever fought a war of this magnitude, or nature, before, and therefore no-one had had to deal with the logistical problems this created.

There were times, however, when these logistical problems showed that there was a level of incompetence higher up the line of command. Matters such as spares being unavailable to repair guns, or simply running out of ammunition, occurred all too frequently. This was highly unsatisfactory when the battery was required to lay down a barrage prior to and during a planned assault, yet the necessary ammunition had not been sent forward.

During his time in France and Belgium with the 12th Heavy Battery, Alex Russell kept his own diary with daily entries from 18 September 1915 until 10 January 1916. He may have kept other diaries over the time of his service but this is the only one that survives in the family archives. It is also accompanied by a notebook and a Book of Rounds in which he recorded shots fired by the battery.

The diary gives a wonderful insight into the life of an artillery officer during World War I. It begins on 18 September 1915 with Russell able to obtain around a week's leave in London. His parents, his sister, his best friend 'Bo' Fairbairn and other friends were in the city at that time, and despite the horrors of war, his diary gives every indication of a carefree young man. Russell was 23 years old at the time, and one who enjoyed life, the theatre, and restaurants, with still a touch of the larrikin persisting, as exhibited by his driving a friend's Morgan car *"furiously"* around the streets of London.

He also noted on 20 September that he *"Drove Ambulance to town with Dad,"* as his father Philip had volunteered to drive an ambulance in France, his own Peugeot vehicle that he had converted to an ambulance. The 'Riponshire' Advocate on 3 April 1915 reported on a rumour that Russell had been seriously wounded but this was discredited by relatives at home. It also stated that *"Mr Philip Russell is now driving a motor ambulance between the front and the hospitals at Havre (France)."* The ambulance had been purchased by Philip with his own money, and he also employed the nurse who accompanied him.

Alex arrived back in France on 24 September, and the entries from one page of the diary, running from 22–25 October 1915, give examples of some typical days for Russell and the battery.

"22
Friday

Went to HQ at 9 AM Returned 5 pm lunch Sale cut wood
Talked about his girl. Poor lad is very bad.

23
Sat

Had a harness inspection in afternoon very good considering AM but especially fine hardly a duty piece anywhere.

24th
Sun

To K.T. misty and cold so could see nothing. News that Estaminet (small French restaurant or café) is going to give up regular meals.
Rained in evening & at night and both dugouts leaked badly. Very miserable.
Stove and lamps arrived

25th
Mon

Dug for an hour or so and finished roof off properly over bedroom not enough overlap on iron and clayy soil forms little damms.
Miserable day & cold
Send for oil"

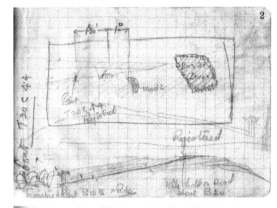

Pages from Alex Russell's Book of Rounds (top & middle) showing his sketch map of a target location and a list of rounds fired

Motor ambulances (bottom), similar to the one provided and staffed by Philip Russell, at Lady Dudley Hospital in France

Australian War Memorial

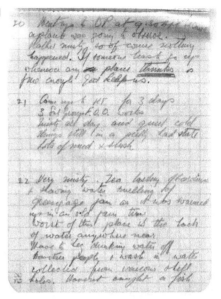

Alex Russell's personal war diary describes a number of amusing and harrowing incidents through a few months of his service in France and Belgium in 1915. The pages show entries for days in September 1915 (above middle) and October 1915 (above right)

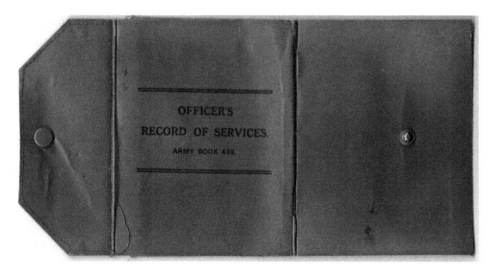

Cover of Russell's Record of Services book (left) and pages showing his personal details, service, promotions and courses taken (opposite page)

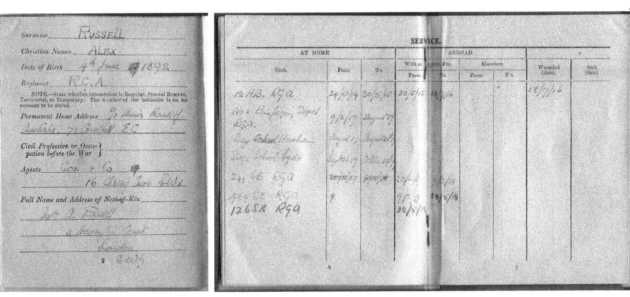

Surname **RUSSELL**

Christian Names **ALEX**

Date of Birth **4ᵗʰ June 1892**

Regiment **R.G.A.**

NOTE.—State whether commission is Regular, Special Reserve, Territorial, or Temporary. The number of the battalion is on no account to be stated.

Permanent Home Address *c/o Union Bank of Australia, 71 Cornhill E.C.*

Civil Profession or Occupation before the War

Agents *Cox & Co.*
16 Charing Cross S.W.

Full Name and Address of Next-of-Kin

W. R. Russell
3 Henry St. Court
London
2 ...

SERVICE.

Unit.	From	To	From	To	From	To	Wounded (date)	Sick (date)
12 H.B. R.G.A.	24/10/14	30/5/15	30/5/15	28/7/16			18/7/16	
No. 2 Reinforcement Depot R.G.A.	9/2/17	August '17						
Gun School Horsham	Aug '17	August '17						
Siege School Lydd	Sept 6/17	Oct. 17						
211 S.B. R.G.A.	Oct 11/17	9/2/18	20/2/18	18/5/18				
404 S.B. R.G.A.	9		9/7/18	18/5/18				
126 SB R.G.A.			28/5/18					

PROMOTION.

SUBSTANTIVE		ACTING	
Rank	Date	Rank	Inclusive From
2nd Lieut.	10/10/14		
Lieut.	1/7/17	Capt.	9/2/18
Captain	25/4/18		28/5/18
Bvt. Major			
Major			
Bvt. Lt.-Col			
Lt.-Col.			
Bvt.-Col.			

PROMOTION.

dates To	Authority	Signature of C.O. or of a Brigade Commander in the case of a C.O.
	III Army G.R.A. (680) dated 28/5/8	*M. Laughton* LIEUT. COL. R.G.A., COMMANDING 71st BRIGADE R.G.A.

COURSES.

Course	Any special authority for a Pass, and where Course was held	Signature of Commanding Officer
Bombing*	Siege Artillery School Horsham	
Musketry*	August 1917	
Lewis Gun*		
Machine Gun	B.C.s Course	
Trench Mortar	Lydd & Salisbury	
Signalling	Sept 6 Oct 1917	
Pioneer	Recommended	
Transport	Gunnery Courses	
Sniping and Scouting	Authority 25/5/18 28/85	
Army Schools		
B.E.F. Senior Officer's Course		
Staff Course		

*Does not include Regimental Course

On 31 October 1915 Russell's battery, under orders, began the move from Kemmel to Albert in the Somme Valley. While only some 60 miles (96km) as the crow flies, the battery needed to take a very circuitous route to get to their destination. The journey took approximately a week from when the guns were pulled out until they were in place again. The men often marched over 20 miles (32 km) in the rain, with the horses pulling the guns along muddy roads. Much of this was at night so that enemy planes could not observe their movements. Such were the conditions when the battery arrived at its new location that one of the guns became stuck in a field at about 6pm on 5 November. This delayed the final installation of the guns at Albert, however, by working through the night the guns were in action again by 9am the next morning. During this movement Alex Russell often had to ride ahead to secure billets, in his diary he mentions one ride of approximately 40 miles (64km). When it became necessary, Alex Russell had to conquer his fear of horses. He did note though on one occasion that he was glad that there had been no fences or ditches to jump.

While at Albert on 15 November, the first snow for the season arrived, "*Quite a nice little fall & reminded me I ought to be getting ready for St M about this time of year*", with "*St M*" being St Moritz where Russell made regular trips while at Cambridge to indulge his passion for skiing. He had first visited St Moritz with the family while at school at Glenalmond in Scotland, many years earlier.

It would appear that during this time he was largely used by the battery as an observer in forward observation posts. Russell had been told that the observation post that he would be using at Albert was a brute of a place, where the observers went for three days at a time. There was no water "*within miles*", and no decent arrangements for cooking. Meals were tinned food and anything else his telephonist might be able to cook. Alex noted in his diary, "*Tea tasting of sardines and shaving water, smelling of greengage jam as it was warmed in an old jam tin. The worst of this place is the lack of water anywhere near. Have to beg drinking water from the howitzer people and wash in water collected from various shell holes. Haven't caught a fish.*" At least he had not lost his sense of humour.

On 28 November, orders were received to move by section to Suzanne to relieve the Fife Highland 4.7" Battery RGA. Right Section pulled out at 4pm and were all clear by 1am. Number 1 gun was stuck badly though, while Number 2 gun took 6 hours to pull out. As the time was now 5am, with the obvious difficulty of reaching the new gun positions before daylight, it was decided

RGA personnel were often forced to haul guns into position by hand, sometimes with the support of horses

to wait until the next night. The final positioning of the guns though was particularly difficult. A motor lorry was needed to pull one gun into place through one foot of deep clinging mud. Six horses were used to pull half loads of ammunitions. Guns were stuck on the sides of the road. Another gun required the lorry after the exhausted horses finally refused to pull any further, when just short of a crest. Lt. Russell managed to get one gun into position, to the amazement of the lorry people when they arrived. He had put fifty men to work to assist the horses, and in this case he said they had all pulled magnificently.

At this location all the dugouts were wet and none had roofs over them. To reach the observation post nearest Maricourt, observers had to walk along 500 yards (450 metres) of what Russell described as the worst trench he had seen, and then along 200 yards (180 metres) of a still worse one. At this point he was only 300 yards (270 metres) from the enemy trenches. This was where Russell spent Christmas night of 1915, and he finally was able to get to bed at 2am.

On Boxing Day, Alex Russell went on leave again to London. He wrote that he "*left Battery 7 am beautifully clean but cart stuck in mud & had to jump out & push. Result mud 1" deep up to my waist. Caught bus at Bray 8 am & train Mericourt* (Mericourt-sur-Somme) *9.30 Had a good brekker* (breakfast) *Arrived Havre 8.40 and London 11 am 27th.*" In London he had a relaxing leave, learnt the foxtrot, saw some shows at the theatre, and commented that no-one ate out in the cafes any more. He took a gramophone back to the battery with him, which proved to be a great success.

At the end of June and into early July 1916, the battery was involved in the attack on Montauban, both with the initial barrage and the ongoing barrage to hamper the German counter attack. The battery was also responsible for silencing some of the German batteries. Their successes included blowing up an enemy ammunition dump, aided by aeroplane spotters and intelligence from the observation posts. An officer was also sent forward with the infantry to maintain contact between the troops and the battery.

During the attack the battery ran out of ammunition and was told that there was no more available. The Commanding Officer was able to "borrow" some ammunition from another battery, however, the supply of ammunition continued to be less than was required. This battle was part of the larger Battle of the Somme, where almost 20,000 British soldiers died, and almost 40,000 were wounded on the first day.

On a number of occasions, the battery was out of ammunition and unable to operate for several hours. Guns continued to break down and no spares were available in France to repair them. At one stage the battery was ordered to concentrate on enemy barracks and roads, which the C.O. thought was the wrong policy for heavy artillery as he believed it was far more important for them to be concentrating on counter barrage activity.

Shortly after this battle, the Germans began firing at the battery. The guns were moved to another location, but not before one man had been injured by shrapnel. The Germans also fired tear gas and other gas shells at them, but the quick donning of gas masks avoided any serious casualties from this. Unfortunately, a shell from the nearby howitzer battery landed short and wounded two men of the 12th Heavy Battery, one had his leg blown off. An official letter dated 9 June 1916 informed Philip Russell that his son, 2nd Lieut. Russell, had been wounded on 4 June, but the Battery's War Diary and Russell's own diary do not mention this, and he likely suffered only minor injuries, if any. The battery then first moved to just south of Carnoy, before moving again to a point north of Maricourt, neither far from their previous position. The guns were in place by daylight on 15 July 1916.

Wounding, Recovery and Training

On the morning of 28 July 1916, two weeks after the battery had moved to their new position near Maricourt, Alex Russell was injured far more seriously when an incoming German 210mm shell exploded near the observation post. He was

buried for some time until rescued by French soldiers. Russell had been overseeing the firing of the battery from a point near a French command post, and when the shell burst a few yards from Russell and threw him into a trench, one of the French soldiers came to tell his commander what had taken place.

Commandant Beurier arranged for Alex Russell to be taken firstly to his own bed, then to the first aid post, and finally into an ambulance. A personal letter written by Beurier to Russell on 14 August 1916 was the first real information that Alex had been able to glean on what had happened to him. He kept the letter with his personal effects that his family now holds:

> "Dear Comrad
>
> It is a great pleasure to me to give you the information you want to know. You were, doubtless, busy to regulate the firing of your battery and, for the purpose situated near my commanding post, when the accident took place: a 210 shell bursted a few yards away from you and threw you in the trench – one of my men came to inform me and I let you be taken to my bed from where my men carried you to the sanitary post and then to the ambulance. I am very glad to hear you are getting better and on the way to health. You may believe that I am very happy, too, have had the good fortune of being able to help you. Please accept my kindest regards.
>
> Yours sincerely
>
> Commandant Beurier"

Alex's daughter Robina, in later recalling this incident, said that her father *"was wounded twice and blown up at his gun site once and buried in mud. He had nightmares about it for the rest of his life."* She also noted that, *"He lay on a railway station in the open all night before being shipped out to England."* Then came a

A German 210mm howitzer of the type that fired the shell that injured Alex Russell on 28 July 1916

seven-month long process of recovery until February 1917, and while he remained on the 12th Heavy Battery's roll during this period, he was not with it in France. He was then given a desk job, which lasted for six months. To explain this, Alex Russell likely suffered a significant, even a potentially life-threatening injury in France. It could not have been psychological, such as shell-shock, or he would never have been sent back to France at a later date in command of others.

There is a strong possibility that when blown into the trench, he suffered a wedging of one or more vertebrae in his spine not far below his neck, in other words a broken back. Certainly, the Army appears to have handled him very carefully. If it was a back injury and any further damage occurred, then he might have become a paraplegic, or died. It is one of the few injuries that would require that length of care, yet once healed might not grossly handicap him in later activities. The spinal deformity is visible in later photographs of him putting on the golf course, and his daughter Robina recounts an incident where Alex went to the tailor for a new suit. At the fitting the tailor angrily tore off the coat because the top was so far from Alex's neck. According to both Philip and Robina, their father's injuries during the war included the loss of a testicle, so clearly the injuries he sustained were quite traumatic.

Russell then spent six months with the No. 2 Reinforcing Depot RGA at Stowlangtoft, near Bury St Edmonds in Suffolk, although his role there is not known. On 1 July 1917 he was promoted to Lieutenant and the following month he was sent to Horsham to undertake a Siege Artillery Course at the Siege School that he completed on 30 August. Russell then commenced a Battery Commander's Course on 26 September at the Siege School at Lydd and another at the Chapperton Down Artillery School near Salisbury, finishing these on 14 October. After completing these courses it was recommended that Russell be given command of a battery in the field.

Letter sent by the French infantry commander Commandant Beurier to 2nd Lt. Alex Russell explaining what had happened to him when an incoming German 210mm shell burst nearby and threw him into an adjacent trench.

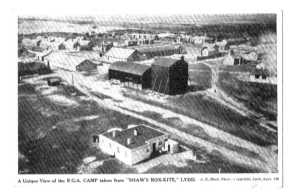

A Unique View of the R.G.A. CAMP taken from "SHAW'S BOX-KITE," LYDD.   A. E. Shaw, Photo., Copyright, Lydd, Kent. 196

A. E. Shaw, Photo., Copyright.   6" HOWITZER IN ACTION, R.G.A., LYDD.   Lydd, Kent

A series of postcards were printed during the First World War showing the various artillery training activities at the Royal Garrison Artillery Siege School at Lydd in Kent (above). Alex Russell undertook a Battery Commander's course there in September and October 1917.

The page from the 12th Heavy Battery's official War Diary (below) with the entry for 28 July 1916 recording that Lt. Russell had been "wounded near the O.P. in the morning."

244th Siege Battery RGA and 484th Siege Battery RGA

On 20 November 1917, some 16 months after his wounding, Alex Russell returned to France to join the 244th Siege Battery RGA with its armoury of six 6" Howitzers. He was transferred again on 9 February 1918 to the 484th Siege Battery, a 4 x 6" gun battery. This battery had gone out to the Western Front in January 1918, becoming a part of the Third Army. Six weeks later, on 21 March, the Germans launched 'Operation Michael', breaking through the British Fifth Army, which began as a rout with the Fifth losing much of their artillery. A series of brave stands and retreats followed. On 25 April 1918 Russell was promoted to the rank of Captain, having been an Acting Captain since 9 March.

The Germans were attempting to capture Amiens, which was the centre of the British supply lines, with important rail and road connections. If lost, then the British would have been unable to mount any strong sustained counter-attack because the necessary logistics could not be met. The British Third Army had made a more orderly retreat, in order to keep contact with the retreating Fifth, and then held firm. Bitter fighting took place as the Germans attacked this flank of the Third Army. At this stage the Australians were thrown in to block the gap. Their roles at Dernancourt, on 4 and 5 of April where 4,000 Australians held up 25,000 German troops, four full divisions, and then at Villiers-Bretonneaux, where 1,200 Australians lost their lives on ANZAC Day 1918 while recapturing that village, are still reverently remembered in France. In the official Australian War History of World War I, Charles Bean mentioned the role of the British artillery in the battle at Dernancourt, their effectiveness and the fact that they were exposed because they had not had a chance to dig in, however, he did not name the batteries.

There is a photograph held in the collections of the Imperial War Museum of a 6" gun from the 484th Siege Battery RGA being transported along the Bapaume-Albert Road on 23 March 1918, two days after the German break-through to the south. Just beyond Albert lay Dernancourt. There was no well-established line in this section at that stage, and German storm troopers were infiltrating through the line where possible, with the elimination of artillery and control posts as their prime objective. As the 484th was in the Albert-Dernancourt area at this time, it is quite likely that Russell's battery was supporting the Australians at Dernancourt. This could well have been the action that led to Capt. Alex Russell being recommended for the Military Cross. Russell remained with the 484th until late May 1918 when he was transferred, with a promotion, and his own battery to command.

126th Siege Battery RGA

On 28 May 1918, Capt. Alex Russell was promoted to the rank of Acting Major and given command of his own battery, the 126th Siege Battery, located at the time at Englebelmer, north of Albert, which was fortunately not under attack after April. Russell took over the command of the battery in troublesome circumstances following the death of its previous commander. The battery was equipped with six 8" mechanised Howitzers, and had gone out to the Western Front in July 1916 where they remained for the duration of the war. There is a photograph of the 126th Siege Battery taken by an Australian War Photographer on 22 August 1918, "near Bray" which is held in the collections of the Australian War Memorial in Canberra. As the 126th was near Bray on 22 August, it must have been there supporting the Australian attack on Mont St Quentin and Peronne.

The fact that a British battery was obviously providing support for the Australians at this time, adds to the likelihood that the British Third Army, including the 484th Siege Battery, had provided similar support to the Australians at Dernancourt. A week after this photograph was taken, the Battle for Mont St Quentin and Peronne commenced, where the Australians were credited with one of the outstanding successes of the war. On July 4, Monash launched the historic breakthrough at Hamel. Russell remained in command of his battery until the Armistice.

Military Cross

In the Supplement to the 'London Gazette' of 3 June 1919 under the heading 'Military Cross' was found this listing, "*T./Capt. (A./Maj.) Alexander Russell, '126th Sge'. Bty., R.G.A*". The date makes this a King's Birthday award, which did not carry citations. It is usually, but not only, awarded for continuing valour, rather than a specific incident. Alex Russell returned to England from Australia in 1922 for his investiture at Buckingham Palace on 21 April.

Alex Russell's Military Cross in its original case. The announcement of the award was made in June 1919 and Russell returned to England in April 1922 for his investiture

A photograph taken by an Australian war photographer of one of the guns of the 126th Siege Battery, Royal Garrison Artillery, on 22 August 1918. At this time the battery was under the command of Major Alex Russell.

Australian War Memorial

The Impact of Russell's War Experiences

It is acknowledged that those who fought in any war remembered what it was like for the rest of their lives, and almost invariably it changed their lives forever. Alex Russell had been closely involved in some of the bloodiest battles of the Great War, the 1st Battle of the Somme and the Battle for Amiens, along with the 2nd Battle of Ypres. He had seen the carnage, the effects of gas, he had lost friends, and was well aware of the incompetence of some officers, both at the unit level, and higher up. He himself had suffered the shock and injuries from an incoming German shell explosion. It is no wonder Alex Russell found it hard to tolerate fools gladly.

Like so many of those who came back from that conflict, Russell certainly did not want to talk about his experiences. He did not join the Returned Services League once back in Australia, but then again his 'comrades' were back in Britain. When a person subconsciously "bottles up" such an important and confronting period in their life, they can lose a great deal of spontaneity, so it is easy to appear aloof and withdrawn. They choose their friends very carefully, and friends need to be people they can implicitly trust to understand should something come out unexpectedly, because anyone who had not been there could never understand the horrors witnessed.

This certainly fits the type of man Alex Russell became after his war-time experiences. His war diaries show the dry sense of humour that he had, and it would appear that this attribute most definitely survived. Under the headline *"Russell's Sense of Humour"* the golf columnist for 'The Herald,' "Par", writing in the 23 March 1927 edition, contended that the understanding between Alex Russell and C. H. "George" Fawcett was a key factor in their amazing string of foursome successes. He went on to write, that after one of their wins Fawcett asked Russell if he could have a lift home, to which Russell sardonically replied *"I've carried you round the links all afternoon and I would not like to spoil it by refusing to take you the whole way".*

Russell himself has said that he had a fear of horses, however, during the war he had much to do with them. They were an integral part of each battery. They pulled the guns. He personally managed to get some guns that were stuck in the mud into place by harnessing two teams of horses to one gun and having fifty men help him. He was rather pleased with himself when the crew of the caterpillar-type machine could not believe what had been achieved just with horses and men.

As a junior officer, when the battery was on the move, it was often his role to ride ahead and organise billets for the battery. In the First Somme offensive, where three million men were involved, they were supported by some 200,000 horses. In the classic book "All Quiet on the Western Front" the hero speaks of the unsettling and terrible cries of the badly injured horses, often with no-one there to put them out of their misery. It is not known if Russell was present when Number 7 horse of 12th Heavy Battery was badly wounded by shrapnel and had to be destroyed.

Was his so-called "fear" of horses more an unconscious expression of an association between horses and his war experience? He seemed not to particularly enjoy going to the races, which was one of his father's passions, although he did attend a number over the years with Jess, who was a prolific race-goer, and he did attend some Western District polo games, but that was almost a social imperative in the district at that time.

His daughter Robina relates a story of Alex and Jess being invited to a race meeting at Flemington Racecourse by the Chairman of the Victorian Racing Club. The closer the Russells came to the course the more erratic Alex's driving became. When Jess commented on this, without saying a word he stopped the car, got out and caught a tram back to the city, leaving Jess to carry on to Flemington alone.

Neither did Russell like cocktail parties particularly as he was not skilled at small talk. When he was blown into the trench he would almost certainly have suffered some degree of hearing damage, and also as an artillery officer he would almost certainly have suffered hearing loss as there were no ear-plugs or muffs in those days, personnel just placed their hands over their ears and turned their heads to one side.

If Alex Russell had a degree of underlying deafness, possibly a hidden shyness, was unskilled at small talk, and was careful in choosing his friends, then how much did these elements contribute to his perceived aloofness? Certainly, stiff 'black tie' cocktail parties would have been a burden to endure. However, he did attend many social gatherings over the years, mostly in the company of wife Jess, who was a very social person, a regular at the races as well as social and charity functions such as fetes, dinners and balls.

Horses were a vital support in most artillery batteries, as seen in this postcard produced in aid of War Bonds

2nd Lt. Alex Russell, RGA (left)

This photograph was taken of British artillery officers at their mess near the town of Kemmel, Belgium c.1917 (below). While the image is not specifically of any of the units Russell served in, it gives the reader a good idea of the conditions he experienced.

Australian War Memorial

Alex Russell's 1924 Australian Open victory was front page news in Melbourne (opposite)

Chapter 4

A GOLFING LIFE

Exactly when or where Alex Russell first played golf is not known for certain. Golf though was a family sport for the Russells. His father Philip was captain of the Geelong Golf Club in 1900 and his mother 'Cissie' was the inaugural ladies' president at Geelong from 1893 to 1894. The parents of 'Bo' Fairbairn, Alex's closest friend, were also deeply involved with the Geelong club. Frederick Fairbairn was captain in 1899, 1905 and 1906 while his wife Rhoda was ladies' president in 1903 and 1905 to 1906. Philip Russell joined Royal Melbourne Golf Club in 1893 and Fred Fairbairn in 1903, while 'Cissie' was also a Royal Melbourne associate. So there was golf in Russell's family, and in his best friend's family as well.

As stated earlier, Alex Russell attended St Salvators Primary School run by P.C. Anderson, the British Amateur Champion of 1893, who was the truly dominant player at the Geelong Golf Club in the early 1900s and a class above the local players. He often took his pupils for walks, and while doing so took a golf stick with him. In Russell's memoirs, written when he was in his sixties, he wrote that Anderson's swing was like poetry, suggesting that Russell was aware at the time of both good and bad golf swings. That he should have remembered this more than fifty years later meant that it must have had a significant impact on him. Did Alex and 'Bo' hit a few shots around the grounds of Osborne House with his father's clubs and balls? There was plenty of space to do so, but we will never know.

The five years Russell spent in Britain is another period where there is uncertainty, but enough coincidences to suggest that he was involved in golf. The first piece of evidence is that he attended Trinity College at Glenalmond, where the school had a seven-hole course of its own. It is nigh on impossible that the young Alex Russell, a keen sportsman and the son of two competent golfers, did not avail himself of the opportunities and experiences offered by Mr Goodacre, who must have been more than an average golfer. When he retired from Glenalmond forty years after Alex had left the school, he settled in Kingussie in northern Aberdeenshire, where they were to name a hole on their course after him, "Goodacre's Garden." How much he was a coach to his young pupils is not known.

What is known for certain is that Alex Russell's name appears in the Royal Melbourne Golf Club's Annual Report of Council of

1915, and on the Honour Board of those who served overseas during World War I. There is no record of precisely when he became a member, but it must have been in 1914.

At this stage the question of how much golf Alex Russell had learnt becomes complicated. At the 1914 Annual Meeting of the Royal Melbourne Golf Club, the members passed the following motion:

> *"The Council shall also be empowered to submit to election each year, as Junior Members, two golfers whose handicaps at the date of their election shall be two strokes or better, and whose ages shall then be not less than 19 nor more than 25 years."*

This raises a complex question, because Alex Russell would have been under 25 at the time this was passed and in 1911 a similar but less restrictive motion had been rejected. It suggests that Russell, who would have been 22 years old at the time, must have been a competent golfer with a handicap of 2 or better. It is possible that Russell had applied earlier and been told he needed to wait until he was 25, but that his name would be placed on the waiting list. His name was re-submitted and accepted soon after the Annual General Meeting and he was elected to junior membership while still at Cambridge University. The waiting list was long enough not to pass up the opportunity.

It can be assumed that Russell almost certainly belonged to another club in order to have had a handicap. The obvious choice would be Geelong Golf Club, which apart from the family ties, had proximity to Geelong Grammar School. However, there is no mention of him in the Geelong Golf Club's record of those who served overseas, but most of that club's records and memorabilia were destroyed in a fire. That Alex Russell joined Royal Melbourne about that time is reinforced by the statement in *'The Herald'* of 11 September 1924, that *"He (Russell) is 32 years of age, and, as a leading player in the Royal Melbourne Golf Club, has been prominent in golf for the last nine years."*

Then follows another period of uncertainty. While Russell almost certainly played golf while he was at Cambridge and represented the university, he did not play in the Cambridge team against Oxford. A number of Melbourne press reports of his first golfing accomplishments in 1919 mention that he played while at Cambridge.

Alex Russell was overseas for seven years, two and a half of these in France, leaving probably about four when he could have played golf, obtaining some experience of English and Scottish courses. This is supported by the fact that not long after his return to Australia in April 1919 following his war service, Royal Melbourne held its first Medal competition on Saturday 26 July 1919, after it had been discontinued for almost five years due to the war. Captain Alex Russell was the winner with a score of 76 – 1 = 75. The handicapper obviously reacted to this, because in September he entered the events of the Victorian Championship Meeting, and was victorious in the Returned Servicemen's Handicap with a score of 78 + 1 = 79.

It was at the 1919 Victorian Amateur Championship that Russell showed he was likely to be a player of the future. At the end of the first day he was lying eighth on 166, four shots behind the three leaders, Ivo Whitton, Foster Rutledge and Bruce Pearce on 162. The following day Whitton (314) played brilliant golf to win by eight shots from Pearce (322), with Rutledge a further shot back. Russell (331) was in a tie for sixth with Lockhart, Quirk and Ritchie. The next day, paired with Rutledge, Russell won the Victorian Foursomes title with a record score of 157. Russell's form had been sufficient for there to be a photograph of him in *'The Australasian'* and mention in an article describing play of the first day:

> *"Russell's long driving was one of the features of the day's play. He seemed to experience no difficulty in getting 250 yards from the tee and at his 12th (478 yards) was pin high in two."*

In 1921 he won the club championship at Royal Melbourne against many of the best amateurs in Australia. His golf had reached a standard where, in 1922, a cartoon of Prominent Victorian Golfers included Alex Russell amongst its number. Similarly, prior to the 1924 National Championships, Russell was discussed amongst those most likely to have a chance of winning, and he went on to dominate the 1924 Meeting.

'Golf' magazine of 10 August 1925, reported how Russell had, a few years previous, the makings of a first-rate cricketer and tennis player, but poor eyesight was a drawback. Only when he was fitted with spectacles, or "Harold Lloyds" as they were described, after the silent movie star, did Russell's golf reach such lofty heights as the national championship.

MAJOR T. F. RUTLEDGE STANDS AT EASE.

Caricature of Major Foster Rutledge (right)

The first known photograph of Alex Russell playing golf was published in 'The Australasian' of 13 September 1919 following his win in the Returned Soldier's Handicap (above right)

State Library of Victoria

Ivo Whitton, of the R.M.G.C. and Metropolitan Club, is considered by most golfers to be easily the best amateur in Australia. He is present champion of both Clubs, Amateur Champion of Australia, Open Champion of Australia twice over.

PROMINENT VICTORIAN GOLFERS

Caricatured by Captain Sydney Dalrymple, M.C.

C. H. Fawcett, commonly "George," is a member of the R.M.G.C. He won the Victorian Amateur Championship one year. Twice partnered with Alec Russell, he has won the Australasian Challenge Shield. He has won trophies all over the place, and is an A1 golfer.

Major Alec Russell, another of the R.M.G.C.'s assets, hits a long, high ball, and plays an interesting game. He won the Club Championship last year.

Alex Russell was in good company with Ivo Whitten and C. H. Fawcett in this series of caricatures of Prominent Victorian Golfers sketched by Syd Dalrymple in 1922

Alex Russell Dominates 1924 National Championships

Royal Melbourne Golf Club – Sandringham Course

To better understand Alex Russell's achievements in 1924, the nature of the Royal Melbourne Golf Club's course at Sandringham needs to be understood. The course was penal with cross bunkers to catch any shot hit thin, there were bunkers on both sides of most fairways to trap the stray shot and while some of the rough was light and sandy, some was severe, and bordering all this were dense tea-tree bushes never cut more than three feet from the ground. At the edge of the tea-tree was bare sandy waste, often containing tree roots. This was no easy course considering its penal character. It was a tough par 72.

Golfers of the day tackled the difficult course playing with twisty hickory-shafted clubs and a wound ball that did not go as far, or bite as well on the greens as today's ball, although the greens would not have been as hard, or as fast, as they are now. The putting greens were considered equal to the best in Australia, if not the best, however, they would have

been nowhere near as true as modern greens. The difference between the par ratings and bogey, this word being used in the context of the period, gives an indication of this difficulty. When looking at Alex Russell's achievements that year, all this needs to be taken into account.

The length of the course for the 1924 Australian Open Championship was 6,321 yards (5,780 metres), with a bogey of 79 and par of 72. The bogey score represented correct golf, the score a competent golfer might aim for on a hole, while par represented perfect golf. Given that this was the Australian Open and the quality of the field was high, par will be given when describing the holes. At that time, club competitions were played against bogey, not par. Hence the handicaps decided by the club's handicapper, were aligned to both stroke and bogey performances – in a bogey competition at this time, competitors played off three quarters of their handicap as listed on the board. The thinking at that time was that any hole of under 500 yards (457 metres) should probably be a par four, the 2nd and 12th holes at Sandringham were allowed to be par fives, due to their special difficulties.

To help visualize the severe nature of the course for those familiar with the Royal Melbourne West Course, the par five 15th hole, which in 1924 was the 4th, provides a good example. In 1924 it was a par four, played from a tee roughly 40 yards (36 metres) forward of the current back tee. The mounds 100 yards (90 metres) short of the green were present in 1924 with a hidden water hazard behind them. Corresponding to the current mounds and rough filled hollows near the start of the current fairway, was a line of steep faced bunkers without the present gap. This was a difficult and unforgiving course for its day.

Australian Open Championship

Prior to the 1924 Australian Open to be played at Royal Melbourne, the newspaper scribes discussed the chances of various players in their golf columns. Alex Russell was named as one who would have a good chance if in form, however, his chances were discounted somewhat as he had just spent two weeks in hospital shortly before the meeting was to start, and had only started to practice again the week before the first round. Either the golf writers over-estimated the seriousness of his illness, or they underestimated Russell, for he was to dominate the meeting, winning the Open Championship, and the Australian Foursomes Championship with C. H. Fawcett, setting new course records during each event. In the Australian Amateur Championship Russell was runner-up after holding the lead in the final after 27 holes, only to lose narrowly with a hole to play.

Card of the Sandringham course from January 1924 (right). For the Australian Championships in September, the course was lengthened to 6,321 yards, an increase of some 105 yards over its January length

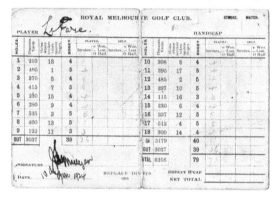

View of the 8th hole on the Sandringham course

State Library of Victoria

Plan of the Sandringham course of the Royal Melbourne Golf Club over which the 1924 Australian Open was played

The Royal Melbourne Golf Club

DAY ONE Thursday 4th September 1924

In the opening round, Russell played brilliantly and set a new course record of 68, which was to stand as the amateur record until the course was superseded by the West Course in 1931. The only time he looked like being in trouble was when his long brassie shot found the bunker at the 12th hole. He just got out but with a brilliant run-up and a putt, managed a bogey five. His long game had been excellent but it was his short game, always up to the hole, that was outstanding. The closest he came to a bad shot was at the final hole, when requiring a four to tie the record, he thinned his mashie off a hanging lie, but the shot ran up and sat on the edge of the hole, narrowly denying him a two and a round of 67.

Every part of Russell's long game had been brilliant but it was his consistency and accuracy on the greens that made his round outstanding. Russell himself said *"I just played like a machine. I felt I was in form all week, but I never expected to get down to 68. It was a very nice round."*

Round 1   3, 4, 3, 4, 3, 3, 5, 4, 3 = 32

              4, 4, 5, 4, 3, 4, 4, 5, 3 = 36 **68**

Due to the large size of the field of 104 competitors, those who had hit off early in the morning round had to wait while the last of the morning round were sent off by the starter before they could start their afternoon round. Russell continued to play steady golf but his putting was not as good as in the morning, finishing with a score of 79.

Round 2   5, 5, 4, 5, 4, 4, 5, 4, 3 = 39

              4, 4, 5, 6, 3, 4, 5, 5, 4 = 40 **79**

At the end of the first day Alex Russell, with his two rounds of 68 and 79 = 147, led the field by two shots from Tommy Howard, the defending champion. On 151 was C.H. Fawcett; 152 Carnegie Clark; 153 Chas. Campbell and Rufus Stewart; 154 Ivo Whitton and W.H. Tunbridge; 155 F.E. Headlam and W. Spicer. Arthur Le Fevre was on 156. The stage was set for Alex Russell's finest hour.

Alex. Russell

DAY TWO Friday 5th September 1924

In the morning round Russell, after a shaky start with a 7 on the 2nd hole, steadied and was out in a respectable 39. Coming home he mostly played consistent golf. Pars for the last three holes meant a good nine of 39 under the conditions and a 78 for the round.

Round 3   3, 7, 5, 4, 4, 4, 5, 4, 4 = 39

              4, 4, 5, 5, 4, 4, 4, 5, 4 = 39 **78**

The two main "movers," both with fine scores of 75, were Carnegie Clark, placing him two shots behind Russell, and Chas. Campbell, the 1922 champion, a shot further back. However, the best round for the morning was A. A. Hancock with a fine 72.

At the Australian Golf Championship, Sandringham, Melbourne. Souter and Russell checking up their cards at completion of the round.

Alex Russell walks from the final green (above) checking his card after his second round on Friday afternoon 5th of September, in the company of playing partner Dan Soutar

Caricature of Alex Russell by Wells from 1924 (above left)

Commencing his final round, Russell was followed by a large gallery but by the time he reached the 7th hole it had dwindled to no more than half-a-dozen. Russell started poorly, taking a five at the 1st after being bunkered and failing to get out. Next he had an adventurous par at the 2nd where he pushed his tee shot and caught trees with his brassie, but an excellent pitch and two putts gave him his five. Par at the next and then he ran up a disastrous eight at the 4th. All chances of winning appeared to have evaporated in one hole. He had hooked his drive and tried to escape from the rough with his baffy, but only moved the ball a few yards. He played a poor third into a bunker from where he played into another bunker, the front left hand pot. On the green with his next but three putts were costly. He made his par three at the 5th, but three-putted again to drop a further shot at the next.

After topping his drive at the 7th, he looked to have no hope, but he recovered well to make his par five. He was starting to look tired, likely a combination of his earlier illness and the gruelling regime of 4 tournament rounds in two days. Russell parred the next two holes to be out in 42. What followed was one of the most remarkable turnarounds in the annals of golf. Carnegie Clark had gone out in 37, so he now led Russell by three shots. Campbell, who had reached the turn in 39, was now equal with Russell.

At the 10th hole, Russell's long putt stopped an inch short of a three, while Clark had a five. The margin was now back to two. Russell then played completely flawless golf scoring seven fours, including a birdie at the 12th, a three at the 14th, and a par five at the 17th, while Clark started dropping shots. By this stage Russell was looking exhausted, but at the 16th he pitched to five feet and his putt just rolled to the left and failed to drop.

Now two shots in front of Clark, with two pars almost ensuring him of victory, the only moment for any anxiety was when he drove past the trees on the 17th and into the rough, but a beautiful brassie second set him up for a routine par five. Needing a par four at the last to maintain his two shot lead, Russell nonchalantly threw his ball onto the last tee, and after a solid par four the 1924 Australian Open Championship title was his.

Round 4   5, 5, 4, 8, 3, 5, 5, 4, 3 = 42

4, 4, 4, 4, 4, 3, 4, 5, 4 = 36 **78**

Carnegie Clark, who had shot 37 on the way out, had come home in 41 for a 78, while Campbell had a 39 coming home to match his 39 out, so all three leaders shot the same score of 78 for the last round. This left the top three placings unchanged.

Alex Russell   **68, 79, 78, 78, = 303**
Carnegie Clark   78, 74, 75, 78, = 305
Chas. Campbell   76, 77, 75, 78, = 306

There was only one person not greatly impressed by his victory. Alex's daughter Robina relates the story that after his win *"my mother rushed into the nursery with "isn't it exciting Alex's won The Open!" We had a rather dour Nanny whose only comment was "Should do – he practices enough!"*

AUSTRALIAN OPEN GOLF CHAMPION.

In the two concluding rounds of the open championship of Australia, played at Sandringham yesterday, Alex. Russell, of the Royal Melbourne club, whose phenomenal play on Thursday morning was the feature of the opening round, maintained his lead, and became open golfing champion for 1924. Inset against the portrait of the champion are the runner-up, Carnegie Clark, N.S.W. (left), and C. Campbell (N.S.W.) who came third, on the right.

Alex Russell, Australian Open Golf Champion, as seen in 'The Argus'

Spectators at the Golf Championship. Left to right: Mrs. Stanley Bruce, wife of the Prime Minister; Mrs. Alec. Russell; Mr. Fairbairn.

OPEN CHAMPIONSHIP OF AUSTRALIA AT SANDRINGHAM.

An extract from the pictorial page for the Australian Open golf (above right) in 'Table Talk' on 11 September 1924 featured the champion Alex Russell and Harry Sinclair (left)

Jess Russell (above) was photographed watching Alex win the Open championship at Sandringham with their two young children Philip and Virginia, along with her father Fred Fairbairn, and the Prime Minister's wife, Mrs Stanley Bruce

Russell (left) recovers from a bunker on the 13th hole in his match with Harry Sinclair in the final of the Australian Amateur

Russell (above) featured in a pictorial spread in 'The Weekly Times' on the Australian Open golf on 13 September 1924

Alex Russell's 1924 Australian Open gold medal (left) in the centre, with casts showing the inscriptions on the obverse and reverse sides. It is on display today in the Royal Melbourne clubhouse

The Royal Melbourne Golf Club

Australian Foursomes Championship

DAY THREE Saturday 6th September 1924

Alex Russell and fellow Victorian C.H. "George" Fawcett, who had also had a good Open Championship, were in brilliant form. Russell's long straight driving and Fawcett's accuracy made them a formidable combination. They set a course record for foursomes with their first round and had the next best round for the day in the afternoon to win by six shots from Ivo Whitton and Eric Quirk. There was a concurrent handicap event based on the morning round and this was also won by Fawcett and Russell (+4) nett 75, from Ross and Tunbridge (+3) nett 78.

Fawcett-Russell   3, 4, 4, 4, 3, 3, 5, 5, 3 = 34

                4, 4, 5, 4, 3, 3, 4, 5, 5 = 37   **71**

In the afternoon, Fawcett and Russell continued their almost flawless par golf, going out in 35 with a birdie at the 7th and a bogey at the 8th. This was the only round of the day to better 75 other than their own morning record-breaking round.

Fawcett-Russell   3, 5, 4, 4, 3, 4, 4, 5, 3 = 35

                4, 4, 5, 4, 4, 5, 5, 4, 4 = 39   **74**

Sunday 7 September was a rest day for the players, with the Amateur Championship starting on the Monday. A weary Russell no doubt appreciated the break.

C. H. "George" Fawcett was a fine amateur golfer, perhaps best known for the champion foursomes combination he made with long-time partner and fellow Royal Melbourne member Alex Russell. Fawcett did not begin playing golf until his twenties and in 1905 he migrated to Tasmania where he won two Tasmanian Amateurs prior to enlisting and serving in France as Lieutenant in the Army. Upon his return to Victoria he joined Royal Melbourne and in 1921 he won the Victorian Amateur and the Club Championship. His biggest individual achievement was being runner-up in the 1930 Australian Open after a move to Royal Sydney. The pairing of Russell and Fawcett also won The Australasian Foursomes Challenge Shield on six occasions.

Alex Russell and C. H. "George" Fawcett as caricatured by H.B. (after Wells) in 1922

The Royal Melbourne Golf Club

C.H. "George" Fawcett (left)

Australian Amateur Championship

Qualifiers for the match play in the Australian Amateur were the top sixteen amateurs in the Australian Open with the draw being an unseeded one, i.e. where a player finished in the qualifying had no influence on the draw, thus 1 did not play 16, 2 plays 15 etc., as happens today. All matches were 36 holes match play – another gruelling event. The draw was:

I. H. Whitton vs E. J. Quirk
A. W. Jackson vs W. B. Tunbridge
F. L. Bulte vs A. Russell
C. H. Fawcett vs J. C. Sharp

Dr K. Ross vs B. Pearce
F. E. Headlam vs Dr L. W. Craig
H. Morrison vs E. G. Schlapp
H. R. Sinclair vs A. A. Hancock

Monday 8th September 1924

Alex Russell vs Fred Bulte

F.L. 'Fred' Bulte, a sixteen year-old lad from Commonwealth Golf Club, was two up at the turn, but was one down to Russell at lunch. In the afternoon, Bulte squared the match with a three at the first, but Russell steadily pulled away with par golf from the 6th after losing a hole by four putting. The match ended on the 14th hole.

The results for the day had been:

I. H. Whitton def. E. J. Quirk 3/1
W. B. Tunbridge def. A. W. Jackson 3/2
A. Russell def. F. L. Bulte 6/4
C. H. Fawcett def. J. C. Sharp 7/5

B. Pearce def. Dr K. Ross 6/4
Dr L. W. Craig def. F. E. Headlam 2/1
E. G Schlapp def. H. Morrison 2up
H. R. Sinclair def. A. A. Hancock 7/6

Tuesday 9th September 1924

Alex Russell vs Ivo Whitton

Needless to say this was the match that aroused most interest, with Ivo Whitton the holder of the title for the last two years and Alex Russell with a chance to make a clean-sweep of all titles at the championships. At lunch the players were all square.

A group photo of some of the competitors in the 1924 Australian Amateur at Sandringham, with Alex Russell at the right of the second row. Other competitors include Eric Apperly, Harry Hattersley and Mick Ryan.

After the break the wind picked up and with Russell playing the steadier golf, turned 3 up. Whitton had reduced the deficit to one at the 13th, then Russell nearly had a hole-in-one at the next, to return the difference to two. The rain was collecting on Russell's glasses, however, the match finished at the 16th when Russell holed a good twelve-foot putt and Whitton missed a slightly shorter one, giving a victory to Russell of 3 and 2 over his arch-rival.

The results of the quarter-final matches were:

A. Russell def. I. H. Whitton 3/2
C. H. Fawcett def. W. R. Tunbridge 2/1
E. G. Schlapp def. B. Pearce 5/4
H. R. Sinclair def. Dr L. W. Craig 4/3

Wednesday 10th September 1924

Alex Russell vs George Schlapp

In his semi-final against E. G. Schlapp, Alex Russell was always in control but nothing could be taken away from Schlapp for the way he played, with Russell running out a 4 and 3 victor. In the other semi-final, Sydney golfer Harry Sinclair defeated C. H. Fawcett at the 16th in a high standard match. While the players had been square at lunch, Sinclair was steadier in the afternoon. Sinclair's putting had been exceptional and one newspaper suggested that his name should be "Sink-Laird"

Friday, 12th September 1924

Alex Russell vs Harry Sinclair

Russell and Sinclair were justifiably the two finalists. Russell had shown remarkable form with patches of brilliance over the previous eight days. Sinclair had played consistently, had scored 70 in the first round of match play, was striking the ball well and putting brilliantly. The previous year he had been runner-up to Ivo Whitton in this event.

Russell was 1 hole up at the turn and was only one over fours, despite two stymies costing him strokes, indicative of the quality of the golf. Over the second nine the lead changed several times and at lunch Russell was 1 up. In difficult conditions, Russell had shot 79 to Sinclair's 80.

In the afternoon at the turn, Russell was 1 up, the margin at lunch. Both players had taken 36 shots. After the 12th the match was all square. At the 14th both players three putted from about twelve feet. Russell was now one down with four to play. Russell pushed his second at the 15th to lose the hole and go two down. At the next he was again in the bunker, but Sinclair three-putted making it a halved hole, with the score now dormie two. At the 17th, Sinclair was in trouble off the tee and took four to reach the green. Russell, with two great woods, was just short of the green and his run-up left him with an eight-foot putt. When Sinclair made six, Russell had two for the hole but surprisingly hit his putt four feet past the hole and missed the return, halving the hole and losing the match 2 and 1.

The next day the 'Sun News Pictorial' newspaper reported the game under the heading of "Russell's Day Off". This seems rather unfair to Russell when one looks at the scores for 27 holes in windy conditions over a very penal course. Also, it was equally unfair to Sinclair, as both men had played high standard golf considering the conditions. The scribes put the deterioration in play after the final turn down to

Alec Russell (Royal Melbourne), open Champion and runner-up to Sinclair (Moore Park) for the amateur title.

nerves. Experienced players at that level, feed off the tension, or they would never have reached that level, however, once physical or mental fatigue enters the equation, then nerves can become a negative factor. Some of the three putts over the last few holes certainly smack of mental and/or physical exhaustion. Newspaper reporters typically prefer to be critical of sportsmen's performances. Russell's putting may have let him down over the last few holes, but he had come within a whisker of making a clean sweep of all three titles. He had dominated the 1924 National Championship Meeting.

TO FIGHT THE FINAL ON FRIDAY.—*Alex. Russell (left), who defeated E. G. Schlapp, 4 up and 3 to play, in the semi-final match for the amateur championship of Australia at Royal Melbourne links yesterday, will play off with H. R. Sinclair (right), who won from C. H. Fawcett.*

Newspaper clipping (above) showing the two finalists in the 1924 Amateur – Alex Russell and Harry Sinclair

Caricature of Alex Russell by Reynolds (left)

As Wells saw the Game between Russell and Schlapp

*A cartoon by Wells following Alex Russell's victory over "Abe"
Schlapp in the semi-final of the 1924 Australian Amateur
Championship. The next day Harry Sinclair did indeed upset
Russell's apple cart.*

*Russell with his young caddy
Leonard Barnett (right)*

Alex. Russell and his caddy

50 'The Sporting Globe' of 6th September 1924 reported that Russell had a young local lad by the name of Leonard Barnett, aged 14 and 4ft. 6in. tall, caddy for him throughout the championship meeting. *"He's a great fellow,"* said young Leonard, although Russell couldn't remember his name, eventually settling on calling him Jerry. *"There is one thing you can always depend on Mr. Russell for one thing, and that is keeping his drive on the fairway….My oath, but he treated me well. After his record round on Thursday he tipped me 15/- and yesterday he gave me 25/- to celebrate the win. All I hope is that I will be carrying for him in the next open championship he wins."*

His Career After 1924

The following year, Alex Russell won the Victorian Amateur, thrashing his opponent in the final, W. H. Bailey, by a margin of 10 and 9. In that year's Australian Open held at the Australian Golf Club's links at Kensington in Sydney, Russell put up a splendid defence of his title, just falling short and finishing tied for third place, 5 shots behind the winner, Fred Popplewell. 'Golf' magazine noted that *"the Victorian amateur is to be heartily congratulated in the magnificent effort he put up in defending his title. On a strange course, with tricky greens, he put up an excellent fight and battled bravely to the end. To get within five strokes of the winner's fine total his display was deserving of great praise."*

Towards the end of 1925, Russell and Arthur Le Fevre, the Royal Melbourne professional, played a four-ball best-ball match against his wife Jess Russell and Mona MacLeod, handing them out 8 strokes. However, the ladies did not need all those shots, winning the match 4 and 3 with a fine best ball of nett 64. Jess made a three at the 13th and a two at the 14th.

In 1926, he was victorious in the South Australian Amateur Championship played at Royal Adelaide's Seaton course. In 1927, he was a semi-finalist in the New South Wales Amateur Championship, and was runner up to Bill Edgar in the Victorian

Amateur Championship. Edgar was later to recount what he thought was the greatest shot he had ever played, as being the two-wood he played at the crucial 16th hole in the afternoon of that match against Russell.

Alex had a magnificent record in foursomes, winning the Australian title twice, first in 1924 with C. H. "George" Fawcett, and again in 1926 with A. W. "Gus" Jackson. Russell won the Victorian State Foursomes title four times, firstly with T. F. Rutledge in 1919, and three times with Fawcett, in 1922, 1925, and 1926. Russell and Fawcett had a remarkable series of successes in The Australasian Foursomes Challenge Shield, donated by 'The Australasian' newspaper, winning an unprecedented six times in the seven years from 1922 to 1927. Each metropolitan club entered a pair for the match play event, with sufficient entries for five rounds for the winners and runners-up. The matches, especially the final, were supported by large galleries at that time. Fawcett was not a long hitter but he was accurate with a wonderful short game, and combined with Russell's length from the tee, this made them an ideal foursomes combination.

Messrs. A. W. JACKSON and ALEX. RUSSELL, 1926 Foursome Champions of Australia.

In 1927, wishing to gain practice for the upcoming Australian Championship Meeting, Alex Russell and Arthur LeFevre issued a challenge to any professional and an amateur from the one club to a 36-hole four-ball better-ball match. In August that year, Ivo Whitton and Reg Jupp took up the gauntlet thrown down by

Jess Russell

Russell and LeFevre, with the challengers victorious by a 2 up margin after storming home to win the last five holes of their 36-hole match at Metropolitan. Russell and Ivo Whitton then teamed up to play a match against F. L. Bulte and Bill Edgar in which the former pair were victorious.

The combination of Alex Russell and F.E. "Peter" Headlam were also very unlucky not to have won the 1927 Australian Foursomes title played at Sandringham. At the 7th hole their ball was stolen after the second shot, which was a blind shot over the hill to what is now part of Royal Melbourne's 18th West fairway. At the time, it was thought the ball had probably been stolen, however, Russell and Headlam elected to go back and play under the penalty of stroke and distance, since they could not be certain as to what had happened. It was later discovered that a small boy in the bushes had stolen the ball. This resulted in a tie with Ivo Whitton and Legh Winser. To further compound the drama, in the play-off at the 4th hole after both had holed out, it was discovered that each pair had played the wrong ball. The matter was referred to the Australian Golf Union, who disqualified both pairs and declared there would be no Foursomes Champions that year. The disqualification of both pairs was later determined by the R&A Rules of Golf Committee as being incorrect, and that a replay should have been ordered.

In 1930, now aged 38, Alex Russell was again runner-up in the Australian Amateur, this time to Harry Hattersley at the Metropolitan Golf Club. In a match watched by almost 1,000 spectators, the gallery witnessed a great display of long driving by the young Hattersley, with Russell not far behind. At lunch Russell was two-up, but failed to produce the same form in the afternoon to go down by a margin of 3 and 1.

Russell was a regular member of the Victorian Interstate Team in the 1920s and 1930s. He twice won the Riversdale Cup, an event of considerable prestige, both then and now. He also won Yarra Yarra's traditional Easter Monday scratch event in 1929, playing on the new course he had just designed. Tied after 36 holes with W. Fowler, the Victorian champion, a 9-hole play-off was to decide the winner. Still tied after these extra holes, it was decided that the match would then continue as 'sudden death'. Russell's birdie three at the difficult 13th (426 yards) decided the event. After playing 48 holes for the day, to birdie the 49th is something only a great and persistent golfer could have achieved. Alex Russell represented his club Royal Melbourne in the pennant team from 1919 to 1931, except for the year 1928 when he declared himself unavailable.

The successful 1926 Victorian team (right)

> "Mrs. Alex. Russell was one of the big gallery that followed the final of the Foursomes Shield competition last Saturday. She was just a little ahead of two women who apparently had only a limited amount of appreciation for the wonderful Alex. "That Russell man!" said one of them. "There he goes again, stymieing that poor little boy. You know he always goes for stymies." Apart from the fact that Alex. Russell is one of the finest sportsmen in the game, those ladies were giving him greater credit than even he merits. If anyone were foolish enough to go for a stymie rather than the hole he would be confronted with a job that is much more difficult than some folk apparently imagine."

'The Herald' 28 April 1926

Three times Russell was club champion at Royal Melbourne, in 1922, 1929, and the last in 1937 when he defeated Ivo Whitton, when these two ageing champions were aged 45 and 43 respectively. To put these three wins in perspective, during those years many of the best golfers in Australia were members of the Royal Melbourne Golf Club. Indeed, the Victorian Golf Association's magazine 'Golf Victoria' published in 2002 an Honour Roll of 25 great Victorian golfers from before World War II, which included Ivo Whitton, Norman Brookes, C. H. 'George' Fawcett, William Nankivell, and Alex Russell, all of whom had been contemporary members of RMGC. Other Royal Melbourne golfers named in the Honour Roll were P. C. Anderson, Hon. Michael Scott, H. A. Howden, Claude Felstead and A. R. Lempriere, however, these players were no longer competing when Russell was a force.

VICTORIAN TEAM, WINNERS OF INTERSTATE MATCH.
*Left to right—*Standing : L. E. Schwartz, E. G. Schlapp, T. E. Headlam, W. H. Bailey. Sitting : A. W. Jackson, I. H. Whitton, (Capt.), Alex. Russell.

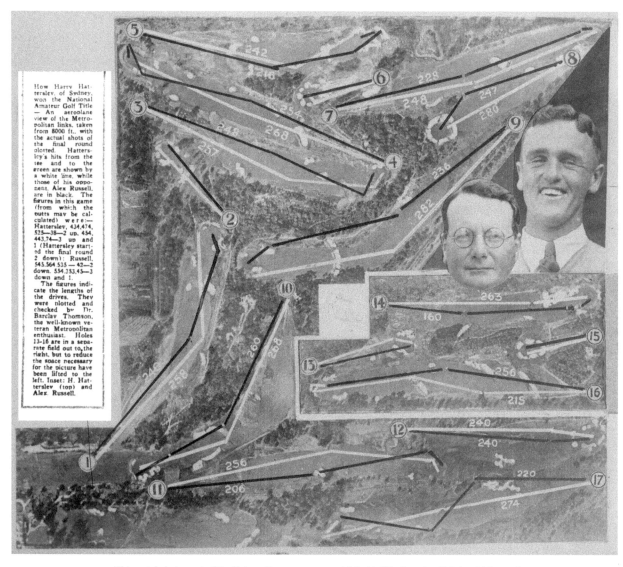

How Harry Hattersley, of Sydney, won the National Amateur Golf Title — An aeroplane view of the Metropolitan links, taken from 8000 ft., with the actual shots of the final round plotted. Hattersley's hits from the tee and to the green are shown by a white line, while those of his opponent, Alex Russell, are in black. The figures in this game (from which the putts may be calculated) were:— Hattersley, 434,474, 525—38—2 up. 454, 443,74—3 up and 1 (Hattersley started the final round 2 down): Russell, 545,564 535 — 42—2 down. 554,353,43—3 down and 1.

The figures indicate the lengths of the drives. They were plotted and checked by Dr. Barclay Thomson, the well-known veteran Metropolitan enthusiast. Holes 13-16 are in a separate field out to the right, but to reduce the space necessary for the picture have been lifted to the left. Inset: H. Hattersley (top) and Alex Russell.

This aerial photograph of the Metropolitan course was published in 'The Sporting Globe' on 24 September 1930 following the Australian Amateur final between Harry Hattersley and Alex Russell that Hattersley won 3 and 1. The white lines depict Hattersley's shots while the black lines depict Russell's. While Russell was considered to be a long driver, he was consistently outdriven by the younger Hattersley.

State Library of Victoria

Russell was elected a member of the Royal and Ancient Golf Club of St Andrews on 13 August 1951, and held that membership until his death in 1961, a singular honour for an Australian golfer. He was also a member at the Barwon Heads Golf Club, the Beaufort Golf Club and the Gala Golf Club in Lismore, Victoria. Alex was made a Life Member of Royal Melbourne in 1933 for his services to the club and he continued to serve as a member of its Council (committee) from 1929 until 1955. He was also made a Life Member of Yarra Yarra in 1928 for his services in designing the club's new course.

Alex Russell played in the British Amateur Championship on two occasions. The first time was at Royal Lytham & St Annes in 1935, losing his first round match to H. E. Taylor (Royal Mid-Surrey) 5 and 4. On the same trip he played in the Open at Muirfield, at least he was an entrant. It is reported that he played one qualifying round at Muirfield but withdrew, with no reason given. In a later trip to Britain in 1938, Russell played in the British Amateur, this time at Troon, unfortunately drawing Cyril Tolley in the first round. Tolley went out in 32 to Russell's 36, eventually defeating the Australian 5 and 3. Tolley was one of the outstanding British golfers between the two wars, winning the British Amateur twice, semi-finalist once, and quarter finalist three times.

Russell kept playing championship events even though his golf was not at a high enough standard for him to be as competitive as he once was. He played in the 1939 Victorian Amateur at Yarra Yarra and qualified for the match play, winning his first-round match comfortably. In the second round, he came up against *"the brilliant Laurie Duffy"* who treated him as he had his first-round opponent. 'The Sporting Globe' noted that, *"the Russell-Duffy match went out half an hour before schedule time after lunch, and when it was suggested that the set time had been advertised, Russell remarked "Who wants to see Laurie beat me 8 and 7?" At the end of the match he cheerfully remarked "I made only one mistake. I missed a 6-footer that would have halved the 29th and thus was beaten 9 and 7 instead of the anticipated 8 and 7.""* Although his golf was waning he most certainly had not lost his sense of humour.

His son Philip only played golf with his father once, other than on their 6-hole course at 'Mawallok', and that was at Royal Melbourne with Ivo Whitton as a third, a daunting experience for a young man. When asked to describe his father's swing, his one-word answer was, *"Perfect."* He also added that *"he swung at the ball, didn't hit it,"* and that when playing on the short 'Mawallok' course he exhibited *"a very, very controlled swing."* After suffering his first stroke in 1950, Alex rarely played golf again.

Alex Russell recovers from a bunker (right) in the 1930 Australian Open at Metropolitan

Course Records

Alex Russell set a new course record for Royal Melbourne's Sandringham links of 68 during the 1924 Australian Open. That record stood for nearly 6 years until shortly before the course was replaced by the new West Course in 1931, when RMGC professional Arthur Le Fevre shot a 66 in March 1930. In that same meeting Russell and his foursomes partner C. H. Fawcett set a new foursomes course record at Sandringham of 71.

At the Victoria Golf Club's Fishermen's Bend course, Russell played in the Open Scratch Medal event held on 26 April 1926, and shot a 69 in the morning round, a new course record. He followed up with 72 in the afternoon, winning the event by a whopping 9 strokes in a field that included Whitton and a number of Victoria's prominent professionals including Reg Jupp and Arthur Le Fevre. Amazingly, Russell also tied for the handicap event even though he was playing off +5. His record score was equalled by A. W. Jackson in 1927, but was never bettered as the club soon moved to its new home at Cheltenham.

Caricature of Russell (above) by Hector Morrison from 1931

Russell also held for a time in 1929 both the 9-hole (36) and 18-hole (76) records at the 9-hole Lismore course of the Gala Golf Club in country Victoria.

Alec Russell (V.) in a bunker.

Russell's Golf Game

A newspaper article once described Alex Russell as someone who was always feared as a match player due to his occasional streaks of great brilliance. *"He appeals to the gallery, because he has a beautiful crisp style with all his clubs, never hesitates, nor plays safe when the green is within reach. His swing with his woods is that happy medium between flat and upright."* He was known for hitting a long and high ball, and at 5 feet 11 inches (180 cm) tall, he was taller than most of his contemporaries and he used this extra height to his advantage.

Afton Morcom, son of Royal Melbourne's esteemed head greenkeeper Mick Morcom and brother of Vern, wrote about Alex Russell's success in the 1925 South Australian Amateur in 'The American Golfer' of March 1926. It was quite a coup to have an article on an Australian golfer published in one of the premier American golf magazines. In the final match, Russell defeated C. Legh Winser, the Australian Amateur Champion in 1921, on his home course at Royal Adelaide, and Morcom had this to say about Russell's swing:

> *"His stance is almost square. His feet seem to have a solid grip of Mother Earth while his knees are slightly bent. About his grip the noticeable point is its looseness. In fact at the top of his swing he opens his hands (a dangerous thing, so a couple of professionals tell him) and at this stage one would have little difficulty in removing the club from his grasp. Like most accomplished golfers he preserves a fairly straight left arm. He addresses the ball with the toe of the club and just after the final waggle gives the club a distinct push away from him.*
>
> *Having amputated his legs and his arms we will now turn to his body. The hips and shoulders pivot fully with the head always giving the impression of acting as an anchor to the swing."*

Of his soft grip, 'The Australasian' noted in 1935 that, *"Alex. Russell in his palmy days, when he could really hit them, used to say that a child might pull the club out of his hands at the top of the swing, so lightly was it held."* Writing in 'The Herald' on 6 September 1924, H. G. Adam described Russell's golf:

> *"Russell above all is a picturesque golfer with ease and grace in all his wooden shots and deadly accurate with his putting when on his game. It is not until one has seen Russell play several rounds that the grace of his swing is apparent. He is a man who impresses more and more every time he is seen in action. Until his calibre is known the casual observer would rank him as a mediocre player with little concentration on his game. There is freedom and ease in everything he does, even in his swinging stride down the fairway."*

Was this perhaps a throwback to his old teacher P.C. Anderson's poetic swing?

Russell's grip (far left) from the front appears quite conventional, but the view from the side shows that he used a reverse overlap grip. At the top of his swing (above) his grip appeared quite loose and his right thumb had slipped off the club.

Alex. Russell, noted amateur golfer and course architect.

A . . .

Five Minutes' Chat with Australian Champions

"PROPER WEIGHT-TRANSFERENCE IS ESSENTIAL" — SAYS ALEX. RUSSELL

By ALEX. RUSSELL, former Open Champion, in a Talk with "Pennant"

ALEX. RUSSELL is not only one of the State's finest amateurs—he is also one of the best thinkers the game possesses. One has only to converse for a few moments with the Royal Melbourne man to realise that his mind, keen and incisive, has delved deeply into the mechanics of the golf shot—the whys and the wherefores of the game.

Encountering him among the spectators at the Williams-Ryan Championship final, I congratulated Russell upon his good showing in the semi-final. It was only at the last hole of that match that he consented to surrender to Ryan.

"Neither of us played good golf," he said; "still, I think I have been playing better recently—thanks to Walter Hagen."

As there seemed something good behind this, I invited Mr. Russell to enlarge upon the subject.

Here is the interesting story that the former Australian champion unfolded:

"It all harks back to a little advice that Walter volunteered to Ivo Whitton," he said. "The American was overhauling Ivo's swing. You'll recall that Ivo's form was a bit sick just at that period. Hagen watched him hit a few shots."

"No, Ivo," he said, "your pivot's not right. You are pivoting your hips too much without transferring the weight to your left heel. You must slide your tail out of the way, otherwise you can't possibly hit against your left side. What's more, you can't get that right shoulder under and through."

That tip, coming from the great Sir Walter, seemed too good to miss. I watched him closely, observing just how he transferred his weight on to that left heel immediately the downward swing began; how he pushed his left hip out of the road, and how he carried out that wonderful 'under and through' movement of the right shoulder. I noted particularly the great distance that Hagen's club head followed along the line of flight. No one out here had anything approaching that remarkable following-up action of his. Soon I set to work applying Walter's principles to my own game, and I can say definitely that improvement resulted."

I could quite believe it. Watching Alex. in the State Championship, one could not help being impressed by his driving, so powerful and sustained.

Here I broke in to enquire whether Alex. thought that this pushing of the club head right out after the ball was responsible for the greater distance that the Americans were reputed to get.

"Well," he answered, "it certainly results in consistently accurate long hitting.

"This weighting of the left heel makes the club head travel along the line of flight. Apart from this it gives greater latitude for a good shot, even with slight mistiming."

Later in the clubhouse he drew my attention to several action photographs of American golfers appearing in overseas magazines. In every instance, whether in ordinary action photographs or "movie" strips, the club head was seen shooting straight out along the line of flight. Those pictorial records also demonstrated amply the other point that Russell had stressed, that the transference of weight to the left heel immediately the down swing is commenced—aided by sliding the hip out of the way—forces the club head to follow along this line.

I mentioned the fact that Victor East, former Royal Melbourne professional, possessed this action in a marked degree.

"Yes," agreed Alex., "and the best present-day example is Mick Ryan. Mick hits against that left side beautifully, and he certainly goes out after the ball.

"Believe me," he added, "that planting of weight on the left heel and bracing of the left side are a great aid to proper balance, and after all, balance is the basic essential of both length and direction in the golf shot.

"Yes," he concluded, "I'm glad I saw Walter Hagen, even if it were only for that one splendid piece of advice that he tendered."

A balanced and comfortable address position (top left)

Russell's swing at impact (left)

A rare interview with Alex Russell on the subject of swing technique (above) was published in the 1 September 1931 issue of 'Golf' magazine

In 1925, Russell visited Brisbane and one writer described his style as being "*beautifully easy, his tee shots are a revelation, and his wrist work deadly. He does not use the over-lapping grip, and brings the whole weight of the body into his strokes. His iron play is equally convincing and accurate.*"

'Pennant,' writing in 'Golf' magazine on 1 July 1925 noted, "*There was Russell standing well up to the ball, his stance being almost square, and the weight distributed evenly over the two feet. When the swing was commenced there was no body movement except that of a fine pivoting action. Rhythm was the keynote. The club went forward and through as it had come back, smoothly and evenly.*"

The golf writer at 'The Referee' newspaper in Sydney wrote in February 1927 that he had photographed a number of golfers and that, "*the two most beautiful and graceful positions, out of dozens, are those of D. G. Soutar and Alex Russell. In each case the picture shows the club head at the instant of impact. Both balls were perfectly hit, and were such that the players expressed the greatest satisfaction......the positions of both men is perfect, and it is doubted whether anyone, even the most critical, could find a fault with anything in the position of either player.*"

Frank Brown wrote about sportsmen's styles in 'The Sporting Globe' in 1928 and used Alex Russell and Bill Edgar as examples of "*free, open wristy swings*". Russell was a noted long driver for his day. In July 1929, he won a long drive competition held at the Northern District Country Championship at Bendigo with one drive of 284 yards (260 metres) and another of 265 yards (242 metres). The 'Sydney Mail' noted after Russell's win in the 1924 Australian Open that "*no other golfer, except perhaps the inimitable Carnegie Clark, gets quite the amount of back spin on the ball that Russell does.*"

Jack Dillon, the doyen of Melbourne's golf writers, succinctly summed up Russell's status in 'The Sporting Globe' on 27 July 1927, stating that:

> "*In Victoria three golfers occupy a class apart. They are Ivo Whitton, Alex Russell and A. W. Jackson.*"

While technique is an important aspect of being a great golfer, temperament is arguably as important. 'Pennant,' in discussing golfing temperaments in 'Golf' magazine noted, "*Take Alec. Russell for example. One cannot imagine that he would ever be a victim to the strain imposed by a tight match. Should his life depend on a single shot one can picture Russell standing up to it, calm, confident and without any undesired tightening of his muscles. That is one of the reasons why Russell is a truly great golfer.*"

Photographs of Russell swinging (top), and chipping and putting (above), featured in a scrapbook kept by his son Philip

'Raith'

In August 1924 Alex and Jess Russell purchased a substantial house called 'Raith' on Fernhill Road in Sandringham from his former foursomes partner Major Foster Rutledge. The house was built sometime prior to 1909 and was situated on a large allotment of 2 acres that only had a driveway access to Fernhill Road but with a wider frontage to Cowper Street. 'Raith' was described as *"a well built modern two-storey timber residence, about 14 rooms, etc., Garage. Hot Water Service, etc."* On the ground floor it had a *"spacious entrance hall, dining-room, sitting-room, double bedroom (with dressing room and bathroom, nursery, sleep-out, maid's sitting-room, kitchen, scullery, pantry, larder, dairy, store."* Upstairs contained a *"smoking-room, double bedroom (with dressing-room and bathroom, single bedroom, three maid's rooms, bathroom,"* while the Outbuildings included *"Laundry, 2 garages, man's room."* The house had *"electric light and gas."*

The driveway entrance to 'Raith' off Fernhill Road was directly opposite the entrance to the Royal Melbourne Golf Club's Sandringham clubhouse, and would have been considered by Russell to be an ideal location so close to the Club. The Russells owned 'Raith' for a little over 10 years, but only lived there until 1932 when they moved to 'Mawallok' and they leased the property to an operator as a guest house. The house and land was placed on the market in February 1935 but did not sell until 1936. In May 1936, under the instructions of Jess Russell, all the contents including furniture, statuary, bronzes, china and paintings were sold at auction. 'Raith' was eventually demolished in 1973 and the land subdivided.

Aerial view of the Royal Melbourne G.C. clubhouse and surroundings (above) from 1933 showing the relationship of the 'Raith' residence to the clubhouse
The Royal Melbourne Golf Club

Brochure for the sale of 'Raith' and its land in February 1935 (right)

Metropolitan Board of Works survey plans from 1915 (below) showing the short walk Russell faced from 'Raith' to the golf club.

Dr Alister MacKenzie photographed on board the SS Berengaria
on 9 March 1926, sailing from New York City to Southampton

Chapter 5

DR ALISTER MACKENZIE & GOLF COURSE ARCHITECTURE

The visit to Australia by Dr Alister MacKenzie in October 1926 for the purpose of designing a new course for the Royal Melbourne Golf Club, whilst a significant event for Australian golf and its golf courses, was a life-changing event for Alex Russell.

Alex Russell's Competence

Russell had been asked by the club in 1924 to prepare a plan for a new 18-hole course at Royal Melbourne, using the land to the east of the 8th hole of the time, with an entrance from Bay Street (Cheltenham Road). This was strong evidence that the club was certainly aware of his interest in golf course architecture. He probably would have first studied this in Britain, and as the dominant course architect in Britain before World War I (and after) was Harry Colt, it is very likely that Alex Russell would have been influenced by Colt's philosophies.

While it is likely that he had read writings by Colt and almost certainly Dr Alister MacKenzie, he would have been more familiar with the work of the former. In 1912 Colt wrote a paper in which many of the same principles can be found as those espoused by MacKenzie in his lectures to the North of England greenkeepers

Contour map of the site for the creation of the new Royal Melbourne course to replace the Sandringham Course. It is believed that Alex Russell surveyed the site using his engineering skills gained at Cambridge and in the Royal Garrison Artillery.

The Royal Melbourne Golf Club

in 1913 and 1914, which formed the basis of his 1920 book "Golf Architecture". Colt and Alison also published their book "Some Essays on Golf Course Architecture" that same year, to which MacKenzie contributed a chapter on labour-saving devices. It is known that Russell had studied Robert Hunter's 1926 book "The Links", as he commended this book to the secretary of Lake Karrinyup in his letter to that club in March 1928. MacKenzie became a partner of Colt immediately after the war, and later Hunter became a partner of MacKenzie. So, it is little wonder, if prior to 1926, Russell had embraced the ideas of Colt, and likely those of MacKenzie, and that the two men, MacKenzie and Russell, should see eye-to-eye when they finally met.

MacKenzie was greatly interested in, and an instructor during World War I on camouflage. It is clear from his war diary that Alex Russell also appreciated the importance of camouflage as his life depended on it when at a forward observation post, so here was another thing in common. In 1925, Alex Russell copied the approach used by Colt of first surveying the land, then drawing a contour plan and finally producing a three-dimensional model of his proposed new course for Royal Melbourne, skills he would have learnt while in the Royal Garrison Artillery. 'Golf' magazine in August 1925 described Russell as:

> *"A clever engineer, he has shown his capabilities in another direction. In the Secretary's office at the Royal Melbourne Course Clubhouse there is a large relief model of the proposed extensions to the Sandringham course. This is Russell's handiwork, and is much admired by all who have seen it."*

Sadly though, both the plan and the model are lost. In fact, according to recollections from his son Philip, Alex set up a large 'sand-box' at his home 'Raith' in Sandringham, in a room dedicated to his golf design activities in which he designed the layout and greens of his courses.

The perception that, prior to Dr MacKenzie's visit, Alex Russell was something of an 'empty vessel' as far as golf course design was concerned and that he learnt all his skills from MacKenzie, is contrary to recorded opinion of that time. While there is no doubt that Russell would have learnt a great deal from the Doctor during their time together, there is abundant evidence that Russell was widely read and quite competent in a theoretical sense before MacKenzie's arrival. His 1926 visit to

"PANTS FOR PINE VALLEY

These days, with Dr. MacKenzie here, practically all our prominent golfers are discussing golf courses, golf holes and golf architecture generally. Everywhere one goes, someone is sketching what he considers an ideal hole, and explaining just what the doctor does to bring about his golfing transformations. Robert Hunter's great book, with its exquisite illustrations of greens and holes and bunkers and such like, has been bought up so ravenously that it is now impossible to procure a copy, and groups poring over it may be seen in every clubhouse. Alex Russell, the former open champion, has been so intrigued by some of the illustrations, particularly some showing views of Pine Valley course in U.S.A., that he will not now be happy until he plays over some of the courses. With feeling and longing that could not possibly be mistaken, he last week look in his expressive and horn-rimmed orbs "I at Sandringham murmured, with a far away just pant for Pine Valley." (Sic) Perhaps Dr. MacKenzie may bring part of Pine Valley to him and locate sections of it on the remodelled Royal Melbourne lay out. He is a man who does such things, and he is very kind."

'The Herald' 3rd November 1926

AERIAL VIEW OF PINE VALLEY.
View of the drive at the first hole; the bunker and green at the second; all of the third, the fourth, the fifth, and the sixth holes; and the long terrifying second shot to the eighteenth green. Although Pine Valley is inland, it has many of the characteristics of seaside courses.

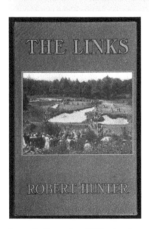

THE FOURTEENTH AT PINE VALLEY. (Crump.)
This green was built in the lake. It is an exacting shot to this island. 164 yards from the tee.

In early November 1926, about a week after the arrival of Dr MacKenzie in Melbourne, 'The Herald' newspaper reported on the enthusiasm that Alex Russell had expressed for the Pine Valley course in New Jersey, USA, based upon the illustrations he had seen in Robert Hunter's – MacKenzie's new American partner – recently published book 'The Links' (above). Russell later recommended the book to the committee at Lake Karrinyup in Perth.

Robert Hunter (right) and some views of Pine Valley taken from his 1926 book (far right)

THE THIRD AT PINE VALLEY. (Crump.)
There is no hole more exacting and thrilling to play well than this one of 184 yards. From the tee the green looks like an oasis in a desert, an absurdly small oasis, although every detail of it can be seen. The green is admirably modelled and of a beautiful design.

Australia allowed Russell the opportunity to further develop and refine his ideas and most importantly, to put them into practice. A theoretical golf course architect is no architect at all, and the budding golf course architect needed projects to get his teeth into and MacKenzie was the catalyst in providing those projects.

The course design that Russell produced for Royal Melbourne in 1924 to 1925 was highly praised by MacKenzie in his letter of recommendation for Russell.

> *"He has made a study of Golf Course Architecture for some years, and on my arrival here I was most favourably impressed with his suggested design for the new Royal Melb. Golf Course as it showed far more originality and ability than the design of any other golf course I have seen since my arrival."*

'The Argus' reported on the announcement of Russell as MacKenzie's new Australian partner on 6 December 1926, saying:

> *"The interesting announcement has just been made that Alec Russell, the well-known Royal Melbourne golfer, who held the title of Open Champion of Australia two years ago, is to be Dr Alister MacKenzie's partner for Australia in the business of golf course architects. As Russell is a civil engineer by profession, he is peculiarly fitted for his new job, and certainly few great golfers know better the good points of a golf course than does the 1924 champion. His model in plasticine for the conversion of the present round at Sandringham into a fresh course embracing the new ground at the club's disposal, which was on view in the clubhouse smoking-room for some months, shows an excellent knowledge of the subject, as well as considerable imagination."*

An article in "Table Talk" on 9 December 1926 provided a similar view on Russell's competence:

> *"Russell is a brilliant man, has travelled extensively abroad, and has for a very long time closely interested himself both in the theory and practice of golf architecture. Rated at plus 5, his golfing standing will immediately give him considerable authority among Australians, and the suggested remodelling of Royal Melbourne, which he submitted to the Club a couple of years ago, so struck Dr MacKenzie that it finally decided him in accepting Russell as his Australian representative."*

In the 'Weekly Times' of 11 December 1926 came further confirmation of his knowledge in the area:

> *"Russell's knowledge and skill to this side of golf has not before been a matter of public knowledge. He is not the sort of man who would spread abroad details of any hobby that was his. But for some years now he has been a close student of*

this subject, and in his travelling abroad he has constantly studied the courses over which he has played. When the subject of remodelling Royal Melbourne was first raised a couple of years ago, he was requested to prepare for the club a complete scheme. This he did and did well. By the work that he did on that occasion he proved conclusively that he had a comprehensive grip of the art of course construction."

The following comments were published in 'Table Talk' on 16 February 1927, following Russell's appointment to design the new Yarra Yarra course:

> *"I expect more from him (Russell) than I would have from MacKenzie had this big task been entrusted to this world authority. MacKenzie would not have bought to it the enthusiasm that Russell will have; he would not have put into it the work the time that Russell will; he would not be so thoroughly possessed of local conditions as the Royal Melbourne man will; he would not have so much to gain by a perfect work, and although beyond doubt MacKenzie's knowledge of his subject is greater at the moment, Russell's store of information is not to be taken lightly. He is likely to cause a very pleasant surprise by what he does on this magnificent piece of land."*

'Golf' magazine in its January 1927 issue reported on his experience of the British courses and lauded his services to the point of the article sounding more like an advertisement:

> *"Mr Russell's reputation as one of Australia's foremost golfers, together with his experience of having played over some of the leading English courses, eminently fits him for the job. He has the time at his disposal, and also the knowledge and ability to carry out the contracts, be they great or small, so that satisfaction is assured to those who may desire to avail themselves of his services."*

An article in 'The Australasian' of 11 May 1927 profiled Charles Lane of the Commonwealth Golf Club and his design activities at that Club and elsewhere, stating that he now joined three other Australians:

> *"..... Alec Russell, S. F. Mann, and H. L. Rymill, who have not just critically noted everything to be seen, in the way of links on the other side, but interviewed and compared notes with the leading course architects from H. S. Colt downwards."*

Perhaps the final word on Alex Russell's competence in this field should be left to Dr MacKenzie himself, who when writing of his Australian tour in the British 'Golf Illustrated' magazine, had this to say about his new partner in the 10 June 1927 issue:

DR. A. MACKENZIE
GOLF COURSE ARCHITECT
Expert in Landscape Work

AMERICAN PARTNERS
—
West of Rocky Mountains
ROBERT HUNTER
PEBBLE BEACH
CALIFORNIA
East of Rocky Mountains
PERRY D. MAXWELL
ARDMORE
OKLAHOMA

MOOR ALLERTON LODGE
LEEDS *ENGLAND*
Telephone 61990

Dear Sir,

    During my visit to Australia I have been impressed with the advisability of taking in a partner whose ideas of Golf Architecture conform as nearly as possible to my own.

    After very careful consideration I have decided that Mr. Alex. Russell, of the Royal Melbourne Golf Club, is far more capable of carrying out these ideas than anyone I have yet met in Australia. He has made a study of Golf Course Architecture for some years, and on my arrival here I was most favorably impressed with his suggested design for the new Royal Melb. Golf Course as it showed far more originality and ability than the design of any other golf course I have seen since my arrival. Moreover, since I arrived here Mr. Russell has been continually associated with me while I have been advising golf clubs, and he has not only drawn some of my plans but has made many valuable suggestions.

    He is one of the very few plus men I know who views the game from an absolutely unselfish standpoint and is most sympathetic to average players who he recognises comprise the majority of club members and on this account alone are entitled to more consideration in the construction of a course than they have been accustomed to receive.

        Yours faithfully,

           ALISTER MACKENZIE

P.S. Please retain this letter for future reference.

Dr MacKenzie's letter of appointment of Alex Russell as his new Australian partner. While the letter is undated, Russell's appointment was announced in early December 1926

"One of the difficulties confronting me in Australia was to make reasonably sure that my advice would be carried out according to my ideas during my absence. For this reason I looked for an Australian partner and was fortunate enough to secure Mr Alec Russell, an ex-Open Champion of Australia, and Secretary to Mr Bruce, the Prime Minister. Mr Russell has already a very sound knowledge of golf course architecture and has studied a good deal not only in Australia but in Britain. He accompanied me and gave me very valuable suggestions during my visits to Australian courses. It had been Mr Russell's intention to go into Parliament, and his name was actually up as a candidate, but he said he would much prefer golf architecture, and I think it possible that in providing attractive golf courses he may do more good for the health and happiness of the community. I have little doubt that Mr Russell, with the help of Morcom, the excellent greenkeeper of the Royal Melbourne Golf Club, will be able to supervise most successfully any work that is entrusted to him."

These extracts show that Russell was not simply considered competent, but that he was highly qualified to carry out any tasks associated with the design of the new Royal Melbourne course and other course projects. His skills are on display in the East Course, about which A.D. Ellis stated, "*... according to highest golfing authorities, could not have been more skilfully performed by anybody.*" Similarly, his works at Yarra Yarra, Lake Karrinyup and Paraparaumu Beach have all stood the test of time and are of a quality far exceeding anything that could have resulted from a 'crash course' in golf design spread over a few weeks.

Indeed, the four major courses with which he was involved in Australia: Royal Melbourne West, Royal Melbourne East, Yarra Yarra, and Lake Karrinyup, all appear in Tom Ramsay's 1981 book "25 Great Australian Courses and How to Play Them". Lake Karrinyup has hosted four Australian Opens and is considered the outstanding course in Western Australia. Paraparaumu Beach was rated 79th in the world ranking in 1999 and hosted the New Zealand Open as recently as 2002 for the twelfth time, where the course was highly praised. Yarra Yarra, while not having hosted an Australian Open, was the venue for seven Women's Australian Opens, and the Ampol and Dunlop tournaments in the 1950s and 60s, as well as Victorian Opens through the 1980s and 90s. A 'strike rate' of this magnitude clearly shows that Alex Russell was far more than simply a competent golf course architect, with the right client and property he could be an inspired one.

To the question *"was Alex Russell just simply a pupil of MacKenzie?"* the answer is certainly a resounding *"No"*. On this matter, Peter Thomson, whose experience and expertise gives him considerable authority, wrote:

"Whether his (Russell's) work was really MacKenzie's by another name is debatable. For mine, he was his own man and, indeed who knows – MacKenzie may have picked up a thing or two from Alex Russell."

Caricature of Dr MacKenzie drawn by Royal Melbourne member, aviator and talented artist Sydney Dalrymple. Captain Dalrymple flew in the Royal Flying Corps in World War I and was club champion in 1935. He had his own plane and often landed it on one of the fairways at Royal Melbourne before a game of golf.

The Royal Melbourne Golf Club

Alex Russell's Number of Course Designs

Another oft-posed question is why did Alex Russell not design more courses than the five main courses he is most often credited with? Research for this book has revealed a number of previously unknown courses and clubs where he had been asked to consult for new courses and the remodelling of existing ones. These courses are listed in a later chapter and depict an architect who was far busier than has previously been understood. There were limits on his design career though. The Great Depression certainly had a major impact on his designing activities through the late 1920s and early 1930s and in 1932 he took over the management of the family property 'Mawallok'. This would have probably reduced the time that he had available to spend on golf course design. Then, World War II took six years out of the prime of his design career, when he ably served his King and country once more.

It is also known that he competed for a number of commissions, especially in Victoria, but was often beaten by local architects such as Sam Berriman and Vern Morcom. Russell's nature appeared to preclude him from "chasing" work and, as a man of independent means, he certainly did not need to rely upon course design for his income, unlike men such as Berriman, whose livelihood depended upon it. After the war, Russell continued to consult to a number of other clubs in Australia and New Zealand regarding course improvements, however, he was never as busy again as in the halcyon days of the late 1920s and early 1930s.

Alex Russell, with his early interest in golf course design, must have been well aware of rumblings from both the United States Golf Association and the Royal & Ancient about infringing amateur status by taking fees for the design of golf courses. Eventually the R&A, as overlords of such matters in the Commonwealth countries such as Australia, decided against any such infringement, and with architects such as Harry Colt, Herbert Fowler and Dr Alister MacKenzie being R&A members of good standing, there was no doubt some internal pressure to resist such a move.

Russell often carried out his design activities without fee. At Royal Melbourne he was a member, and so a fee would not have been expected, nor appropriate. At Yarra Yarra the agreed fee for the new MacKenzie & Russell partnership was £75, with MacKenzie likely receiving half, or perhaps all.

At Lake Karrinyup, when asked about his fee he replied, *"How about a bottle of whisky?"* For the new course in Canberra, where his client was the Federal Capital Commission, Russell charged a commercial fee. Paraparaumu Beach in New Zealand paid for

Alex Russell

MACKENZIE & RUSSELL
GOLF COURSE ARCHITECTS

DR. A. MACKENZIE

MOOR ALLERTON LODGE

LEEDS. ENGLAND

ALEX. RUSSELL

" RAITH, " SANDRINGHAM

VICTORIA

his fares from Australia, and he stayed near the course with Stronach Paterson, with his only reward being a silver hip flask.

Other clubs where it is known that he charged a fee include Glenelg in Adelaide, where he was paid £25 to inspect the course and provide a report with his recommendations. He charged a fee at Riversdale to redesign their course, and at Peninsula as well. The lack of payment on some of his projects would have had a further consequence. While Russell may have been prepared to provide his services for nothing, MacKenzie almost certainly would not have, because it was his profession and his livelihood.

MacKenzie would not have made Alex Russell his partner so that he could give Russell free advice for him in turn to give free advice to clubs. Some clubs claim an association with MacKenzie because Russell used the *'MacKenzie and Russell'* partnership stationery. Perhaps, but unlikely, Russell may have paid MacKenzie out of his own pocket for advice and for the use of the letterhead, however, even if this was so, the advice would have been given to Russell not the club, and therefore, it would not alter the fact that it was purely an Alex Russell course. It is likely though, that with MacKenzie living and working in America from around 1929 and his involvement with various partners there including Robert Hunter, Perry Maxwell and Chandler Egan, that Australia post-1926 was a long way from the front of his mind.

The new firm of MacKenzie & Russell, Golf Course Architects, was formed and Alex Russell embarked upon his new career with considerable passion.

Mr. H. S. Colt, the golf architect.

The letterhead of the new MacKenzie & Russell partnership (top)

Harry Colt, the great English architect (above), was a considerable influence on Alister MacKenzie, and in turn, Alex Russell. This portrayal of Colt was drawn by the great caricaturist Charles Ambrose and published in 'Fry's Magazine' in December 1909.

The trio responsible for making Royal Melbourne's West Course the greatest golf course in Australia, a crown that it still wears proudly to this day

Chapter 6

ROYAL MELBOURNE GOLF CLUB'S WEST COURSE

In 1911, the Royal Melbourne Golf Club purchased 60 acres (24 ha) of land abutting the south-east corner of its Sandringham course, however, any utilisation of it was delayed by the advent of World War I. Post-war there was uncertainty about how the Sandringham area would develop. It was as much a holiday destination as an outer suburb at that time and this was further compounded by problems in locating a new clubhouse. Following the further purchase of land in November 1923 that provided access to what is now the main paddock of Royal Melbourne, Alex Russell was asked in November 1924 by the club's Council to submit a design for a course using this new land as a point of entry to the location of the clubhouse.

The residential clubhouse (above) at Royal Melbourne where Dr MacKenzie stayed during his 1926 visit to Melbourne.

A.T. Brown

At the same time, A. T. Brown, a mining engineer and club stalwart, was also asked to submit a plan of the new course. He had prepared an earlier version back in 1922 using a different point of access, with his suggested clubhouse position located at the site of the present 10th green and 11th tee on the West Course. Brown's later plan was very similar to his 1922 version.

After first surveying and preparing a contour plan of the property, Russell then produced a plasticine model of his design. That Russell was skilled in map-making is clear from an entry in his war-time diary that he had produced a map for his battery. Russell's plan, submitted in February 1925, was described in the Council minutes as a scheme. Being called a scheme, it probably contained more than just an 18-hole course, and may well have included an additional 9-hole course and tennis courts. Both models were on display at the club for some time and Russell's modelling work was commented upon by the press of the day as being *"distinctly brainy. The one he constructed for his proposed lay-out for the new Royal Melbourne course was very well done, and received unstinting praise from Dr MacKenzie."* After both models were submitted to the members it was decided to seek the best person available regardless of cost. As is well known, Dr Alister MacKenzie was selected by Royal Melbourne to design its "New" (West) course.

The Club's Sandringham Course was a mixture of both antiquated and modern golf course design elements, as seen here in this photograph of the 14th green c.1909 (above)

The Good Doctor

When MacKenzie arrived in Melbourne in late October 1926 he stayed in the residential Royal Melbourne clubhouse, a close neighbour to Alex Russell who lived directly across the road from the main entrance to the club in his house 'Raith', at 2 Fernhill Road. Since both were Cambridge men who served

Dr MacKenzie (right) was photographed by a newspaper photographer upon his disembarkation in Melbourne from the SS Otranto on 26 October 1926. It is the only known photograph of MacKenzie taken while he was in Australia.

DR. A. MACKENZIE.

in the British Army during World War I, Russell in the Royal Garrison Artillery and MacKenzie in the Royal Engineers, they had much in common beyond their shared passion for golf and golf architecture. Together they discussed the possibilities of the proposed course and Russell accompanied MacKenzie on his visits to other clubs, with discussions and dinners likely at both the club and in Russell's home.

It is clear from MacKenzie's writings that he knew when he selected Alex Russell as his Australian partner, he was leaving the task of completing the new course in good hands. MacKenzie also knew, and stated publicly, that M.A. "Mick" Morcom was one of the best course curators and constructors that could be found anywhere. Before leaving Melbourne in late November, MacKenzie had Morcom construct one of the holes for the new course, which he described as a short hole of the Eden type, a version of the famous 11th hole on the Old Course at St Andrews, and one of the most copied holes in all of golf. This hole became the renowned par three 5th West, arguably the greatest one-shot hole in Australia. MacKenzie later wrote about the creation of this hole in the 27 May 1927 issue of 'Golf Illustrated' magazine:

> *"While I was in Melbourne Morcom commenced the construction work on the new course, and he made a new short hole of a somewhat similar type to the Eden hole at St Andrews, which new hole is, I think, the best example of artificial work I have ever seen on any golf course, and will certainly be better than any short hole south of the Equator."*

At the Extraordinary General Meeting (EGM) which authorised the Council to proceed with the alterations to the course as recommended by MacKenzie, the club also showed its faith in Russell when the members voted in favour of the following determination, *"Mr H. M. Ross and Mr Alex Russell be appointed to supervise the carrying out of Dr MacKenzie's plan."* Three months later the two men were authorised to depart from Dr MacKenzie's plan where necessary. From reading the Council minutes, it is apparent that departures occurred on several occasions, with some of the changes from MacKenzie's description of the course being rather significant ones.

Early Sketch Plan

Dr MacKenzie wrote an article about the new course he had designed for Royal Melbourne for the 'Herald' newspaper before leaving Australia and it was published on 29 December 1926. While the outward nine as constructed broadly

corresponds with what materialised, the inward nine certainly does not.

Perhaps of interest is that MacKenzie starts his description of the layout under the heading **NEW HOLE** and then commences at the 5th hole (new). A sketch plan of the Royal Melbourne course was discovered in the club's archives as recently as 2005 and was almost certainly drawn by MacKenzie himself. Furthermore, the plan is consistent with MacKenzie's description in the 'Herald' article. While the eighteen-hole layout is in his hand, the other lines indicating possible routings for the additional 9-hole course are in a 'ball-and-stick' format. However, the 'flag-stick' drawn in the first hole of the 9-hole course is very much in MacKenzie's style, suggestive that he drew a 9-hole routing on this plan as well.

An obvious question arises as to why the sketch plan differs from the one on the wall in Royal Melbourne's clubhouse? At one stage, the corner of the present 11th Hole (West) was part of an extensive swamp, which extended for about 400 metres south of the club's boundary. Apart from rainfall, this swamp was fed by a small soak near the current corner bunkers. Anyone building a house in Ardoyne Street adjacent to this area, still needs to be careful, if excavating for a garage under the house, due to the high water table. Aerial photographs taken in 1931 and in 1936, do not show any houses in the area where the swamp existed. However, the 1936 photograph shows an area where soil and vegetation have been removed.

As no house was built there in the next 15 years, it is reasonable to suggest that the land may have been cleared to assist in its drainage. On 27 November 1927 the Council, along with Alex Russell and Hugh Ross, inspected proposed changes to the 16th and 17th holes, amongst others. This would appear to have been the time when the changes to 10th, 11th, 17th and 18th holes were considered.

Extract from MacKenzie's sketch plan showing his proposed one-shot 5th hole with an exaggerated 'T' shaped green

The Royal Melbourne Golf Club

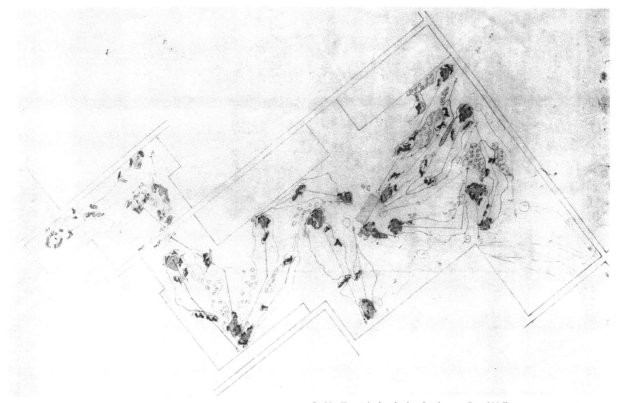

Dr MacKenzie's sketch plan for the new Royal Melbourne course was drawn in pencil by him and
also contained an outline of a possible 9-hole course

The Royal Melbourne Golf Club

The 9-Hole Course and the roles of MacKenzie and Russell

In the 'Herald' article referred to above, MacKenzie wrote that the club was blessed with spare land that could be used for a 9-hole course, perhaps even 18-holes.

> *"The ample space available at Royal Melbourne makes it possible to give members something that is a great asset and an additional attraction; that is a subsidiary short course of nine or even 18 holes. The boon this will provide to the novice desiring to improve his game in*

> *seclusion, safe from the continual 'fores' called by the more experienced players, can be well imagined."*

MacKenzie then also elaborated on the benefit to women golfers of such a course.

On the other hand, the 9-hole course was always treated as a separate enterprise in the minutes of the Council meetings. On 17 March 1927, three months after MacKenzie had left, mention is made in the minutes under the heading 'Nine Hole Course':

> *"In consequence of alteration of site of Clubhouse and the purchase of new land* (Bumpford's block) *the nine-hole course to be redesigned."*

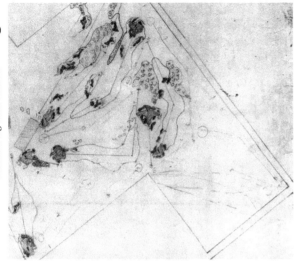

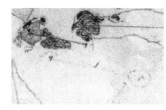

Closer view of MacKenzie's 9-hole layout (far left)

The first hole of the 9-hole layout (left) is sketched out in characteristic ball-and-stick manner, with the flagstick drawn in MacKenzie's distinctive hand

The Royal Melbourne Golf Club

At first sight this suggests that MacKenzie designed only the West Course, and the 9-hole course, on which construction was started but never completed, was designed by Russell. However, in a recently discovered article in the 'Yorkshire Post' of 5 April 1927 of an interview with Dr MacKenzie soon after his return to England from his world tour of 1926 and 1927, he discussed aspects of the project to design a new course for the Royal Melbourne Golf Club. The article noted that, *"Dr MacKenzie (sic) made a new 18-hole course and left with them* (Royal Melbourne) *a layout for a 9-hole course capable of extension to 18 holes."*

If the 9-hole layout had been MacKenzie's, it would be strange if it then needed to be redesigned. This suggests that the 9-hole course was designed by Russell, but that MacKenzie had significant initial input. The first four holes of the 9-hole course depicted in the 27-hole plan, with modifications, were eventually utilised as the first four holes of Russell's East Course. In support of this, MacKenzie set out two lines of play in his final plan of the 18-hole course, while there is only a single line of play shown on the 9-hole layout.

These give conflicting impressions. That the 9-hole course had not actually been designed by MacKenzie, as it would seem unlikely that he would design a 9-hole course that then needed to be re-designed due to where he had located the clubhouse. It appears more logical that a 9-hole course, which had been part of Russell's 1925 scheme, had to be re-designed because

Russell's clubhouse had probably been close to where the practice putting green is located today. The minutes of Council also give the impression that MacKenzie was contracted to only design an 18-hole course.

However, re-examination of the sketch plan, which obviously was not his final plan, shows a 'flagstick' in the first green of what appears to be lines searching for enough holes to make a nine. This 'flagstick' is virtually a MacKenzie trademark, drawn in his own particular style. The final plan would have been more 'finished', have the 'card' for all the holes, and almost certainly his signature. The siting of his holes on this plan have been indicated with very faint pencil marks. Almost certainly the 9-hole course sketched out, to accompany the more detailed sketch plan of the 18-hole course, was drawn by MacKenzie and not added at a later date by Russell, or others. The nine holes as seen in the 27-hole plan are different because of the extra space obtained by the later purchase of Bumpford's block. Whether MacKenzie used any of Russell's holes from his 1925 scheme and was finding extra holes to replace those that had been lost to the clubhouse and some holes of the "New" course, will never be known. Yet if this was so, it would explain the Council minute that the 9-hole course needed to be re-designed. Holes 3, 7, 8 and 9 in the sketch correspond to holes 2, 5, 8 and 9 in the 27-hole plan. If this was the 9-hole layout MacKenzie had suggested, then only one of the holes in the sketch shares the general location of an East Course hole, MacKenzie's 3rd, which is today's 2nd East. When finally constructed, this hole was strategically quite different to that depicted in the 27-hole plan.

Although there are significant differences between the nine holes as suggested by the sketch, from the holes in the 27-hole plan, it is clear that MacKenzie certainly had input into the 9-hole course as originally envisaged, and on which construction was started but never completed. However, Alex Russell would almost certainly have had a much greater role in designing that nine than with the 18-hole course and, as explained in the March 1927 Council Minute, MacKenzie's 9-hole course had to be redesigned.

'Final' 27-hole Plan

The final 27-hole plan, which hangs on the clubhouse wall, was 'discovered' in 1982, along with one similar plan that has a title of 'Approximate' written on it. At first glance the two maps look as if the same person has drawn them. However, inspection of the originals indicates that the two maps almost certainly were drawn by different people.

The 'Approximate' plan retains all the old Sandringham bunkers and has only one line of play and the work is typical of other drafting carried out for the Club by the architectural firm of Sidney Smith, Ogg & Serpell. The final 27-hole has the same layout and yardages but the bunkering is different, especially as many of the Sandringham bunkers have been deleted.

This 'Approximate' plan, drawn sometime between April 1928 and November 1929, almost certainly represents a plan sent by the club to MacKenzie with the suggested altered layout. It was probably amended by club stalwart H. M. Ross, and MacKenzie's response regarding the bunkering, was effectively MacKenzie's sign-off as an approval. Therefore, while Russell and Ross both made significant inputs into the design of the West Course, it was still essentially a MacKenzie course in its overall concept.

However, there were three holes that Russell needed to change. The 1st and 3rd holes had to be altered in order to leave room for the 17th East, and the 12th hole was later extended in 1950 to provide an additional par five. The present par three 16th West hole, while using the same routing as the Sandringham hole, differs from MacKenzie's hole and as Dr Martin Hawtree wrote in 2003:

> "The present design is a complete Russell/Morcom invention even if the original green was used, and is even more of a bogey 4 than the original scheme."

Philip Russell believed his father had a major role in the design of the West Course. He thought that his father was not bothered by all the credit being given to MacKenzie, and if he was, he never showed it.

While Russell was highly qualified in a theoretical sense to carry out any tasks associated with the redesign of Royal Melbourne, what he obviously lacked was the practical experience of translating plans onto the ground. At Royal Melbourne he had the ideal man to assist him in this regard, talented head greenkeeper and constructor "Mick" Morcom. Morcom had experience in building the many alterations that had been made over the years to the club's Sandringham course, and in 1925 he

had constructed a new course for the Kingston Heath Golf Club to a design by the Scottish émigré professional Dan Soutar.

Russell certainly had an influence on MacKenzie in formulating their plans for the West Course and after MacKenzie had left Australia, set about implementing those plans with Morcom, once the question of land acquisition and clubhouse location had been settled. Doubtless, interpretation of the plans was necessary and modifications were required to meet changing site conditions and additional land, but Russell carried out the detailed design work and construction supervision with aplomb.

Nearly five years had elapsed from the time of the Doctor's visit until the West Course opened in 1931, ironically never to be seen by the man widely credited with its creation, apart from the one hole he built before leaving Melbourne. What is often disregarded is that Russell's solo works at Yarra Yarra and Lake Karrinyup were finished up to two years prior to the completion of the West Course.

The Sporting Globe's golf writer Jack Dillon succinctly summed up the West Course's design accreditation in an article he wrote in September 1933 previewing the upcoming Australian Championship meeting. He wrote:

> "Although the "voice" in the creation of the course was that of Dr Alister McKenzie (sic), the "hand" was that of Alex. Russell and the latter would never have made the course quite what it is if it had not been for the knowledge, skill and enthusiasm of M. A. Morcom, whom McKenzie, in an English paper, referred to as the finest curator in golf."

A sketch of Dr. Mackenzie, the British golf architect, who is at present in Melbourne re-modelling the Royal Melbourne course and advising on the treatment of other links. The drawing is by Captain Dalrymple, the scratch golfer of the Royal Melbourne Golf Club.

1926

A 1926 caricature of Dr Mackenzie drawn by Royal Melbourne's Syd Dalrymple

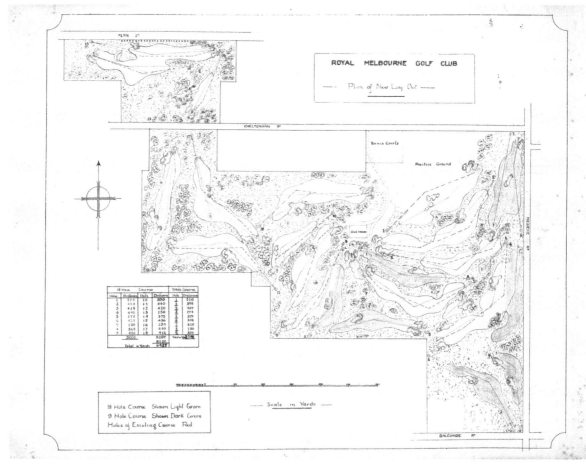

Construction and Criticism

Initial works of clearing and preparing the ground for the new course had begun by the time of the Annual Report being released to the members on 27 June 1927, and was described as being *"well in hand, and will be pushed ahead under the able supervision of Mr Alex. Russell and Mr H. M. Ross, to whom the thanks of the Members are due for the time and attention they are giving to this work."*

It is important to note that while work commenced on the new course, play was continuing all the while over the old

Sandringham course, although with some interference where existing Sandringham holes had to be modified for the new course. In August 1927, the Council decided to defer planting the new course until the next season as severe drought conditions were affecting the course, while in November decisions were still in train regarding alternative holes for the new 16th and 17th.

In December 1927 Alex Russell resigned from the two man sub-committee responsible for supervising the construction of the new course. Hugh Ross, the other member of the sub-

The 'final' 27-hole plan (above) contained alternative lines of play for each hole on the main course and a more detailed 9-hole layout

The Royal Melbourne Golf Club

committee, was a well-known pastoralist and an excellent golfer. At the age of 75 he had comprehensively broken his age with a wonderful round of 70. However, it is also clear that he was a man who held strong opinions, from which he would not back down. Russell's reasons for resigning were significant, according to Jack Dillon, who in 1931 wrote that *"at one stage it was found that the plans as left by McKenzie had to be modified. So drastic were some of the amendments that Alex Russell (who is a partner of Dr McKenzie) decided to dissociate himself from the work."* Russell at this time was not a member of Council, and in the matter of disagreement it is apparent that the Council member's views won out and he saw no other option than to resign. Dillon stated that Ross then stepped solely into the breach of overseeing construction of the new course.

In March 1928, the minutes recorded that a plan of the new course was to be *"prepared by Mr Ross to mark out the alterations to Dr MacKenzie's Plan."* The Annual Report released in June 1928, noted that, *"During the year the ground for all the new fairways has been ploughed and thoroughly worked and should be in splendid condition for planting early spring."* In October 1928, Ross was authorised to *"make arrangements to plant the new greens with similar turf to that in the practice green at 1st tee."* In June 1929, the next Annual Report stated that, *"Development has progressed steadily and appearance of the new fairways is encouraging – so much so that the Council expects the New Course will be ready for play by the time the new Club House is built."* Work was certainly proceeding on the new course under the direction of Hugh Ross.

It would appear that Russell was not involved with the West Course for all of 1928 and the first part of 1929 at the very least, no doubt concentrating instead on his other design projects and the family property at 'Mawallok'. Coincidentally, Russell elected to make himself unavailable for Royal Melbourne's pennant team in 1928, deciding instead to play for the Corangamite Golf Union (Western District) in the Country Golf Shield competition, in a team full of famous Western District family names including Currie, Manifold, Fairbairn and of course, Russell.

This period was quite tumultuous for the club as the Council's plan for a new clubhouse on the hill was narrowly rejected by the membership in 1929 for a second time, leading to a fresh election for Council members in September 1929. Russell stood and was elected with the greatest number of votes of any candidate, but Ross decided not to stand. Russell was immediately appointed to the Greens Committee and was

straight back in the driver's seat for the West Course. Minutes of Council meetings for September and November 1929 show that he suggested alterations for the site of the 18th green and driveway, as well as to the 3rd and 4th holes of MacKenzie's course.

Ross and Russell had jointly overseen construction during 1927 until the disagreements that led to Russell's resignation. Ross then took over responsibility for this task during 1928 and 1929 until Russell's return following his election to Council in late September 1929. From that time until the opening of the course in July 1931 the West Course was Russell's sole responsibility. It is testament to the construction skills of Mick Morcom and to the supervisory talents of both Alex Russell and Hugh Ross that the final result was such a seamless one. Ross was re-elected to Council in 1933 and became captain for 1934-35, however, he resigned that position mid-term after an acrimonious disagreement with Council.

Alex Russell

In late 1929, the South Australian golf architect Herbert L. "Cargie" Rymill had a series of articles published by 'The Sporting Globe' that critically reviewed several of the top courses in Sydney and Melbourne. In the 6 November 1929 edition, his review of Royal Melbourne's new course was published. It is clear from the review that Rymill was viewing a far from finished course and it is also apparent that "Mick" Morcom took him around the new holes. Some of Rymill's observations are worthy of note:

> "The new Royal Melbourne course will be a great improvement on the present one.....There will be some remarkably fine holes. The bunkering round the greens is quite in keeping with that on the latest courses in the U.K., Morcom, the head greenkeeper, having the requisite expert knowledge. Some of the greens on the faces of rises I would have preferred to have terraced with irregular slopes, instead of having one slope or grade. The entrances to the green also should have had diagonal slopes with "drawing" to the pots to attract the ball when the incorrect shot was made."

At the time of Rymill's visit, the original Sandringham holes had not yet been modified and he was quite critical of two of the existing short holes that were to be incorporated, with modifications, into the new West course. These holes were the Sandringham 5th (now the 16th West) and the Sandringham 9th, the old Mount Misery hole which became the 7th West for a few years before being replaced in 1937 by a new short hole set to the north and designed by Ivo Whitton:

> "As two of the old short holes, the fifth and the ninth, will be included in the new course, I explained to Morcom that they are very poor types and need improvement. Cutting away the face of the bunker four feet, lowering the front portion of the green, and having a diagonal ramp up to the back portion of the green would greatly improve the ninth.
>
> The fifth is at present a very uninteresting hole. It could be made an excellent hole of the "Mutton Chop" variety, with the bulge or nose on the back right corner. The green should be shifted to near the ti-tree on the right and raised on to a plateau."

Herbert L. "Cargie" Rymill (left), the founder and architect of the Kooyonga course in Adelaide, was a noted critic who was not afraid to voice his honest opinions on other courses

Rymill stated that he could not understand why a short 9-hole course had been squeezed in to the detriment of a few holes on the main course and suggested that it would be far preferable to purchase some additional land to allow an additional 18-hole course to be laid out. In fact, the club already had this plan well in hand and announced the purchase of additional land not long after Rymill's visit. He also suggested that the proposed permanent clubhouse site was a mistake given it had an inland location on the site where the current par three 7th West hole lies today. Rymill much preferred a perimeter location alongside the road, and the Club eventually gave up that inland position when they relocated the 7th West to this spot in 1937.

The Annual Report of 26 June 1930 noted that a number of greens of the Sandringham course would be re-turfed the next autumn and that temporary greens were being prepared for when they were taken out of play. Interestingly, the report referred to what is now the West Course as the "MacKenzie Course" while the East Course was described as the "Cheltenham Course." Alex Russell was also thanked for his *"time and attention"* to the laying-out of both the new courses, *"besides research work in the direction of improving or fairways and greens"*:

> "On the "MacKenzie Course" the fairways have been kept cut and the greens have been formed and sown, and are progressing very well. The fairways will be top-dressed next Spring, and should be in fine playing condition by the Autumn of 1931."

Golf writer Jack Dillon penned an expansive piece on the new West Course in the 21 January 1931 issue of 'The Sporting Globe', some 6 months before it officially opened. The article was accompanied by the first published detailed plan of the course, complete with bunkering. He noted that most of the new course was already playable and that many rounds of *"experimental play"* had been enjoyed, and would no doubt continue to be enjoyed until the course was opened. He noted that two of the replacement greens for the old Sandringham holes were already back in use for the general play that was still going on over the Sandringham course. He wrote of the unique character and personality of the new course:

> "Essentially this character comes from the manner of the making of the new course. Mostly in the cases of the holes of the other courses, the bunkering and the features were added to the holes. At The West Course the holes were superimposed on locations selected as ideal for those holes. Natural features on simply wonderful sea-side golfing country (possibly Melbourne's first real sea-side

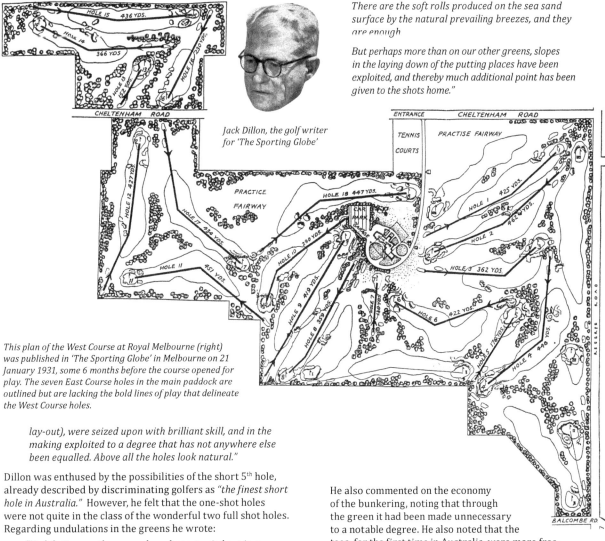

There are the soft rolls produced on the sea sand surface by the natural prevailing breezes, and they are enough

But perhaps more than on our other greens, slopes in the laying down of the putting places have been exploited, and thereby much additional point has been given to the shots home."

Jack Dillon, the golf writer for 'The Sporting Globe'

This plan of the West Course at Royal Melbourne (right) was published in 'The Sporting Globe' in Melbourne on 21 January 1931, some 6 months before the course opened for play. The seven East Course holes in the main paddock are outlined but are lacking the bold lines of play that delineate the West Course holes.

lay-out), were seized upon with brilliant skill, and in the making exploited to a degree that has not anywhere else been equalled. Above all the holes look natural."

Dillon was enthused by the possibilities of the short 5th hole, already described by discriminating golfers as *"the finest short hole in Australia."* However, he felt that the one-shot holes were not quite in the class of the wonderful two full shot holes. Regarding undulations in the greens he wrote:

"Undulations on the greens have been carried out in a manner reticent, and in a decidedly more moderate way than at others of our championship courses. In fact, to some obsessed with the rather overdone "rolling" greens, the putting places may appear flat. That, they simply are not.

He also commented on the economy of the bunkering, noting that through the green it had been made unnecessary to a notable degree. He also noted that the tees, for the first time in Australia, were more free-form in shape and not rectangular, and *"in most cases at the West Course are as near to rectangular as the greens are to perfect circles. It adds a delightful touch."* Dillon then added a description of the holes, with comments generally about their relationship with the old Sandringham holes:

"There is an admirable "get-away" fairly straight ahead hole of 425 to 361 yards as the opening proposition. Spaciousness of fairway from the tee, which marks practically all the holes with a second shot, is conspicuous at this hole. But the spaciousness, while it gives the ordinary golfer his chance, does not help the real golfer to score par figures, for, if he does not take the best line at every long hole, his shot home is either extremely difficult or impossible. This first hole is, but to a less degree than most of the others, a bent hole.

Hole 2 (462-416 yards) comes back to the clubhouse in a WSW direction, and is somewhat suggestive of the fifth at Yarra Yarra.

Over to the east, and then sharp round to the left, goes the third (362-322 yards) to a green that slopes away.

To Ivo Whitton was given the credit for many of the features of the fourth hole (448-394 yards) by Alex Russell. This is, perhaps, the best hole on the course. It is distinctly dog leg, with a big natural hazard up on the rise on the right to be carried from the tee, and as much of the corner near the woods has to be cut off as is safe.

Then comes the shot across the valley (176-143 yards) to a green that is set delightfully, trapped skilfully, and contoured with great cleverness.

Again back to the clubhouse the player is taken by the sixth (422-372 yards), and the green is located on the spot below the rise to the right of the old eighth fairway, where on big occasions the galleries sat to watch the eighth green being played, and to wait for the shots to Mount Misery. Best of all is the fairway shaping is that at this hole. This sixth appealed to me as a priceless piece of work. Unless the corner is taken, and the ideal "bay" reached, the shot home is either to be a super one, or is impossible. The wee bit of pull at the end of the perfect shot home is a detail that is notable, and called for at several of the holes, if they are to be played perfectly.

Follows, but for a while only, the old ninth (Mount Misery). This will later be replaced. The old tenth will be in The East Course.

The eighth (359-329) will be to a green to the right of the present tenth.

Back to the clubhouse, the ninth (419-344 yards) will take the player from the present eleventh tee, but verging off the old fairway up to a delightful location to the right, and on the hill. Here again, although helped by the swing in of the land, there is called for that little piece of draw for the perfect getting home.

Starting "home," the first hole is a full smack across the valley now in front of the present eleventh green and up to a rise, where the green is a short pitch away round the corner to the left – a gem of a hole that long markers may not appreciate. It is 290-272 yards.

From a new high tee a hole of 451-418 yards is played to the new green made at the back of the old 12th.

The twelfth (427-374 yards) is from a new tee to the left, to the old thirteenth green remodelled.

A new short hole of 152-132 yards is played across the rough at right angles to the old short fourteenth.

The fourteenth is the old fifteenth remodelled, then is played the old fourth remodelled, and it is followed by the old fifth remodelled.

Two slashing fine holes end the round. From the old sixth tee the seventeenth (434-349 yards) is played. A good drive will get down just short of where the bunkers were in front of the old sixth green, and there is left a nice smash across the old twelfth fairway to a new green on the rise in new country to the left of where the drive from the old twelfth tee finished.

For the eighteenth (447-397 yards) the drive is made over the big high corner where the old twelfth tee was, and down to the old seventh fairway past the bunkers that were out of range from the seventh tee. Then the shot home is to the remodelled old seventh green.

Dillon found something to criticise in the short holes of the new course, something that is widely recognised as one of the strengths of the course today. Even before the course opened for play it was noted that the Mount Misery hole would be replaced and so Dillon was not reporting on the final group of one-shot holes:

Even in a masterpiece of art a layman finds something that appeals to him as not quite his ideal. On this great golf links I was a little disappointed in the short holes. Maybe my state of mind was not fitting, after those great longer holes, for, after all, a one shotter is only the tail end of a perfect two shotter, for appreciating the short holes. I do not say that the one shotters are not first class good holes, but to me they do not appear of equal merit with the other propositions.

With all due modesty I am prepared to admit that those who designed these holes have forgotten more than I know. But I think it is the shape of the greens in which I find the lack.

Not in their contour, not in their placing, not in their bunkering did I miss anything, but I do feel that somewhat of a swing round in their setting, and elongating in their shaping, would make me more satisfied with the thirteenth and the fifth. I do not think Russell is completely happy about the thirteenth, but the fifth has been pronounced expertly as the best one shotter we have."

The next Annual Report dated 31 March 1931 summarised progress during the year with the West Course and noted that:

"The 4th, 5th, 12th, 13th and 15th greens of the old Course have been re-designed, and the greens turfed with the bent and fescue mixture from the turf nursery. This almost completes the West Course, which will be put into play as soon as the Temporary Club House is ready for occupation....The above work has had close and constant supervision from Mr Alex. Russell during the whole of the year, and to him the Members are indebted for the energy and interest he has shown in club affairs."

In June 1931, the Victorian Governor Lord Arthur Somers, together with his wife Lady Somers, played a preview round over the new West Course, yet to open to its members. The Vice-Regal couple played with Alex and Jess Russell, and *"holes were put in the greens and discs laid on the tees specially for the occasion. His Ex. hit the ball so well that he came away with the idea that the course was magnificent, the surroundings sylvan, the birds in the trees the best whistlers he had ever heard – and he came back the next day and had another round."*

'The Referee' noted in April 1931 that:

"It is stated authoritatively that the new West course of the Royal Melbourne Club will be open for play in July. The temporary clubhouse will be completed in June, and Alex. Russell, Committeeman in charge of the construction of the links, states that he will be able to let players loose on the course in July. Interest in the new venture has been evinced all over Australia, firstly because Royal Melbourne is probably Australia's premier club, and secondly it is constructing two courses, a thing previously unheard of in the country."

Views of the recently opened West Course featured in 'Golf in Australia' magazine's August 1933 issue. At the top is a view from the tee of the one-shot 5th West, which MacKenzie had Morcom construct for him before leaving Melbourne. The bottom photograph depicts the same green, but looking from the hill behind the green back towards the tee. Note the sandy hollow shaped by Morcom at the rear of the green separating the green from the hillside.

The Royal Melbourne Golf Club

Open at Last

The club held a farewell function at the old clubhouse on Wednesday 1 July 1931 and the final competition round over the Sandringham course was played on Saturday 11 July, with Alex Russell and Ivo Whitton fittingly tied with a fine round of 74 each. Members cleaned out their lockers and transferred them to the new clubhouse the following Monday. This can be considered the first day that the new West Course was officially in use, although members had been unofficially playing over the new course for some months prior. The club's Annual Report dated 16 June 1932 indicated that it was *"brought into play in July, 1931, and has met with universal commendation."* It further noted that *"The Council wish once more to record their appreciation of the manner in which Mr Alex. Russell has devoted his time and talents to the supervision of the construction and maintenance of the two courses, and also of the excellent work done by our Green-keeper (Mr Morcom)."*

In October 1931, one of Victoria's premier golfers, A. W. Jackson, who regularly contributed a golf column to 'Table Talk,' wrote full of praise for the new West Course:

> *"Those who have played over the new course at Royal Melbourne are loud in praise for the latest and best work of Alex. Russell. The constructional work has been artistically carried out by Morcom and the playing of the course gives members the greatest of pleasure."*

'The Sporting Globe' noted in January 1932 that:

> *"Royal Melbourne's new West course, despite its youthfulness, has fairways that are wonderfully covered. That lay-out is probably the most pleasant in Australia for golf, and the brilliant skill with which it has been laid out makes it one of our best tests of the game."*

Oblique aerial view from 1941 looking over the 'temporary' clubhouse and showing the 18th West green at the right and Russell's 18th East at the left. The roadway was made to the site of the planned 'permanent' clubhouse that was eventually abandoned. The 2nd West green lies at the top of the photograph.

The Royal Melbourne Golf Club

At the same time, it also reported that "Mick" Morcom had recently suffered a heart attack and had been ordered to take a month's rest, noting that *"the breakdown has probably been the direct result of concentration on the huge task of preparing the two new championship links of the R.M.G.C."*

Perhaps the most considered view on the new course was that of the amateur great and Royal Melbourne stalwart, Ivo Whitton, who wrote an article for the 'Sydney Morning Herald' about the Australian Championships in September 1933:

> *"A few remarks about the course may be of interest to Sydney golfers. Possibly, judging from the practice scores, golfers who have not had the chance at seeing or playing on the new course at Royal Melbourne would have decided that it must be a very easy course. Possibly in fine weather it is; but it is a course that calls for exact placing of the tee shots. There is really only one drive and pitch hole, and with the other two-shot holes, which are mostly about 400 yards to 460 yards, if the tee shot is not perfectly made it is almost impossible for the average length player to get up in two. If the tee shot is hit well, but not quite perfectly placed, it is still possible to get up in two, but a most difficult second follows.*
>
> *I have no hesitation in saying that I consider this lay-out one of the finest courses I have ever played on – always interesting and always giving fresh problems to the player. The course, with a few alterations, is practically as laid out by Dr McKenzie during his trip to Australia some years ago. The experience I have gained in the four years we have been on the new course is that it is a much easier course for practice rounds than it is for actual card and pencil play."*

Royal Melbourne and Victorian amateur great, Ivo Whitton

These comments by Whitton confirm that the course was very much what MacKenzie claimed it would be in his 29th December 1926 *"Herald"* article, and that it was essentially MacKenzie's design, despite some necessary alterations by both Russell and Ross.

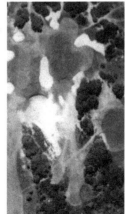

1933 view of golfers putting on the 7th West green, (far right) known as 'Mount Misery,' and a 1936 aerial view of the hole (right). This was a hole that MacKenzie and Russell decided to retain and modify, but its highly terraced and undulating green proved too controversial and the hole soon became known as 'Russell's Folly.' It was replaced in 1937 by a new short hole to a design by Ivo Whitton.

The Royal Melbourne Golf Club

Alex. Russell

Aerial photograph of Royal Melbourne's West Course from 1936 (above). The layout is clearly one still in transition from the Sandringham Course.

The Royal Melbourne Golf Club

A less than flattering caricature of Alex Russell (left) from 1930

Over the ensuing years there have been few changes that significantly affect the overall strategies of the holes on the West Course. If Russell, or one of his contemporaries like Ivo Whitton, was to return today they would not be asking, 'Where has a particular hole gone, the old one was much better than this?' rather it would be the general changes they would be commenting on mostly. The West Course at Royal Melbourne was pronounced by Jack Dillon as *"Australia's Best Links"* some six months before it opened, a mantle which it has never lost in the ensuing 85 years. It remains a lasting testimony to the skills and inspiration of MacKenzie, Russell and Morcom. Sadly, MacKenzie never returned to see the completion of the wonderful course he had designed on his visit to Melbourne back in 1926.

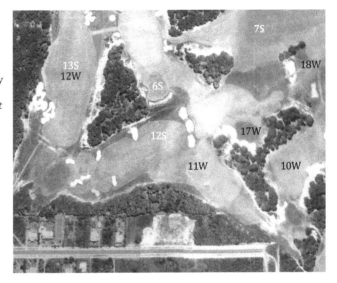

This extract from the 1936 aerial (right) clearly shows how a new first half of the dogleg 11th West was spliced onto the old straightaway Sandringham 12th hole. Similarly, the old Sandringham 6th green can still be seen, with a new dogleg left spliced onto the end as the 17th West hole playing to a new green.

The Royal Melbourne Golf Club

View of the 9th West green during the 1963 Women's Commonwealth Golf Tournament

The Royal Melbourne Golf Club

3rd West – View to green

4th West – View from tee

5th West – View from tee

15th West – View to green

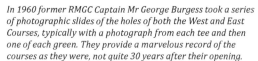

In 1960 former RMGC Captain Mr George Burgess took a series of photographic slides of the holes of both the West and East Courses, typically with a photograph from each tee and then one of each green. They provide a marvelous record of the courses as they were, not quite 30 years after their opening.

The Royal Melbourne Golf Club

8th West – View from tee

18th West – View from tee

Classic MacKenzie-Russell-Morcom fairway bunkering on the par five 12th hole on the West Course. Alex Russell later designed and built a new green for this hole, moving it back and to the left. It opened for play in 1953.

Oblique aerial photograph of the Royal Melbourne courses from 1936 looking to the west across the East Course in the foreground and the West Course in the distance. In the lower foreground is the 10th East green with its diagonal approach bunkering, and above it is the 11th East with its expansive bunkering that was later considerably reduced. In the right hand lower corner lies the 17th green of the adjacent Victoria Golf Club's course, and above it that course's 12th and 13th holes. This photograph, part of a series of oblique and vertical aerial photographs of the course, was taken by Air Vice Marshall (Sir) Richard Williams of the RAAF, who had served with distinction in the Australian Flying Corps in World War I.

The Royal Melbourne Golf Club

ROYAL MELBOURNE GOLF CLUB'S EAST COURSE

English golf course architect Dr Martin Hawtree, in a report to the club in 2003, commented upon Alex Russell and the East Course:

"The East Course suffers from a great many disadvantages, by comparison with the West Course. There is no second starting point, many road crossings, a very suburban boundary, a rather flat topography for at least two-thirds of the course. It is lasting testimony to the genius of Alex Russell that the course seems to override many of these problems to become indeed some members' preferred course. As Russell's first course, it is a wonderful achievement that few other architects have come near. It is fascinating to sense Russell imbibing the ideas of MacKenzie and then developing them in his own particular way. This is what gives the West and East Course their subtlety of variation upon a common theme of architectural reference. Russell undoubtedly had immense good fortune, as indeed did MacKenzie, in the craftsmanship of Morcom and later Crockford. But the ideas represented by Morcom must surely be Russell's. We never have any doubt that we are at Royal Melbourne but there are new developments here on the East Course which are not just to do with a different soil type and topography. Here was Russell's chance to prove himself and he did it well".

Hawtree incorrectly refers to the East Course as Russell's first course. In fact he had already designed the new course for the Yarra Yarra Golf Club that opened for play in December 1928, the new Lake Karrinyup course in Perth that was first played in 1929, along with a new 9-hole course at Summerland on Philip Island that opened in 1930. This is not to mention his day-to-day involvement in supervising the construction of the West Course, which would have involved countless design decisions. Yet while Alex Russell made a significant contribution to the design and construction of the West Course, his role with the East Course was entirely different. Dr Alex Ellis, in his 1941 history of the Royal Melbourne Golf Club, summed up Russell's all-encompassing role in the following, succinct manner:

"In 1933, Mr Alex Russell, who for years had devoted practically the whole of his time to the supervision of the construction of new holes for the West Course, and to the architecture and construction of the East Course, was elected an honorary life member. He was solely responsible for the design and lay-out of the East Course, work, which according to the highest golfing authorities, could not have been more skillfully performed by anybody."

The idea of having two courses was not something that the club all of a sudden decided upon in 1929. Members had been suggesting the idea for some years, however, the general feeling was that the land was not available for such an endeavour, and if it was, it would be too expensive for the club to consider. The son of a long-serving Council member of the club, Tom Trumble, a solicitor and an ordinary member, overcame several difficulties and privately obtained options over the land that lay to the east of Reserve Road in Black Rock. It is upon this 78 acres (32 ha) of land that two-thirds of the East Course is sited.

A Special General Meeting was held on 1 November 1929 to consider the acquisition of this new land and the creation of another 18-hole course. Russell addressed the meeting and the minutes recorded that:

"Mr Alex. Russell seconded the motion and briefly dealt with the situation and the suitability of the land and soil. He said a first class eighteen hole course could be constructed by using some of the nine hole course marked out on the Club's present area in conjunction with the area proposed."

The 'Argus' newspaper, shortly after the meeting, reported on this new land acquisition for the club, noting that:

"The Royal Melbourne Club intends that the new course shall be at least the equal of the MacKenzie course, which is already far advanced towards completion. At the same time it is bound to be largely dissimilar in character. According to Alick Russell (to whose design and under whose supervision the new course will be constructed) and Ivo Whitton, the new country resembles the area upon which the Metropolitan links has been laid out more than the land already in use at Sandringham.

The land now acquired adjoins the present eighth fairway, and extends along Reserve Road, close to the Victoria Club's property, reaching a point within about five minutes of the Cheltenham railway station. It is of the very best golfing soil, and will accommodate 12 holes of the new round. The other

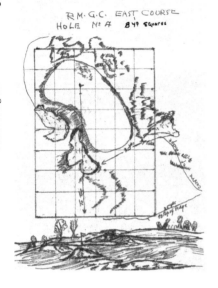

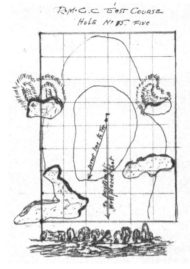

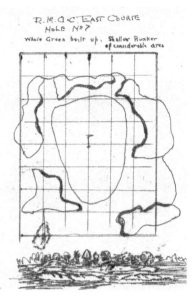

A selection of Alex Russell's ink green plans for the East Course. Each plan also contained a perspective sketch of that green.

The Royal Melbourne Golf Club

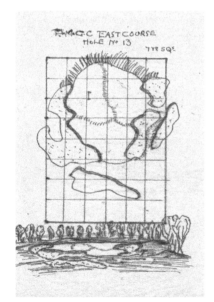

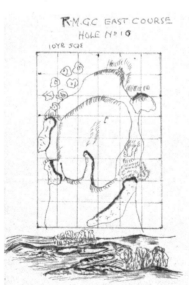

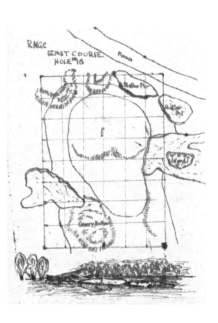

six holes will be in the adjoining block, into which nine rather indifferent holes have already been squeezed. Three of these will be merged, and a magnificent championship course will be thus formed."

The additional land for the East Course was purchased in late 1929 after the West Course had already been laid out. However, Russell probably had little opportunity to lay out a clockwise course routing without severe internal dangers to players. It could be argued that it would have been possible in the far paddocks, but if some areas of lower-lying ground that become soft and wet after rain were to be avoided just in front of greens, then the anti-clockwise routing was a preferable one as these areas were then located in the carries. When the East Course was laid out it was largely surrounded by open paddocks and market gardens, while Reserve Road and Morey Road were sandy tracks, so the anti-clockwise lay-out of holes was not considered a problem at the time.

Construction and Opening

Little time was wasted between acquiring the land and starting construction of the second course. It would appear from the 'Argus' report that Russell had figured out by November 1929 that the new land could hold 12 good holes, allowing him to reduce the additional nine holes that were already laid out on the main block back to six. However, in the final analysis he decided upon seven holes in the main paddock and 11 in the newly acquired land. Russell prepared a set of green plans in ink for each of the greens on the new course, with each depicting a plan of the green and surrounding bunkering, as well as a perspective view of the green as seen from the fairway. However, there is no known overall course routing plan, and if Russell prepared one, as it would be expected he would have, then it sadly has not survived.

On 12 November the green committee was authorised *"to take the necessary steps for laying out and starting construction"* of the new course. The Annual Report of 26 June 1930 referred to what is now the West Course as the "Mackenzie Course" while the East Course was described as both the "Second Course" and the "Cheltenham Course." It gave a brief report on the status of the latter:

> *The "Second Course" has been laid out, and most of the clearing and ploughing has been done. Owing to the easy nature of the ground the cost of construction should be well under the estimate of £8500 given to Members at the Special Meeting when the purchase of the land for this Course was approved. The Course should be fit for play in the Autumn of 1932."*

The club's next Annual Report dated 31 March 1931 reported on the ongoing progress with the East Course. It is of interest that the

Royal Melbourne's talented head greenkeeper M.A. "Mick" Morcom (right) was described by Dr MacKenzie as "the best greenkeeper I have come across in Britain, America, or Australia."

The Royal Melbourne Golf Club

Two of the primary implements used by Morcom and Russell in constructing the two Royal Melbourne courses were a disc plough (below) and a pan scraper (bottom). These are on display today adjacent the main driveway at the club.

projected opening of the course had been pushed back from autumn into winter:

> "The construction work of the East Course is complete, except for the formation and sowing of the greens. That work will be done this Autumn, and the course should be ready for play in the Winter of 1932."

Jack Dillon reported in 'The Sporting Globe' on 2 December 1931 on progress with the East Course:

> "Greens are now well turfed and being cut, and fairways growing solidly and are completely defined for the new East course of the Royal Melbourne GC. Indications are that according to the original plan, the second championship lay out of Victoria's premier golf club, will be ready for play next June. The combination fescue and bent greens are now practically as good as those on the West Course."

In June 1932, Dillon once more reported on the new course:

> "The layout is expected to be ready for the official opening late this month. Some good judges have pronounced it better than the West Course. Recently it has been completely topdressed. Fairways have come on well, and the greens are up to the high standard of the west course."

The course was opened for member play over the weekend of 18 to 19 June 1932 and Dillon followed up with an article the next week about it, full of praise for the course and its architect:

> "About twelve months ago, members of Victoria's premier golf club, Royal Melbourne, moved to, and played over for the first time, their great new West Course, a magnificent conception of Dr Alister

MacKenzie and Alex. Russell. It was brought into being under the clever supervision of the latter with the brilliant work and assistance of Australia's greatest golf curator, M.A. Morcom.

Over the last week-end members played over, for the first time, the club's new East Course, the great conception of Alex Russell, translated into actuality by him and the same talented Morcom. Both courses are among the greatest of Australia's championship links. My first impression of the East Course is that it is a better links than the West Course and something "quite different" from any other course in the land.

MORE ADVANCED

After going carefully over the holes on Saturday, in the company of the club's secretary (Mr Benson Lewis) and half a dozen other members of R.M.G.C., my impressions may be thus summed up:

The Alex Russell who conceived this course is a more advanced, experienced and mature golf architect than he was in any other work he has done; the layout is longer, more difficult, more varied, over better country generally, more picturesque, and a better test of golf than the West course; when this course is matured in turf, and final touches have been made here and there in bunkering, it will probably be among our modern links what the old R.M.G.C. course at Sandringham was in the pre-MacKenzie days, namely – second to none in Australia.

According to the card, the yardage of the holes is: 325,422,393, – 210,348,160 – 520,470,353 – 3201; 466,360,440 – 139,430,308 – 169,542,418 – 3272; total 6473 yards. But at several holes there may be 40/50 yards added. With the possible exception of the 13th of 139 yards (the most beautifully located and attractively set short hole in Australia), the four one shotters are difficult above the average, but exceptionally fine. The lowest par (within reason) that could be set is 73. There is just a chance that the 12th of 440 yards may work out a long par-4 but the 18th will be one of the most difficult par 4 holes we have.

The superlatively turfed greens (fescue and bent with possibly more bent than was included in the West Course mixture that proved so fine) are in area not set so generously as on the other course. But they are cleverly and subtly undulated and moulded, often with great golfing point.

WILL CAUSE A "HUMP"

However, on the saddle shaped green at the 16th there is a "hump" running in the direction of the hole that may prove as annoying as some of the much criticised 7th green of the West Course.

There is hardly a "straight-ahead" hole on the course. But the many bent holes differ from the West holes in that the chances of cutting corners are extremely rare, and the point of the holes does not encourage such play. Blind shots are practically non-existent. Two drives are in a sense blind, but the ball that does not go in the right direction for the safe fairway may be watched.

The now dormant couch has been thickly planted, and has gripped well. When it comes up again later in the year there should be a great mat of turf. The English and other grasses for winter are coming on well."

Alex's son Philip recalled being out on the East Course with his father during its construction:

"I do remember being out on the East course because Jocky my dog was with me, and Dad and Morcom, who was the curator, Dad and Morcom were designing the East course and I was getting Jocky caught down a rabbit warren and Dad said what's wrong and I said the dog's down the hole and I can't get it out. Well, Dad said I would fix that and Dad took him by the tail and pulled him out. I can remember that quite clearly, that was on the East Course.

The 27-hole plan on display in the clubhouse, comprising the West Course plus the 9-hole course, became redundant, as far as the nine-hole layout was concerned, when the East Course was planned. Russell had pointed out at the Extraordinary General Meeting that some of the holes from that nine could be used in the new course.

The first four holes were essentially the first four holes of that 9-hole course, which was partly constructed, but over which there is no record of formal play ever having taken place. The first hole was a modification of the old 10th hole of the Sandringham course. When used as part of the East Course, the fourth of these holes had to be shortened by about seventy yards. In a 1931 aerial photograph, the proposed earlier 4th green is clearly visible. The current 16th green was in place, but this was not part of the original 9-hole course. The 2nd and 3rd holes both show

bunkers in the plan, but in neither case were there ever any drive-bunkers positioned. Aerial photography in the 1930s shows how the area was initially devoid of trees. Subsequent photographs, however, indicate that extensive tree-planting had taken place.

Russell's delightful par three 16th hole on the East Course was not a part of the original Composite Course. It was a question of using the 4th East or this hole as the 16th Composite, and the 4th East connected better to the previous hole. During tournaments when the Composite Course was in use, players walked from the 16th green (4th East) to the 17th tees past this spectacular short hole, and it was often commented upon by passing players that it would be a thrill to get the opportunity to play it competitively. Finally, it was incorporated into the Composite Course for the President's Cup in 2011, partly because players had requested to play it, but also a matter of gallery control. Russell's hole performed more than admirably.

The Australian Open Championships of 1953 and 1963 were played over the course, while, in 1983, it was the venue of the Australian PGA Championship. In 1983, the professionals were

English golfer Mrs J. B. Walker approaching the 12th green on the East Course during the final of the Australian Ladies' Amateur championship in 1935

The Royal Melbourne Golf Club

full of praise for the course and many expressed the view that they had enjoyed 'The East' even more than playing the Composite Course.

A final comment by golf architect and historian Fred Hawtree, father of Martin, perhaps sums up Russell's position. In writing about Harry Colt, whose approach to golf-course design almost certainly influenced Russell, and MacKenzie before him, Hawtree declared:

> *"Above all, his courses have stood the test of time, his own touch-stone. A Colt golf course is still just that—not a quasi-landscape, but a natural haven for the eternal joys of true golf."*

The courses of Alex Russell, the East Course and others he designed, can equally be measured by the same criteria.

Alex Russell

Aerial photograph from 1936 showing the East Course holes in the main paddock that lie west of Reserve Road

The Royal Melbourne Golf Club

Oblique aerial photograph (left) from 1936 of the East Course's 18th green showing Russell's spectacular bunkering

English golfer Mrs J. B. Walker plays out of a greenside bunker (bottom) on the 3rd hole of the East Course in 1935. The 4th East green can be seen at the upper left.

The Royal Melbourne Golf Club

Aerial photograph from 1936 showing the East Course holes in the two paddocks that lie east of Reserve Road

The Royal Melbourne Golf Club

18 E

2nd East – View to green

13th East – View from tee

12th East – View to green

16th East – View to green

In 1960 former RMGC Captain Mr George Burgess took a series of photographic slides of the holes of both the West and East Courses, typically with a photograph from each tee and then one of each green. They provide a marvellous record of the courses as they were not quite 30 years after their opening.

The Royal Melbourne Golf Club

18th East – View to green

In the authors' opinions the 16th East is one of the finest short holes in Australia. Its pedigree was further confirmed when it replaced the 4th East as the 16th hole in the Composite Course for the 2011 President's Cup.

Oblique aerial view c.1930 over the 7th fairway and the Yarra Yarra clubhouse taken by Charles Pratt, a pilot and photographer for the Airspy company. The 18th green lies above the clubhouse and the 5th green to its left. Note the shadow of Pratt's plane on the 7th fairway and the tank-stand at upper right from which the photographs of the 18th hole were taken (refer page 99).

State Library of Victoria

Chapter 8

YARRA YARRA GOLF CLUB

The club first began in Eaglemont in 1898 as the Eaglemont Golf Club, before moving to Rosanna in 1911 to become the Yarra Yarra Golf Club, playing at first over a 5,000 yard (4,500 metre) course laid out by M.G.B. Jefferson. By 1925, the club was losing members and the committee was convinced that the state of their clay-based course compared with newer ones on sandy soil was the primary reason for the decline, so it decided to investigate the matter of moving to a sandy location.

A Move to the Sandbelt

In December 1926, an estate agent was invited to address the committee and he considered that the sale of its Rosanna land could yield the Club around £60,000. Three members of the committee viewed *"every block of land available for golfing purposes between Cheltenham and Oakleigh"*, eventually deciding upon land at East Bentleigh bordering Warrigal Road and just to the west of the Commonwealth Golf Club's new course at Oakleigh. Nine separate parcels comprised the 121 acres (49 ha) of sandy, market-garden land. Alex Russell, along with Harry Alexander, the club's greenkeeper, and John "Jock" Young, the professional at nearby Commonwealth Golf Club, were requested to inspect the land and submit reports on its suitability. Rowley Banks, the Yarra Yarra professional, also inspected the land prior to purchase.

Russell submitted his report on the Bentleigh land to the club on 4 February 1927 and an extract from it was recorded in 'The Sporting Globe' on 12 February:

"The whole of the property is covered with easy undulations which are of just sufficient steepness to make interesting holes without entailing hill climbing of any sort. The soil is a sandy loam, and much of it has already been under the plough and a considerable portion is market gardens now. There would be little work necessary before planting the fairways. The area is well supplied with water, good mains running along the boundaries and much piping is already in position. There are many suitable sites for a club-house; but one in particular stands out, and this site would enable each nine holes to begin and end at the club-house."

Russell's report clearly impressed the committee as four days later, just over a month after Dr MacKenzie had left Australia bound for New Zealand, he had secured for the new partnership of MacKenzie & Russell their first commission. An article by "Back Spin" in 'The Sporting Globe' newspaper of 9 February 1927 suggested that Alex Russell would be entrusted with this design prior to the official announcement. Interestingly, the article went on to discuss the necessity for Australia to import golf architects:

"Australians usually are able to hold their own in most walks of life, so there seems no valid reason why we should have to import our golf architects. In any case, why should we have to copy slavishly methods that have been used in Great Britain? Why not assert our individuality, and set up some new standards of our own? Perhaps Russell will give us a lead in this regard. Whatever he offers us, we hope it will be on new and progressive lines as opposed to stereotype  *methods. Should he make a success of his first venture in this line, a wonderful field should unfold itself for him."*

ALEX. RUSSELL, Vic.,
1st, 3rd, Open Championship of Australia, 1925,
Kensington, Sydney, N.S.W.

On 7 February, the club held a special meeting of members to address the question of the planned move. The meeting heard that a few years earlier Yarra Yarra was considered to be the fourth club in Melbourne but had since been supplanted by Kingston Heath, Woodlands and Commonwealth. The club's income was also down compared to Commonwealth since its move.

Alex Russell was invited to attend and asked to address the meeting to give his views on the land and his design for the course. During the meeting, committeeman E. W. Scott spoke in favour of the move. Scott was the Australian manager for Yorkshire Insurance and was also a member of the Metropolitan Golf Club. He knew very well the benefits of a sand belt location for a golf club. Scott's address noted that on the Friday before the meeting he, along with the president, Harry Alexander and Rowley Banks had:

> *"met Mr Russell there to inspect the property. He gave us his opinion. He says the area available of 121 acres is practically all excellent golfing country, being of sandy loam, eminently suitable for the growing of fine golfing grass. He says this*

area is capable of the construction of an 18 hole course, and it is of a convenient shape as well. He also says that the whole of the property is covered with undulations which are just of sufficient steepness to make interesting holes. In discussions with Mr Russell I said to him "Would I be over-stating the mark in saying that the ground is capable of forming the finest golfing links in Australia?" He said "You would, because there is one better, and that is Seaton." But he also said "it is better land than the Metropolitan, better than the Commonwealth or Kingston Heath, better land than the New Victoria, and you can make the finest golfing course you could ever see on that land.""

Despite some opposition, three motions: to sell the Rosanna land, to purchase the Bentleigh property and to raise funds as needed to develop a course and clubhouse at Bentleigh, were put to the meeting and these were carried comfortably by 129 votes to 37. The reports on the land were formally tabled at the committee meeting on 8 February, and at that meeting the decision was made to take up the options and purchase the land.

The purchase proceeded and the club ended up paying around £150 an acre for its new home, far more than they had originally hoped for. It would appear that the market gardeners drove a hard bargain, as overall the land cost the club around £18,250. The old course and clubhouse at Rosanna was eventually sold in 1936 for £10,250, well less than the £60,000 the club was told it could expect to receive back in 1926.

MacKenzie & Russell's First Commission

The committee minutes of 8 February recorded that Messrs. Meudell and Gillespie were to be instructed to survey the land and *"That Alick* (sic) *Russell be appointed Architect to the laying out of the new Course."*

'The Argus' newspaper in its 10 February 1927 edition reported that the Yarra Yarra Golf Club had entrusted Alex Russell with the task of designing its new course:

> *"The area of the site is 121 acres, and with the exception of about three acres of slightly swampy land, the whole is eminently well suited for conversion into a course that, when completed, will compare favourably with any in the metropolitan area. The expense of laying out the holes has been estimated at £8,000, but as the land is already cleared and cultivated market-garden land, this is considered by*

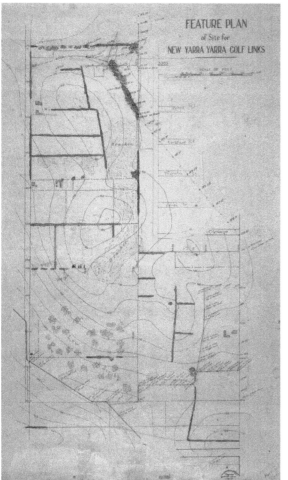

Contour survey plan for the new land at Bentleigh also showed the vegetation, including a number of hedges and expanses of bracken

Yarra Yarra Golf Club

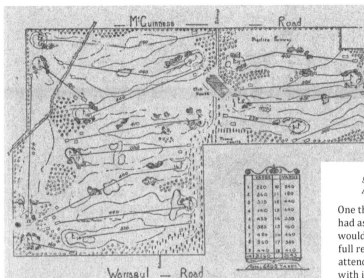

Plan of the proposed new Yarra Yarra course at Bentleigh accompanied an article by Jack Dillon in the 'Sporting Globe' on 17th December 1927. It was likely drawn by a newspaper artist based upon Russell's plan.

State Library of Victoria

good judges to be a very pessimistic estimate, and that probably £5,000 will be found to be nearer the mark. In support of this view it has to be stated that a main water supply pipe runs on every side of the property .A few days ago Alex Russell, in company with H. G. McRoberts, E. W. Scott, and the club's professional, Rowley Banks, and greenkeeper A. Alexander (sic), inspected the land, and were thoroughly satisfied with what they saw, as well as the rosy prospects it holds for the future. Russell has supplied the club with a report in terms which are most gratifying to the club. The report indicates that the soil is of an exceptionally fine variety for the purpose in view, and that its contours are excellent, supplying as they do undulations of sufficient slope without involving anything that might be called hill climbing."

'The Sporting Globe' article on 12 February noted that:

"Alex Russell has been given the new course to model. This will be his first effort since he joined partnership with Dr A. MacKenzie to build a championship links in Australia. He has virgin country to mould, and will not be hampered by the clearing work usually associated with the preparation of a great course. He has the advantage of being able to vision all the holes, as the country stretches before him. Russell has made a study of golf course construction for some time

as a hobby, and with his knowledge of the game and its demands, he should mould the area into one of Australia's finest courses."

One thing that all these reports made clear was that the club had assured Russell that once his plan was approved they would not interfere in the construction process, allowing him full rein over the course he was to design and build. Russell attended the committee meeting on 17 February and discussed with its members both the land at Bentleigh and his design for the course, presenting them with *"a rough design for a 6,300 yards round with a longest hole of 490 yards, the good points of which deeply impressed the Committee. At the same time the matter will be left entirely in the hands of Russell, who intimated that he would be greatly disappointed if the completed course did not attain to first class championship class."*

He said that he had not definitely decided that the layout he had shown them was the best possible one, and that he hoped to arrive at a final decision within the next week. Russell would then take the committee over his final course on the ground. At its meeting on 8 April, the committee determined that, *"It was unanimously decided to adopt the amended design for the layout of the new course"*, indicating that Russell had indeed developed an improved design in the meantime.

There is no evidence to suggest that Dr MacKenzie saw the land for Yarra Yarra prior to leaving Melbourne on the 30 November 1926, as it had not been selected by this time. Hence, Alex Russell bore full responsibility for the development of the new course. Although Russell's communications are on MacKenzie and Russell stationary, evidence supporting any involvement of MacKenzie in its design relies on a single press report in 'The Australasian' of 23 April 1927 that indicated Russell's plans had been sent to MacKenzie for his input:

"The design of the round embracing, of course, the scheme of hazards, grassy mounds, and hollows, as well as sand bunkers, is now in transit across the seas for MacKenzie's inspection."

The same article stated that construction was well under way. There is no evidence of any formal advice to Russell back from MacKenzie. In 1968, S.M. "Barney" Allen, a past captain of the club, stated in a letter that:

"*Surveyor's plans of the Bentleigh property were sent to Dr Alister McKenzie (sic) with a request to submit a design for a course. This he did and appointed the late Alex Russell as his representative. My informant was the late L.G. Shaw who gave months of his business time to watch the Club's interests in regard to the course construction.*"

This statement by 'Barney' Allen is inconsistent with the club's minutes, since the three reports on the land by Russell, Alexander and Young were dated 4, 4, and 6 February 1927 respectively, with 'The Argus' on 10 February 1927 stating the site had been first inspected only a few days earlier.

By this time MacKenzie was onboard the 'S.S. Maunganui' traversing the Pacific Ocean en route to San Francisco, having departed New Zealand on 1 February 1927, a week before the club's final decision to purchase the land was made, and prior to the decision to have a survey of it prepared. Neither is there any mention of a request to MacKenzie in the club's minutes, nor of any response.

It should be remembered that there was no airmail service to New Zealand at that time, however, there was a Trans-Tasman cable available for telegrams. The committee may have made contact with MacKenzie, well before even having the land inspected, taken out any options, or obtaining the member's approval and placed a purely hypothetical proposition to him, but this seems quite unlikely and is unsupported by any evidence.

MacKenzie was on the move through this period, travelling to the United States after New Zealand, prior to his return to England on 1 April 1927. Leeds would have been the only reliable address to which any plans could have been sent. From all the meeting minutes, and the newspapers of the time, Alex Russell is the only person given credit for the design of Yarra Yarra's new course.

Making a New Links

The club wasted no time to begin the process of constructing its new course. Greenkeeper Harry Alexander was reported by 'The Herald' on 9th March to be "*located at Oakleigh and actual work has already commenced. For the last few days men have been busily engaged demolishing the hedges that are on the property, a huge scheme of tree planting will be begun very soon, and in a few days*

the actual construction of the holes will be started. An ideal site has been allocated by the architect for the clubhouse and a practice fairway of fine dimensions has been provided. Seven holes have been designed on the Centre Road side of the club-house site, and eleven on the larger area on the other side." What is little known, is that Yarra Yarra was the first of Alex Russell's projects to go into construction, as the building of the West Course at Royal Melbourne was delayed for some time due to issues relating to the clubhouse location and purchase of additional land.

It is possible that Royal Melbourne's talented curator and constructor "Mick" Morcom had an involvement in aspects of the construction of the new course. 'Golf in Australia' magazine reported in early 1927 that, "*It is a great opportunity for Russell, for he has been given carte blanche in the matter. With men like Morcom around to advise him he will not be short of help in his deliberations.*" When Alexander resigned in June 1927 after a few months supervising the new course construction to become the greenkeeper/professional at the newly formed Heidelberg Golf Club, the committee asked Alex Russell for his opinion in regard to the appointment of his successor. Russell arranged to bring Ernest Johnson, who had previously worked under Morcom at Royal Melbourne, to the job and to lead the construction crew. Due to Morcom's Royal Melbourne commitments, it is likely any assistance from him, if it occurred, came in the form of brief visits during the construction phase.

In June 1927, it was reported that a Fordson tractor had been purchased with a special plough and disc cultivator, and that all the necessary clearing and ploughing had been completed. Planting of the fairways would commence in August, using an ample supply of couch grass that had been arranged at minimal cost to the club. Two bores were also being sunk on the property by the Mines Department. Horse-drawn scoops were used to supplement the tractor. When the soil was brought onto each green it was placed onto large iron plates kept hot by fires underneath in an endeavour to destroy any grass and weed seeds. A plantation sub-committee headed by Leslie Brunning, the well-known Melbourne seed merchant, ably assisted by former nurseryman George McEwan Duncan, began the task of tree planting in the areas between fairways.

In December 1927, the golf writer for 'The Herald' visited the course to view its progress and reported that clearing, fencing and repeated ploughing had been completed, while "*limes and fertilisers have been put into the ground, the new holes, with greens, fairways, bunkers and all features according to a clever plan by Alex Russell have been set, and three months after setting*

A series of three photographs were taken of the 18th hole at Yarra Yarra from the tank-stand during an inspection of the course and are undated. However, given the progress that can be seen, they were possibly taken at the time Alex Russell conducted a guided tour of the course in April 1928 as reports of this tour indicated that the greens had not yet been sown. The generously wide fairways are well covered with couchgrass. The features of greens, tees and fairways are annotated with their relevant hole numbers.

Yarra Yarra Golf Club

the covering of thick couch on the fairways is wonderful…..Russell has provided many real feature holes in his lay out."

Drainage was necessary on the 8th and 14th fairways, with the low area on the 8th lifted with sand taken from a nearby part of the property. At this stage of construction it was anticipated that all the works would cost in the order of £7,000. The report also commended the club's new greenkeeper Ernest Johnson, *"who was for some time under M. A. Morcom at Sandringham, and later in charge of Royal Park, is doing fine work and showing commendable enthusiasm in the big undertaking."* This report also contained the first published information about the length of Russell's holes at Yarra Yarra:

"The yardage of holes on the new lay out is: Out: 220, 360, 315, 140, 435, 385, 405, 560, 440 – 3260. In: 340, 180, 440, 440, 330,160, 450, 385, 410 – 3145 – 6405. From the plan it may be gathered that there is great variety, many bent holes, and excellent bunkering arranged for. The actual country has been cleverly exploited, and allowed to dictate the length of the holes, location of greens and tees, and has to a great extent indicated the best positions for bunkering. Very nice judgement has been shown in the selection of short hole sites."

Later in December 1927, the golf writer J. M. Dillon wrote about a recent visit he had made to the course at Bentleigh and his article in 'The Sporting Globe' was accompanied by an illustration of the first plan of Russell's new course, a reproduction of what appears to be the original plan drawn by Russell. Dillon noted that he had heard that the country was flat and barren before he had visited it but the undulating nature and the fine growth of couch grass disabused him of these notions. Some 8,000 trees had been planted by this time, with thousands more to come. He added:

"To the fullest the roll of the country has been exploited. Alex Russell has had a wonderful opportunity, and as far as can be judged at this stage, he has made a truly fine job. More than likely it will firmly establish his reputation as Australia's first and greatest real golf course architect. From the club house site the whole of the links can be viewed. The opening hole is just a fine "get away" one of 220 yards, and the proposed bunkering scheme will make it a first-class iron or baffy one-shotter. A real feature will be the 360 yards bent second. Other holes with any amount of scope for the placing of shots, and the taking of alternate routes in proportion to the player's skill, make the round one of great promise. There are three short

holes – the 4th, 11th and 15th – and, ranging from 140 to 180 yards, they have given Russell great scope for the making of golf propositions in which he revels. Each appears to be a beautiful hole…..A study of the plan reproduced will give an excellent idea of the skilful way in which the country has been used."*

Alex Russell was invited to speak to the members at an Extraordinary General Meeting held at Queen's Hall in Collins Street, Melbourne in the evening of 29 March 1928. The minutes of the meeting recorded the general thrust of Russell's address:

"Mr Alex Russell – The Club's Course Architect was introduced by the Chairman. Mr Russell in a brief speech informed members that he could say quite a lot, but it was rather difficult to talk about his own job. He was, however, more than satisfied with the progress made and was convinced that Yarra Yarra would have a 1st class course. Comparisons were odious, but without mentioning any names, he thought our fairways were already better than any others in the metropolitan area, with one possible exception. The Course was being spoken of in golfing circles throughout Australia, and he had already been asked to and had shown two interstate Greenkeepers over it. Several good players who had seen the course had been kind enough to say there were several very good holes. The course would be fit to play over in October next and should be in very fine order by January."

Dillon revisited Yarra Yarra on Saturday 19 April 1928, as part of a group of *"representative golfers"* who were invited to cast their eyes over the new links. He posed the question as to whether Russell could produce something at Yarra Yarra to rival the fine work of Dr MacKenzie and other well-known golf course architects. His answer was a resounding yes, saying *"what I saw more than came up to my expectations"* and further describing that the members waiting for their new course were *"like a lot of youngsters anticipating the gifts of Father Christmas."* Of the one-shot holes, Dillon was unanimous in his praise, saying that after the 3rd hole:

"Follows one of the exceptional short holes for which the links is certain to become noted. It is about 140 yards long, but there is a subtleness about it that has marked Russell's short hole – and other work – throughout. There is a right to left slope, which calls out for cut on the shot if the green is to be safely held. Nasty places are on the left. Bad parts are on the right. If the shot is well steered and too long it will encounter much bother.

RUSSELL'S FAVOURITE

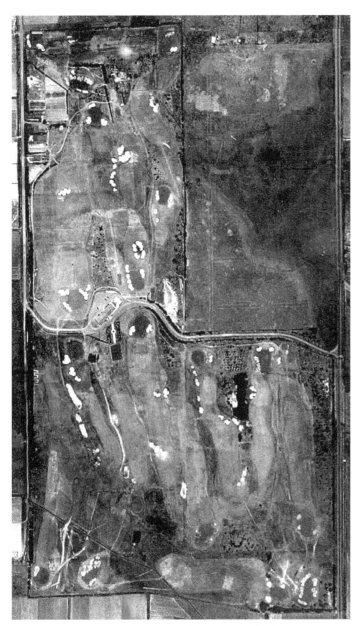

The short hole that, of the four one shotters, appealed mostly to me was the 180 yards 11th. The green is skewed round, and right in front and up against the putting place is a line of nasty and effective looking hard traps. A full iron with stop is the shot called for. Those unwilling to take the risk will have a pitch back on the extreme left end, where they may rely on an accurate chip for a 3. Russell's favourite short hole is his 160 yards up hill one – the 15th – to a green that has a level patch and then a step up to the putting area proper."

Alex Russell conducted a personal tour for the group of influential golfers and journalists that visited the course that Saturday, *"pointing out the features of the different holes. The greens, although formed, are not yet grassed, and their character, therefore, cannot be fully judged, but one could see that, clothed in smooth turf, they will make a splendid show, and it can be taken for granted that they will lack little in scientific construction,"* according to Harry Culliton, the golf writer for 'The Australasian.'

When it came time to sow the greens, Morcom was asked to undertake this work in person. The minutes of the committee meeting held on 19 March 1928 indicated that they were awaiting the return of Alex Russell from Western Australia, where he was laying out the new Lake Karrinyup course, before sowing the greens and that *"it was hoped to obtain the services of Morcom of Royal Melbourne to do the actual sowing, as it was considered doubtful whether the Greenkeeper Johnson was capable of planting such fine seed."* Presumably Morcom was brought over to sow the greens, although the minutes do not specifically record this. It would appear quite probable that he did. The greens were grassed with Sutton's Mix, from English seed merchants Sutton & Sons of Reading. This mixture was used with much success at Royal Melbourne by Russell and Morcom, when the new greens of both the West and East courses were sown a year or two later. The resultant putting surfaces at Yarra Yarra were given the highest praise. In later published recollections of club member and former nurseryman George McEwan Duncan, he noted that the greens at Yarra Yarra were in fact sown with *"a special mixture which the Club imported from Suttons, the English seed merchants. The base of this mixture was South German Bent, but also contained Red Fescue and Hard Fescue. One interesting incident occurred – when the 9th green was in its young stage, a violent gale blew it out of the ground, and we had only two months before opening day....However, we pinched a bit of turf from each of the other seventeen greens and turfed the bare green, with the result that on the opening day this green was equal to any."*

Aerial photograph of the Yarra Yarra course from 1933. Note the chains of bunkers that Russell built on holes such as the 5th, 9th and 16th.

Yarra Yarra Golf Club

In August 1928, the committee was deliberating as to when to open the new course and clubhouse, with a date of 15 December 1928 being projected as a likely date given that the Spanish Mission style clubhouse was expected to be fit for occupancy in October. One committeeman was opposed to opening the course this soon and had consulted Mr Charles Lane from Commonwealth, "Jock" Young and George McEwan Duncan who all said the greens would not be ready until March 1929. Alex Russell had written to say that, *"the course would be in a playable condition by December, but would be better in January."* The committee then pushed back the opening to 15 January 1929, but later revisited this decision and brought it back to the original date in December, no doubt due to improved growing conditions in the spring.

A report in 'The Herald' newspaper a few days before the opening meeting gave revised lengths for the new holes. These were the distances included on the course card for the first few years:

"The yardage of the course is, 225, 365, 348, 135, 429, 358, 424, 542, 439 – 3265 out; 340, 186, 404, 426, 385, 165, 462, 400, 465 – 3233 in. The total is 6498 yards. For a while the 12th hole will be played as one shotter."

View across the 7th green to the clubhouse. Note the square corner to the green in the right foreground.

State Library of NSW

Open for Play

Russell's creation at Yarra Yarra opened for play to its members on 15 December 1928, with over 100 members playing on a fine, but windy day. It was clear from the outset that the group of one-shot holes that Russell had designed were quite outstanding, a reputation they have carried forth to this day. In its report on the opening meeting, 'The Argus' suggested that it was *"marvellous to find the fairways and greens so thoroughly well established, and as good as they are, considering that it is only 18 months since the first sod of the new course was turned."*

Alex Russell was elected the first Life Member of the Yarra Yarra Golf Club in 1928 in recognition of his services to the Club

On the opening day, Alex Russell was honoured by life membership at Yarra Yarra Golf Club, in appreciation of his services in delivering them such a fine golf course. 'The Argus' described the award as a *"graceful compliment"* for his *"splendid and painstaking work in designing the links and superintending its construction,"* while the entry in the club's minutes reads:

> *"Although the Committee in ordinary circumstances did not think life memberships altogether desirable, they were unanimous in their desire that members should pass the necessary resolution appointing Mr Alex Russell a life member, as a token of their appreciation of the signal services he had rendered to the Club at a negligible fee."*

Club records show that this 'negligible fee' was in fact the sum of £75, paid to the firm of MacKenzie and Russell in January 1929. Possibly Russell forwarded half, or even all the fee to MacKenzie, keeping nothing for himself.

High Acclaim

Praise for the new course from the golfing press of the day can be best illustrated by 'Jack' Dillon, the golf writer for 'The Sporting Globe' in Melbourne. Some extracts from Dillon's articles about the course included:

> *"The design was handed to the most competent expert here."*

> *"Brilliantly he has come through the test, and his reputation as a great golf architect is definitely made."*

> *"No.11 is, I think, the most difficult and intriguing one shotter in Victoria."*

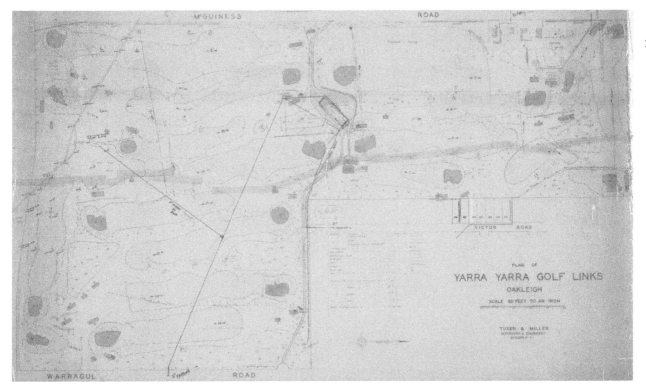

"Walter Hagen and Joe Kirkwood played at Yarra Yarra. Without qualification, they stated that the greens at Bentleigh were easily the best they had played over in Australia…..Furthermore, they stated that the course was one of championship calibre, and rated it so, in golfing value, better than any course that they had seen outside Victoria."

And from 'The Sun' newspaper:

"Alex Russell, who designed the links, has done his job well. When Yarra Yarra take over they will have one of the best links in Australia."

'The Argus', 'The Australasian', 'The Herald', and 'The Age' newspapers in Melbourne all had highly complimentary reviews of Russell's first design effort. 'All Tennis & Australian Golf' magazine in its 1 February 1929 issue reported on the enthusiasm of Mrs Nellie Gatehouse, the prominent Melbourne woman golfer and president of the Victorian Ladies' Golf Union, Miss Mona MacLeod and Miss Hay, who undertook the setting of the women's scratch score for the new course.

Mrs Gatehouse commented, *"During all the years I have been making scratch scores, this is the first course I have ever been on where the ladies tees have been out in the correct spots without having to be altered in any way."* The article further commented

Survey plan of the course (top) by Tuxen and Miller surveyors in 1935 accurately depicted the golf features only a few short years after the course was built

Yarra Yarra Golf Club

that Russell had studied the wants of the woman golfer, and that perhaps *"his wife had a finger in the pie where this was concerned."*

But probably the most telling of all critiques was that of South Australian golf architect and *"well-known links expert"*, Herbert L. "Cargie" Rymill, who penned a series of reviews of several of the major Melbourne and Sydney golf courses for 'The Sporting Globe' newspaper in late 1929 and early 1930. In his article on the new Yarra Yarra course, published on 27 November 1929, Rymill wrote:

> *"Yarra Yarra is the latest of the additions to the links assets of Victoria. Because of this, and the fact that the work was, from the conversion of virgin country to the completion of the links, carried out by Mr Alex Russell, I was particularly anxious to see the new course.*
>
> *When one considers that little over two years ago this country was just market gardens, it is wonderful to contemplate what has been accomplished. For such a comparatively uninteresting piece of country, a truly fine lay out has been brought into being. Russell's green formations and bunkering round the green are particularly good and equal to that seen on the best links at home.*

High praise indeed, from a man who always appeared to be hard to please. Rymill was, however, disappointed in the placement of the fairway bunkering, suggesting that it would have been *"much better if it had been done along the lines followed by Mr C. Lane, of Commonwealth, with more variety, and dictating that every shot should be placed for the obtaining of the easiest line to the hole."* He was very impressed by the par threes though, and said that:

> *"Taken as a whole, the one shotters are of a very high class, and as good as will be found on first class courses anywhere. The irregular shaping of the greens, and the cunningly sloped diagonal plateaus or terraces, had great variety. The whole surface of the greens are visible from the tees, so that the player may see exactly where the hole is placed. There is no seeing of the top of the flag only, as one finds too frequently elsewhere."*

This aspect of visibility of the greens was one of Dr MacKenzie's favourite subjects that he no doubt passed on to Russell during their shared time in Melbourne. Rymill found the idea of bunkerless greens, as at the 10th and 14th at Yarra Yarra, to be excellent and noted that it provided variety and made judging of the distance of the approach shot quite difficult. He added that there was the classic justification of the bunkerless nature of the final hole on The Old Course at St Andrews for so doing. He was impressed by the excellent quality of turf on the greens, saying that:

"It consists of creeping bent and fescue. Considering that the seed was put down only 18 months ago, what has been done at Yarra is a great lesson to other green Committees who have weedy fescue greens. I have an idea that some of the greens at Kooyonga were the best in Australia, but I must give the palm to the greens at Yarra Yarra as far as Australia is concerned."

In February 1929, Russell wrote to the club outlining what he saw as necessary course work, with the committee deciding *"to inform Mr Russell that the work was proceeding on lines suggested in his letter. Also decided to thank Mr Russell for his letter and his interest in the work on the course."*

The official opening of the new course and clubhouse that took place on Saturday 23 February 1929 was a grand affair with over 500 invited guests, and the club's Annual Report recorded that *"nothing but praise was heard of the splendid achievement which has culminated in the new Yarra Yarra."*

Of Alex Russell's contribution, the report stated that, *"the result is a monument to the ability of Mr Alex. Russell, under whose supervision the work was carried out."*

H. L. "Cargie" Rymill was a South Australian golf course architect who had a hand in the original layouts of the Royal Adelaide, Kooyonga, Glenelg and Grange courses

*Aerial view looking over the Yarra Yarra course
and clubhouse c.1936 from the booklet "Golf
Courses of Victoria" with the greens numbered.*

Some seven years later, on 3 December 1936, Alex Russell made a subsequent inspection of the course at the request of the committee and was reported as being well satisfied with its condition. The club manager reported on his visit, stating that in regard to greens, Russell *"strongly recommends all humps to be removed from the greens always keeping in view the question of drainage. He suggests the Committee should consider the setting aside each year a sum of say 20 pounds for this purpose, and in time the whole of the greens will be free of this trouble. This has been done at Kingston Heath with the result that the greens are more or less perfect. He considers Kingston Heath the best links in Australia. He strongly urges the spike roller at all times as this is most beneficial to the greens."*

It would appear that, in using the term *"humps"*, Russell was most likely referring to minor inconsistencies in the green surface rather than designed larger undulations. He also recommended that the lips of some of the rear bunkers should be raised to stop people from being able to putt out of bunkers, suggesting that, *"Putting out of bunkers is simply not golf."* Two bunkers on the 4th and 11th greens were then altered as he had instructed. In his view the bunkers should be raked every week and deeply enough for aeration purposes.

Alex Russell's first solo design effort at Yarra Yarra was a tour-de-force and paved the way for a career in golf course architecture. Undoubtedly he learnt much while making the Yarra Yarra links, lessons he took with him into his subsequent designs.

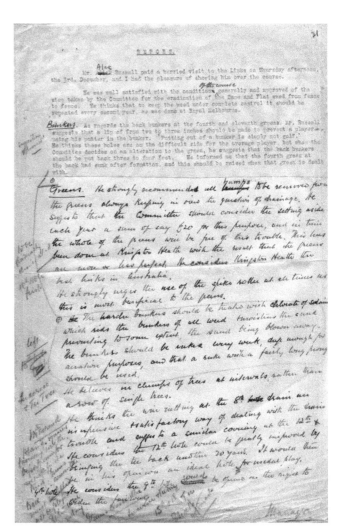

Alex Russell (left) inspected the course on 3rd December 1936 (above). The Club Manager took him around the course and noted his suggestions in this report

Yarra Yarra Golf Club

Alex Russell's 11th at Yarra Yarra, one of the finest par threes in Australia

Yarra Yarra Golf Club

1942 painting by Victorian artist Harold B.
Herbert of the Riversdale Golf Club's 18th hole

Chapter 9

RIVERSDALE GOLF CLUB

Riversdale Golf Club originated as the Surrey Hills Golf Club in 1892, playing in leased paddocks north of Mont Albert railway station, making the club the second oldest in Victoria. In 1908, due to encroaching development that was threatening the course, the club moved to Camberwell. This was to be the Riversdale Golf Club's home until 1927, when a move was once more necessary due to neighbouring development pressures.

After considering many different locations, the club purchased the St John's Wood Estate at Mt Waverley on the corner of Huntingdale and High Street Roads and a new course was laid out to a plan by "Jock" Young, the club's professional.

Railroaded

The club's greens committee determined at its 12 May 1927 meeting that Mr Alex Russell should be asked to plan and supervise the bunkering. Russell agreed to do this for a fee of £20 and 5% of any work undertaken on his recommendation. He also asked for a survey plan of the course. A month later, due to a threat to the club's occupancy of its land from a new railway line to Glen Waverley that was proposed to run through the centre of the course, the club decided to place Russell's plans on hold. However, it was also agreed that Russell should be asked to draw up an alternative plan of the course, allowing for the railway as it was planned at that time, and also another version if the line was moved further to the south, something one of the directors hoped to achieve. This modification occurred some six months

"Jock" Young

later, when the railway line was re-aligned to the southern end of the property. By June 1928 the directors had copies of Russell's plans and by August the arrangements with Russell were confirmed at a directors' meeting.

So, while the new course opened for play on 1 October 1927, after relocating to St John's Wood, the club was soon forced to reconfigure its new course considerably to accommodate its reduced footprint. However, this was to prove a blessing in disguise, as Young's course was considered by many to be rather uninteresting.

Some 22 acres (9 ha) of land, affecting eight holes, was finally transferred to the Railways Department in November 1929, leaving the club with a balance of 132 acres (53 ha), with the consequential need for the practice fairway to be put into use for new golf holes. An alternative practice fairway was to be built to the south of the railway line but this land was later relinquished by the club.

A new railway station, called Jordanville, was to be sited opposite the links. Riversdale's financial situation benefited considerably from the compensation for the acquired land, and the land they now held was of much greater value, while access to the course would be improved by the adjacent station. "Jock" Young was by this time the professional at Commonwealth Golf Club and was one of three people asked by Yarra Yarra to comment on the suitability of their proposed new site at Bentleigh. Riversdale made the wise decision to entrust the redesign of their course to Alex Russell for a modest fee of £52-15-0.

Jack Dillon, the golf writer at 'The Sporting Globe', wrote about the redevelopment on 5 June 1929 under the heading "Riversdale Takes Wise Advice" and clearly he had seen Russell's plans for the course when he wrote:

Photograph of Alex Russell (left) playing in the Riversdale Trophy on 3rd June 1929

"The Riversdale Club has been up against difficulties. In a big way these difficulties have been faced. More than likely Riversdale will show the way to those who build on clay. One of the most reassuring signs to date has been the calling in of Alex Russell to advise on the new layout. Fortunately, the new railway goes right through the course and dictated a rearrangement of holes – to say nothing of a re-valuation of the land. Than Russell there is not to my knowledge in Australia a more competent golf architect. With him and the competent home club green keeper, a course of exceptional class has been designed and in 12 months this club should have something exceptional in clay courses."

Just prior to the opening, 'All Tennis and Australian Golf' magazine reported on the progress at Riversdale in their 1 February 1930 issue:

"The new links at Burwood are now looking a picture. When the bushway scheme – under the direction of Alex. Russell – is completed the course will be right up in the championship class. Only one thing is now needed to put the links on a level with the other leading clubs, and that is the opening of the new railway next to the course."

Russell's Turf Knowledge

Alex Russell's involvement at Riversdale, as with his other courses, went beyond just drawing plans. He had a sound knowledge of agronomy, and advised Riversdale on matters such as preparation of fairways, their top-dressing, and sowing of the greens. The Victorian Golf Association Green Research Committee established an experimental plot at Riversdale. Russell was the long serving representative for Royal Melbourne on that committee and he provided Riversdale with

Extract (above) from the Greens Committee Meeting Minutes for 11th April 1929. Items 4 and 5 refer to Russell's comments on the size of the 17th green and his visit to the course "today."

a letter setting out the advantages and disadvantages of sowing seed, or laying turf for the greens.

It was eventually decided to sow the greens with a mixture of couch and bent. The seed needed to be mixed, as directed by Russell, prior to sowing, again with directions from him on how this was to be carried out. Clearly, he did not choose Sutton's Mix, as was used at Royal Melbourne and Yarra Yarra. Russell did not do things without a reason, so presumably the slightly different conditions at Riversdale required a slightly different combination of grasses, no doubt, based on those grown in the experimental plot. Such use of test plots to find the most suitable grasses had been practiced by him at Royal Melbourne and Lake Karrinyup. The Riversdale course, while having some sandy areas, is mostly based on clay and Russell introduced the use of a spiked roller. The success of this can be judged by the subsequent newspaper comments, especially those of Joe Kirkwood in March 1930.

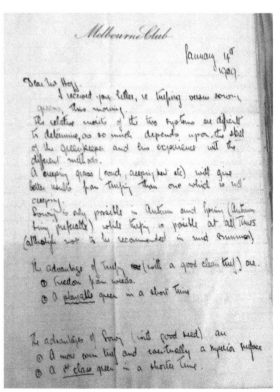

First page of a letter from Russell to Riversdale's Mr Norman Hogg dated 4th January 1929 (below) and written on Melbourne Club notepaper

Hagen and Kirkwood

Riversdale's new holes came into play on Saturday 29 March 1930 and the revised course was opened by an exhibition match that afternoon starting at 2pm, with Walter Hagen and Joe Kirkwood taking on two of Victoria's best amateurs in Ivo Whitton and Mick Ryan. A gallery of around 500 watched proceedings and a special train was put on to take spectators out to the course. Hagen and Kirkwood comfortably accounted for the amateur pair, winning the four-ball match by a margin of 5 and 4. Hagen shot a brilliant 66 and Kirkwood a 71. Ryan shot 75 and Whitton a 79, and they did well not to lose by a greater margin. A report in 'The Age' on 31 March gave a detailed account of the opening match and also included the lengths of the rearranged holes:

> "The yardage of the rearranged holes at Riversdale is as follows:-
>
> 1st, 190 yards; 2nd, 436 yards; 3rd, 145 yards; 4th, 344 yards; 5th, 430 yards; 6th, 443 yards; 7th, 468 yards; 8th, 389 yards; 9th, 352 yards. Out, 3197 yards. Par, 37.
>
> 10th, 230 yards; 11th, 391 yards; 12th, 298 yards; 13th, 500 yards; 14th, 120 yards; 15th, 494 yards; 16th, 407 yards; 17th, 200 yards; 18th, 312 yards. In, 2952 yards. Par 35.
>
> Total, 6149 yards. Par, 72."

Riversdale had been Kirkwood's old club and he was lavish with his praise of what Russell had achieved. At the end of the match Kirkwood gave his customary trick-shot exhibition. Having visited the course in the days leading up to the match, Kirkwood was impressed with the state of the turf on the greens and the thick grass that now covered the fairways. He later wrote a letter of thanks to the club, and noted:

> "I have watched with much satisfaction its advancement in its new location, and was particularly pleased to note the fine work that was done on the links even since my previous visit in 1928. When the further minor improvements which, I understand, Mr Alec Russell has in view, have been completed, the course, in my opinion, will be one of the best inland links in Australia. Exceptionally good work has been done in choosing the sites for the greens, and the fairways have been carpeted with an excellent mat of grass."

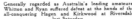

Generally regarded as Australia's leading amateurs, Whitton and Ryan suffered defeat at the hands of the all-conquering Hagen and Kirkwood at Riversdale last Saturday.

Victorian amateurs Ivo Whitton and Mick Ryan (right) lost their match to Hagen and Kirkwood

Walter Hagen and Joe Kirkwood (far right) travelled the world together giving exhibitions and earning a handsome living

More Praise

Clearly Russell had in mind some small enhancements to his course. 'Tennis and Golf in Australia' magazine was similarly laudatory:

> *"The upheaval caused through this same railway cutting right across a big section of the links proved a blessing in disguise. In planning out the necessary new holes the Committee decided to call in Alex. Russell as golf course architect. No wiser step could have been taken. The Royal Melbourne man, who has now built up a big name in his new profession, made a splendid job of the work set him to do. The new holes would be a credit to any course in the world."*

And further on:

> *"Alex Russell cannot only get results but seems to have the gift of getting them quickly. The fairways, greens and tees give the impression of a thoroughly matured golf links. The whole course is nothing more or less than a beautiful green carpet. The natural undulations and slightly hilly nature of the country make Riversdale one of our most sporting lay-outs."*

'The Argus' suggested it was fortunate that the railway had cut off the most undesirable of its land on the south side of the line. It added:

> *"Of the country remaining, which is ample for a first-class course, Mr Alex Russell has made the most, and the new holes offer far superior golfing problems to the player than the old layout offered."*

On 29 May 1930 'Table Talk' noted that Russell had designed seven new holes for Riversdale as a result of loss of land to the railway:

> *"The seven new holes planned by Alec Russell make Riversdale a much more interesting proposition than formerly, as those who play in the open meeting during King's Birthday week-end will find."*

Caricature of Alex Russell by Hector Morrison

The Riversdale Open Meeting was held in June and was contested over a course that had been drenched by 2 inches (50mm) of rain over the week-end. 'The Age' reported that:

> *"The undulating character of this excellent golfing country, however, affords a fairly natural drainage, and there was little evidence of anything in the way of water-logged soil save at the eighth, where some of the approach shots were caught just in front of the green. Par is 72 for the new Riversdale layout, which was rearranged by Alex. Russell and opened by Walter Hagen a few months ago. Yesterday's conditions, in spite of the absence of rain and heavy wind, made par just a trifle too stiff a proposition for the field."*

In October 1930, Jack Dillon was glowing in his praise of the great improvement in the Riversdale course wrought by Russell:

> *"The golfers from other clubs, who on the Riversdale links last Saturday took part in the shield games, were wonderfully impressed by the improvement that has been effected on the links at St John's Wood, Burwood. No links in Victoria has been revolutionised to the extent that the Riversdale lay-out has in the past two years.*
>
> *During the June open meeting the fairways were thickly covered, and the greens had a fine mat of turf that looked exceedingly good to the eye. However, on that occasion the greens were on the tricky side. Since then the fairways have improved considerably, and the greens have thickened and become as good to the putter as they were to the eye, formerly – and that is really good.*
>
> *Alex Russell's plans and the admirable work of the greenkeeper, supplemented by the untiring enthusiasm and hard work of the club's captain (Norman Hogg), put members greatly in debt.*
>
> *Much of the fine growth that has been brought about at Riversdale is attributed to an experiment that has provided a full success. Fairways and greens have been rolled with a spiked roller. These numerous and deep punctures in the soil have had the effect of aerating the grasses and stimulating their growth. As the method is natural and includes no artificial forcing of growth, the effects are likely to continue."*

Dillon was again unstinting with his praise when he wrote of Riversdale's advance in 'The Sporting Globe' in March of 1931:

> *"But now members of Riversdale may, without any qualifications, say that they get more pleasure from taking*

their golf on their own links than it is possible for them to get anywhere else, even at Metropolitan or Royal Melbourne. By the wise, consistent and unselfish work of officers and staff of this club, and through the advice of Australia's greatest links architect, Alex Russell, Riversdale has been revolutionised.

When it was first opened at St John's Wood, Burwood, the layout was uninteresting, and it was confidently forecast that it would be one of those clay courses where turf would never be of a first class quality. Now the holes are interesting, what bunkering has been done is well done, and on greens, tees and fairways the turf is thick and up to the standard of that on the best links here.

In discussing Riversdale links these days, there are necessary no limitations or qualifications in describing it. It is a truly delightful place for a game of golf."

The 1936 publication "Golf Courses of Victoria" noted that the land cut off from the course by the railway line was used as a practice fairway with specially marked targets at 50-yard intervals making it the most up-to-date round Melbourne. The course also boasted an expansive dam and a turf nursery, as well as a turf test plot laid down by the Greens Research Committee of Victoria:

"The fairways have been cleverly graduated around the hills of this undulating course. What Riversdale lacks in level stances it makes up in panoramic views, the terraced slope of three levels of greens (13th, 14th, 15th and 16th), as viewed from the high 12th hole presenting an unusual feature of golfing landscape."

When located at Surrey Hills, the club instituted an open amateur competition known as the Surrey Hills Gentlemen's Championship, Gold Medal. This competition was the second oldest in Australia, and continued as the Riversdale Cup, an event with a proud history and an honour board containing many of the great names of Victorian and Australian golf. P.C. Anderson won the title three times, while his brother Mark was the inaugural winner. Others to have hoisted the cup aloft include The Hon. Michael Scott, Ivo Whitton four times, and Alex Russell twice. In more recent times winners have included Mike Clayton, Aaron Baddeley, Robert Allenby and Ryan Ruffels.

There have been changes to the course over the years, yet Russell's routing has generally been maintained where possible. As with a number of Russell's courses, the first hole is a short

hole to 'get the field away'. Walter Hagen opened the course back in 1930 with a near perfect tee shot that finished only 12 feet (4 metres) from the hole on the first. Riversdale, as with all of Russell's courses, has a fine collection of par three holes.

Finally, as John Boundy, the club's historian and archivist, wrote:

"Alex Russell's legacy lives on at Riversdale. We are the beneficiaries of a wonderful layout that continues to challenge golfers of all standards. Our course has certainly stood the test of time with the basic layout virtually unchanged over the past eighty five years."

Page from the 1936 publication "Golf Courses of Victoria" describing the Riversdale Golf Club

Discovering Alex Russell

1945 Aerial Photograph
of the
Riversdale Golf Club
The area delineated in orange indicates
the land lost to the railway

1st
2nd
17th
18th
10th
14th
3rd
9th
8th
15th
4th
11th
16th
13th
7th
6th
5th
12th

RAILWAY

*Aerial photograph of Alex Russell's Riversdale
layout some 15 years on from its opening*

The 2nd, with entrance drive on right,
and Clubhouse in background

The 7th,
from green to tee

Scenes of the course from a booklet published by the club in 1948. At top left is the view from the 2nd tee, while top right the photograph is taken behind the 7th green looking back down the fairway. At bottom left is the view of the par three 17th, with the 18th tee view at bottom right.

Aerial Panorama, showing SUMMERLAND (on Phillip Island) in Foreground, and indicating Relative Geographical Positions

Chapter 10

SUMMERLAND GOLF LINKS

Phillip Island, at the mouth of Victoria's Western Port Bay, has long been viewed as an ideal holiday destination for Melbourne's masses, and one man, Melbourne consulting engineer and later the inaugural Shire President of the Phillip Island Council, Albert K.T. Sambell did much to develop the island as a tourist mecca which continues until this day.

The western end of the island was more isolated and remote from the established townships of Cowes, Newhaven and Rhyll, leading to the spectacular Nobbies, a chain of small rocky islands trailing off the westernmost point. Irish immigrant Patrick Phelan first purchased land here in 1870, cropping it for chicory and grazing sheep and cattle. Over the ensuing years he purchased a number of adjoining land parcels until, by the time of his death in 1913, he owned all of the western peninsula of the island along with a large parcel on the eastern side of Swan Lake, a total of 617 acres.

After Phelan's death, this land was scooped up by Sambell who had a much grander vision for the land than farming, and he was willing to pay over three times the current going rate for farmland to secure the peninsula.

A.K.T. Sambell and the Phillip Island Holidays Development Company

Albert Keaston Trenavin Sambell was born near Violet Town in north-eastern Victoria in 1879. He developed an early interest in engineering, and when he was employed as the municipal engineer at Tallangatta at the age of 23, he was the youngest man to be appointed to such a role in the state of Victoria to that time. He later held the post of municipal engineer in a number of rural councils and was instrumental in developing the water supply projects for the Mornington Peninsula and the Flinders Naval Depot.

Sambell first acquired land on Phillip Island in 1912, purchasing 455 acres (184 ha) of land near Ventnor on the northern coast of the island facing Western Port Bay and here he later built a substantial house known as Trenavin Park. After acquiring Phelan's land in 1914, Sambell slowly began to purchase the first pieces of the holiday and recreation jigsaw that his landholding on the western end of the island would ultimately fit into. That initial piece was the ferry service to the island.

As an isolated island, the only way to access it was on the ships belonging to the Phillip Island Shipping Service that ran from Stony Point, adjacent to the Flinders Naval Depot on the eastern shores of the Mornington Peninsula, today's HMAS *Cerberus*. He acquired this service in 1917 and then controlled the only commercial means of accessing the island.

Over the years he continued to invest in the service, bringing in newer and larger ferries, while passenger numbers to the island increased from 12,000 in 1923 to 25,000 in 1926, a doubling in just three years. Sambell also eventually purchased the two hotels on the island, the Isle of Wight Hotel and the Phillip Island Hotel, both in Cowes. By the mid 1920s the Victorian economy was sufficiently buoyant to encourage land speculation and Sambell saw that his land bank on the western end of the island could be developed to meet a need for coastal holiday residences.

Summerland

In July 1926, the firm of Sambell, Candy and White, Surveyors, advertised in the Melbourne newspapers a call to Surveyors, Architects and Town Planners for designs for *"A New Township for Phillip Island"* and offering 90 guineas worth of prizes for the best designs. Prospective designers were asked to *"Submit designs for an extensive area situated at "The Nobbies," Phillip Island,"* and that a new 500 foot (150 metre) long jetty would be constructed in the adjacent Cat Bay at which a steamer, one of Sambell's fleet, would call in regularly.

Albert Keaston Trenavin Sambell, engineer, developer, entrepreneur and Shire President

Philip Island & District Historical Society

"Golf Links, Tennis Courts and Other Sporting Facilities" would also be provided, while the site was described as *"Ideal, and Provides Unlimited Opportunity for Distinctive Design."*
Which firms were awarded the first prize of 75 guineas and the second prize of 15 guineas are not known, but soon a separate development company, The Phillip Island Holidays Development Pty Ltd with a capital of £40,000 was established,

The SS Alvina, one of the ferries of the Philip Island Shipping Service owned by Sambell

and later that year surveyors began working to lay out the access road and establishing a network of roads and housing allotments.

In the early days of the island there was only an unmade track through this peninsula and out to The Nobbies, more than a two-hour trek by horse and cart from Cowes, following the same route that today's highway takes. The road, previously called Nobbies Road, that gave early visitor access to the surf beach near Swan Lake and the nesting area of the colony of Little Penguins, was renamed by Sambell's wife Eleanor as St Helens Road. Sambell also constructed a road down to that surf beach, today's Summerland Beach, and with it gave visitors to the island direct access to the penguin colony. Three local residents started a guided tour service that would meet visitors at the Cowes ferry and drive them out to the beach for a personal viewing of the penguins at sunset, and so began what soon became known as the Penguin Parade.

By late 1927, Sambell's development company had settled on the design of their township, which was far more than a simple speculative sub-division, containing as it did a commercial strip along the coastal road and a residential hinterland. In early January 1928 the company began to market the new development that it called 'Summerland'. The company prepared a lavish 16-page brochure entitled *"Ideal Summerland On the Nobbies, Phillip Island,"* complete with maps and a coloured aerial view of the island showing the location of Summerland. The map of the initial phase of development also showed the location of the land that had been *"Reserved for 18 Hole Golf Links Designed by MacKenzie & Russell."* This is the first clue that Sambell and his investors were quite serious about the golf component of their development.

Golf on Phillip Island

Golf was probably played on Phillip Island in the 19th century, but not in any organised form. Six golf courses were laid out on the island before the present one, and these are all now long gone. One was associated with the Isle of Wight Hotel in Cowes, which had been purchased by Sambell. The rudimentary course was laid out *"within three-quarters of a mile of the town, on undulating ground, commanding spacious views of Westernport,"* according to an article in 'The Argus.' The article covered the opening of the new course

by His Excellency the Governor of Victoria, the Earl of Stradbroke, in November 1921, and noted that His Excellency played a game on the links later that day with Sambell and two other men.

By the time the Summerland links was playable, there were still three other golf courses in use on the island, which, according to the golf writer for the 'Sporting Globe,' Jack Dillon, he found *"to be just as rough and relatively of no attracting powers outside the immediate locality, as I expected from the accounts I received. However, in the matter of the fourth course I received a pleasant surprise."* That surprise was Alex Russell's Summerland Golf Links.

The Summerland Golf Links

The timing of the planning of Sambell's new development at Summerland in 1926 and 1927 could not have been any better for Alex Russell. In December 1926, it was announced that he had been appointed the Australian partner of Dr Alister MacKenzie on the back of MacKenzie's hugely successful Australian foray that year, and the new firm of MacKenzie and Russell was open for business.

It is not known if Sambell was a serious golfer but he played well enough to play with the Governor who certainly was, and so he was likely to have heard of the 1924 Australian Open champion Alex Russell and his new career. Regardless, the fledgling firm of MacKenzie and Russell soon had a new commission to design an 18-hole golf course at the eastern end of the Summerland development.

The project was briefly reported upon in the 1st September 1927 issue of 'Golf' magazine:

> *"We are informed that there is a scheme afloat for the construction of a first-class course for Phillip Island. Experts, who have inspected the proposed site, and a couple of the State's leading golfers were most enthusiastic regarding the nature of the country to be utilised. It is the nearest approach, they say, to the genuine links country that they have seen anywhere in Australia."*

The involvement of Alex Russell as the designer of the course was not released until the brochure was made public in January 1928, and an extract from Russell's report to the company was included on one page of the brochure entitled *"A Perfect Golf Course in an Island Setting,"* accompanied by a photograph of the site that was captioned "A Beautiful Stretch of Golf Country":

> *"In a magnificent scenic setting, and possessing many distinctive features, the golf course at SUMMERLAND will be a masterpiece – one of the very finest in the whole of Australia. The links, which will be in easy reach of your own front door, will be greatly enhanced by natural hazards and bunkers,*

A Beautiful Stretch of Golf Country

A Picturesque Portion of Swan Lake

IN a magnificent scenic setting, and possessing many distinctive features, the golf course at SUMMERLAND will be a masterpiece — one of the very finest in the whole of Australia. The links, which will be within easy reach of your own front door, will be greatly enhanced by natural hazards and bunkers, which will provide interesting problems for the thoughtful golfer, while offering an excellent test for the beginner.

The scheme provides for a modern golf house to add the required note of distinction and charm to a course which will take its place among the favoured few of the Commonwealth.

In the opinion of Mr. Alex. Russell, the well-known champion and golf architect (now partner of Dr. MacKenzie) there is no finer golfing country in Victoria. The greens and fairways, in their situation and formation, are exceptionally fine; and of such character and condition as to attract golfing enthusiasts from far and near. In his own words: "I have seen and played on practically all the first-class courses in Australia, and have been shown many proposed sites for golf courses, and can confidently say that not one of them has such good natural features as this area has, or so nearly approaches the great seaside courses in England and Scotland. There is no doubt that a championship course can be constructed here which will have no superior in Australia."

A Perfect Golf Course in an Island Setting

At your door— A Sportsman's Paradise!

"There is no place where the young are more gladly conscious of their youth, or the old better contented with their age."

WE leave it to Robert Louis Stevenson to describe the fascination of this Island paradise. Unique among Australian resorts, SUMMERLAND is most adequately described by the word "versatile." Tourists readily admit that, among the existing resorts of Victoria, there is none which offers such a variety of attractions. Here will be established an exclusive Sports Club, under the management of a committee which will include Alex. Russell and other well-known golfers, the membership of which will be confined to those who purchase a residential site or sites. As soon as a reasonable number of lots have been sold, the recreation grounds and sports areas will be handed over to the members of the club, and will become their joint property to govern as they think fit.

From the actual proceeds of the sale of each block the owners will pay into a fund, which they have provided, the sum of £10, payable in two moieties: the first after 50 per cent., and the second after 75 per cent. of the purchase money is paid. From this fund the owners will be recouped from time to time, the actual amount expended by them to date of payment going towards the erection of buildings, and laying out and maintaining parks, gardens, golf course, and recreation grounds. The balance (if any) will be held for the use and benefit of the club, as its committee may deem desirable.

which will provide interesting problems for the thoughtful golfer, while offering an excellent test for the beginner.

The scheme provides for a modern golf house to add the required note of distinction and charm to a course which will take its place among the favoured few of the Commonwealth.

In the opinion of Mr Alex. Russell, the well-known champion and golf architect (now partner of Dr MacKenzie) there is no finer golfing country in Victoria. The greens and fairways, in their situation and formation, are exceptionally fine; and of such character and condition as to attract golfing enthusiasts from far and near. In his own words:

"I have seen and played on practically all the first-class courses in Australia, and have been shown many proposed sites for golf courses, and can confidently say that not one of them has such good natural features as this area has, or so nearly approaches the great seaside courses in England and Scotland. There is no doubt that a championship course can be constructed here which will have no superior in Australia.""

The brochure also indicated that an exclusive Sports Club would be formed as part of the development, "under the management of a Committee which will include Alex. Russell and other well-known golfers, the membership of which will be confined to those who purchase a residential site." The plan was to hand back the golf course and other recreation areas to the club once a sufficient number of blocks had been sold, with the owners paying the sum of £10 from the proceeds of the sale of each block into a fund from which they would draw from time to time to recoup their expenditure on the erection of buildings, the construction of the golf course and other recreation amenities.

Two pages from the Summerland brochure from January 1928 (above) describing the golf course to be designed by Alex Russell and the Sports Club committee of management that was proposed to include him

State Library of Victoria

The site for the golf course was at the eastern end of the Summerland development and in behind the Summerland Beach where the penguins went into and came out of the ocean each day. In the end, this proximity to the penguin colony would be, along with World War II, one of the main causes of the eventual demise of the course. The holes stretched out as far as the shores of Swan Lake and two holes of the course were to the north of the main road, separated from the balance of the course.

Fortuitously, Alex Russell's plan for the Summerland links has survived, being a rare example of a signed and dated Alex Russell routing plan, in the collection of the Phillip Island & District Historical Society. The plan is dated *"15. 12. 27"* and includes a card of the course. Also, in the manner of his mentor Dr MacKenzie, Russell just included the length of each hole with no reference as to bogey or par figures. This card has been subsequently marked up to show which were the nine holes constructed first, as sadly the remaining nine were never realised.

The land was sandy and contained broken sand dunes and grassed-over old dunes, as well as drainage courses leading out from Swan Lake. The ocean was not far away, on either side

of the course, and Russell must have been reminded of some of the coastal links in Britain when he first set foot on the site sometime in 1927. A clubhouse and lodge building was to be located on the new easternmost road of the development that led down to the beach and the penguins, with delightful views across the golf course and along Summerland Beach.

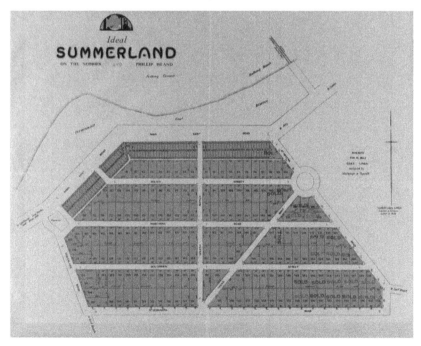

Detail of the course card and Russell's signature on his plan of the course (top)

Alex Russell, the designer of the Summerland Golf Links course (above)

Subdivision plan (left) of the Summerland development. The note at right reads "Reserved for 18-hole Golf Links designed by MacKenzie & Russell"

State Library of Victoria

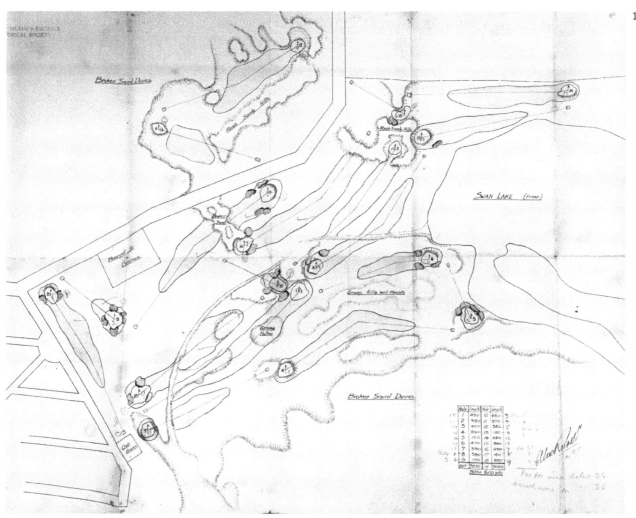

*Alex Russell's hand drawn layout plan of the
18-hole Summerland course. Original signed
plans of Alex Russell are extremely rare.*

Philip Island & District Historical Society

Construction

A report entitled *"A Visit to Summerland"* graced the pages of the 'Frankston and Somerville Standard' newspaper on 6 January 1928 and described the Summerland development as:

> *"the new model township that is in the process of formation out at the nobby end of the Island and we were surprised to see the amount of work that had been put in and the progress made in the way of laying out the roads and the planting of them with ornamental trees, while a golf house is in the course of erection. The selection of the site for this has shown great wisdom for the view from the verandah is one of the finest to be found along the southern coastline of the whole island."*

On 27 January 1928, 'The Herald' reported in its golf column on the new course and added that "Mick" Morcom, Royal Melbourne's famed curator, had been down to view the site, no doubt at the urging of his friend Alex Russell:

> *"There recently has been an enormous amount of effort in making Phillip Island, in Western Port, a powerful attraction for holiday makers. Naturally no resort these times is nearly complete without golf. Already two links have been opened on the island. A third, that in connection with the Summerland Estate, near the Nobbies, promises to be something exceptional. Alex. Russell, former national open champion, and perhaps the leading golf architect of Australia, has been greatly impressed by the links that is being made there. He has given it as his opinion that the land selected for a links is as good as any in Victoria, and, with the great natural advantages, a championship course could be made. M. A. Morcom also has been greatly intrigued by the site chosen."*

The jetty at Cat Bay (below) that Sambell built to service his Summerland development went out of use soon after it was built as the mooring proved too difficult to manage

Phillip Island & District Historical Society

It also noted that good progress had been made on building the jetty on the Western Port Bay side of the development. 'The Age' reported on 8 February 1928 that:

> *"Work has commenced on the new golf course at Summerland. It is hoped that five holes will be ready at Easter and the full eighteen holes will be in excellent playing condition next season. When this course is completed there will be three courses on the island, and golfing enthusiasts will be fully catered for."*

This estimate though was well off the mark and in June that year the company announced in the pages of the 'Frankston and Somerville Standard' newspaper:

> *"that their nine hole course will be ready for play next spring and that a water supply will be provided for each green before next summer. A café is also under construction and will be opened for the convenience of visitors next summer."*

In April 1928, the company advertised for operators to run the guesthouse that formed part of the golf clubhouse, and in 1931 the guesthouse was enlarged to accommodate more guests. Notably the course was now described as a 9-hole course and it was apparent that the company had decided to only construct this initial nine and leave the remaining holes until a future stage.

Water was planned to be laid on to each green, and in December 1929 the Shire of Phillip Island, now a new council solely for the island and headed by its first Shire President, none other than Sambell himself, granted permission to the company to lay water pipe to the Summerland golf links from Green Lake, located just to the north-east of the two holes on the northern side of the main road from Cowes. This was subject to the approval of the engineer, which in this case, was no doubt a formality given that it was the Shire President's company.

Postcard of Summerland Golf House

Rees Jones, constructor and greenkeeper of the Summerland Golf Links, holding a pair of penguins

Phillip Island & District Historical Society

The golf holes were constructed and maintained by local man Mr Rees Jones, with assistance from his son Les and other local farmers. Jones was a good golfer, playing off a plus 2 handicap and later won the 1938 Club Championship of the Summerland Golf Club. During construction Rees lived for two years in a tent and a tin shed with his wife and two children. Many cubic yards of Merri Creek soil were imported on to the golf course site in a measure to try and provide 'improved' soil conditions from the existing native sands. Local farmer Rupert Harris and his brother Gren, who worked their family property near Ventnor, were also employed by Sambell in the construction of the course. They took out to Summerland a sledge, two draught horses and a dam scoop, which they used to form the bunkers. Irrigation water was pumped from the spring at Green Lake, now known as Flynn's surfing area, and was reticulated to the course from a large holding tank on a dune nearby.

Opening

After a good deal of hard work in establishing turf in this sandy country, the course finally reached a playable condition in early 1930 and Sambell decided to open the 9-holes at Summerland with a professional tournament to be held on 23 April, for which the company put up prizemoney of £50. Twelve of Victoria's leading professionals were invited and the event was well covered by the Melbourne newspapers. A week before the event 'The Sporting Globe' reporter visited the island to check out the new course and he wrote:

> *"At the week-end I visited this course, and was pleased to discover nine excellently laid out and well kept class golf holes. Alex. Russell was the designer, and he did a sound job. Without any exaggeration, it may be said that this course could become one of the most popular in Victoria. At the present time there is very good turf on the greens, water is laid on, and the fairways are coming on promisingly. I am sure the professionals will be as pleasantly surprised next week as I was on Sunday. The course is eight miles from Cowes, and the road is good."*

The professionals, including "Jock" Young, Arthur Le Fevre, George Naismith and Reg Jupp, played a practice round on the Tuesday before tackling 36 holes of stroke play, four trips around the 9-holer. 'The Age' commented that:

> *"The visitors played over the picturesque course today, and were agreeably surprised at the excellence of the layout and the freshness of the turf. An up to date watering system has been introduced at all the greens, which are in good order throughout. So far nine holes have been constructed, and the Committee is very wisely concentrating on establishing the work begun, which was undertaken under the expert supervision of Alex. Russell. Excellent golfing country has been selected, with a splendid sandy subsoil, and if the present sound policy is maintained the course should mature into an admirable seaside links.*
>
> *Par for the 18 holes is 68. Some of the holes have admirably exploited the scenic effects of the country, notably the ninth, which is played towards the beach. The fourth and fifth, both blind holes, have to carry the saddleback of a large sand hill from the tee and opened out into miniature valleys on the way to the green. Large galleries witnessed the visitors at play today."*

'The Argus' described the course as:

> *"still somewhat in the rough, but the intrinsic interest of the round is already very great. The undulating terrain is of the most approved pattern, with brush covered sand dunes on all sides and many beautiful nooks for the putting green."*

The company supported the publicity for this event with paid advertisements, espousing the Summerland course as the *"most attractive one out of Melbourne"* and that visitors should reserve accommodation at Sambell's Isle of Wight Hotel in Cowes, where the professionals were put up during the trip.

The day of the tournament saw the course freshened up by some overnight rain and the morning scores were good, with Horace Boorer, Le Fevre and Jupp tied for the lead on 71. The afternoon scores worsened, likely due to a freshening breeze, and Boorer ended up tied for first prize, after an afternoon round of 77, with Ernest Wood who shot rounds of 75 and 73. The 'Argus' report of the tournament noted that the other 9 holes had *"been laid out and would gradually come into play,"* suggesting that a start may have been made on building the remaining holes. After the day's play, the prizes were awarded to the winners by Sambell in his role as Shire President.

IF GOLFERS ONLY KNEW that the
SUMMERLAND GOLF COURSE
Is the most attractive one out of Melbourne. They would reserve accommodation at the **ISLE OF WIGHT HOTEL, COWES,** and enjoy the well grassed fairways, watered greens and interesting design.
INCLUSIVE WEEKLY TOURS. £5/15/-   Ring F5708, or Cowes 1.

Newspaper advertisement for the new Summerland course from April 1930

Harry Culliton, Riversdale identity and golf writer, attended the tournament and wrote glowingly of the new course and its similarities to Scottish links in 'The Australasian' newspaper on 3 May 1930:

> "The occasion was the opening of the Summerland links, laid out some three years ago by Alex Russell, over terrain that could scarcely fail to delight the heart of any player possessing an eye for the truly beautiful and interesting in golf holes. For the land in use is rolling links country that, if it were geographically possible, might be part of the eastern Scottish seaboard. At any rate, the imported professionals, J. Young, Arthur Le Fevre, and the Thomsons (these brothers used to golf on what is perhaps the finest natural links in the world – Macrihanish, on the west coast of Scotland), share that opinion with me. My own game, too, such as it is, began on a links, Dornoch, Sutherlandshire, of such rare quality.... So we were able to judge the new course by the very highest standards.
>
> Naturally the course has a long way to go before the rough places become smooth, and the fairways and greens have settled down to their final perfection, but all the elements are there, and it requires only time and proper attention to develop them into a splendid and attractive links, and one that is pervaded by the true golfing atmosphere."

Description of the Links

Jack Dillon, the golf writer for 'The Sporting Globe' newspaper, visited the Summerland links a few months after the opening tournament and was pleasantly surprised by what he found, providing the only known hole-by-hole description of the course. In his review article published on 7 June 1930 he wrote:

> "In the nine holes of the Summerland links I discovered a golfing place that is certain to interest followers of the game. Very fine golf country has been admirably used by the designer, Alex Russell. Greens have been sown with good turf and well looked after. At present these putting places present surfaces as true and suitable for golf as will be found outside the metropolitan area.

Postcard of the Summerland Surf Beach (right)

The Summerland links is not part of a registered club, but early steps are to be taken to include it among our registered courses. Then it should immediately become popular with linksmen, and it will certainly add to the appealing holiday charms of the island. Some of the holes would advantageously fit in on the championship links of the city.

Hole 1 – The opening hole is a straight-ahead drive and pitch of 345 yards, an admirable length for a first hole.

Hole 2 – There follows an iron shot of about 160 yards on level country, and at present without notable feature.

Hole 3 – Of considerable golfing merit is the third, of 480 yards. There is some fine natural bunkering to be carried with the second wood shot.

Hole 4 – The fourth of 270 yards is the first hole in the exceptional country. The drive is made straight ahead to a cleared patch, and a nice short pitch is left to an interesting green. However, the main feature of the hole is the fact that the man who fancies his driving ability may take a risk and shoot straight ahead for the green over high and rugged sand hills. The short cut does not call for tremendous hit, but if it comes off it gives a thrill of course, the short cut means a blind drive.

Hole 5 – Somewhat similar is the position that a player may take from the tee at the 380 yards fifth. He may go safely out to the right to a cleared position, or he may "give it a go" and drive over sand hills to get an easy and shorter shot home if the drive comes off.

SUMMERLAND SURFING BEACH

Hole 6 – All the advantages of a naturally bunkered piece of country for a one-shotter are found at the 111 yards 6th. This hole looks quite an uninteresting proposition by reason of the fact that there is at first glance, just a tee and a nice little green near enough to look simple. But that pitch must get the green or real trouble follows. Sand hills on the left, rugged country on the right, nasty, desperate places at the back, and none too sweet spots short, reveal themselves to those who fail to make the pitch as it should be made.

Hole 7 – Another blind tee shot is encountered at the 430 yards 7th, which in some ways is reminiscent of the 8th at Royal Melbourne.

Hole 8 – Then comes a good one-shotter of about 160 yards up to a plateau green.

Hole 9 – To my mind the ninth is the most cleverly laid out hole of the present nine. The drive may be sent as far as one can hit along a tongue that gets narrower the further it goes, and the perfectly hit tee shot stops on a plateau which gives an ideal location for the pitch home. A drive off the line gives plenty of natural troubles.

While actual selection of places for holes has been well considered, there has up to date been no serious effort to titivate and generally give point and beauty to the bunkering round the greens. Russell will, doubtless, do this in the competent manner of which he is capable. When that work is done the course will provide a test that will give any amount of trouble to the best, and as much pleasure to all as can reasonably be expected from a course. While the country is rugged and truly seaside, there is remarkably little climbing called for in the round."

Settling In

In early October 1930, it was announced that the Summerland links would host the Cowes Golf Club's first annual Open Meeting later that month. The entry form contained *"an attractive plan of the course at Summerland,"* and the report noted that *"it is not many months since a professional contest was held over this course, and one and all the visiting tutors expressed themselves as well pleased with the site selected, and with the enterprise in the construction of the links designed by Alex Russell."* Sambell put on a special steamer to bring golfers across from Stony Point for the event.

A 1931 report on the attractions of Phillip Island noted that the new golf course at Summerland was *"one of the best seaside links in Victoria"* and that it was *"now in perfect condition."* The second annual Open Meeting was again held at Summerland in May 1931 and a report from Jack Dillon in 'The Sporting Globe' suggested that it was a course *"that those who have not visited are recommended to try. They will find it a pleasant surprise. Alex. Russell laid it out in great golfing country. With the exception of Barwon Heads and Warrnambool, it is as fine a test as will be found outside the metropolitan area."*

In January 1932, 'The Sporting Globe' reported on improvements made to the course, *"Recent improvement to Summerland links, at Phillip Island, will be appreciated by players during the open meeting there. The blind tee shots at the fifth and*

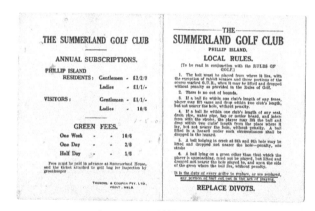

Card of the Summerland Golf Club from 1937

Discovering Alex Russell

1930s aerial photograph (above) showing the Summerland course, the Golf House, the surf beach and the Cat Bay jetty

Phillip Island & District Historical Society

seventh holes have been eliminated, and the fifth fairway is now well grassed." Precisely how these blind shots were eliminated, the report failed to mention. A subsequent article noted that the course had been well-patronised by holiday golfers over the 1931 Christmas period.

Summerland continued to be a popular holiday destination through the 1930s and the guesthouse, known as either Summerland House or Summerland Golf House, with its spectacular views down the coast, continued to be high on the list of choices when staying on the island. Sambell continued to promote his Isle of Wight Hotel in Cowes and his Summerland House, as well as the golf course in the advertising that his ferry service undertook.

The Summerland Golf Club was formed, with a course card from that year showing the name of the new club, while in 1939 its third Open meeting was held, indicating an establishment date around 1936 or 1937. Sambell's son, also A.K.T. Sambell, was one of the club's vice-presidents in 1938. However, it appears that the club itself did not survive past the onset of World War II as the club's championship honour board, still held by the family of Rees Jones, stops at 1939.

Postcard of the Penguin Parade at the Summerland Surf Beach (right)

Petering Out

The course was not able to be kept open during World War II, and suffered another blow shortly after the war when golfers from Cowes wanted a closer course in the days of petrol rationing. A site was chosen near Cowes and a public meeting was called in 1947 but the project was turned down. The majority of those present wanted to re-establish the now out-of-use Summerland links. Summerland was still owned by the Sambell family and they managed to get the golf course back into some semblance of playable condition and golf recommenced. Later that same year, the Cowes proposal re-emerged and another meeting gave it the go-ahead. The land was still available and a company was formed to purchase the land and construct a golf course, and is the course of today's Phillip Island Golf Club. Reports about the island's attractions still mentioned a golf course at Summerland as late as 1951, but it likely fell out of use shortly after, reverting to farmland.

Unfortunately, the Summerland development was not an ongoing success. Few houses were built on the first stage of 282 allotments that Sambell's company developed, but enough lots must have been sold to warrant an additional area being subdivided in 1933. Further subdivisions were made in 1951-52, 1954 and 1962, yielding a total of some 773 lots, but as late as 1985 Summerland was home to only 183 houses, a motel and a shop.

Prioritising the Penguins

From the time of the first guided tours to view the penguins at Summerland Beach, the popularity grew and soon a Chevrolet bus, the first tourist bus to be registered in Victoria, was needed to bring the tourists out from Cowes to view the nightly parade of the penguins.

FAIRY PENGUINS PARADE AT SUMMERLAND BEACH

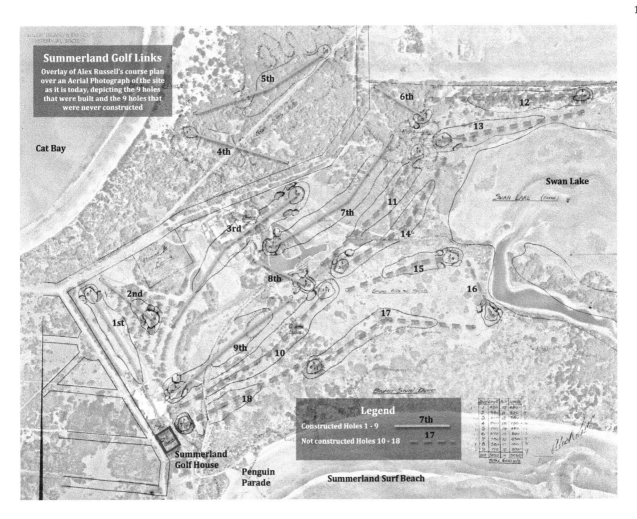

Summerland Golf Links

Overlay of Alex Russell's course plan over an Aerial Photograph of the site as it is today, depicting the 9 holes that were built and the 9 holes that were never constructed

Cat Bay

5th

6th

12

13

4th

Swan Lake

SWAN LAKE (Fresh)

1st

2nd

3rd

7th

11

14

15

16

17

8th

9th

10

18

Summerland Golf House

Penguin Parade

Summerland Surf Beach

Legend

Constructed Holes 1 - 9   7th

Not constructed Holes 10 - 18   17

It had become apparent to many residents and visitors that the destruction and isolation of the penguin's breeding grounds onshore at Summerland would eventually result in the collapse of the colony, and the first conservation measure was the donation of a 10 acre (4 ha) parcel to the State of Victoria around 1950, specifically for penguin protection. The establishment of the bridge to the island in 1940 unleashed a new influx of tourists and by 1955 it proved necessary to establish a much larger reserve. Fences were then upgraded and viewing areas erected. The Penguin Parade's management was then taken over by the Shire of Phillip Island in 1961, before being placed under State Government control in 1981.

For many years, the Penguin Parade lacked permanent off street parking and this was provided as a commercial venture by the Reith family on the site of the old 1st hole of the Summerland golf links. Elaine, Sambell's youngest daughter, had married Dr Alexander Reith and together they owned the land where the golf course was located, as well as an old house that the 2nd and 3rd holes of the course skirted around. Their farm was called 'Lammarwells.'

The Reiths had plans to replace the old run-down house with a new house closer to the coastal dunes and the edge of the penguin reserve, but their planning application in 1961 was refused, not once but twice. Following protracted legal battles the family eventually sold their land to the State Government in 1979, and with this land acquired, the government set about constructing a Visitor Centre and permanent car parking to cater for the steadily increasing visitor numbers.

The first moves to begin a buy-back of land at the Nobbies end of the Summerland Peninsula to add to the penguin reserve commenced in 1974. Most Summerland properties were acquired between 1985 and 2010, with all buildings now demolished. Today, it is estimated that over 32,000 penguins live in the colony, making it one of the largest in Australia and an increasingly popular destination for both local and overseas visitors.

Extract from a 1933 Tourist Map of Phillip Island showing the Summerland golf course location (right)

Some Golf Course Archaeology

Surprisingly there is still some evidence of the golf links remaining on the ground at Summerland and the Penguin Parade has not yet obliterated all evidence of the old course. One of the most obvious remaining features is the tee of the par three 6th hole. Today this feature sits within an area of turf near the head of a walking trail that leads to Swan Lake. The Kikuyu turfed area here is quite large, and local lore is that the grass escaped from the golf course. The banks at the sides of the tee are apparent and its alignment is towards the general area where the green was sited. A clearing next to a large dune some 100 metres away is probably the old green location. Jack Dillon described this hole as 110 yards (100 metres) in length with a green that had sand hills at its left. The 4th and 5th holes that were on land to the other side of the main road from Cowes have now been reclaimed by scrub and the alignment of today's road cuts right through these holes. A flattish plateau in open ground could be the site of the 3rd green, but other later works such as pond excavations, workshop buildings and car parks appear to have obliterated any traces of the other golf holes. The clubhouse building is long gone too, but the views from its exposed location are spectacular still today and it is little wonder that this position was selected.

One of the last known advertisements (below) for Summerland House and the golf links from the immediate post-war years

Ideal
SUMMERLAND
on the Nobbies
Phillip Island

"*The Land of Somewhere We Long to Go*"

A Sad Demise

Alex Russell's Summerland course was rated by good judges as one of the best courses in country Victoria and he must have been thrilled by the sandy linksland site he was given so soon after coming into partnership with Dr MacKenzie. Unfortunately, his full 18-hole course was never realised, and the holes he planned along the banks of the Swan Lake would have been spectacular. A.K.T. Sambell's vision of making the Summerland Peninsula a holiday playground never fully eventuated, with a number of factors conspiring against the course's longevity. The penguins of Summerland were the ultimate beneficiaries of its eventual demise.

View of Summerland today looking down to the surf beach and the Penguin Parade. The approximate location for the Golf House would be in the left foreground of the photograph

The Scene of the State Golf Championships.

An aerial view of the Lake Karrinyup course, where, commencing next Monday, the 1934 open and amateur golf championships of Western Australia will be decided.

Chapter 11

LAKE KARRINYUP COUNTRY CLUB

Prior to 1927, there had been a number of discussions in Perth about forming a country club, but it was not until July 1927 that Arnold Hodder, the Honorary Secretary of the Perth Golf Club and a real estate agent, came across an area of Tuart forest land at North Beach, some 16 km north of Perth, and the idea was able to be realised.

Tuart forest has an over-storey provided by the Tuart gum (*Eucalyptus gomphocephala*), a large eucalypt growing to around 10 to 15 metres tall in the north, and to 40 metres in the southern area of its natural habitat range. These forests can be found from approximately 200 kilometres north of Perth to Bunbury in the south, and confined to a narrow coastal strip where there is a deeper layer of limestone topped with sand.

At Lake Karrinyup, apart from the Tuart trees, there was also red gum, while the undergrowth was generally light and contained 'prickly-bush'. Sandy loams and yellow sand supported grasses cropped by cattle, with clover around the 30 acre (12 ha) lake, and the limestone subsoil was rarely apparent at the surface. The market gardens in the adjacent areas made it apparent that this would be ideal golfing territory, with a beautiful lake to provide water as well. Tuart forests are mostly open and home to many species of native animals and birds, and it is little wonder that Lake Karrinyup was to declare its property a game preserve, and the abundance of birds proved this to have been a perceptive decision.

Hodder thought about this site for a short time before showing it to two of his friends, Dr Ralph Crisp, captain of the Perth Golf Club, and Keith Barker. A foundation committee was formed that comprised several influential Perth businessmen and professional men, and they coined the name 'Lake Karrinyup', a corruption of the local name for the area and its lake, 'Careeniup'. Options on the land were taken, and a prospectus circulated on 19 August 1927. Four weeks later, fifty members had been secured, but twenty more were needed for the scheme to be viable and with only eight days to go before the options expired, a frantic search for more members was carried out. With the numbers secured in the nick of time, the land, comprising some 353 acres (143 ha), was purchased at a cost of £10 per acre. Members had the option of buying one of

fifty half-acre blocks of land for £50, or taking out an interest-bearing debenture of the same face value. A General Meeting on 30 November elected the office bearers and a committee of the new Lake Karrinyup Country Club. Its Notice of Incorporation then appeared in the 'Sunday Times' on 8 January 1928.

Both Alex and Jess Russell were well known to Keith Barker through golf and he often visited them when in Melbourne on business with the A.G. Spalding & Co sporting goods firm that he represented. Barker was asked by the new committee to contact Russell on his forthcoming trip to Melbourne, with a view to having the firm of MacKenzie & Russell design the club's new course.

As a representative for the A. G. Spalding & Bros. sporting goods firm, Keith Barker knew Alex and Jess Russell well and invited Alex to Perth to design the new course for the Lake Karrinyup Country Club

Lake Karrinyup Country Club

Russell readily agreed and the appointment was announced at the new club's first general meeting on 30 November 1927.

Visiting the West

Russell arrived in Perth on Wednesday morning 15 February 1928 on the Great Western express train, the forerunner of today's Indian Pacific, and at the railway station he was met by the club's president, Dr Dixie Clement, secretary Arnold Hodder, treasurer Bert Meecham, and captain Keith Barker. His arrival in Perth was considered newsworthy and he was interviewed at the station by some Perth newspaper reporters, including one from 'The Daily News':

> *"Discussing the necessity of having expert advice before building a golf course Mr Russell said that no one thought of building a house or laying out public gardens without getting expert advice, and the same advice applied in the case of golf courses. "You have only to see the mistakes made in Victoria alone in the construction of golf courses to realise the need for expert advice. Greens have been put down and have to be shifted. There are four or five new courses in Victoria. New South Wales has a few and Canberra is building a new course. I prepared plans for a new 18-hole course there, which will have wonderful scenery around it......Discussing his work in this State, Mr Russell said he expected it would be a week before he could express a definite opinion on the ground at Lake Karrinyup. He was going to see it this afternoon. One course he had recently designed had appeared quite simple at first but had resolved itself into a jig-saw puzzle, which had taken days to solve. Mr Russell expects to be about a month in the State."*

Russell also discussed the current crop of young golfers in Australia and how he thought golf was booming in Australia, but had a long way to go to catch up with other countries such as England and America. He was also quoted as saying about the Lake Karrinyup property:

> *"The joyful part is the size of it. Elsewhere one is asked to do great things with 150 acres, including the club house. Of the 360 acres here, only 15 are taken up by the lake, and one should be able to do something with the rest."*

Sweating it Out

His promotional duties complete, and wasting no time, Russell visited the site that afternoon with club officials. He was to spend the next four weeks during a heat-wave walking

Newspaper clipping from Russell's arrival in Perth on 15 February 1928

the property with Keith Barker and Bill McLean, understanding the nature of the terrain and planning his holes.

Barker later reported on an early policy alternative advanced by Russell, concerning the location of the clubhouse at either the lakeside or on the northernmost hill. Russell explained that:

> *"You have two choices – either you can have the clubhouse by the lakeside with the course laid out on easy lines, it will be hot in summer and you have to build a considerable roadway into it – or you can have your clubhouse here where we stand, a magnificent panorama, cool in summer, short access from the road but you will have to play up to it twice."*

MR. ALEX RUSSELL,
Golf architect and champion player

The club elected to choose the high ground and Russell set about his design work in earnest, measuring, assessing, taking notes and sketching over four gruelling weeks in the Perth summer heat, contending with the dense Tuart forest, sand and the ever-present flies. In doing this he was assisted by James Tinlin, who had learnt his craft as a greenkeeper at North Berwick in Scotland before emigrating to Western Australia and becoming the new club's construction foreman. He stayed at Karrinyup until December 1928 when he left for a post as the head greenkeeper at Mt Lawley, being replaced by A.E. Faul.

Russell was interviewed by 'The Daily News' on 25 February and was asked for his first impressions of the site and the project in general:

"'Providing a sufficient number of members stand behind the club, there is no reason why a really good golf course should not be put down at Lake Karrinyup', said Mr Alex. Russell, the well-known Victorian player, today. Mr Russell is designing the lay-out of the links for the new Lake Karrinyup Country Club.

After looking over the site, Mr Russell is impressed with the natural possibilities. As he describes it, the course will not be a first-class seaside course on undulating country. But he knows of only one other place where natural conditions are so favourable. Water is to be had in plenty for the initial cost of a pumping installation. The importance of this asset can be realised when it is known that 25,000,000 gallons of water a year are used to keep the Seaton course in S.A. in perfect condition all the year round.

Mr Russell is designing the eighteen-hole course; but he is also making provision for an additional nine-hole course that can be put down in the future when the club has grown sufficiently. As he points out, the club has been fortunate to obtain freehold, and at a low price, ample land which in similar proximity to the capital in New South Wales or Victoria would cost at least £100 per acre Owing to easily available water supply, Mr Russell considered it should be possible to turf the course and have it in playing condition in twelve months."

At the end of each day Russell, Barker and others would retire to either the nearby Osborne Park Hotel or the Ocean Beach Hotel for a well-earned thirst quencher or two. Russell drew a general plan and a set of detailed green plans for the club to follow. His plans also included the provision of a 9-hole practice course that did not eventuate until many years later.

J. E. TINLIN, WHO CONSTRUCTED THE ORIGINAL GREENS AT KARRINYUP.

In the manner of his mentor Dr MacKenzie at Royal Melbourne, Russell personally supervised the construction of one green, the par three 8th across the lake, which he felt would become a famous one-shotter, and then left the club to their labours.

The Scot J. E. Tinlin, who supervised construction of the course until his departure for Mt Lawley in December 1928

Heading Home

On 7 March Russell gave a small dinner party at the Hotel Esplanade for various club officials, including Keith Barker. Before leaving Perth, Russell was asked if the bunkers could be dug by hand using shovels and his reply was that they would look like someone had been at it with a teaspoon! After excavating one bunker this way the club resorted to the proven method of horse and scoop.

Russell had advised the club to establish some experimental plots to see which grasses would be best for the greens in the difficult Perth climate. Grasses trialled were Chewing's Fescue, Kentucky Bluegrass, Crested Dogs-tail, *Paspalum compressum* and Creeping Bent. The fine New Zealand Fescue was eventually chosen for the greens, and the Kentucky Bluegrass and the Creeping Bent trialled in the approaches. Russell advised that the black loamy soil from the swamp, as a drought had almost dried out the lake, be used for top-dressing.

Initially Russell had planned that the current 10th hole would be the opening hole, but later he decided to reverse the nines as the first hole would then become a short par four followed by two longer holes, which would help to spread out the field. Russell later used a similar strategy of a short two shot first hole on the East Course at Royal Melbourne, just under 330 yards, while his opener at Cottesloe was similarly 334 yards.

Both Yarra Yarra's and Riversdale's first holes were challenging par threes. Originally the first hole at Paraparaumu Beach was the current 10th – a wonderful hole of just under 300 metres – but with houses and out-of-bounds on the left it made an unsatisfactory first tee shot for the round and the nines were reversed in Russell's remodelling. So, at Lake Karrinyup, Russell continued his preferred strategy of using a short four to start the course.

On the 13 March 1928, Russell provided the club with a five page hand-written report, a general layout plan and drawings for each green. His report set out explanations of his intentions, along with a number of instructions. As Russell never set out his golf design philosophy in a book or article form as many other architects had done, before and since, the reports he prepared for Lake Karrinyup and Paraparaumu are very important as indications of his philosophy.

Russell initially only included championship tees, and advised that temporary forward tees should be built first, as it was hard to know exactly where to place the tees until the course

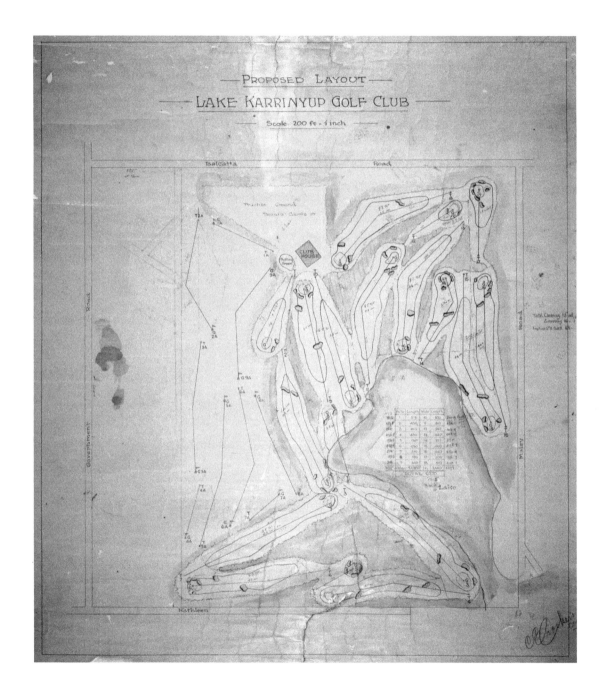

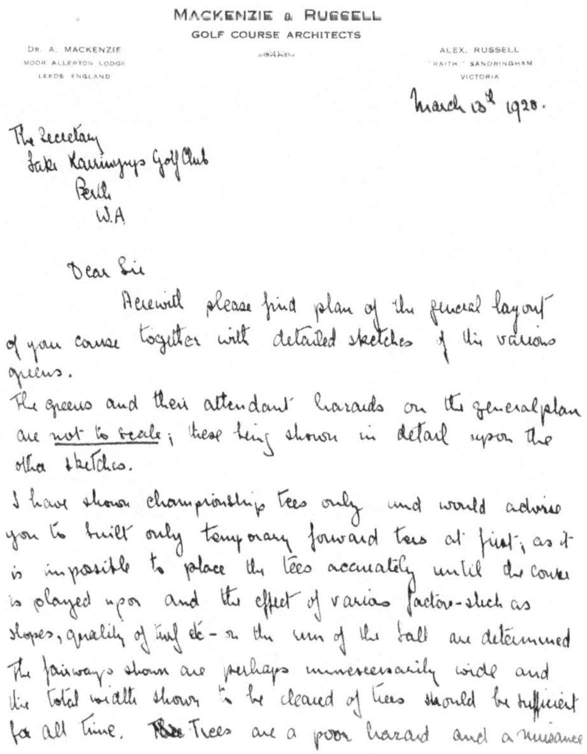

MACKENZIE & RUSSELL
GOLF COURSE ARCHITECTS

Dr. A. MACKENZIE
MOOR ALLERTON LODGE
LEEDS. ENGLAND

ALEX. RUSSELL
"RAITH," SANDRINGHAM
VICTORIA

March 10th 1928.

The Secretary
Lake Karrinyup Golf Club
Perth
W.A

Dear Sir

Herewith please find plan of the general layout of your course together with detailed sketches of the various greens.

The greens and their attendant hazards on the general plan are not to scale; these being shown in detail upon the other sketches.

I have shown championship tees only and would advise you to built only temporary forward tees at first, as it is impossible to place the tees accurately until the course is played upon and the effect of various factors—such as slopes, quality of turf &c—on the run of the ball are determined. The fairways shown are perhaps unnecessarily wide and the total width shown to be cleared of trees should be sufficient for all time. Trees are a poor hazard and a nuisance

Two of the five pages of Russell's handwritten report to Lake Karrinyup from March 1928

Lake Karrinyup Country Club

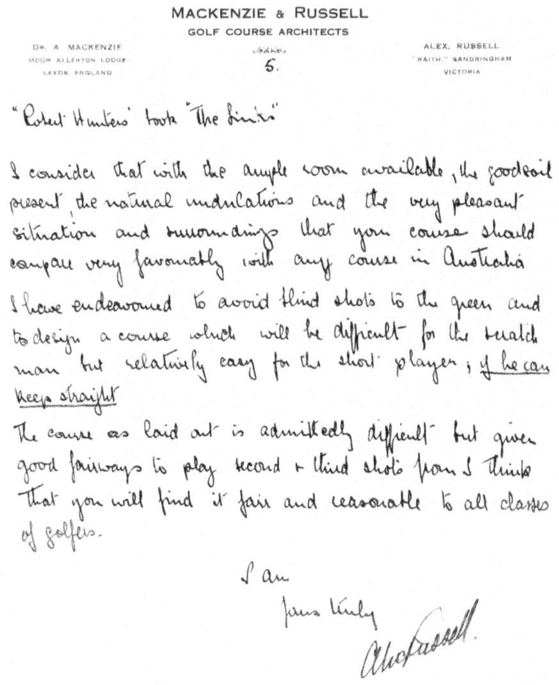

MACKENZIE & RUSSELL
GOLF COURSE ARCHITECTS

Dr. A. MACKENZIE
MOOR ALLERTON LODGE
LEEDS. ENGLAND

ALEX. RUSSELL
"RAITH," SANDRINGHAM
VICTORIA

5.

"Robert Hunters" book "The Links"

I consider that with the ample room available, the good soil present, the natural undulations and the very pleasant situation and surroundings that your course should compare very favourably with any course in Australia

I have endeavoured to avoid third shots to the green and to design a course which will be difficult for the scratch man but relatively easy for the short player, if he can keep straight

The course as laid out is admittedly difficult but given good fairways to play second + third shots from I think that you will find it fair and reasonable to all classes of golfers.

I am
Yours truly
Alex Russell.

Alex Russell's 1928 overall plan of the course (opposite)

Lake Karrinyup Country Club

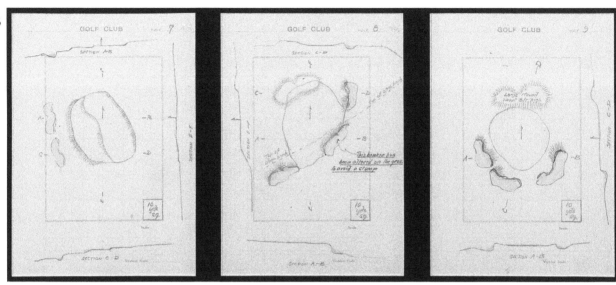

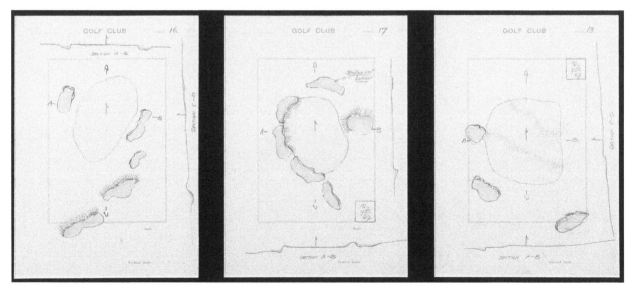

A selection of Alex Russell's 1928 green plans. Note his use of diagonally positioned bunkers on a number of greens.

Lake Karrinyup Country Club

had been played. The fairways were to be wide and trees needed to be cleared far enough back from the centreline of each hole to be sufficient for all times. He considered that, *"Trees are poor hazards and a nuisance on account of fallen leaves and I have therefore shown a large width between the trees and the fairway"*.

The greens were to be large, and while this meant increased costs for watering, it allowed bold undulations to be incorporated in the putting surfaces. While his green plans were drawn to scale to allow accurate scaling of the size and shape of the various features, the vertical scales were provided more as an indication of what he was envisaging. The slope of each green was not to exceed 1 in 14, with no local slope greater than 1 in 7, and that there should be many relatively flat areas provided in which to cut the hole. A player should not have to aim outside the hole with a firmly hit three-foot putt. Again Russell appears to have opted for fescue and bent grasses on the putting surfaces, as he had done at Yarra Yarra and was shortly to do at Royal Melbourne.

With his bunkers, Russell specified that the formation work should be done with a horse-drawn scoop and left as rough as possible, as this would provide a more natural appearance. With respect to the rough he called for *"a tufty and binding plant which will prevent the sand from blowing and will not matt over and cause lost balls."*

The final page of the report highlighted many key points of Alex Russell's overall philosophy of golf course design:

"It is essential if the full enjoyment is to be got out of the game that all artificial hazards and formation work be made as natural as possible.

Exceedingly good examples of this work are to be found in Robert Hunter's book "The Links".

I consider that with the ample room available, the good soil present, the natural undulations and the very pleasant surroundings that your course should compare very favourably with any course in Australia.

I have endeavoured to avoid blind shots to the greens and to design a course which will be difficult for the scratch man but be relatively easy for the short player, if he can keep straight.

The course as laid out is admittedly difficult but given good fairways to play second and third shots from I think that you will find it is fair and reasonable to all classes of golfers."

Building Karrinyup

The ensuing construction of the course proved most difficult. The cost of clearing the fairways at £11 an acre was more than the cost of the land, and sixty Italian clearers camped behind the current 15th green and manfully went about their task. The clearing began in May 1928 and some 800 to 1,000 tons of timber was removed from the course, while planting of couch grass on the fairways commenced in August. By September, 'The West Australian' noted:

'The remarkable progress made in the development of the links of the club is subject for comment. It is just over twelve months since Arnold Hodder, the secretary, and also secretary of the Perth club, discovered the site. He considered for a while and then launched the present scheme, which has been an unqualified success.'

A team of 60 Italian labourers cleared the course
Lake Karrinyup Country Club

A later 1934 newspaper article stated that the work of building the course commenced straight after Russell's design was received in 1928, *"Clearing and ploughing and planting, fencing, reticulation, etc., were all proceeded with and were completed by September. The pumps were turned on and the course was watered for the first time that November. Fescue seed was sown on the greens the following May and the course was thrown open for play on July 1, 1929."*

A detailed description of the holes on the new course still under construction was given in the 5 August 1928 issue of the 'Sunday Times' by its golf writer *"T. Box."*:

"The greens are being shaped in readiness for planting at both Karrinyup and Mount Yokine. As the former will evidently be our premier course in the near future let me conduct you in fancy around it and warn the budding scratch men of the dangers they must face. You start with a testing one shotter, rather like the fifth at South Perth, with a gentle valley instead of the foreground of trees and with a slope on the right, inviting entry from that quarter to a rising green. That done, you open your shoulders to a 425 yarder down towards the lake, to a rising open green guarded by three mound bunkers, triangulated, with a big one, short, to trap a pulled second on the lakeward slope. A parlous hole. On to the 3rd, 465 yards away along the lake shore, with a natural green of bold undulations needing little bunkering. The fourth, 420 yards, has a plateau green, the approach to which is guarded on the right by a little knoll, and which ends in a run-off. Reach that and you will need a courageous fourth to earn a five. Number five is a gem, a short 130 yarder, with a small green, 22 yards by 33, guarded by three bunkers, a right, a left, and a laggard's trap. Heigh ho! We shall swear horribly there, at ourselves. At number six, 430 yards uphill to a big green, flanked by two pot bunkers on the right, and eke a hollowed mound by a big mound and trap on the left, the call is for a longer second than you and I can summon, drifting a little as it dies. Perhaps some day, with a following wind. Number seven, a three shotter down hill a bit, has an interesting plateau green, the inner green being on the right at the back behind a diagonal fold. Left, towards which the ground trends strongly, there are two awe-inspiring traps. Number eight is of terrifying excellence.

None but the brave deserve the green, one hundred and ninety yards away, but over an arm of the lake. Up a steep bank and through a 16 yard opening, a combination of a water-carry with the 12th at Fremantle and a bolder version of the first green at Perth, without the side ditch. Strong men will burst into bubbles at this. Play to the ninth is 340 yards and therefore to a close kept green, pots in front and a mound behind its wide waist. Number ten is a 370 yarder lakewards to a boldly undulated green, two pots on the down side, left, a run-off at the far end, like the Avenue at Fremantle improved by bunkers, but less steep beyond. The next, number eleven, is a superb dog-leg, a shade reminiscent of the Seaton Crater in that a splendid drive up hill may permit a man of mettle to go for the green. If he flinch in doing so, the third will be out of pot bunkers,

on the right with more awaiting him over the green on the left. But if he follows through and gathers his second the hollow of the green will nurse his ball along as it does at 14th at Perth. The plateau green at the 12th has guardian bunkers in front and on the right and a fall away behind, as a short hole should -140 yards. The far end of the green undulates kindly, but try to lay the putt back from it dead, and it may prove cruel. Thirteen is another dog-leg, 440 yards long. The green calls for a long second with draw, to enter a sanctuary guarded on the left near corner and the right far one, and others at the waist. Being a 270 yarder, the fourteenth is inside a ring of four mounds. A longish carry to the right leaves an opening to the bold. The easy carry, left, ends in front of a pitch shot as at the Perth second. The fifteenth is 460 yards, to a green openly laid between two mounds. The main interest I fancy, will be in playing for position with the second, over a cross bunker, left, which will call for a strong carry. Perhaps the best hole on the links is number sixteen, with a double fold in the fairway, 440 yards to a green guarded similarly to the eleventh. At the seventeenth you face, as a climax, a modified Redan, the famous North Berwick 200 yards hole calling for a strong draw, to a green heavily bunkered on all points but the S.E. corner. Then to the last, uphill 410 yards to a double plateau green, between Scylla and Caryidis, formidable pots at the entrance. The architect, Alex Russell, has certainly spread us a feast of interesting and yet eminently fair and friendly greens. May he win an Australian championship on them, and I be there to see!"

In March 1929, "The West Australian' gave a progress report on the establishment of the course:

Great strides have been made in the preparation of the ground of the Lake Karrinyup Country Club and it is hoped to commence play in June. About this time last year Mr Alex Russell, the well known golf architect, spent four weeks in laying out the course. Clearing was commenced in May, and couching in August. To-day the tees are fully grassed and ready for play. The greens are well covered and all have been mown and rolled. The fairways are also well covered, and mowing operations will be carried out as soon as the winter rains permit. Each day during the summer 38 sprinklers have been in use throwing about 25,000 gallons per hour. The water is drawn from the lake without noticeably affecting its level. Plans for a two storied residential club-house are in course of preparation and the building will be completed

*by the beginning of the 1930 season. It is understood that
a site for a polo ground has been approved by well-known
polo players, and the Committee is considering the early
preparation of it. Tennis courts will also be laid down. There
is a good road now from Perth to the club, and motor drives
have been formed within the club boundaries. One of the
attractions of the course is the varied scenery. The lake itself
makes an attractive background from many vantage points.
The large tuarts, jarrahs and redgums scattered between
and around the fairways are fine examples of their type. The
undergrowth is exceptionally light, giving the whole a natural
park like effect."*

While the new club was yet to be officially opened as the
clubhouse was incomplete, play had commenced over the new
course in July 1929, with "The West Australian" reporting that,
*"Many players have visited the course on Sunday afternoon and
they all expressed surprise at the wonderful progress that has been
made."* On the 19th November, 'The Daily News' commented,

> *"At Lake Karrinyup the country club have a magnificent
> course, which despite the fact that the first tree was cut
> scarcely two years ago, is already playing quite well, and
> by next season should be in 'tip-top' condition. With the
> completion of the palatial clubhouse it will be a course
> second to none in the Commonwealth".*

Opening

The official opening by the Lieutenant Governor, Sir Robert
McMillan, took place on Sunday 18 May 1930. *"T. Box"* of
"The Sunday Times" waxed lyrical about the views from the
clubhouse and around the lake, that the new grass had yet to
mature fully but when it did it would do so magnificently, *"and
then the new club's well-earned triumph will be complete."* The
'West Australian' the following day described it as, *"A red-letter
day in the history of golf in Western Australia. Golfers now have a
course which can be described as fine as can be found anywhere."*

Barker, who was the new club's first captain, later described the
Lake Karrinyup Country Club as having been *"conceived in the
days of prosperity and born in the days of depression."* The club
had grand plans for a polo field, a short 9-hole course, a bowling
green, and a variety of other sporting facilities, but with the
onset of the Depression and some of the expenses being higher
than expected, these other plans were shelved. In 1931, it was
reported that periodically members donned bathing suits and
harvested golf balls from the depths of the lake.

"Mashie Niblick," writing in 'The Daily News', covered the 1932
season opening and suggested that:

> *"Lake Karrinyup has made really astonishing progress.
> I spent the day there playing golf, walking over the
> beautifully turfed fairways (in between visits to the rough),
> and putting on greens thickly matted with fescues."* And
> *"The golfing community is indebted to the enthusiasts who
> made this project not only a possibility but an actuality."*

GOLF CHAMPIONSHIP AT KARRINYUP.

A competitor driving over the lake from the eighth tee in the State open golf championship meeting, which began at the Lake Karrinyup links yesterday.

*View of the 8th hole from the 1934 W.A. State Open, note how high the
water level is in the lake*

Out West Again

In 1933, the club decided to ask Alex Russell back to Perth to
conduct a review of their new course, but found him a difficult
man to pin down as the wool clip that year at 'Mawallok' was
higher than anticipated. Russell was booked to fly across,
arriving in Perth on 19 November 1933 on the mail plane from
Adelaide. He departed eleven days later, travelling back to
Melbourne by sea on the coastal steamer S.S. Karoola.

He stayed at the Weld Club and first undertook a brief review of
the Cottesloe Golf Club's course and then spent the remainder

of his visit assessing the course at Karrinyup, providing the club with a comprehensive report on 30 November. In this report he made general comments about the excellence of the course, noting in his covering letter that the report contained his impressions *"formed after a close inspection of the course over a period of ten days."* He considered that three greens required reconstruction and for championship play he advised that all the two-shot holes needed extending, with the course needing a hole of 460 yards to stretch out the second shot. *"For ordinary play – including many competitions – the course needs shortening. New short tees are needed at many holes and ladies' tees at nearly all."* Russell suggested that the championship tees should only be used about four times a year. For the ladies' tees, he frequently suggested they be set 30 yards forward, but at one hole he recommended 50 yards. Russell was critical of the Karrinyup bunkers:

> *"Practically all bunkers are too small and too narrow. One of the most important things is to <u>increase the area of bunkers to make them more visible and more alarming</u>. <u>The mounds at the back of bunkers are nearly all too abrupt,</u> the bunker on the left of the 5th green being the most obvious exception. This makes them unnatural looking and also hard to upkeep. <u>The sand should run up the face of the bunkers more:</u> lessening grass cutting costs and making bunkers more visible. Bunkers generally should be large in area but shallow especially if not near the green."*

Russell underlined the important items twice, shown above as bold and underlined, while single underlined items were less important. The remainder could be dealt with over a period of years. He then detailed the changes that he regarded as necessary at each hole, and at the end of his report he summarised the work that was required:

> *"LIST OF WORK MARKED AS IMPORTANT*
>
> <u>New Tees</u> at 3rd, 4th (2), 6th, 11th, 16th, 18th
>
> <u>New Ladies Tees</u> at 3rd, 4th, 5th, 9th, 12th, 13th, 14th, 15th, 16th, 17th
>
> <u>New Bunkers</u> at 3rd (2), 4th (2), 5th, 6th, 7th (2), 10th, 13th, 14th
>
> <u>Enlarge Bunkers</u> at 2nd, 3rd (3), 6th (2), 7th (2), 10th, 11th(2), 12th, 14th, 18th
>
> <u>Mounds Removed from Bunkers</u> at 2nd, 5th, 15th, 16th (2)
>
> <u>Sketches attached</u> 1st, 5th, 8th, 17th"

By the end of 1933, all of Russell's proposed alteration work had been completed by the club. In April 1934, the 'Western Mail' newspaper reported that:

> *"Up till just before Christmas, 1933, Mr Russell had not seen the result of his work in 1928. When he did he was delighted and made very few alterations to his original plan. These alterations consisted of the levelling of three greens, taking bumps out of two, building several forward tees for ladies and a few for men, enlarging existing bunkers and creating a few new ones. All this work has now been done and once again the State championship is to be held at Karrinyup this year."*

In the lead up to the 1938 W.A. State Championships the 'West Australian' newspaper gave a detailed description of the changes made in 1933 and the course as it stood in 1938:

> *"The course is one of the best in Western Australia from the point of view of bunkering. During his second visit, Mr Russell commented that some of the bunkers had been made too small, and some too deep....The sixth hole is unaltered. Of this hole Mr Russell said that it was one of the best on the course and as good a par four as he knew.......The 17th is the 'show' hole of the course. When Mr Russell was making a preliminary inspection of the land he seized on this portion of the course and insisted that it must be used, whatever became of the rest. It might be said, therefore, that the course was built round the 17th hole."*

Russell visited Karrinyup at other times in the 1930s, on his way to and from England, often playing the course with his wife Jess. In February 1935, he played the course with Jess on the way back to Melbourne from England on the 'Otranto', and *"he spoke in eulogistic terms of the course,"* while in September that year he visited Perth again on the way home from England. In October 1938, he spent a day *"in Perth, having returned to Australia by the liner Orcades after a visit to Europe. He left Perth yesterday by the mail plane Kyeema for the eastern States."*

The DC-2 mail plane 'Kyeema' in which Alex and Jess Russell flew back to Melbourne on October 1938

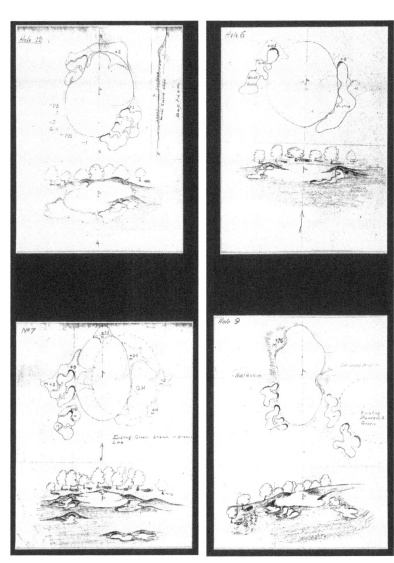

While undated, it is believed that these green plans date from Russell's return visit to Lake Karrinyup in 1933. The style of the drawings, in particular the perspective views of each green, closely match the green plans that he had drawn or year or so earlier for the East Course at Royal Melbourne.

Lake Karrinyup Country Club

During World War II the clubhouse at Lake Karrinyup was taken over by the Women's Auxiliary Australian Air Force, who occupied the building from Anzac Day 1942. Despite efforts to maintain the greens, eventually the entire course was abandoned. After the war, the course had effectively been reclaimed by the bush and a mighty effort was needed to rehabilitate it and open it for play, with 9-holes eventually reopened in late 1946. In August 1947, Bert Meecham put forward the idea of inviting Alex Russell back to inspect the course. To facilitate this, additional clearing of the roughs took place ahead of his visit.

In September 1948, Russell and Ivo Whitton visited Perth on behalf of the Australian Golf Union to report on the suitability of the Perth courses to host the Australian Championships in the near future. During this visit, Russell and Whitton inspected the Lake Karrinyup course on Wednesday 8 September, with Russell revisiting it on two further occasions and Whitton once. Both men felt that significant alterations to Karrinyup would be needed to make it a suitable championship venue, and fortunately the club agreed. Russell wrote a separate hand-written report to the club dated 11 September 1948, outlining his recommended modifications. These included lengthening and re-bunkering, along with some green alterations.

A bulldozer was made available, and by March 1949 all the reconstruction work was complete. It is believed that this is one of the few times Russell's work was implemented using heavy equipment and quite a contrast to the days of horse and scoop at Royal Melbourne. An article in 'The Daily News' on 2 March 1949 reported on Russell's final course alterations at Karrinyup:

Discovering Alex Russell

Extensive alterations to the scenic Lake Karrinyup Country Club golf course at Balcatta to make it suitable for future national championships are now almost complete. All earthwork alterations – re-bunkering, lengthening of the course and fairway changes – have been completed. Much new grass is still to be planted. Karrinyup Club captain W. D. Seale said today that during the last two months about 2000 tons of soil had been shifted. Main alteration to the course was the addition of 280yd., bringing the total length to 6420yd. On the lengthened holes, the fairways have been brought back the same distance as the tees. Melbourne golf architect Alex Russell who, with Ivo Whitton, inspected the course during the State open championships last August, suggested the alterations to the club. Bogey for the course (74) will probably be raised one or two strokes — most likely on the fourth and 11th. Alex Russell, who designed the Karrinyup course in 1927, said last year that "Lake Karrinyup would be equal as a test of golf to any course in Australia if the present alterations were made.""

Keith Barker wrote a memoir in 1969 about the creation of the Lake Karrinyup Country Club and its course. He had this to say of his friend Alex Russell:

"He was an original thinker and had no hidebound ideas. He was all for alternative routes for the middle and longer markers. He strongly urged us to use the front tees while the going was heavy. He had a keen eye for ground and hated anything artificial.....He introduced an "heroic carry" on the 7th and revelled in the criticism this brought forth – "a hole is not worth a damn if no one comments on it one way or another" he used to say. Another saying he had about golf holes in general was "if it has to be blind make it bloody blind." He spent a lot of his student days on famous Scottish courses where every so called rule of golf architecture is broken – particularly on the most famous one."

HOLES	Yards	S.S.S.	Strokes Allotted
1	229	4	15
2	428	5	13
3	451	5	7
4	397	4	1
5	130	3	17
6	413	5	5
7	510	5	9
8	198	3	3
9	326	4	11
OUT	3082	38	
10	362	4	6
11	378	4	2
12	149	3	18
13	415	5	16
14	271	4	12
15	457	5	8
16	414	5	10
17	193	3	4
18	381	5	14
IN	3020	38	
OUT	3082	38	
Total	6102	76	

The alterations were a success and the course was chosen to host the Australian Championships in 1952, with Norman Von Nida capturing the Australian Open with a record four round score of 278, followed by a successful hosting of the Australian Interstate Teams Matches, the Australian Amateur and Australian Foursomes. Lake Karrinyup was finally on the national stage.

Course card from 1935 (above)
Lake Karrinyup Country Club

Alex Russell in 1934 (right)

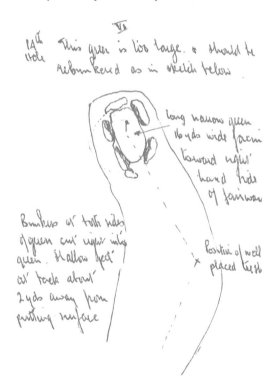

A page from Russell's 1948 report with his recommendations for a remodelled and rebunkered green for the 14th hole

Lake Karrinyup Country Club

Aerial photograph of the course from 1941

Lake Karrinyup Country Club

Card *of the* Course

Out	In
1. 220 yds	10. 320 yds
2. 349 yds	11. 130 yds
3. 355 yds	12. 304 yds
4. 149 yds	13. 365 yds
5. 274 yds	14. 135 yds
6. 131 yds	15. 255 yds
7. 293 yds	16. 461 yds
8. 318 yds	17. 319 yds
9. 423 yds	18. 246 yds

Total 5,049 yds

Legend

1929 holes
1937 holes
2001 references
modern greens & tees

1942 Aerial Photograph
of the
Paraparaumu Beach Golf Links

1942 aerial photograph showing the course at it was just prior to Russell's first visit in 1949. The original 9 holes from 1929 are shown in white, with the yellow lines depicting the later 9 holes that were added in 1937.

Overlay by Mark Guiniven

PARAPARAUMU BEACH GOLF CLUB

Paraparaumu Beach is located on a majestic stretch of linksland some 50 km north of the New Zealand capital, Wellington. The idea for a golf course on these sand dunes first came about in 1929, when a group of local residents decided to accept an offer from the owners, Messrs. McLean Bros., to use a parcel of land near the beach as a golf course. "The Evening Post' newspaper reported in its 17 June 1929 issue that, *"The ground, which has been under preparation for several months, is now almost ready for play, and it is hoped to hold the official opening in about six week's time. The course is in an ideal situation for summer and winter golf, and contains the full 18 holes, over a distance of about 3 ½ miles."*

The First Course

The landowners shortly after decided to sub-divide their property, and George Nathan, Stronach Paterson, Douglas Whyte, Jack Francis and H.R. Chalmers, all successful Wellington businessmen, purchased the land, along with the golf course, as part of a wider sub-division of prime beachside real estate that they proposed to develop. They formed the Paraparaumu Beach Golf Links Estates Ltd in 1930. An advertisement for the sale of sections in the sub-division in October 1930 indicated that *"A splendid 18-hole golf course, adjoining the sub-division, is being laid out (10 holes now being played over) under the supervision of Mr J. Watt, Professional, of Heretaunga."*

Some 200 acres (80 ha) of beachfront land was divided into sections with 120 acres (50 ha) retained for the golf course. A club was formed and in 1933 the Paraparaumu Beach Golf Club was elected as a member club of the New Zealand Golf Association. It was some years though before the full 18-hole course was in play, opening in November 1938. The first course had small greens encircled by three strands of wire to keep the sheep off the greens, with the sheep providing mowing and fertilising services. Much of the course maintenance was carried out by volunteers, and during World War II, Rod Marsh, the club's greenkeeper, was the only paid member of the green staff.

A New Club and a New Course

After the war, Chalmers wanted to sub-divide the company's golf course land for further residential development, but Paterson,

Whyte and Francis had a different vision and purchased the land in 1948 on behalf of the golf club. Sufficient interest was gained from local golfers, and debentures raised the necessary funds to achieve this. This effectively meant the formation of a new club and today the club considers 1949 as the date of its establishment. It was soon determined that the course needed to be thoroughly overhauled and Whyte contacted his good friend Sloan Morpeth, a renowned New Zealand amateur golfer, golf architect, and golf administrator who was at the time living and working in Melbourne as the secretary for both the Commonwealth Golf Club and the Australian Golf Union. He put forward the name of Alex Russell as a suitable architect.

John Hornabrook, three times New Zealand Amateur champion, twice winner of the New Zealand Open, and a foundation member at Paraparaumu Beach, recalled in his book 'Golden Years of New Zealand Golf' that he had met Alex Russell in Melbourne in 1948 and told him:

> *"what they were setting out to do at Paraparaumu and got him interested enough to be willing to come over and work on the course layout. This cost the Paraparaumu club only his fare over and a silver cigarette case. Even if he had required a large fee it would have been a good investment for the club. He was a magnificent judge of golfing country and had a deep understanding of how to make the best of it and produce a course which, while testing to the good player, wasn't overly cruel to the average run-of-the-mill weekender."*

Stronach Paterson (above left) and Douglas Whyte (above right) were two of the prime movers in establishing the new golf club and luring Alex Russell to New Zealand to redesign the course

Russell was then engaged to redesign the golf course at Paraparaumu so that it would be capable of hosting the country's premier golf events with the goal of making it *"comparable to the best championship courses of Australia, Great Britain and North America."* Douglas Whyte was an outstanding amateur golfer and a very capable businessmen, holding the chairmanships of both Golden Bay Cement and the Bank of New Zealand, as well as being the Chairman of the New Zealand Golf Association. Whyte ruled the club with an iron fist for 25 years, and along with head greenkeeper Jack Hunt, they would be responsible for bringing Russell's plans to fruition.

Across the Tasman

Alex Russell arrived in New Zealand early in 1949 aboard the trans-Tasman steamer the 'RMS Wanganella' and he spent six weeks at Paraparaumu, a long time for him for preliminary design work on a course. His visit likely occurred after the club's first Annual General Meeting held on 12 February 1949. By April 1949 his overall sketch plan had been drawn up more formally, suggesting that his 6-week visit took place through March and into early April of that year.

This was not Russell's first trip to New Zealand though, as he had been playing captain and manager of the Victorian team that travelled to New Zealand in April 1930 to play in the Kirk-Windeyer Cup matches at Shirley Golf Club in Christchurch. Russell did not ask for any remuneration, merely that the club pay for his passage. He stayed locally at the Paterson's family home on Golf Road with Stronach and his son, also Alex, who was at the time the club's secretary. Russell received a replica

Local young amateur golfers John Hornabrook (far left) and Ian Ewen (left) assisted Russell in his investigations of the site by hitting balls for Russell to gauge distances and the influence of the wind

of the silver hipflask owned by Stronach that he had admired.

As soon as Russell saw the land, he knew it was capable of being one of the best golf courses in the world. He was supplied with topographical mapping of the land prepared by trainee survey cadets from the Army and aerial photographs supplied by the New Zealand Air Force. The extended time on site allowed him to supervise directly sufficient work to make it clear to Whyte and Hunt how he wanted the earthworks formed so that they would appear natural. This was an attribute of all his designs stretching back to the MacKenzie, Russell, and Morcom approach at Royal Melbourne some 20 years earlier.

Russell went out each morning armed with a 5-iron, a bag of balls and his topographical map, hitting balls in all directions to ascertain distances, the effect of different winds and the run of the ground. However, these shots were those of a 57-year old who had suffered a number of strokes. When Dr MacKenzie and Bobby Jones were laying out their Augusta National course in Georgia, Jones hit a number of tee shots to work out the landing areas on many of the holes. So too at Paraparaumu Beach, Alex Russell made use of the services of four of the region's leading young amateurs, Guy Horne, John Hornabrook, George Roberts and Ian Ewen. Russell asked them *"to walk the sandhills with him, each of us carrying a few clubs and playing shots from given points directed by the architect. Those exercises helped him determine his final plan,"* Ian Ewen later recalled.

Russell had these golfers hitting various shots to suggested landing areas from tees and to proposed green sites, with the relationship between the landing areas and the setting of the green being of great importance to him. Ewen recounted his memories of that time:

> *"Par 4s (1) At nearly every par four he aimed to have a flat area on the fairway where the pro or scratch amateur player would drive to and have a straight shot to the green. A hooked, sliced or mishit drive would most likely finish on a slope or have a bump or bunker between the player and the green.*
>
> *(2) On most par 4s he planned that the best place to approach from would be the centre left side of the fairway."*

Ewen commented that every hole was laid out to be reachable in two shots by the long hitter. His recollections cover a number of holes, but one in particular illustrates how minor changes can alter the very character of a hole. He pointed out that the lower part of the 6th green had since been enlarged and

R.M.S. "WANGANELLA"
Huddart Parker Line

was being used for a pin position for half of the time. Ewen suggested that the lower section was never meant by Russell to be used for a hole location, and explained how this negated the design of the hole since the hazards only protect the top tier, not the lower tier. *"It is the only hole on the course with a genuine two tier green. It was purposely laid out as a challenging approach shot hole because of its shortness."* He noted that *"Russell gave very special attention to the placement of bunkers, using the natural contours of the sandhills to best advantage while at the same time taking into account the severity of the coastal winds and their ability to blow sand from the hazards."*

In his report, Russell noted that he had attached a, *"Sketch plan of the proposed new lay out and detailed sketches of greens which need alteration. Owing to lack of time they are I am afraid only sketches. The vertical scale of the green sections is exaggerated."* While the original sketch layout plan has been lost, the club has a more formalised version of this plan that appears to have been drawn by a local surveyor or draftsman, which is dated April 1949. It holds a copy of his report, together with 11 of his green plans.

Continuing, Russell set out several general matters that needed to be addressed in his view, such as laying water to all greens and tees, and eliminating the Paspalum and Rats-tail grasses. One item of interest, especially considering how undulating the course has remained, was that he suggested, *"Smoothing out many of the steep bumps and hollows on fairways"*. Perhaps 'softening' may have better expressed his intentions as the fairways were certainly not smoothed out.

Russell was clearly aware of the costs involved, and he set out priorities accordingly as to what might be done subject to finances. First came the general matters, then he suggested the bunkering to holes where the greens did not require alteration, and the addition of new championship tees. He then proceeded to set out his views on bunkering: *"Generally speaking no green is bunkered heavily on both sides with the exception of those drive and pitch holes where some bunkering is necessary."*

He then continued:

> *"Bunkers have been shown in the sketches as large and formidable. It might be wise, until it is known how much the sand will blow, not to make them full size. If this is done the part of the bunker nearest the pin or centre of the fairway should be made first. I feel that if heavy sand impregnated with salt is used in the bunkers it will not generally blow away but a rough grassy hollow can be substituted if absolutely necessary. Faces of bunkers can always be sodded if necessary."*

The report contains a list of changes hole-by-hole and there is evidence that he reversed the nines as well, as he prefaced his comments for the first hole with, *"Hole 1 Present 10th,"* continuing in this manner for all 18 holes.

Construction and Opening

After a six week stay in New Zealand, Russell returned to Australia, leaving the work up to Whyte and Hunt to undertake and interpret his plans, sketches and written instructions. Work began around the spring of 1949, and was undertaken in such a manner to allow play on the course while the modifications were made. First to be done was the re-bunkering of the holes that were not proposed to be altered, followed by the more significant reconstruction tasks.

Alex Paterson, Stronach's son, recalled that a darker, loamy soil was imported from the Manawatu region so as to provide some more "body" to the native sands in the construction of the new greens, in a similar manner to the importation of Merri Creek soil at Russell's Summerland Links on Philip Island in Victoria. Perhaps this was a suggestion of Russell's in both instances.

The 'Levin Chronicle' newspaper reported on the opening of the new clubhouse in its 27 May 1950 edition and commented upon progress of the remodelling of the course:

> *"Reconstruction of Links*
>
> *The club's links are rapidly being brought to the stage where they will be one of the finest, if not the finest in the country. The club bought the links about 18 months ago from the Paraparaumu Golf Links Estates, Ltd. Twelve months ago it asked Mr Alec Russell, golf architect, of the Royal Melbourne Golf Club, to re-design the course, and he said then that without his doing much, it was already one of the finest in New Zealand.*
>
> *In the final plan, the fifth hole will be played from a new tee. The eighth will be a completely new hole. It has been sown and will be in use next year. The tenth has been lengthened 60 yards by putting the tee back.*
>
> *The twelfth will be a completely new hole and will be in use next year. The thirteenth is to be redesigned and a start will be made on this next year. At the fourteenth a new green is to be formed and this will probably be done this year. The fifteenth will be another new hole. The tee will be shifted back and there will be a new fairway. The green has been reformed and will be ready for use next year.*
>
> *The sixteenth is a new hole; it has been prepared and will be made use next year. The seventeenth is being altered and will be ready for use next year. Holes that have not been changed have been re-bunkered. When reconstruction is complete the championship course will be approximately 6400 yards in length."*

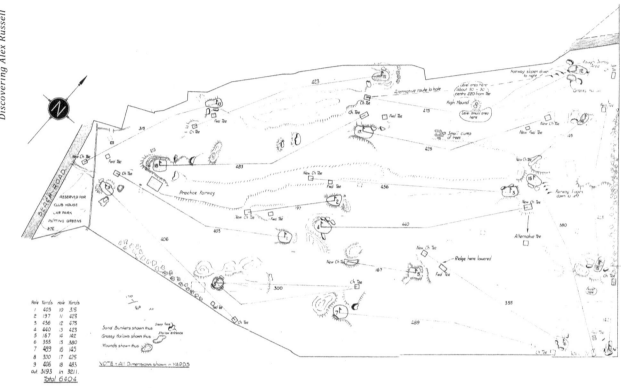

Hole	Yards	Hole	Yards
1	403	10	315
2	197	11	423
3	456	12	475
4	440	13	423
5	167	14	142
6	355	15	380
7	489	16	145
8	300	17	425
9	406	18	483
Out	3193	In	3211
		Total	6404

Sand Bunkers shown thus

Grassy Hollows shown thus

Mounds shown thus

NOTE : All Dimensions shown in YARDS

PARAPARAUMU BEACH GOLF COURSE

SCALE: 2 CHAINS TO 1 INCH

APRIL ~ 1949

*Alex Russell's sketch layout plan for the reconfigured course was
drawn up more formally by a local draftsman or surveyor in April 1949*

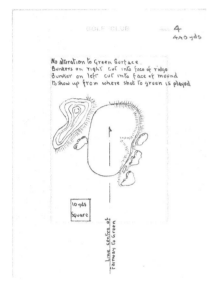

GOLF CLUB 4
440 yds

No alteration to Green Surface.
Bunkers on right cut into face of ridge
Bunker on left cut into face of mound
to show up from where shot to green is played

10 yds
Square

Line Centre of
Fairway to Green

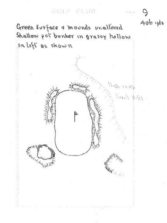

GOLF CLUB 6
365 yds

Small green. Slopes at back & sides unaltered
Green surface unaltered
Slope from front level to back level much
more gradual

10 yds
Square

2 yds

Line Tee to Pin

Plateau on left of fairway to hold good drive
Several deep grassy hollows to be reduced.

GOLF CLUB 9
406 yds

Green surface & mounds unaltered
Shallow pot bunker in grassy hollow
on left as shown

A selection of Russell's Green Plans

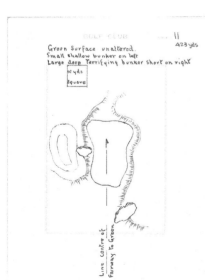

GOLF CLUB 11
423 yds

Green surface unaltered.
Small shallow bunker on left
Large deep terrifying bunker short on right

10 yds
Square

Line Centre of
Fairway to Green

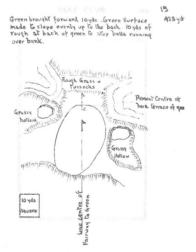

GOLF CLUB 13
423 yds

Green brought forward 10 yds. Green surface
made to slope evenly up to the back. 10 yds of
rough at back of green to stop balls running
over bank.

Rough Grass &
Tussocks

Present Centre or
back terrace of green

Grassy
hollow

Grassy
Hollow

10 yds
Square

Line Centre of
Fairway to Green

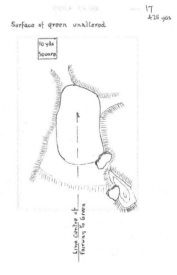

GOLF CLUB 17
425 yds

Surface of green unaltered

10 yds
Square

Line Centre of
Fairway to Green

Many of the holes referenced in this article suggested that they would be brought into play *"next year"*, being 1951. However, the club's 1950 Annual Report, prepared in June 1951, noted that their limited amount of labour had affected the speed at which Russell's plan could be implemented:

> *"The formation of the new 8th, 12th, 16th and 17th holes was completed and the greens and fairways sown. Owing to unfavourable weather conditions the fairways have not progressed as well as we would wish. The relaying of the new 15th green was completed by our own staff and a much improved hole is now in play. Unfortunately the work of improving the course has been seriously hampered by shortage of labour. For the past six months our regular Greens Staff has been reduced to two and consequently no new work has been commenced.*

In 1951, Paraparaumu played host to an invitational tournament that was the forerunner to the long running Caltex event. Comments from the competitors about the course showed that it was still raw in parts but would only improve given time. The 1952 Annual Report, issued in mid-1953, noted that *"the course is nearly finished"* and that the club would be applying to host the 1954 New Zealand Open. They were eventually granted the Open in 1959. It appears that some works were carried over into 1953, with no official re-opening of the remodelled course. The best that can be surmised from the available information is that the remodelling took place from 1949 to 1953 as resources and staffing allowed, with the more major works of new fairways and greens undertaken earlier, while the work of making new tees and adding bunkers was done as time permitted.

Construction in progress on Russell's new 13th green at Paraparaumu Beach (above and top), with Douglas Whyte and greenkeeper Jack Hunt posing with their work

The home green (left). Note the small bunker hunkered down into the side of the dune, out of the wind, and with its turfed face

Back Again

When Alex Russell returned at the club's request in 1952, some three years after his first visit, the course works that he had set out were still not fully complete. After inspecting the course, he wrote a report on his findings and recommendations, dated 6 May 1952. He suggested only minor changes to the links and complimented Whyte and Hunt, saying that, *"I found my ideas and suggestions had been translated exactly as I conceived them."* Russell had known that the sprawling bunkering of his designs at Royal Melbourne and Yarra Yarra were not appropriate, nor sensible on this windswept links. He kept his bunkers small and pot-like, while on some holes he eschewed bunkering altogether, rather letting the close cut slopes of the adjacent dunes provide the hazard. Here was an example of Russell's site appropriate design sensibilities at work.

His concerns about the fine volcanic sand blowing away in the wind were confirmed by time, and sodded bunker faces, smaller bunkers, and replacement with hollows were necessary in some places. Russell acknowledged this when he returned in 1952:

> **"Bunkers.** *It is obvious that the method constructing the bunkers was wrong and that most of them will have to be turfed on the steep side. This will make them look less formidable but will not detract from their value as hazards."*

Even keeping the bunkers small wasn't enough to restrict sand blow with sand flashed faces. Russell then went into detail of how the grassing of the bunkers should be carried out, so that the grass could still be cut by mechanical means. Later, he discussed particular bunkers that blew badly and suggested that they be replaced by grassy hollows, but again he stressed that it must be possible to cut these mechanically.

As at Lake Karrinyup, Russell suggested that the back tees only be used on special occasions such as medal rounds and championships, as he felt the course would play very long when the fairways were slow. He was also concerned about allowing the course to become overly lush, stating that, *"I hope you will be able by judicious manuring to keep the fairways turf close and springy, and not let it become soft and lush. This will not be easy at the bottom of hollows."*

Somewhat surprisingly, Russell was critical of the extent of closely mown turf around the greens, and said that he felt *"that a wild shot to the green often gets off too easily as there is too much closely cut turf around the greens and not enough rough. More rough would make the little chip shots to the pin more difficult. There is splendid rough growing on lots of mounds and sandhills which is just the type needed closer to the greens."*

Paraparaumu has always been renowned for the quality of its par three holes, a feature in common with all of Alex Russell's courses. Norman Von Nida described the 5th as *"one of the finest and toughest short holes in the world,"* causing the club to promptly name the hole after him. The 2nd hole, despite being blind, is held in high regard, while the 14th green eventually needed to be moved for safety reasons when houses were constructed bordering this hole. A new hole was then designed by Sloan Morpeth.

Alex Russell designed several courses on what are links-type sandy soils, but in designing Paraparaumu Beach he created a true links, in a true links environment. One senses that all of his love of golf in Scotland gained expression at Paraparaumu. While it is still Russell, it is quite different from any of the other courses he designed, perhaps apart from the Summerland Links on Phillip Island.

When the wind blows at Paraparaumu, as it usually does, it becomes a difficult course as the golfer must be accurate at all times, positioning for the next shot, as going for the flag or even the green from a poor position can be costly. The running ball and the undulating fairways means the ball does not always end up where you expected, or even hoped. This might sound daunting, and in some ways it is, but this course provides great enjoyment, even if the score might be climbing faster than the golfer's ego would prefer. The thought of how to play one's next shot is Scottish seaside golf encapsulated. As Russell himself said, *"Golf without thinking is not golf."*

In September 1951 the club hosted an exhibition match led by Peter Thomson. The match featured (above right) Phillip Scrutton (a fine British amateur and friend of Thomson), George Roberts (who had also hit balls for Russell), John Hornabrook and Thomson. Next to Thomson are Stronach Paterson and Douglas Whyte. The card from the match (right).

Aerial photograph delineated with the holes for the 1959
New Zealand Open held at Paraparaumu Beach

Favourable Comparisons

A number of writers and players have gone on record favourably comparing Paraparaumu Beach with Scottish courses on the roster for The Open Championship. Ian Ewen, one of those who hit test shots for Russell when the course was being designed, was awarded a Cambridge Blue for golf, having competed against Oxford in 1935-36. He had played many of the top courses in Britain and had this to say, "*In my opinion Paraparaumu demands more difficult shots on numerous holes than some of the famous British links where the British Open is played.*"

In September 1954, Ian Ewen, speaking to Henry Longhurst, the doyen of British golf writers and commentators, compared the course with Prince's course at Sandwich and Longhurst could see his point. Longhurst, after saying the course was still too new and the tournament had been played in appalling conditions, had this to add, "*It seemed to me, though, that Paraparaumu, judged by any standard in any country must in a few years become a tremendous shoulder opening course, on its day, of extending the Sam Sneads of this world and, among less mortals, separating the men inexorably from the boys.*"

Bob Charles, New Zealand's famous left-hander expressed a similar view, "*It is New Zealand's only course which compares with the links styles used for British Open roster. True it is short, but only for the professionals and championships – but for sheer golfing pleasure at club player level, I can't find many better courses in the world. It's an incredible challenge.*"

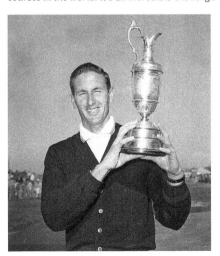

New Zealand's Bob Charles proudly holds aloft his 1963 Open Championship trophy that he won at Royal Lytham and St. Annes. Charles holds the Paraparaumu course in high regard for its true British links characteristics.

Providing the golfer remembers that golf is not just about making the best of good luck, but is at least, if not more, a matter of handling bad luck and awkward lies, then all will agree that this is a great course. It is one where not only the best player will almost always come out on top, but will have been enjoyed by all. On this course, being the best player also means having the imagination to work out what shot to hit and then having the skills to execute what they have conceived.

While luck can be a factor, as it can at most links courses, the course is not unfair. No course hosts twelve national opens if it is unfair. This is a course one plays hole by hole, or perhaps shot by shot, since the course changes as often as the wind and the weather. Not only is it a great stroke play course, it has all the attributes of a great match-play course, be it a championship, or a four-ball between friends with little more on it than the first round of drinks.

One member, Bob Northcote, a Scot who had played many links "*at home*", credited Paraparaumu Beach with not having one bad hole, but that it was missing one thing, "*There should be a wailing wall near the 18th green where those players who had had a bad day could pause and let their emotions flow.*"

Douglas Whyte, a central figure in the creation of the club and the course, always maintained the course had put Paraparaumu Beach on the map. It can equally be said that the oil company Caltex provided the club and its course with international recognition. Initially the Caltex tournament was to run for five years, in the end it ran for eighteen. During that time, the winners list contained many internationally recognised names: Peter Thomson (5 times, twice in a tie), Bob Charles (4 times, once in a tie), Kel Nagle (3 times, once in a tie), Dave Thomas of Wales (twice), Maurice Bembridge of England and Australia's Billy Dunk, who also won the New Zealand Open that year at Paraparaumu.

Paraparaumu Beach was one of the select group of courses that was featured in the 1960s television series 'Shell's Wonderful World of Golf', with a match between New Zealand legend (Sir) Bob Charles and the American Bob Goalby in 1962. The only other course selected in Australasia was Royal Melbourne's West Course, hosting a match between Peter Thomson and Gary Player.

There are many who still regard Paraparaumu as the best course in New Zealand. Talking about Chisholm Park in Dunedin, Greg Turner commented, *"I think, that after Paraparaumu Beach, it's the second best links course in New Zealand,"* while in the most recent New Zealand rankings the course was placed third best in the country. For many years the course was ranked in the Top 100 in the world but has since dropped out, probably a result of two factors – new highly publicised courses being placed above it, and a diminished exposure for Paraparaumu. Russell's youngest daughter, Robina, after living in New Zealand for a time, was eventually persuaded by a friend to go and play the course, given that her father had designed it. She enjoyed the course but found it difficult, later recalling that her father *"must have had a nasty streak I never knew about."*

There have been numerous accolades for Paraparaumu over the years, perhaps the most succinct one came from Gary Player, winner of nine major championships, who said, *"This is a great golf course, a great, great golf course."*

Peter Thomson, five times winner of 'The Open Championship', nine times winner of the New Zealand Open, five times winner of the Caltex Tournament held at Paraparaumu, and one who has great respect for Russell's courses, was made a life member of the club in 1961. He also wrote the foreword for the club's history book, and his last paragraph tells us how the great golfer feels about the course:

> *"We had nothing like it in Australia, which must have struck Alex Russell, who did the layout for an undisclosed sum, which it might be guessed was such a modest figure, that it would be better counted as a gesture of love. Russell of course knew his golf from his Australian Open win and his playing at Royal Melbourne and St Andrews. Course designing approaches an artform, especially done in a perfect modelling medium like volcanic sand. Russell must have been ecstatic.*
>
> *What was left after his departure was a gem of enjoyment, a monument to the game and a gift for the future. When we all turn to dust, "Paraparaumu" the Golf, should be still lying there as it was when the first golfers came by, with Kapiti an off-shore island standing guard to see that no one steals it away. And the winds will ever blow to test the golfer's will and integrity. Paraparaumu will be famed for a century yet."*

The undulating and tumbling contours of Russell's 6th hole at Paraparaumu Beach

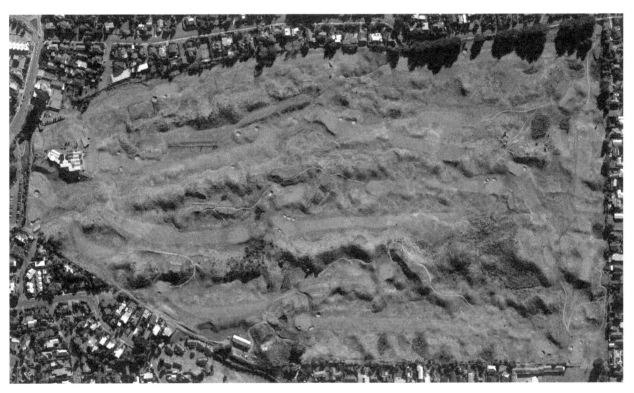

*This 2015 aerial photograph shows up the course's
dramatically rumpled terrain and the dune spines
that run through the course*

Alex Russell

Chapter 13

RUSSELL'S OTHER COURSES

The following courses with an involvement by Alex Russell in either their design or redesign have been listed after extensive research by the authors. Further information on any of these courses would be welcomed. As would be expected, Russell was particularly active in his home state of Victoria, especially in its country regions.

VICTORIA

Albert Park Golf Club *Melbourne, Victoria*

As well as its course at Caulfield, the Melbourne Golf Club had laid-out a 9-hole course at Albert Park around 1891. In 1899, with the now Royal Melbourne club about to concentrate its activities on a new course at Sandringham, a new club was formed, the Albert Park Golf Club, with a 6-hole course laid out in the park. In 1931, the club was able to obtain a lease of a further thirty acres from the Albert Park Trust, and Alex Russell was asked to extend the course to 18-holes. 'The Sporting Globe' reported in its 11 November 1931 edition that:

> *"Work is now in hand to make the course a full one. Alex Russell has been commissioned to fit in the new nine holes, and to remodel the old ones. The approval of the park authorities has been obtained....Because of the great popularity of the links, its low overhead and the fine manner in which the finances have been handled, Albert Park is one of the very few clubs in a position to embark on new work at the moment."*

A few days after this report the 'Weekly Times' noted that:

> *"Permission has been obtained from the Park Trust, and plans have been prepared by Mr Alex. Russell, to remodel and extend the Albert Park golf links to an 18 hole course. The park-side course is now composed of nine holes. These holes are to be improved, and an additional nine holes are to be laid out and constructed. During the period the Albert Park Golf Club has been in permissive occupancy of the portion of the park used as a links, more than £20,000 of golfers' money has been expended, and the country has been transformed from an unsightly rubbish dump into the most attractive portion of the great park."*

The land for the extension had been used for grazing and the terms stipulated that the land *"could not be alienated by fencing"*. The club had to spend £500 a year on maintenance and beautification of this land, in addition to their rental of £250 a year. Further, they were required to provide nine additional cricket wickets and practice pitches. According to the Keysborough Golf Club's history book, Russell was originally of the opinion that there was only enough room for fifteen good holes, but the terms of the lease stipulated that an 18-hole course was to be constructed and Russell eventually modified his plan to fit in the additional holes.

It took some years to extend the course, and in September 1934 it was reported that the terms of the agreement had not yet been fulfilled, with the club warned by the South Melbourne Council that unless the extension was undertaken the additional land grant would be rescinded. This must have had the desired effect, as the Mayor of South Melbourne officiated at the opening of the full course and their new £8,000 clubhouse on 25 July 1936.

When the time came in 1947 for the club to move to a greenfield site at Keysborough, Sam Berriman, the man responsible for putting C.H. Alison's design on the ground at Huntingdale, was selected ahead of Russell to design their new course, now the Keysborough Golf Club, and their old course at Albert Park was taken over as a public course.

Ballarat Golf Club *Ballarat, Victoria*

The club was founded in 1895 on Crown land that was part of Ballarat Common, and in 1909 the 9-hole course was extended to 18-holes. In October 1929, Alex Russell, of the MacKenzie and Russell firm, was engaged by the Ballarat Golf Club to provide advice *"concerning the improvement of the putting greens, bunkering of the greens and the course and general course improvements."* Russell developed a five-year plan for the club that involved an annual expenditure of around £200. The club's history book recorded that:

> *"The Russell reconstruction plan involved many changes to the course and affected every hole except the third. For example, in enlarging and developing the eight green, 118 cubic yards of soil were ploughed, broken up and transported to the green, a further 45 cubic yards of soil was scooped to the green, 38 yards of ashes were mixed with 10 cubic yards of soil and sand as topdressing and two and a half bushels of grass seed were added.*

*Characteristic Russell bunkering on
the final green at Ballarat c.1940*

*During the early 1930s work continued progressively with
tee placements changed and more clearly defined, greens
raised and enlarged and new bunkers carefully placed
and former ones remodelled......By 1937 work under the
plan had been completed at a cost of almost £1200 and
widespread satisfaction was expressed at the final results."*

In October 1930, the club held its annual Open Meeting and
Harry Culliton noted in 'The Australasian' that:

> *"For one thing the rather "countrified" aspect of the links
> has disappeared before the excellent bunkering scheme
> carried out during the year to designs by Alex. Russell. This
> is not yet complete, but it will proceed in due course. An
> instance of the improvement made is the short hole known
> as Clarke's trap. This, although interesting enough, had
> been a very crude affair, a flat square green placed inside
> a sort of zareba [a thorn fence surrounding an African
> village] as foreign to modern golf course architecture as
> could well be imagined. The appearance of the first and
> second holes too has been improved beyond recognition."*

"Backspin", writing in 'The Referee' in Sydney on 22 October,
commented that:

> *"Recent visitors to the Ballarat meeting were greatly
> impressed with the wonderful improvement in the
> character of the links, brought about by the bunkering
> and remodelling scheme carried out by Alex Russell.
> Obsolete bunkering systems are soundly condemned
> by city players visiting rural links. It is high time that a
> number of other clubs undertook the task of replacing
> such golfing atrocities as wire-netting bunkers."*

Two years later Culliton observed:

> *"Alex Russell is to be heartily congratulated upon making
> an excellent imitation of a silk purse out of something
> very like a sow's ear, speaking of golf courses from the
> point of view of the fastidious modern golfer. The course
> is now an excellent round. The old "potato-pit" bunkers
> have been swept away and new, symmetrical hazards,
> well placed and sand filled, have displaced them."*

Barwon Heads Golf Club *Barwon Heads, Victoria*

Philip Russell recalled that his father redesigned the 16th hole
at Barwon Heads, in what year is not known. However, the
committee apparently took a dislike to one of the new bunkers
that he said was rather bluntly named "Russell's Asshole", and
had it filled in. There is a brief mention of Russell in the club's
history book as providing *"support for Victor East's work at
Barwon Heads,"* but it does not elaborate further. In any event
East was involved with George Lowe in laying out the course
that first opened in 1922 and while it is possible Russell
assisted Lowe at that time, it is considered unlikely. He almost
certainly made some contributions to the design of the course
in the immediate post-war period when he served on the
committee and was both captain and president.

Beaufort Golf Club *Beaufort, Victoria*

The club was formed in 1889 with Alex Russell's father Philip
Russell one of the founding members, as the Russell property
'Mawallok' was located close to the town. Alex's son Philip
Russell stated that his father made some alterations to the
course at Beaufort, likely in the mid 1930s after Alex had
returned to live at 'Mawallok'. In 1936, the course was described
as having *"large sand greens"* and *"heavily bunkered fairways."*

Beechworth Golf Club *Beechworth, Victoria*

At its annual meeting in April 1928, the Beechworth Golf Club
*"decided to at once extend the present 12-hole course to an 18-
hole course, and Mr Alex Russell, the prominent golfer, will be
asked to design the lay-out of the new course."* Russell must have
been engaged to undertake this work, as a later article in 'The
Sporting Globe' on 14 December 1938 discussed the sporting
facilities of the town of Beechworth and noted that, *"Under the
direction of Mr Alex Russell, one of the leading golf architects
in Australia, a new 18-hole course was laid out a few years ago
at Baarmutha Park."* The Beechworth Golf Club's course was

described in 1936 as being laid out on interesting undulating country with sand greens and was well bunkered.

The Beechworth course c.1940

Bendigo Golf Club *Bendigo, Victoria*

The club was established in 1901 as the Bendigo Golf and Bowling Club. 'The Riverina Recorder' newspaper on 8 February 1930, in reporting about the new course for the Swan Hill Golf Club that Alex Russell was designing, also commented on some of the other course design projects that Russell was currently involved with, *"Mr Russell has recently been engaged in designing plans and lay-out of golf courses for Colac, Ballarat, Bendigo, and the new Royal Melbourne clubs."* The 'Weekly Times' of 3 May 1930 reported on the opening of the Bendigo club's season and noted that:

> *"The links were in perfect order. The club is rearranging its course under the direction of Mr Alex. Russell, the golf architect, the object being to confine the whole 18 holes to the club's own property. New bunkers have been installed and other improvements made to meet the new scheme, which will be carried out in sections as money becomes available. Improvements carried out in the last two years have cost £1000, of which £700 has been provided out of revenue."*

This suggests that the remodelling of the Bendigo course began some time in 1928. 'Golf' magazine of 1 November 1931 reported that, *"Alex Russell has prepared a scheme for remodelling the bunkering of the Bendigo course. This is now being put into operation."* In 1937, it was reported that the course had well-grassed fairways but still retained sand scrape greens.

Brentwood Golf Club *Melbourne, Victoria*

The Brentwood Park Golf Company owned 103 acres (42 ha) of land two miles (3 km) east of the Kingston Heath course and 'The Argus' of 6 September 1930 described it as a *"fine tract."* The land was to be taken over by the Brentwood Golf Club *"and will be formed into a course. Mr Alexander Russell has inspected the land. It is expected that a temporary nine-hole round will be playable in about a month."*

On 10 September, the Sydney newspaper 'The Referee' noted in a short article that *"Like Eric Apperly in Sydney, Alex Russell is becoming equally known as a golf architect in Victoria. The two latest are Brentwood Park (103 acres), two miles east of the Kingston Heath links, and the new Dromana Country Club...."* The Brentwood Park course never eventuated.

Colac Golf Club *Colac, Victoria*

Golf was first played in Colac around 1880, when some of the town residents played over a rudimentary 9-hole course with barbed wire fencing around the greens to keep out the cattle. The Colac Golf Club was formed in 1897 and official permission was granted to lay out a 9-hole course on the racing and recreation reserve a few years later, located *"on a hill a mile and half to the south of the town"*, which became known as the Racecourse Links. The reserve was first gazetted in 1865, with an area of 145 acres (59 ha), and later further expanded to 174 acres (70 ha).

In 1926, the club expanded its course to 18-holes, to a design by its club professional Angas Polson, and 'The Sporting Globe' reported that since the full course was in use there had been *"a remarkable increase in membership."* The new course was 6,047 yards (5,530 metres) in length and involved *"great changes in the old course."* Despite the report noting the congratulations Polson had received on his layout at Colac, the club must have seen some deficiencies in it and decided to contact Alex Russell to visit the course and give his opinion on possible improvements. Russell would have been well-known in Colac, located in Victoria's Western District, and once news of his foray into golf course architecture was made public in late 1926, the club would have no doubt been aware that he could assist

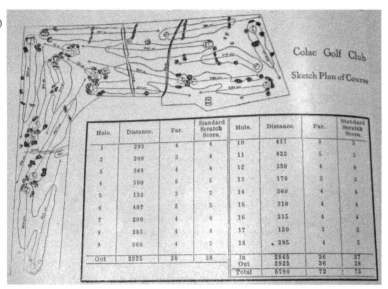

Sketch plan of the revised Colac course and a card of the course (left) published in 'Golf' magazine in October 1929

Hole.	Distance.	Par.	Standard Scratch Score.	Hole.	Distance.	Par.	Standard Scratch Score.
1	293	4	4	10	417	5	5
2	200	3	4	11	422	5	5
3	368	4	4	12	350	4	4
4	500	5	5	13	176	3	3
5	132	3	3	14	360	4	4
6	497	5	5	15	310	4	4
7	290	4	4	16	315	4	4
8	285	4	4	17	130	3	3
9	360	4	5	18	385	4	5
Out	2925	36	38	In	2865	36	37
				Out	2925	36	38
				Total	5790	72	75

them with their improvement plans. In 1927, the club requested permission from the trustees of the Colac racecourse reserve *"to secure a plan for a new golf course. Mr Russell, of Melbourne, has been commissioned to submit a plan,"* according to an article in 'The Argus' on 9 January 1928. However, Russell must have been engaged as early as October 1927 as 'Table Talk' reported on 13 October that Colac was one of the projects that Russell was involved in, suggesting that *"These days Russell is kept busy making and redesigning golf courses. Those in hand include Canberra, Yarra Yarra, Colac, Narrandera and Warrandyte."*

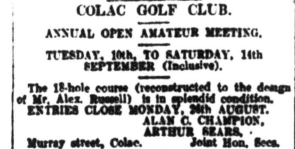

1929 newspaper advertisement for Colac's Open Amateur Meeting (above) noted that the course had been "reconstructed to the design of Mr Alex. Russell"

In June 1928, the trustees of the racecourse reserve *"informed the Colac Golf Club that there was £100 available for immediate expenditure in connection with the reconstruction of the links in accordance with the plan prepared by Mr A. Russell, of Melbourne. More would be made available as money came to hand."* Whether any of this money was received by Russell as a fee is conjecture. 'The Age' reported on 16 July that *"Colac racecourse trustees have decided to carry out Mr A. Russell's scheme for new golf links at the racecourse reserve in co-operation with the golf club."* There is also a suggestion that Russell may have been assisted at Colac by Mrs Eleanor 'Nellie' Gatehouse, a well-known identity in Victorian ladies' golf and President of the VLGU for a number of years, but exactly what her role was is not known. (Mrs Gatehouse's grandson Jamie said his grandmother introduced mounds into some golf courses which became known colloquially as *"Mrs Gatehouse's bosoms"*.)

A subsequent report from nearby Camperdown in their 'Chronicle' newspaper on 20 December 1928, headlined *"Colac Golf Club – Progress of New Course,"* gave a good idea of the extent of the works. It advised of a report from the sub-committee *"supervising the reconstruction of the links"* that was presented to a full committee meeting. Some relevant aspects of the report included:

> Some £205 had been expended to date.

> The new greens had been ploughed and roughly formed, and were in the process of being cultivated and cleared of weeds prior to sowing. How many new greens were being constructed was not recorded.

> The bunkers had all been formed and some were completed, with some having to be built higher and others drained.

> The new fairways were ready for mowing, and *"would be cut in accordance with Mr Russell's plan."* This is suggestive that construction must have started some months earlier.

> The drain across the old 1st, 12th and 14th fairways was widened by around six feet.

> Water had been laid on to the 11th green at a cost of around £20, but the cost of connecting other greens would not be as great as there were existing pipelines in the vicinity.

> A new mower was to be purchased.

When exactly the reconstructed course was reopened for play is unknown, but it appears that it was back in play some time towards the middle of 1929, as evidenced by advertisements in August of that year placed by the club in 'The Argus' for their upcoming Annual Open Amateur Meeting promoting the fact that *"the 18-hole course (reconstructed to the designs of Mr Alex. Russell) is in splendid condition."*

'The Riverina Recorder' newspaper, in reporting on 8 February 1930 about the new course for the Swan Hill Golf Club that Alex Russell was designing, also commented on some of the other course design projects that Russell was currently involved with, *"Mr Russell has recently been engaged in designing plans and lay-out of golf courses for Colac, Ballarat, Bendigo, and the new Royal Melbourne clubs."*

'The Argus' reported on the women's country championships that were held at Colac by the VLGU in June 1930 and suggested that, *"The course must be one of the best outside Melbourne. It was laid out by Mr Alec Russell over very suitable sandy soil except for four or five holes, which in this respect are less favoured than the rest. The beautiful surroundings too, greatly enhance the pleasure of the round. This is only the second season there, but greens and fairways are in splendid order."* In 1936 the Colac course was described as having *"large well-grassed greens"* and *"mown fairways, nicely bunkered."*

Croydon Golf Club *Melbourne, Victoria*

At a meeting held on 28 August 1925, a group of local golfers took the decision to form a golf club and to take up the option to purchase land at Croydon. The Croydon District Golf Club was then established, with their first course of 9-holes laid out to a design by professional David Young, and some two years later the course was extended to fourteen holes. By playing four holes twice, 18-hole competitions could be conducted. The next step in the club's evolution was to add a further five holes, closing the original 7th hole in the process, to the designs of Alex Russell.

'The Sporting Globe' in its 2 April 1932 issue noted that, *"One of the most popular, particularly for week-end play, of the "just out of town" golf links, is that at Croydon. At present there are fourteen well-kept and interesting holes, and work is going on in the construction of the final four which will be available for play in a few months."* Croydon's 18-hole course was first played in December 1932, with a length of 6,128 yards (5,603 metres) and a par of 73.

Dromana Country Golf Club *Dromana, Victoria*

An old grazing property on the foreshore at Safety Beach, on the Melbourne side of the Dromana township on the Mornington Peninsula, was taken up for the purposes of a new residential development in the mid 1920s. Seven miles (11 km) of roads were made and in 1928 these were used by the Royal Automobile Club of Victoria for acceleration and speed tests. A report on the tests in November 1928 noted that, *"alongside the portion of the estate where the tests will be held are areas reserved for a golf course and an aerodrome,"* and that Mr McLaren of the Light Car Club expected that Safety Beach would be made *"a regular rendezvous for motorists and golfers"*

On 5 September 1930, 'The Argus' reported that:

> *"DROMANA – Nearly 70 acres at Safety Beach has been set aside for a golf course, and a club has been formed under the name of the Dromana Country Golf Club. The designing of the course is left to Mr A. Russell and the links will be open about the middle of December. It will be available to visitors and members alike."*

'The Referee' newspaper in Sydney picked up on 'The Argus' report a few days later, noting that Alex Russell had two new projects in Victoria, being Brentwood Park near the Kingston Heath course and *"the new Dromana Country Club, where nearly 70 acres of the Safety Beach estate will open in December. It will be difficult to keep one's mind on the game for the course is encircled by the race-track for cars, and there is an ideal landing ground for aeroplanes behind the clubhouse."*

'The Argus' then reported a few days before Christmas 1930 on the development of the *"New Links at Dromana. Golfers and others from all parts of the peninsula attended the opening of the new links of the Dromana Country Golf Club. The course, which is in a rough state is situated at the foot of Mount Martha, and the nine holes all command beautiful views of Port Phillip Bay, Arthur's Seat and Mount Martha. The nature of the soil and the layout of the course proved a surprise to the many golfers. The club is applying for affiliation with the V.G.A."* A report in 'The Age' noted that the enterprise behind the course belonged to Mr H.S. MacLaren and his associates.

The course was constructed on part of Bean's Safety Beach property which was thickly vegetated with clumps of reeds, silver tussocks and bracken fern, and in its early days the course was very rudimentary. By January 1933 the course had improved and another official opening of the 9-hole course took place, with the President of the Shire of Flinders officiating. A report in the 'Weekly Times' noted that, *"although it will be some time yet before the greens are in perfect condition, the new course already provides a good test of golf. The holes are attractively planned, fairways well grassed and bunkers cleverly placed."* A café on Marine Drive served as a temporary clubhouse until a purpose-built clubhouse could be constructed. A contemporary report in "The Sporting Globe" also noted that the club had progressed considerably, *"and now has a sporting lay-out of nine holes. Trees have been planted and the course lends itself to interesting developments."* A temporary water supply saw water pumped into a tank from where it was trucked out onto the course to water the greens.

In September 1937, the Southern Development Company, the owner of the land the golf course was sited upon, advertised for applications for *"occupancy of Dromana Golf Course, including residence, use of course, equipment, fairway and green mowers, tuition,"* with further particulars available from the company or the Dromana Golf Club.

The following year, 'The Argus' reported that the Southern Development Company, with its 200 acres (80 ha) of land at Safety Beach, had sunk a bore and that arrangements had been made to lay pipes from the bore to the golf course. It also noted that *"provision has been made for the nine-hole golf course to be extended to 18 holes,"* but whether that extension ever took place is not known. In 1941 the name of the Dromana Country Golf Club was struck off the Register of Companies in Victoria and the company dissolved in September 1941. The company had been first registered in February 1934.

Anecdotal evidence of some local residents indicates that the course occupied the land that eventually became the A.V. Jennings Horizon Estate around 1990, with many golf balls unearthed when the subdivision was being cleared. Interestingly, the last mention of the club was the annual meeting held at the end of 1938.

Gala Golf Club *Lismore, Victoria*

The Gala Golf Club played over the 9-hole private course with turfed greens established on the 'Gala' estate of Mr Edwin

Currie near Lismore, only 60 km from Russell's 'Mawallok'. Philip Russell recalled that his father assisted the Currie family in the layout of this course. Currie was the president of the club and Alex Russell was a club member and served on the greens committee in 1933. Jim Fairbairn, the cousin of Alex's wife Jess, was also a member. In addition, Alex donated a cup played for in the club championship. The course's fairways were laid out across the property's paddocks, while the clubhouse was an old tin shed with a stone fireplace and a gravel floor, with rough wooden tables and benches, true farm golf.

Grange Golf Club *Stawell, Victoria*

The Grange Golf Club at Stawell first contacted Alex Russell for his advice in 1956 when they were developing a new course on leased land. The club's secretary, Jack Jones, was entrusted with the responsibility of engaging a golfing expert to design their new 9-hole course and he turned to the well-known Western District identity, Alex Russell. Jones visited Russell at 'Mawallok' and was shown over the private 6-hole course. He explained a number of aspects of the course and gave Jones excellent advice according to the club's history book, *"much of which was incorporated in the nine hole layout of the Grange and later on when the course was enlarged to 18 holes. Mr Russell was not an advocate of long holes but emphasized that design was just as important as length. He explained that it was necessary for a golfer to think before he played his shot particularly from the tee. He said that a golfer must learn to place his shots and this was why design was most important."* The new course opened for play in January 1957, making this work in Stawell likely Alex Russell's last foray into golf course design.

Kew Golf Club *Melbourne, Victoria*

The Kew Golf Club was encountering regular flooding problems on its course adjacent to the Yarra River and 'The Sporting Globe' reported on the club's plans in its 29 October 1932 edition, noting that:

> *"To obviate the risk of interruption to play consequent upon occasional floods, the Kew Golf Club has decided to purchase 50 acres to the left of the present 7th green. All the land is higher than that now susceptible to flood waters. Next week Mr Alec Russell, links architect, will inspect the country and advise the Committee of a plan for incorporating new holes and remodelling the present layout."*

A few days later, 'The Argus' filed a similar report. Russell did inspect the course and the proposed new land for the club early -

in November 1932, and a report in 'The Australasian' on 19th November described his findings:

"KEW LINKS

The round of the delightfully situated links of the Kew club, several holes of which picturesquely skirt the Yarra at East Kew, will shortly be radically altered so as to obviate the disastrous ravages accompanying the periodical invasion by the flood waters from the river. These not only altogether cut off the members for weeks from enjoyment of a large section of their course, but incidentally involve expensive work restoring order again over the large area affected. Mr Alex Russell, the golf course architect (former open champion of Australia), recently inspected the course, seeing it for the first time, and was most agreeably surprised with its fine quality and appearance. Fifty acres adjoining the club's property on the east side are under offer to the club, and Mr Russell has now advised their purchase. The proposal is to abandon the six holes which are subject to flood, and utilise the now acquired land for the construction of six new holes to replace them. Mr Russell, who is highly optimistic about the result of the alterations, is now working on the plans of the lay-out."

With Russell giving a favourable report and working on the design of the new holes, it is surprising that the club then decided not to proceed with the acquisition of the new land. In 1937, they went ahead with suggested improvements to their current course that "Mick" Morcom had made some time earlier. The club eventually purchased the additional land to the east, some three decades later.

Long Island Golf Club *Melbourne, Victoria*

The directors of the Long Island Estates company approached Russell in October 1933 asking if he would inspect their Frankston property and assess its potential for country club development. This he did and his report of 15 November 1933 was full of praise for the site but expressed reservations about its financial viability with the adjoining Peninsula Country Club close-by. The club still has the letter and accompanying report that he wrote following his inspection, with the text reproduced in the club's history book:

Dear Mr Hiscock

I enclose brief report of your Frankston area. At the same time I feel I must call your attention to the financial side of the question.

About 40 acres will be absorbed in fairways and I think that 50 pounds per acre will be a moderate allowance to bring cleared country into good fairway.

Then there is green construction and water mains to greens. Water is essential for greens in that class of soil. Lastly there is bunker construction. This can be tackled gradually but some bunkers must be constructed at once if the course is to be sufficiently attractive.

Finally there is the Peninsula Club competing next door and so far as I know is in some financial difficulties. I do not want to be too pessimistic but my advice is to consider carefully the possible revenue before spending too much on construction work.

Yours sincerely,
Alex Russell"

His report was short and similarly to the point:

"Re the area I inspected recently near Frankston known as the Racecourse paddock. There is no doubt, that you have there, a piece of first rate golfing country.

The area – 119 acres – should be sufficient for a full eighteen hole course, the contour of the country would make an interesting layout assured, and couch grass should do well on this type of soil.

The area is nicely timbered and is conveniently situated to both road and rail.

I can confidently recommend that a first class eighteen hole course could be constructed on this area."

On 9 December, Russell refused the job to design their course, writing to Hiscock simply that, *"I regret that I am unable to undertake the layout of your course as I cannot spare the time,"* with the job being awarded to G.B. Oliver, an expatriate Scotsman who had also laid out the Paterson River course. The new course that became the Long Island Golf Club opened for play in 1937. What was occupying Russell's attention in late 1933, apart from his property 'Mawallok', is not known.

'Mawallok' Private Golf Course *Near Beaufort, Victoria*

Around 1935, Alex Russell laid out a 6-hole golf course on his 'Mawallok' property near Beaufort, located at the bottom of the garden and to the north of the main residence. His son Phillip described the course at 'Mawallok' as a 6-holer that was played a second and third time by the use of different tees. The Russells gave names to each of the six holes: First, Short, Long, Rocky, Lake and Home. While Philip recalled his father being an excellent golfer, he never was able to make a hole-in-one at 'Mawallok', despite hitting to within an inch at the Lake hole during one round. Phillip also noted the course's excellent condition, its creative design and the fact that it was great fun to play, not just for the family, but for the many visitors. In 1939, a letter from a greenkeeper applying for a position at Long Island Golf Club in Melbourne wrote *"I am at present senior greenkeeper to the private golf links of Major Alex Russell on his Mawallok estate. Major Russell is considered a foremost authority on greens preparation and maintenance....our greens, fairways etc, are second to none in Victoria at the present time."*

Alethea Russell recalled some aspects of the Mawallok course, noting that her mother-in-law Jess took out a large tree on the Long Hole while Alex was away, which made him furious once he returned and noticed it gone:

Early photograph of the Home hole green in front of the house at 'Mawallok', note its square shape

"One of the more famous things that happened on Mawallok Golf Course was the pine tree on the, well, the holes didn't have numbers, they had names. The first, the short, the long, and on the long there was a pine tree that was right in the way. It was always called the damn and blast tree. And my mother-in-law always wanted it down and my father-in-law wouldn't listen, he went away once and she had it removed. It was a wonderful golf course, it really was."

Of the Rocky hole she noted that *"if you didn't get it where it was supposed to go, you would end up anywhere after it hit a rock. It was all rocky except the green and tee really. Very interesting and the next hole was across the lake."*

After World War II, Les Beardsell, who had served with Philip in Libya, Greece and Crete, was responsible for the upkeep of the course. In November 1952, Alex and Jess Russell opened 'Mawallok' to the public for a garden fete to raise funds for the construction of a hall for Girl Guides and Boy Scouts in Beaufort. It was opened by the Victorian Governor Sir Dallas Brooks and Lady Brooks, who stayed the weekend as guests of the Russells. Over 1,000 people attended and one of the attractions was an exhibition match over the 6-hole golf course by Ossie Pickworth and Major Russell, one of the very few times that Alex played golf after his first stroke in 1950. The course was let go for a number of years when new owners

By 1949 the Home green (left) had been expanded into a more circular form. Two of Russell's young grandsons assist in the top-dressing of the green.

took over after Philip sold the property, but has in recent times been reinstated.

Interestingly, the following notification was printed on the 'Mawallok' score cards, suggestive of Alex Russell's dry sense of humour:

"ANYONE DESTROYING RARE PERSONS, PLANTS OR SHEEP WILL NOT BE ASKED AGAIN."

Northern Golf Club *Glenroy, Victoria*

In August 1930, 'The Age' newspaper reported on the Northern Golf Club's open meeting and noted that their course had undergone considerable change since the previous year, with the addition of two new holes. It also noted that the club's *"enterprising Committee proposes shortly to confer with Alex. Russell regarding a system of bunkering to meet the requirements of the new course."*

At its meeting on 2 October 1930, the committee passed the following motion:

> *"Motion: that the layout of the whole course be submitted to an expert. Secretary to report expense."*

Alex Russell was the expert consulted, as correctly predicted by 'The Age' back in August. However, Russell's fee of £100 proved too expensive for the club, and his services were not engaged. The minutes of the Committee meeting held on 12th November 1930 noted that:

> *"The Secretary reported that he had communicated with Mr A. Russell, Golf Course Architect, on the question of re-modelling the course. Mr Russell quoted 100 pounds. It was decided to take no action."*

It was evident though that the club still needed advice on its course and in 1935 "Mick" Morcom was consulted but his plans were not proceeded with. The following year both A. W. Jackson and Sloan Morpeth were asked to report on the course and Jackson's proposals were accepted, although his new holes, when built, did not garner complete satisfaction.

Peninsula Country Golf Club *Frankston, Victoria*

An 11-hole course was developed by the Tower House Golf Company on an undulating 460 acre (186 ha) site at Frankston, to a design by the St Andrews native G.B. Oliver, who was also one of the directors of the company. The course opened for play in December 1923 and the following year the Peninsula Country Golf Club was formed to take over the property from the company, extending the course to 18-holes to Oliver's designs. The full course opened for play on 25 September 1926, but it only lasted until early 1928 when the 8th, 9th and 10th holes, the last to be completed, were taken out of play. One temporary hole was created by dividing the 14th into two par fours, and another by creating a short par three, the 9th, from near the old 8th tee to the 10th green. Clearly the new club was dissatisfied with Oliver's work.

Alex Russell was asked to assess these temporary holes and recommend changes to the course in general. Commissioning this review at a cost of £25 was one of the last actions of the

Card of the 'Mawallok' course that involved three loops of the 6-hole layout. Local Rules were emphatically declared as "NONE."

chairman of the foundation committee Alex Macneil before he handed the reins over to Edwin Russell, and was seen as further proof of Macneil's lack of confidence in Oliver as a designer. Certainly the course was out of balance in terms of bogey or Standard Scratch Score (SSS), the measure by which amateur men were then rated for handicap in Victoria. Jack Dillon, writing in 'The Sporting Globe' on 5 January 1929, noted that:

> *"Recently the Committee decided to obtain the services of Mr Alex Russell, the noted golf architect, in connection with considering the best procedure to complete the links. Than Russell they could not have got a better man, and it will be with considerable interest that the recommendations of this expert will be awaited."*

Alex Russell was well-credentialed for the task. At Peninsula he recommended the creation of three new holes and alterations to a number of other holes that were implemented by the course green staff over seven years. The first was the addition of what is now the 16th South to become the new 7th hole. The tee of the original 7th became the 8th and was moved to near the members' tee on the current 17th South. The new 9th became a short hole playing slightly downhill to the reshaped 10th green. There was then a short walk to the 10th tee, the old 11th.

The original 12th and 13th holes remained unchanged but were played as the 11th and 12th. Russell liked the two temporary holes created by dividing Oliver's 14th hole. The 13th was a par four from the old 14th tee that later became the ladies tee when the members tee was constructed higher up the hill. Russell moved the temporary green to where the green of the 1st South is today. The 14th, now the 2nd South, was played from the present ladies' tee. It was a short par four which played initially to the old 14th green. These changes were the first instalment of Russell's alterations and brought 18 holes back into play.

The 'Argus' on 24 October 1929 reported that *"Recently the course was rearranged on the advice and plans of Alick Russell, and it now ranks very high among the links of the State."* A subsequent report in 'The Sporting Globe' on 26 November 1930 indicated that *"the bunkering scheme of Alex Russell"* was not yet complete.

After the untimely death of club president Sam McKay, the new president General H.W. Grimwade rearranged the priorities and pushed to complete Russell's recommendations. The dog-leg and present green were added to the 14th in 1935. A greenside bunker of the old 14th was retained and reshaped to become a fairway bunker on the new hole. The green and bunkers on the 15th were also remodelled in 1935. The other Russell change was

at the par four 4th where he had expressed his dissatisfaction at the placement of the green, as for scratch and low markers the approach shot to the green was long and blind. Work on rectifying this began in 1935 but because of poor weather the new green did not open until the summer of 1936-37. Throughout this activity, the course remained open with only the minor inconvenience of temporary greens and tees.

Portsea Golf Club *Portsea, Victoria*

Golf in Portsea began with a 9-hole course laid out by "Jock" Young on land first identified by club stalwart and then captain of the Riversdale Golf Club, A. W. Relph, back in 1923. Young was professional at Riversdale at the time, before his move to Commonwealth in 1924. The land was purchased by the Portsea Lands Company Pty Ltd that Relph and a group of his friends had established and the course opened for play to holiday golfers in December 1924.

The Portsea Golf Club was formed on 1 January 1926, leasing the course land from the company, with Relph as the inaugural captain. An additional hole, designed by Bill Meader of the Victoria Golf Club, was added early that same year, bringing the total up to ten. By September, the 2nd and 6th holes had been lengthened and at this time the course was 2,715 yards (2,486 metres) long and the bogey for the 10 holes was 40.

In December 1928, the club, at the instigation of its president A. O. Barrett, paid Reg Jupp, the Metropolitan professional where Barrett played his city golf, to review the course and he suggested some alterations. Relph and Barrett had a number of disagreements concerning the course in these early days.

Relph's son noted that every time his father arrived at the course it seemed that Barrett had changed some more holes. In early 1929, Relph engaged Alex Russell, who had undertaken bunkering and remodelling work at Riversdale, to prepare a report on expanding and improving the now 10-hole course, and to design new greens and remodel others. In June 1929, the committee had agreed to Russell's suggestions, with new greens proposed on the 1st, 7th, 8th and 9th holes, and new tees planned for the 2nd, 4th

Arthur Relph, Portsea's inaugural captain

Portsea Golf Club

Copy.

MACKENZIE & RUSSELL.

Golf Course Architects

June 10th, 1929.

The Honorary Secretary,
Portsea Golf Club.

Dear Sir,

I enclose plans of Green 1, 3, 4, 6, 8 and 9 which are
new or have considerable alterations.

Green 2 is left unaltered at present.

Green 5 should have the steep bank on the left eased off and turfed
when funds are available.

Green 7 is in a new site further on than the present green, but the
slopes are good and it only wants top-dressing heavily in
the hollows to make it more level.

The new 8th hole is short - 90 yards - but I do not think too short
It will be much cheaper to construct than a green on the
previously proposed site.

As I suggested, I will leave the suggestions for the new 12th
hole until I get the sketch of the course from the surveyor.

The plans are only sketches and should not necessarily be
adhered to exactly. The squares on the sketches are approximately
10 yard squares.

I am,

Yours sincerely,

(Sgd.) Alex. Russell.

Copy.

PORTSEA GOLF CLUB.

GENERAL.

1. All slopes to be gentle.

2. No straight embankments or straight lines
of any sort round the greens.

3. Greens to be flat and almost level within five
yards of the pin at least.

4. All the mounds shown should be sufficiently low
and broad to be cut with the mower.

5. The immediate approaches to the greens need
attention generally. The small bumps and
hollows flattened and the turf improved.

----

and 9th. His report noted that he would leave his suggestions for the 12th hole until he had received a plan of the course from the surveyor. The brief report concluded with a page of general recommendations, containing points from 1 to 5.

Two additional men were put on to assist in implementing the alterations. 'Golf' magazine noted in its 2 December 1929 issue that *"the altered lay-out, as designed by Mr Alex. Russell, has made a wonderful improvement in the links, and has added considerably to the natural attractions of the course both as a test of golf and for the enjoyment of the game."*

In May 1930, the committee had approved alterations to the 2nd, 7th, 8th 10th and 11th holes and the following month further changes were approved to the 7th, 9th and 11th, but how many

of these were Russell's proposals is unclear. By June 1930 the differences between Relph and Barrett had deepened, with Barrett having commissioned a further report on the course by Reg Jupp and in August, Barrett submitted a plan he had devised to extend the course to 15 holes. Relph was strongly opposed to extending the course past 12 holes and the committee agreed with him, with Barrett resigning in protest.

A copy of Alex Russell's two page report (above) – brief and to the point – to the Portsea Golf Club dated 10 June 1929

Portsea Golf Club

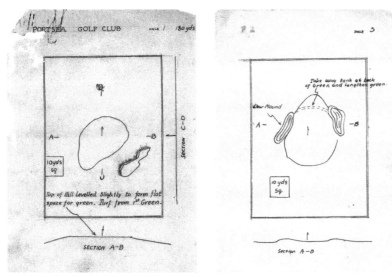

A selection of Green Plans prepared by Alex Russell for the Portsea Golf Club

Portsea Golf Club

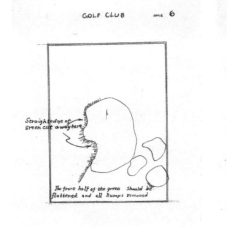

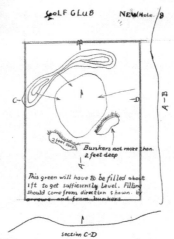

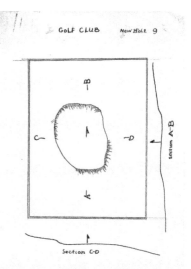

A report in 'The Sporting Globe' on 3 December 1930 suggested that *"last year Alex Russell advised on methods of bunkering the holes and the lay out is now well on the way to being one of the most popular in Victoria."* 'Golf' magazine in February 1932 reported on the Summer Meeting that had recently been held by the club on its remodelled course. At the time of writing one more new hole had been added, the one-shot 8th, with an additional hole, the new 5th, in the course of construction that would bring the total up to 12. The new 5th, a short hole of 110 yards, and sited on the hill in the centre of the course, was funded by A. O. Barrett who had once more become involved with the course. 'Golf' magazine reported:

"The Remodelled Course

The remodelling of the 7th, 8th, 9th and 10th holes carried out during the year has added much character to the general layout, and the course now provides a good test of golf to the back-marker, while those with the concession of many strokes are able to enjoy their game without spending half the time digging their way out of sand bunkers and impossible jungle. The 7th hole has been lengthened, and is now five hundred yards long, and being undulating right from tee to green, requires firm and well-placed shots in order to get the correct figures. The 8th, an entirely new hole, is an intensely interesting pitch of about one hundred and fifty yards, slightly uphill. The green is large and naturally undulating, and many experienced golfers have expressed the opinion that this hole is equal to any 3-bogey hole of its kind on metropolitan courses. The 9th hole is now played from a tee where a view of the fairway can be obtained in place of the blind drive that formerly caused many lost balls. The tee at the 10th hole is also better placed, and the approaches to the green much improved.

The object of the founders of the club was to provide pleasant golf for everybody, and, acting on the advice of Jock Young, who originally laid out the links, and Mr Alec Russell, who later advised the Committee on extensions and alterations, every possible use was made of natural hazards, which are sufficiently difficult of negotiation to reward a good shot and penalise a bad one."

The club holds a collection of Russell's green plans in their archives, six of which were reproduced in their history book. Two of these contain the annotation "New Hole" suggesting Russell was responsible for at least one of the new holes at Portsea as well as other alterations to the existing holes.

In addition to Alex Russell, a myriad of cooks had a hand in the pot at Portsea. Apart from Barrett and Reg Jupp, "Jock" Young returned in 1933, laying out a new tee and green on the 12th

hole and lengthening the 3rd. Then A.W. Jackson extended the course to 14 holes in 1947, with a final extension to 18-holes undertaken by Sloan Morpeth in 1965.

Sandringham Golf Links *Sandringham, Victoria*

There is a common myth that the second nine holes at the current Sandringham Municipal Golf Course was part of Royal Melbourne Golf Club's old Sandringham Course, but this is not the case. When the club developed the land east of the practice green to Reserve Road and extending south to Balcombe Road for new golf holes, which it had owned since 1911, it sold to the developer T.M. Burke Pty Ltd the three parcels of land that contained the first three and the last three holes of the old Sandringham course. The sale took place in 1929, with the club to retain occupancy until the date of settlement in June 1932. In the interim the club could continue to use the land for golf.

With the onset and worsening of the Depression, the Burke company found itself in some financial difficulties and was unable to take possession. In 1931, the club leased the blocks to Messrs. Watt and Aikmann who planned to use the land for a 9-hole public course. Alex Russell was engaged to create three additional holes in the three paddocks that once housed the 1st and 18th holes, the 2nd and 17th holes, and the 3rd and 16th holes of Royal Melbourne's Sandringham layout. The Argus' reported in its 6 July 1931 edition that *"six of the present holes of the Royal Melbourne club's old course, and three new holes laid out by Mr Alex Russell, all running over ideal golfing country, will be formed into a new public golf course at Sandringham. The course will be opened about the middle of the month and will provide one of the finest links of the kind in Australia. The present residential clubhouse of the Royal Melbourne club, with all its very complete appointments, will be available for persons using the course."*

The article also suggested that the Brighton Golf Club, which at the time played over the public course at Elsternwick, was considering relocating to the new Sandringham course. If the new Russell holes were to ready for play in July 1931, work on building them must have commenced several months earlier.

Newspaper advertisement (right) for the new Sandringham Golf Links from June 1932

The syndicate also took over Royal Melbourne's six grass tennis courts and made these available for hire to the public.

The 6 April 1932 edition of 'The Referee' newspaper contained a paragraph on an exhibition match held over the 9-hole course on Saturday 2 April, noting that *"four professionals entertained a large following on the old Royal Melbourne, now the Sandringham public links."* The four professionals were all local Victorians, namely Charlie Conners and Bill Fowler who took on the Thomson brothers, Hugh and Don, with the Thomson brothers appointed as the professionals at the new public links. That month, 'The Sporting Globe' reported that *"as far as excellence of playing conditions are concerned the nine-holes layout at Sandringham stands out among our metropolitan public courses, The turf there is as good as can be found anywhere in Australia. For years the holes were part of the classic Royal Melbourne course."* Green fees for the 9-hole course were an affordable 1s.6p.

WHERE TO PLAY GOLF.
IN *MELBOURNE*

Sandringham Golf Links
(Late Royal Melbourne)

AUSTRALIA'S FINEST PUBLIC COURSE

Practice Nets and every facility for Golfers

Palatial Residential Club House

Ideal for Interstate Visitors.

Full particulars from Manager, Fernhil Road, Sandringham.
'Phones: XW 1566, 2577

Newspaper advertisement for the course (above) from June 1932

Longevity of tenure, though, was something the course lacked. In October 1933, it was reported that the public golf course would be closing as the purchase by Burke of the three blocks was complete, *"and the Sandringham Golf Links subdivision will be commenced as soon as the necessary arrangements can be concluded. It is proposed to subdivide the first paddock, on which the golfhouse stands, first. This will include about 15 acres, and will be divided into about 70 allotments."* Arrangements were put in place quite quickly and Burke arranged for the sale of 73 allotments by public auction held on 2 December 1933.

Oblique aerial view of the third paddock (above) from 1940-46 showing the new Russell holes that were added. At lower right can be seen the 14th green on Royal Melbourne's West Course. The Royal Melbourne Golf Club

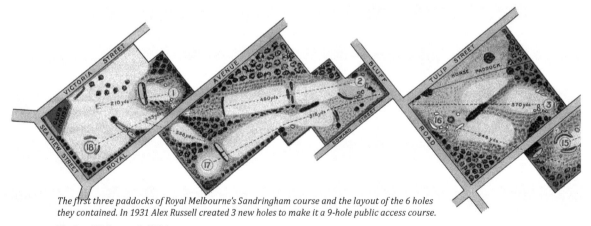

The first three paddocks of Royal Melbourne's Sandringham course and the layout of the 6 holes they contained. In 1931 Alex Russell created 3 new holes to make it a 9-hole public access course.

The Royal Melbourne Golf Club

Legend
Sandringham Public Holes post-1931 ——————— 2nd
RMGC Sandringham holes pre-1931 - - - - - - - 17

1945 Aerial Photograph
of the
Sandringham Public Golf Links
Showing its relationship to Royal Melbourne's West Course and the later Sandringham Muicipal Golf Course. The two paddocks where the holes were located correspond to the second and third paddocks of Royal Melbourne's old Sandringham Course. Holes 2 and 17 were located in the second paddock with holes 3 and 16 in the third paddock.

Layout of the Sandringham Golf Links once the first paddock – where it is understood Russell added one additional hole – had been developed for housing. The original form of the course had 9 holes, then for a period it was 12 holes, then back to 9 holes again, until all its land was developed for other uses post-war.

SANDRINGHAM GOLF LINKS.

ARE STILL AVAILABLE FOR PLAY.

12 HOLES, 1/6.

1935 advertisement for the Sandringham Golf Links (left) noting that 12 holes were now available at a cost of 1s/6d.

However, the golf course did not immediately close. Advertisements for the facility ran through 1933, 1934 and into 1935, and give some idea as to the status of the course. In late 1933, the advertisements noted *"that the Full Course is Still Available for Play and Will be Until Further Notice,"* while one from August 1934 noted that *"Although the famous old Clubhouse is to be Demolished, the Full Course will be Available to Golfers for Some Time to Come."* By 1935, these advertisements were suggesting that the course was still open, but by now it had been extended to 12 holes.

Examination of a 1945 aerial photograph of this land shows that Russell ingeniously added five new greens into the second and third paddocks, to go with the existing four greens, giving 9 holes. Perhaps for a short period after 1935, the holes on the clubhouse paddock were still available, allowing for the 12-hole course as advertised.

The second and third paddocks were eventually purchased in the late 1930s by the Sandringham Council, and remained as golf holes for some years, however, by the 1950s, with holes only remaining in the second block, this was an informal arrangement. It was here that the long-serving Royal Melbourne professional Bruce Green first started playing the game. In 1946, the Sandringham Council indicated that it wished to acquire and develop all the area between Bluff Road and Reserve Road, Tulip Street and Cheltenham Road. The scheme included housing for returned servicemen, a golf course, and other recreational facilities. This acquisition was to include all of Royal Melbourne's land north of Cheltenham Road – the land where the 13th to 16th holes of the West Course are sited.

The club entered into negotiations with the Sandringham Council and the acquisition of its land was thankfully avoided. However, with compulsory acquisition still possible at that stage, the matter was treated very seriously by the club's council, and Alex Russell urged it to purchase all the blocks of land where the practice fairway now exists. Russell drew plans for four new holes, using this and other club land as a contingency, should

The course of the Swan Hill Golf Club lay in the centre of the racetrack (right) until Russell designed a new 18-hole course on a site 3 miles out of the town

the club ever lose the holes across the road. The hospital was eventually built on land near the old Sandringham 2nd green and 17th tee, and opened in 1964. The third paddock was subdivided for returned servicemen's housing in 1947-48.

Thus there was in existence for a few years in the 1930s, a 9-hole public course that used six holes of Royal Melbourne's original Sandringham Course in the first three paddocks with three new holes added by Alex Russell. A later phase that used only the second and third paddocks was also of 9 holes, but the course in this phase contained only four original Sandringham holes with five new Russell holes. However, it is important to note that no part of the current Sandringham Municipal Course was ever part of Royal Melbourne's old Sandringham Course, nor was it part of the temporary 9-hole public course from the 1930s.

Swan Hill Golf Club *Swan Hill, Victoria*

When the club's 9-hole course on the racecourse, originally laid out by professional 'Dick' Banks from Albert Park in 1912, became too congested, a new site was found some three miles out of the town, a Mallee and Murray Pine covered sandhill. 'The Riverina Recorder' reported on 8 February 1930 that *"The Swan Hill Golf Club, since acquiring 111 acres of land on the cemetery road, have made arrangements to have the new links set out by an expert. The services of Mr Alex. Russell, golf architect, of Melbourne, have been obtained for the work. Mr Russell has recently been engaged in designing plans and lay-out of golf courses for Colac, Ballarat, Bendigo, and the new Royal Melbourne clubs. The Swan Hill Golf Club has decided to have an 18-hole course."*

The new course was opened on 22 May 1930, and in 1935 Mr Gervase Carre-Riddell built some new greens and added bunkering. The routing of the course had changed little since Russell first laid it out. However, when in 1991 a new course opened at Murray Downs Resort, the Swan Hill Golf Club moved to the new course and became Murray Valley-Swan Hill Golf

Wangaratta Golf Club *Wangaratta, Victoria*

The Wangaratta Golf Club established a 12 hole course on land about a mile (1.6 km) from the centre of the town, and around 1930 they acquired an additional 20 acres (8 ha), formerly a part of the High School farm. The 'Weekly Times' reported in March 1933 that six new holes were then laid out on this additional land, and that *"the whole course, which has an area of 90 acres was laid out under the supervision of Alex Russell."*

The 18-hole course was around 6,000 yards long (5,486 metres) and was irrigated with water from the nearby Ovens River, making it the only country course in the region to mow its fairways. 'The Sporting Globe' noted in its 24 January 1934 issue that *"The club intends to make further improvements to the links, in the lay-out of which they have been advised by Mr Alex. Russell."* In 1936, the course was described as having *"grass greens, fairways in good condition."*

Warrandyte Golf Club *Warrandyte, Victoria*

An article in the Melbourne weekly magazine 'Table Talk' by its golf writer A. W. Jackson, the former Victorian Amateur Champion, on 13 October 1927, discussed Dr MacKenzie and his new partner Alex Russell. Jackson wrote that *"Russell has overseas experience in the matter of golf course construction to support his ability of knowing what should be done on a golf course from an eminent player's point of view. These days Russell is kept busy making and re-designing golf courses. Those in hand include Yarra Yarra, Colac, Narrandera and Warrandyte. He has also had a call from West Australia."* No detail has been found as to what work Russell may have done at Warrandyte. The course was closed in 1981.

Women's Golf Club *Melbourne, Victoria*

In October 1927, Mrs Newton Lees, the president of the Victorian Ladies' Golf Union and the 1924 Australian Ladies' Amateur champion, called a public meeting to be held on 10 October for women interested in forming a golf club in Melbourne exclusively for women. At her own expense she had secured options on around 100 acres of land in the Melbourne sand-belt at Cheltenham for the purposes of establishing a new course. The cost of the land alone was given as being over £8000.

An article in 'The Sporting Globe' on 12 October 1927 indicated that the land had been *"pronounced by men like Alex Russell, M. A. Morcom and Ivo Whitton to be ideally suited for golfing purposes,"* and the proposal was well supported by the 100 women who attended the meeting, with over 40 lady golfers prepared to commit £100 each for foundation membership. A committee was formed of prominent women golfers, including Mrs Nellie Gatehouse, the sister of Mrs Lees, and Miss Mona MacLeod.

This committee met on 24 October, and a report in 'The Age' noted that, *"There has been the possibility of securing land at Cheltenham at most advantageous rates, and it was thought that could the money be raised the proposition would prove a commercial success. Although £5000 had been promised, it was thought that the proposition was too large to be undertaken at present, especially as the option for the land expired on 1st November, and the meeting decided that the proposal should be abandoned."* Sadly, the prospect of another Russell and Morcom new course in the Melbourne sandbelt was extinguished.

The sisters Mrs Newton Lees and Mrs Austin Gatehouse (below centre, and right) were the two main proponents behind the Women's Golf Club

Mr Alex Russell.

MRS NEWTON LEES, GEELONG
National Champion Woman Golfer of Australia

MRS A. GATEHOUSE (Royal Melbourne),
Holder of the Championship Title.

WESTERN AUSTRALIA

Cottesloe Golf Club *Perth, Western Australia*

The Cottesloe Golf Club was established in 1908 and made their home at Cottesloe Beach with a course of 9-holes known as the 'Sea Links' that was co-designed by Peter Corsar Anderson, Alex Russell's first schoolmaster and the 1893 British Amateur Champion. In 1904 P.C. Anderson was appointed the Headmaster of Scotch College in Perth and he was to play a major role in the formation of the Cottesloe Golf Club. His habit of taking pupils on walks, swinging a club as he went, has been mentioned earlier, and he continued this habit at Scotch. As a result, a significant number of the members of the new club were Scotch College old boys. Anderson was also involved in the design of the first 9-holes of the (Royal) Fremantle Golf Club.

By 1924, the inadequacies of the 9-hole course were apparent and in 1928 the club purchased land at its current location at Swanbourne. A new course was designed by the club's recently appointed Scottish professional David Anderson, with input from two members, Tom Stevenson and Bill Rees, and opened in the middle of 1931. However, there was a good deal of dissatisfaction with the course, both from members and the golfing press, notably due to the straightaway holes that went up and over the dunes, resulting in many of the holes having blind tee shots and approach shots to the greens.

A minute from the new course committee back in December 1927 had referred to a possible visit from *"Mr Russell, Golf Architect"* and it is quite likely that Alex Russell first saw the proposed land for the new course at Swanbourne on his first visit to Perth in early 1928. Again, Russell's friend Keith Barker, was probably instrumental in arranging the visit. However, it appears that Anderson's designs were well advanced and the club did not pursue an involvement by Russell until after the new course was open. In September 1932, the club wrote to Lake Karrinyup hoping to obtain the services of Russell *"towards the end of the year."*

In the end this took over a year to arrange, with Alex asked for his advice on the Cottesloe course when he was in Perth in November 1933 inspecting the progress of his course at Lake Karrinyup. Russell pointed out that a few blind shots were common in Scotland but the number at this course was far too excessive. Russell's brief was modest, and he proposed a few minor alterations that made little difference to the major structural problems that could only be resolved by a significant re-design. He did though propose the possible acquisition of additional land on the northern boundary.

Cottesloe's special committee maintained contact with Russell over the next few years, and in October 1935 work was reported

Keith Barker (left) assisted in arranging Russell to visit the Swinbourne course of the Cottesloe Golf Club in 1928

as having just commenced by 'The West Australian' newspaper on 25th October on *"a comprehensive bunkering scheme and alterations to the location of certain tees in accordance with the recommendations of Mr Alec Russell, who visited and reported on the course about two years ago. It is also anticipated that the major scheme which entails fairly extensive alterations to certain holes, and the creation of several new ones will in all probability be on the way to completion during the coming summer."*

Under this new scheme, the entire layout was to be changed, with the holes now to run between the dunes rather than over them. This would also make playing the course far less tiring and considerably quicker. Alternative routes of play for many holes were provided by Russell in his suggestions. Russell provided sketch plans for all the greens but sadly these have not survived. The report in 'The West Australian' laid out the details of the scheme, which can be summarised as follows:

- Relocation of the tees on the 4th, 6th, 14th and 16th holes to eliminate blind tee shots.
- Bunkering to the 5th, 7th, 8th, 09th, 11th, 12th, 13th, 15th, 17th and 18th holes calling for improved accuracy and judgement.
- New tee and remodelled green to the 2nd hole.
- Remodelled green to the 5th hole.
- New greens to the 6th, 9th and 13th holes, with lengthening of the 13th.
- Lengthening of the 18th, and eliminating blindness on these holes.
- An entirely new 1st hole of the dog-leg type *"of about 330 yards with the fairway heavily bunkered and green well guarded."*
- Existing 1st hole to be used as a practice ground.
- 3rd to be a new one shot hole of 140 yards.
- Existing 10th is to be scrapped and replaced by a new 13th hole of 130 yards.
- Present 13th extended to 400 yards.
- 17th extended to 460 yards and fairway and green bunkered.
- 18th straightened out and lengthened to 415 yards.

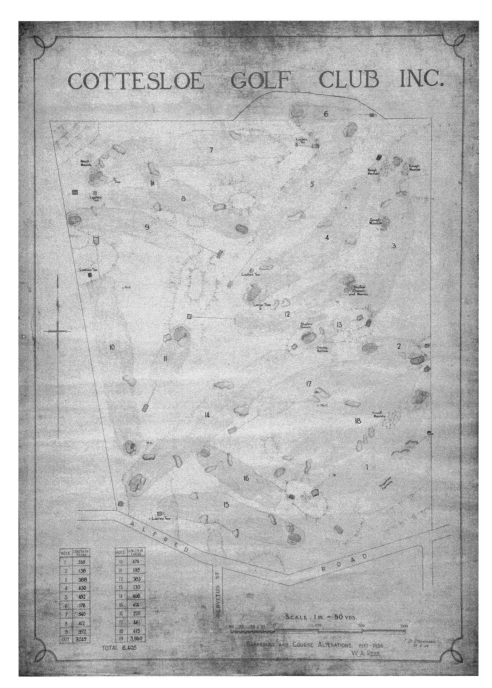

Plan of the course alterations proposed by Alex Russell in 1935-36 and drawn up by Cottesloe member Bill Rees

"There is not the slightest doubt that the course, when completed, will be a very attractive lay-out....It will possess a course completely free of blind tee shots and will only have one hole where the green is not entirely visible at a distance of 150 yards and under."

The works were implemented over a period of years, commencing with only those holes that required rebunkering, and the course remained in play throughout the remodelling. A plan of Russell's layout was drawn by a club member Bill Rees, probably using Russell's various sketches as a guide and is today displayed in the clubhouse. In April 1938, the club moved to formally play over Russell's redeveloped course, and on 30 June 1938 the 'Western Mail' newspaper reported:

"Last Sunday was the first occasion on which many of the professionals had played over the new Cottesloe lay-out, and like all golfers who have played the course this year, were loud in their praise of the altered course. Now, with the Cottesloe bogey reduced from 75 to 73, the course has not only become a very pleasant lay-out, but a rigid test of golf. With the introduction of the new bogey, there are no holes at Cottesloe where the ordinary golfer can hope to win strokes back from bogey."

Between 1959 and 1960, alterations were made to the layout so that there could be two loops of nine instead of Russell's 18-hole loop. Recent significant course alterations have meant that little of Russell's design remains, however, most of his original routing is still used. Judging from Cottesloe's history book there is still significant appreciation at the club of Alex Russell's contribution to the development of its course.

The Western Australian Golf Club (Mt Yokine) *Perth, Western Australia*

While he was in Perth commencing his design work for Lake Karrinyup in 1928, Alex Russell was also approached by the newly formed Western Australian Golf Club to modify and bunker their 18-hole course at Mt Yokine. The course was in the process of being laid out by Eustace Cohen, a founding member and local architect, who began to specialise in golf course design later in his career. Once more, the approach to Russell most likely came from Keith Barker, a foundation committeeman of both Lake Karrinyup and WAGC, with whom Russell had walked many miles around the site for the Karrinyup course in the heat of summer and had grown to know him well.

'Golf' magazine reported in their 1 October 1928 issue that, *"the layout... has since been approved and improved by Messrs. MacKenzie and Russell, the golf course experts"*, and later referred to, *"...the excellent scheme of bunkering by Messrs. MacKenzie and Russell."* The report also noted that the new course had sixty bunkers *"well and skilfully placed."* Russell's contribution to the WAGC course is not widely known.

An article in 'The West Australian' in May 1928 suggested that *"after the various fairways had been planned and staked out, the well-known golf architect, Mr Alex. Russell, of Melbourne, inspected the links and suggested alterations which have been carried out..... The fairways are now all roughly cleared to the width of 66ft. That was done originally so that they could be altered according to future requirements or experts advice. According to Mr Russell 50 feet is a wide fairway and 40 feet a narrow one."* The report also included an extract from Russell's report to the club:

"With regard to the general possibilities of your land, I feel sure that no difficulty will be experienced in constructing a very satisfactory course upon it. There is an excellent situation, overlooking Perth, the length of the course is ample, and there is no doubt that those responsible for the general layout expended considerable time and thought upon it, with the result that there will be many interesting holes, a great variety of shots, and few blind holes."

Grassing of the new course was expected to begin in August of that year, with the work supervised by Cohen's firm Eales, Cohen and Bennett, who also designed the clubhouse. The new course was open the following year. While the club's history book does not name Alex Russell as the designer of their course in the late 1920s, the article in 'Golf' magazine and

Eustace Cohen and Keith Barker, pictured at Lake Karrinyup together (far left), and Eustace Cohen, (left) building architect, golf course architect and the original designer of the Mt Yokine course

various newspaper articles make it quite clear that the firm of MacKenzie and Russell were involved with improvements and bunkering to the course. On comparing the yardages of the holes in the magazine article with yardages given for the 1952 layout in the club's history, the sequence appears to be the same, except that most of the holes are slightly longer. Russell may well have left space for these extensions, considering he had told Lake Karrinyup that the tee positions should not be finalised until the course had been in play for a while. The first hole at Mt Yokine is a one-shot hole designed to get the field moving, a common Russell opening strategy.

View showing No. 2, 8, 17 and 18 Fairways.

Site for No. 1 Fairway, Green and Practice Fairway, before clearing.

The holes summarised are (with par figures on distances):—

1st—	182 yards, par 3		10th—	357 yards, par 4
2nd—	393 yards, par 4		11th—	170 yards, par 3
3rd—	325 yards, par 4		12th—	283 yards, par 4
4th—	343 yards, par 4		13th—	352 yards, par 4
5th—	319 yards, par 4		14th—	367 yards, par 4
6th—	528 yards, par 5		15th—	312 yards, par 4
7th—	422 yards, par 4		16th—	132 yards, par 3
8th—	500 yards, par 5		17th—	464 yards, par 5
9th—	191 yards, par 3		18th—	478 yards, par 5

Out—3203 yards, par 36.   In—2915 yards, par 36

Total—6118 yards, par 72.

The course, generally, is very intresting, and calls for a great variety of shots. It is hard to offer choice of selection without having played over the links several times, but the fourth, sixth, eighth, eleventh and sixteenth holes are the ones which stay in your mind as a memory of Mount Yokine, and with the excellent scheme of bunkering by Messrs MacKenzie and Russell, I am inclined to think most talk at the "19th" will be about the 11th and 16th holes.

There are sixty bunkers in all, well and skilfully placed. The course is being thoroughly grassed by modern methods, and no money or trouble is being spared to make the links an up-to-date championship course. I can forsee much pleasure for members and visitors to these links. The promotors are to be congratulated on the success of their efforts to produce a course planned on modern lines.

The new Western Australian Golf Club's course at Mt Yokine featured in a three-page spread in the 1 October 1928 issue of 'Golf' magazine.

It included three views of the course under construction, as well as a card of the holes. It also noted the "excellent scheme of bunkering by Messrs MacKenzie and Russell" and that the new course had 60 bunkers that were "well and skilfully placed."

Site for No. 1 Fairway, Green and Practice Fairway, after clearing.

Albury Golf Club *Albury, New South Wales*

The Albury Golf Club was established in 1899 with a course on Albury Common and in 1906 some 106 acres (43 ha) of undulating land was secured at its present location to the north of the town. Shortly after this, the course was extended to 18-holes. A report in the 'Sydney Morning Herald' on 3 September 1929 was headlined *"Renovations at Albury"* and described the planned alterations to the course:

> *"Arrangements have been made by the Committee of the Albury Golf Club to secure the services of A. Russell, golf architect, of Royal Melbourne, to visit Albury on September 14 with the view to securing a new plan of the course, also a system of bunkering and putting down new greens and lengthening the course to the full professional course. When the work has been done Albury will have a course which will compare more than favourably with some of the metropolitan courses."*

In June 1931, the 'Wagga Wagga Express' reported on the upcoming Riverina Championships that were to be held at the Albury course the next month and noted that much work on improving the greens and fairways was underway:

> *"The links total 6,127 yards, with a par of 72, and difficult scratch score of 75..... The most striking feature of the course, which last year was re-laid by Mr Alex. Russell, the well known Melbourne professional (here the report is in error), is the good distance of every hole. They are not hard when the proper distance shots are played, but a weak tee shot, or through the green, pays the penalty, for the player then has to do something phenomenal to recover, or put up with the extra stroke. The short holes – there are six of them – all have interesting and contrasting features.....The first and tenth tees are now near the clubhouse, and allow for two starting points. The links are in ideal surroundings with an abundance of natural bunkers, whilst the undulations have been utilised to the best advantage. The turf provides good fairways where any club can be used according to the distance desired whilst the greens are both interesting and pleasing, and reflect the vast amount of work that has been done on them this season. The Albury Golf Club has every reason to feel proud of their links."*

The Australian Golf Club Sydney, New South Wales

After leaving earlier homes at Moore Park, Queen's Park and Botany for a permanent location at Kensington in 1905, the Australian Golf Club availed itself of the services of Dr Alister MacKenzie in December 1926 to inspect their course and advise upon improvements, which according to the club's 1927 annual report, were not considered drastic. The cost of undertaking MacKenzie's proposals, including his fee, was only just over £500.

By the late 1930s there was a general feeling that the course needed lengthening and that there were too many drive and pitch holes, with some work on tightening the course occurring in the lead-up to the 1937 Australian Championship meeting held at Kensington. Alex Russell visited the course in May 1939 at the club's request to prepare a remodelling plan. According to a later report, *"Russell pointed out that the short course, in the centre of the playing area, possessed natural features for an ideal course."*

Russell presented the committee with his plan and they were initially disappointed with his proposals for five short holes and Russell subsequently agreed for the 6th hole to be extended to a 340 yard (311 metre) dogleg two-shot hole to eliminate this issue. In July 1939, a special meeting of members was held that approved Russell's remodelling plan, however, due to the onset of World War II, the plans were deferred. It is not known if any of Russell's proposals were implemented after the end of the war.

Russell was quoted during his visit to Sydney by Hector Morrison, writing in the Sydney 'Telegraph' in May 1939, as suggesting that sand bunkers might become obsolete, a report that was picked up by a number of other newspapers across the country.

Narrandera Golf Club *Narrandera, New South Wales*

The club was formed in 1905 and played on a 9-hole course close to the town. In July 1912, a new 9-hole course was laid out south of the town near the Murrumbidgee River, on an area known as Brewery Flat. After several floods, the club decided to move during World War I, to a new 9-hole course located on Narrandera Racecourse. Some years later, the committee could see the limitations imposed by having their golf links on the racecourse and put a proposal to members that the club should acquire its own property.

In 1927, a new company, the Narrandera Golf Club Limited, was formed to purchase the nearby Powell's paddocks alongside the racecourse. Initially the racecourse holes were retained and nine new holes laid out on the closest paddock, until a further nine were laid out in the far paddock and the club could play its new 18-hole course in 1928.

An article in the Melbourne weekly magazine 'Table Talk' by its golf writer A. W. Jackson, the former Victorian Amateur Champion, on 13 October 1927, discussed Dr MacKenzie and his new partner Alex Russell. Jackson wrote that *"Russell has overseas experience in the matter of golf course construction to support his ability of knowing what should be done on a golf course from an eminent player's point of view. These days Russell is kept busy making and re-designing golf courses. Those in hand include Yarra Yarra, Colac, Narrandera and Warrandyte. He has also a call from West Australia."*

New South Wales Golf Club *Sydney, New South Wales*

The New South Wales Golf Club at La Perouse had Dr MacKenzie design its new course in 1926 and they called his partner Alex Russell to Sydney in 1931 to inspect the completed course, only lightly bunkered, and critique the existing bunkering plan. This Russell did, and he also is known to have made suggestions for remodelling some of the greens, while on others he suggested locations for new greens, generally beyond the current green locations. It would appear that he did not prepare a report, as the committee meeting minutes include detailed notes from one of the committee members who went around the course with Russell on the day of his visit. Some selected extracts include:

> *"The First: A splendid hole, as is every one of our short holes, comparable with anything he had seen.*
>
> *The Fifth: Splendid hole. The gully to the left would be improved by the forming of grassy hollows.*

The spectacular site at La Perouse of the New South Wales Golf Club's course (above), modified by Eric Apperly in 1935-37. Little was done to the course following Russell's 1931 visit.

> *The Seventh: Does not like this hole at all, and considers it unwise to spend money on improving the green. Suggests bringing tee forward to the ladies tee, making the green to the 8th fairway with bunkers on either side of it, and with an opening of 10 yards by 30 yards.*
>
> *The Twelfth: Does not consider the existing green can be made much good. When funds permit, would recommend scooping out behind, and making open green larger.*
>
> *The Thirteenth: Considers the formation about 60 yards through existing green, ideal for new green. Terracing up from existing green to proposed green. The 14th tee would then be carried back, making it imperative to play two shots to open up hole.*
>
> *The Eighteenth: Leave existing green, flatten out on right and terrace down, making large green up to an including portion of rough, leaving it open at the rear with bunkers in front.*
>
> *Bunkers: Wherever giving trouble with regard to blowing out, allow them to be grassy hollows, and at the 14th, the bunker on the left to be filled in and made a grassy mound, or to be doubled in width and made a grassy hollow. The 9th bunker, he would take out to where previously filled, and make a grassy hollow."*

It would appear that few, if any, of Russell's recommendations were taken up by the club, and within a few years much of the course was significantly modified by Sydney architect and golf architect Eric Apperley from 1935 to 1937.

HEARTY CONGRATULATIONS were showered on Alex. Russell after winning the open golf championship of Australia at Royal Melbourne yesterday. E. L. Apperly (right) is seen adding his.

Alex Russell and Eric Apperly were fierce competitors on the course and good friends off it. In this newspaper clipping (above), Apperly offers his congratulations to Russell after his 1924 Australian Open victory

AUSTRALIAN CAPITAL TERRITORY

Red Hill Golf Links *Canberra, ACT*

Alex Russell's golf design activities eventually took him outside Victoria to other Australian cities, and the first of these trips was to Canberra, the new Australian capital, in September 1927. 'The Argus' wrote of Russell's trip in its 27th September 1927 issue and noted that:

> *"With the arrival of each new party of public servants the membership of the golf club has increased until the existing nine-hole course has become inadequate to meet the demands placed upon it. It is beautifully situated at the rear of the Hotel Canberra, but the club has been forced to consider the advisability of moving to another site, where an 18-hole course can be established. The former Victorian open champion, Mr Alex Russell, is at present in Canberra at the invitation of the club and the commission to report upon the new links and to make suggestions for their lay out. It is proposed to retain the present links for visitors and to transfer permanent residents to the new site."*

'The Argus' followed up with a subsequent report on 20 October that indicated that the preferred site was to be at Red Hill:

> *"Work has been begun on the new permanent golf course at Canberra. The site, which was selected on the recommendation of Mr A. Russell, former open champion of Victoria, who has been entrusted with the task of laying out the course, is at the rear of Red Hill, and for the present only nine holes will be provided. Eventually, however, an additional nine holes will be laid down."*

Similar reports appeared in the 'Australasian,' the 'Canberra Times' and 'The Age' newspapers, while a report in 'Golf' magazine in its 1 November 1927 edition stated that:

> *"Alex. Russell is becoming more engrossed every day in his new-found business of golf course architecture. He recently paid a visit to Canberra to see how things were progressing in the golfing line up there. Evidently he wants to make sure that his friend the Prime Minister, Mr Bruce, is provided with a decent class of links on which to take his recreation, now restricted almost exclusively to the Royal and Ancient Game."*

It would seem very likely that Russell's good friend, Prime Minister Stanley Bruce, for whom Russell served as Private Secretary in 1923, had arranged for Russell to be appointed as the golf course architect for this new project. As it was a government undertaking under the auspices of the Federal Capital Commission, the paperwork for it still resides in the National Archives in Canberra, providing a detailed and fascinating account of the project and Russell's role.

Russell first visited Canberra in September 1927 to inspect three sites at Majura, Western Creek and Red Hill in the company of the Commission's Surveyor and John Irving, the greenkeeper at the existing Canberra course near the Hotel Canberra. In a three-page letter on MacKenzie & Russell letterhead dated 29 September, Russell considered that *"the best available area appears to be just south of Red Hill, and although the soil conditions are not ideal a course here would be protected from westerly winds to some extent, would have water mains close to it and would command good scenery."*

He suggested that it would be an expensive and lengthy task to construct a good course on this site, primarily due to the difficulties in establishing a turf on the *"rather clayey"* soil to withstand the severe frosts and hot summers of the Canberra climate. Russell stated that it would be difficult to estimate the cost of construction accurately, but that for a sum of between £4,500 and £5,500, exclusive of the water supply costs, a good course could be built. He felt that it would take at least two years to build *"and probably longer, for the fairways to become fit for play."* He noted that there was turf of a fair quality on about half of the site at the time and he believed that the first nine holes could be laid out over this area. These holes could possibly be ready for play during the following winter. He noted that if the Commission decided to proceed, he could return to Canberra in *"about three weeks time and peg out the necessary fairways; these can then be topdressed and manured and possibly sown in early autumn."*

Russell returned to Canberra in October and went over the land in detail with Irving, who Russell understood would be overseeing the construction work on the new course. He wrote on 24 October 1927 that he had left Irving with, *"a plan of the course and detailed sketches of each of the nine greens and their hazards."* He explained to Irving *"exactly what should be done, and I am quite confident that he will be able to carry out the work in accordance with my wishes."* Russell suggested that Irving be allowed to come to Melbourne and *"inspect some of the work done on recent courses here; as a better idea of the type of bunkers and greens can be obtained in that way."* He enclosed his suggestions as to the best sequence of works, grass types and best times for sowing, and also told Irving *"to let me know when the greens and hazards are formed so that I may personally put any finishing touches on them that may be required."*

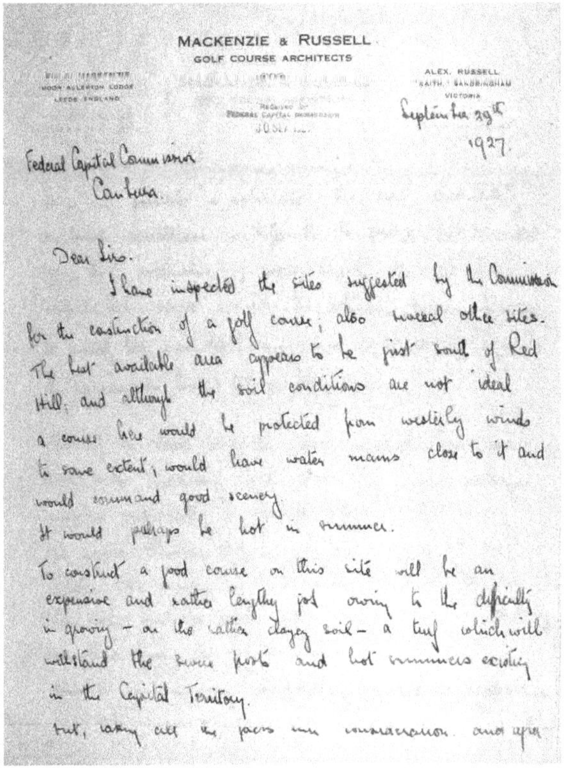

MACKENZIE & RUSSELL
GOLF COURSE ARCHITECTS

DR. A. MACKENZIE, MOOR ALLERTON LODGE, LEEDS, ENGLAND

ALEX. RUSSELL, "RAITH," SANDRINGHAM, VICTORIA

September 29th 1927.

Federal Capital Commission
Canberra.

Dear Sirs.

I have inspected the sites suggested by the Commission for the construction of a golf course; also several other sites.
The best available area appears to be just south of Red Hill; and although the soil conditions are not ideal a course here would be protected from westerly winds to some extent, would have water mains close to it and would command good scenery.
It would perhaps be hot in summer.
To construct a good course on this site will be an expensive and rather lengthy job owing to the difficulty in growing – on the rather clayey soil – a turf which will withstand the severe frosts and hot summers existing in the Capital Territory.
but, taking all the facts into consideration and after

MACKENZIE & RUSSELL
GOLF COURSE ARCHITECTS

DR. A. MACKENZIE, MOOR ALLERTON LODGE, LEEDS, ENGLAND

ALEX. RUSSELL, "RAITH," SANDRINGHAM, VICTORIA

2.

It is not possible to estimate the cost accurately as local conditions are difficult to judge; but I would say, that, exclusive of water supply, the cost of an eighteen hole course would be between £4500 & £5500.
It would take at least two years, and probably longer, for the fairways to become fit for play.

The turf on about half the area is quite fair now; and with topdressing and manuring would perhaps improve sufficiently to permit play.
It would therefore appear possible to lay out an eighteen hole course so that nine holes would use this area; and to make these nine holes fit for play sometime during the next winter.
This is not a very satisfactory method of construction but, taking all the facts into consideration and after

MACKENZIE & RUSSELL
GOLF COURSE ARCHITECTS

DR. A. MACKENZIE, MOOR ALLERTON LODGE, LEEDS, ENGLAND

ALEX. RUSSELL, "RAITH," SANDRINGHAM, VICTORIA

3.

further reflection, I think that this is probably the best way out of the difficulty.
If the Commission decides to go on in this matter I can return to Canberra in about three weeks time and peg out the necessary fairways; these can then be topdressed and manured and possibly sown in early autumn.

I am
Yours truly
Alex Russell

Russell's inspection report on the Red Hill site of 29 September 1927

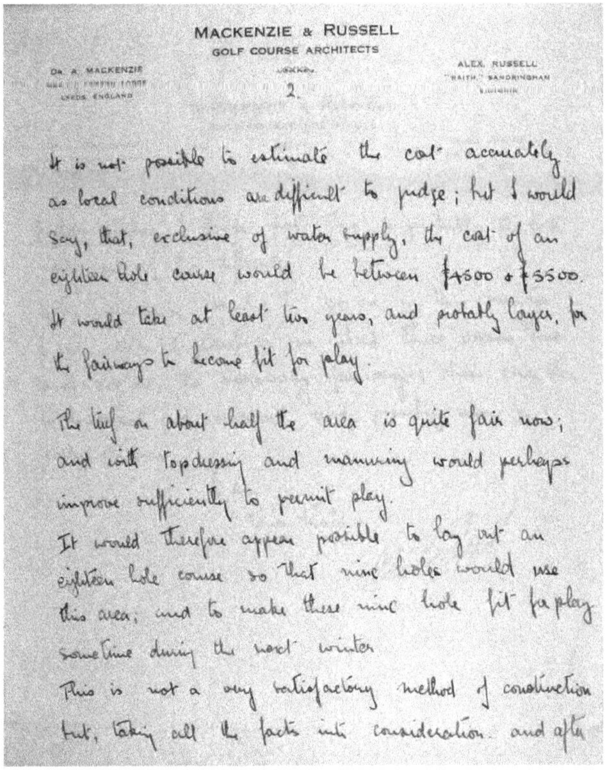

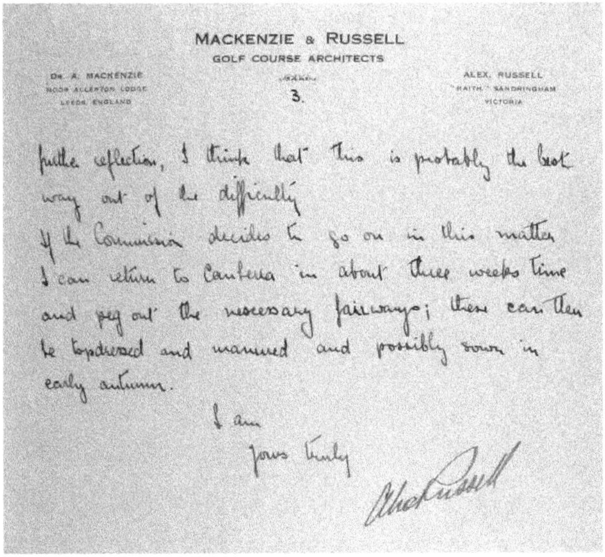

Discovering Alex Russell

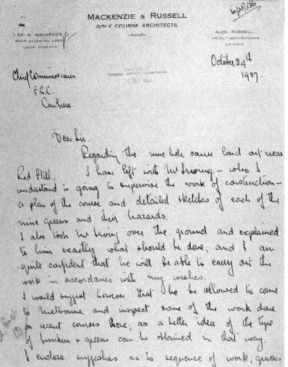

Russell's letter and suggested sequence of work of 24 October 1927

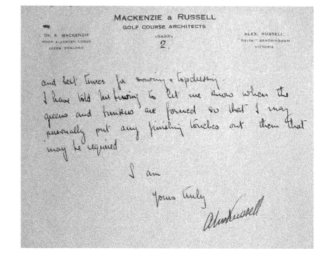

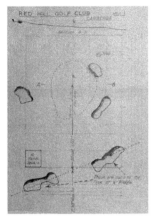
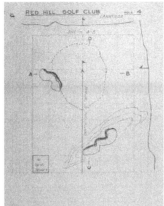
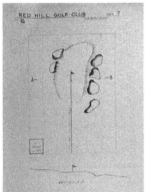

Green plans for the new Red Hill course drawn by Russell, together with two MacKenzie & Russell invoices

The Commission's engineers were then tasked in November 1927 to prepare estimates of cost for the construction of an access road, the provision of services and the clearing and construction of greens, tees and fairways. Based on Russell's plans and sequence of works, Irving estimated the construction of the nine holes would cost some £2,500 and a requisition form for this amount was lodged with the Commissioner. Interestingly, Irving's estimate noted that there were five fairway bunkers shown on Russell's detailed plan of the holes.

The Commission's Superintendent of Parks & Gardens, Mr Alex Bruce, expressed concern in a memorandum to the Acting Chief Engineer dated 30th November 1927 that *"it was apparent that a very considerable slaughter of fine trees"* was about to take place, especially on the fairways of holes 1 and 9, and suggested that these holes be re-routed. In January 1928, Irving and Bruce came to Melbourne and inspected a number of the most recent courses at Russell's suggestion, including Victoria, Commonwealth, Metropolitan and Kingston Heath. Russell then personally showed the two men around Yarra Yarra on 12 January, which was then under construction.

Russell again visited Canberra in April 1928 and on 1 May 1928 he submitted a MacKenzie & Russell invoice for £20 Preliminary Fee and £20/6/0 for train and hotel expenses, and this was paid by cheque at the end of June. Then in March 1929 Russell, claimed his full fee of £150 for laying out the nine holes, being 5% of the estimated cost of construction. This caused no end of consternation amongst the Canberra bureaucrats as they could find no record of any written agreement between the Commission and the firm of MacKenzie & Russell. It was eventually paid, even though the course was not constructed, but for the wrong amount of £160 and the Commission's accountant wrote to Russell firstly in June and then again in August and September requesting that he send them back a cheque for £10. Russell eventually returned a cheque and tersely expressed his displeasure at their incompetence by writing on the letter, *"Please note that you took over 12 months to pay this account and then paid it wrong. AR."*

The course at Red Hill which Alex Russell designed was never built. However, the site did eventually become a golf course in 1947, when the first nine holes of the Federal Golf Club were built over the same land to a design by the professional James H. Scott of Elanora, also a noted golf course architect.

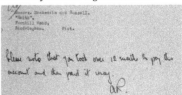

Russell's terse handwritten note back to the bureaucrats

SOUTH AUSTRALIA

Glenelg Golf Club *Adelaide, South Australia*

Alex Russell came to Adelaide in 1929, ostensibly to play in the Australian Amateur at Seaton where he lost in the quarter-finals, but also to inspect the new course of the fledgling Glenelg Golf Club. For a fee of £25, Russell visted the Glenelg course, sited on Adelaide's coastal sandbelt, on the afternoon of 29 August, after having played a four-ball exhibition game with Ivo Whitton there in the morning. He forwarded his report in September, and although it has since been lost, later press reports indicated that *"he pronounced the country perfect from a golfing point of view and as sporting a course as he had seen. He recommended early adoption of the alterations contemplated when the drift sandhills had been conquered."* Club minutes record that Russell had recommended that a lease on additional land be obtained, with the option of purchasing at a later date, for the further extension of the course as suggested in his report. This additional land was not obtained and Russell's scheme at Glenelg sadly never eventuated.

MINUTES OF A GREENS SUB-COMMITTEE MEETING HELD ON THE
COURSE AT 11 A.M. ON WEDNESDAY, 6TH JUNE, 1951.   85

- - - - - - - - - -

PRESENT: Ian McLachlan (Chair), C.T. Hargrave, D.K. McKenzie,
and the Secretary, J.H. Thyer.

The President (T.S. Cheadle) and Vice President (C.L. Winser) were
in attendance.

APOLOGY: W.R. Chambers.

The Chairman read a letter conveying recommendations from Alex
Russell after his visit to the course and referred to previous
recommendations by Alex Russell and the McKenzie reports.
Greens were then visited.

No. 5.-   The advantages of moving the green bodily towards the
railway line were analysed.

It was finally decided to prepare a temporary green in front, then
to lift the green about three feet with sand and re-turf; work
is to be done in the Spring if possible.

No. 8.-   It was decided to build a mound about three feet high
on the left of the green closing the opening to 16 yards; a
bunker to be built into the mound on the outside and facing
towards 19th Fairway.

Crater (No. 11).-   Entrance to be closed by building a shallow
bunker on the left, the spoil to be used to bring the shoulder
of the knoll on the left out and to the green.

A shallow bunker to be constructed on the right of the green and
beyond the present NO THOROUGHFARE mounds.

No. 15.-   The bunker on the left to be raised at back about two
feet to show up, point to be extended six feet towards fairway,
and near edge lowered.

Bunkers at back of green to be made grassy hollows with green
sloping gently into them.

GENERAL.

It was agreed that these works should be carried out as and when
the present programme permitted, but that each item be supervised
by a member of the Greens Committee.

Royal Adelaide Golf Club *Adelaide, South Australia*

Russell, as Dr MacKenzie's Australian partner, also visited the Royal Adelaide course at Seaton a number of times in his professional capacity, the club having records of inspection visits by him in 1929 and 1951. Minutes of the committee meeting on 20 September 1929 noted that the firm of MacKenzie & Russell had submitted a report for suggested alterations to the course, including rough sketches for alterations to some of the new greens. It is likely that this inspection had taken place at the same time in late August 1929 as the Glenelg inspection, following the Amateur Championship at Seaton. If so, Russell was well positioned to pass comment on the course having just played over it competitively.

An article written by Jack Dillon, the golf writer for Melbourne's 'Sporting Globe' newspaper, was printed in 'The Advertiser' in Adelaide on 7 September 1929 and was quite critical of the remodelling of the Seaton course that had been undertaken in accordance with MacKenzie's plans. At the end of Dillon's article, 'The Advertiser' published this paragraph:

> *"It is only fair to say that Mr Alex Russell, who is partner to Dr McKenzie (sic), expressed views diverging from those of Mr Dillon as regards the "lack of imagination" shown in carrying out Dr McKenzie's recommendations with regard to the Royal Adelaide course. He has supplied the club with a report on the course, and, although this is not yet public, the opinions he expressed prior to leaving Adelaide were entirely in favour of the manner in which the scheme had been carried out up to date and such alterations as he had suggested the club Committee already had in view, but had not had time to put in force before the open meeting. The executive of the club, moreover, has every confidence in Reeves, the head greenkeeper, and his ability to interpret the McKenzie plan as well as anybody anywhere."*

After a long hiatus, Russell was again invited to inspect Seaton, visiting on 24 May 1951, and he made *"certain suggestions which he had promised to forward in writing."* By June he had submitted his report that addressed a number of modifications to existing greens and bunkers, and it appears that most of these were carried out. In 1956, the club honoured Alex Russell with Honorary Life Membership for his services to the game.

Minutes of the Greens Sub-committee of the Royal Adelaide Golf Club for 6th June 1951 (left), noting Alex Russell's visit and his recommendations

RUSSELL THE GARDEN DESIGNER

A little-known aspect of Alex Russell's design activities included garden design. At 'Mawallok', the Russells had further developed the beautiful garden originally designed, in part, by William Guilfoyle and Alex had laid out a 6-hole golf course around 1935. Prime Minister Stanley Bruce had a £20,000 Spanish Mission style mansion built for him in 1926-27 on a 400 acre (162 ha) land parcel in Frankston, south of Melbourne. The estate was known as 'Pine Hill' and featured a stile that gave Bruce convenient access to the neighbouring Frankston Golf Club.

Around 1928, Alex carried out the design of a splendid garden for Bruce, his friend and mentor. Bruce, like Russell, came from a wealthy, influential and conservative Victorian family and both men shared similar interests in the military, classical music, Roman history – and of course golf. Russell carried out

the task with his usual brilliance and precision, and from all accounts, the 'Pine Hill' garden became known as one of the finest in Victoria. Russell had been influenced by the great gardens of England, in particular those of the Royal Botanic Gardens at Kew. It is understandable then that he designed an 'English Country Garden' for Bruce, who was an Anglophile of the first order.

WHEN THE PRIME MINISTER— —GOES TO THE COUNTRY

Prime Minister Stanley Bruce (top right)

Feature article on Bruce's new Frankston residence 'Pinehill' in 'The Home' magazine of 2 April 1929 (above)

*Evening shadows highlight the dramatic contours
around the par three 5th green at Russell's
Paraparaumu Beach course in New Zealand*

Chapter 14

GOLF DESIGN PHILOSOPHY

General Philosophy

Perhaps one of the greatest things about the two Royal Melbourne courses is that each of the 36 holes are completely different strategically, no two greens are the same, and all holes are playable by a wide variety of players, with all enjoying their game. This is something both Dr Alister MacKenzie and Alex Russell aimed for, and achieved, in their other courses. However, there is a marked continuity between the two RMGC courses. There is no sense that "these are MacKenzie holes" or "these are Russell holes," again no doubt due to the commonality of the design and construction partnership of Russell and Morcom.

Despite enjoyment for the players being paramount to MacKenzie and Russell, both Royal Melbourne courses have the capacity to distinguish between the very good, the good, the average, and those of varying lesser ability, and not just between the very good and the good, with the rest being unimportant and left to cope as best they can, using a "that's what a handicap is for" approach. As MacKenzie put it in his 1926 reference for Russell:

> "He is one of the very few plus men I know who views the game from an absolutely unselfish standpoint and is most sympathetic to average players who he recognises comprise the majority of club members and on this account alone are entitled to more consideration in the construction of a course than they have been accustomed to receive."

Probably for this reason, the dramatic carry bunkers of the West, once heroic carries with a couple of exceptions, do not occur on the East Course. Russell was limited in the land area at his disposal and carry bunkers would have left too little space for safe passage past them by the player who was unable, or unwilling, to attempt the carry.

Keith Barker, one of the founders of Lake Karrinyup and a personal friend of Russell, wrote in his 1969 recollections "*Lake Karrinyup: As It Was In The Beginning*" of some of Russell's design philosophies:

> "He was an original thinker and had no hidebound ideas. He was all for alternative routes for the middle and longer markers. He strongly urged us to use the front tees while the going was heavy. He had a keen eye for the ground and hated anything artificial."

He introduced an "heroic carry" on the 7th and revelled in the criticism this brought forth – "a hole is not worth a damn if no one comments on it one way or another" he used to say.

Another saying he had about golf holes in general was "if it has to be blind make it bloody blind." He spent a lot of his student days on famous Scottish courses where every so called rule of golf architecture is broken – particularly on the most famous one."

View from the tee on the 6th hole of the West Course (top) taken by George Burgess in 1960. These diagonal carry bunkers were not there when the West Course was first built – Russell added them a few years later in 1934-35. The aerial photograph (above) demonstrates that carrying the staggered bunkers from the tee delivers a great advantage for the courageous golfer over one who plays safely left of them. However, judgement of the amount of the carry to 'bite off' needs to be precise or the tee shot may finish on the far side of the fairway, a far less favourable line of approach to the steeply sloping 6th green.

The Greens of Alex Russell

It would be unwise to examine Alex Russell's work in relation to his greens, or indeed his bunkers, in isolation. In both there appears to be a transition through 'MacKenzie and Morcom at Kingston Heath', 'MacKenzie, Russell and Morcom at the West Course', 'Russell and Morcom at the East Course', 'Russell and Johnson at Yarra Yarra', with others being more in keeping with those at Yarra Yarra.

One golf course architect has commented that apart from the routing, after that, one was lucky to have 40 per cent of what had been envisaged, because so much depended on the shaper. Therefore, it is appropriate to quote the 'The Sporting Globe's' golf writer Jack Dillon, in relation to Royal Melbourne's West Course:

> *"It was McKenzie's original general plan. The real work of finalising and designing the holes was undoubtedly Russell's. But without M.A. Morcom, probably the most competent curator in any club anywhere, the work would not have been in quality anything like it is".*

This view of the 4th East green demonstrates how the spread of the mounds into the putting surface produces a rolling edge.

Again, one wonders which golf course architects had the most influence on Russell when it came to designing his greens. Martin Hawtree has stated that the greens of the 'Yorkshire MacKenzie' are different from the greens of the 'American MacKenzie', and that the greens at RMGC are more in keeping with those that MacKenzie later designed in America. The most significant difference being the use of a rolling edge that flows into the green, rather than having mounds within the green. While their philosophies were similar, Colt believed in 'rolling edges', while MacKenzie preferred mounds within the greens. American architect Jeffrey Brauer on this subject wrote:

> *"My mentors always shaped greens with mounds on the inside curves of the greens, whereas Colt put mounds on the outsides of the greens producing a rolling edge, that made the whole green more natural and appealing."*

MacKenzie had Morcom construct two greens while he was in Melbourne, both short holes, the 15th at Kingston Heath and the 5th West at Royal Melbourne. Both these greens, when firm and fast with today's green speeds, have slopes that are right on the edge of what is and what is not acceptable. However, it should be remembered that 80 years ago mowers did not cut as closely as they do now. The 5th at Royal Melbourne has a rolling edge, though much less so now than originally, or even 20 years ago.

All the greens at Royal Melbourne are different, and it is unlikely that someone will stand on a green elsewhere at a Russell course and say this green reminds one of a green at another of his courses. In all cases the greens appear to fit naturally into their locations. The tilt of the green, for instance, is in the same direction as that of the land. In his report to Lake Karrinyup, Russell wrote that the slope of the green should not exceed 1 in 14, with no local slope greater than 1 in 7, and that there should be many relatively flat areas in which to cut the hole. A player should not need to aim outside the hole with a firmly struck three foot (one metre) putt. However, as Dr Martin Hawtree has pointed out:

> *"Greens (East) are considerably smaller than on the West Course, averaging 467m² as opposed to the West Course's 537m². Greens are on the whole more artfully conceived and elaborated on this site. Whereas one may feel that some greens on the West Course simply had to be mown out from the*

existing site, here one sees ingenuity and artifice the whole time. Always the existing slope of the land is worked with but subtly transformed and re-contoured. The surrounds are equally well contoured, tending to develop further away from the greens than on the West."

Hawtree's observations require two comments. Firstly, the size of the East Course greens depicted in Russell's green plans are much larger. At the time of construction, the club's finances were under pressure because of the Depression and so perhaps economies were required. Secondly, Hawtree was looking at the greens in 2002 and 2003, by then the intrusions from the rolling edges had been so reduced that some green area had almost certainly been lost. It also reinforces the views of MacKenzie and Russell that all artificial works should look natural. If it is more the first point rather than the second, then Hawtree's comment stands as an indictment of what has been allowed to happen, a common theme across old courses where the green area gets progressively reduced over time. For some reason, while there were losses of mounds in the greens of the East Course, it did not seem to be so marked. This may be a function of the East Course greens being smaller, and again it is no doubt due to the larger greens of the West Course that the loss is most noticeable.

Apart from 11th East, which was located in somewhat lower ground, no green at Royal Melbourne is built significantly up above the level of the surrounding ground. To a much lesser extent, 13th and 14th West and 13th East have been raised slightly. With the last of these it was a matter of necessity, given its location adjacent to an old swamp, hence all the old swamp gums surrounding it. In several cases, the greens are set on the top of a rise, a characteristic of some of Colt's greens. Examples are 2nd East, 10th West, 12th Yarra Yarra, and less markedly 10th East, 15th West, and MacKenzie's 15th green at Kingston Heath.

The natural looking green site at the 14th East has had its left side raised above an area that, after heavy rain, could become quite wet until it was effectively drained in the 1970s

When greens were cut into the side of a hill, this allowed Russell to create a slope that fed the ball into the green, if hit from a certain angle. This provides an alternative for the player who cannot carry the ball to the green and stop it there, and is perhaps best illustrated by 4th East and 9th West. The latter green was moved from MacKenzie's proposed site and is therefore a Russell modification, this banked effect could not have been used at the original site.

The 9th West was a long, mildly three-tiered green, with two small subtle steps, which have been lost when this green was re-laid. This has meant that while the overall slope of the green is the same, the three pinnable areas now are part of a general, and therefore, more severe slope than before. It would depend on Russell's definition of a firmly struck putt with some current placements, if his dictum that *"no firmly struck three foot putt should have to be aimed outside the hole"* is still as true as it once was. Sometimes the greens are cut into the front of the hill as with 5th West and 6th West, the latter green being moved from its original site, both of which are fine examples of Morcom's skilful use of cut and fill construction.

By using this same technique, Russell avoided having a steep step in the greens, however, such steps are something he did use from time to time, with the construction of 10th East, 6th Paraparaumu Beach and 15th greens at Yarra Yarra all showing large and distinct steps in their putting surfaces. These three holes do not have raised ground spreading forward of the green's location; they are all set into a ridge with a significant fall. To have introduced a steeply raised approach out in front of the green, similar to 5th West or 6th West, in such a location would have looked unnatural.

Like MacKenzie, Russell set the plane or general tilt of his greens towards the point from which the approach should be played, almost always towards one side of the fairway or the other, and which side will be the more advantageous often depends on the pin position. The plane in most cases has a gentle fold running through the green that accentuates the difficulty for a player approaching the green from the wrong side.

The contours of the greens are created by the faces of the bunkers and mounds feeding into the greens from the side, with mounds within the greens being rare, only 11th West has this feature in the work of MacKenzie and Russell. However, the boldness of the contours and the rolling edges have been greatly

The 9th West green seen in 1960 (left) is a long, mildly three-tiered one, with two small, subtle steps. As can be seen the green has been artfully set into the side of the hill with dramatic bunkers on the low side.

The Royal Melbourne Golf Club

The 15th at Yarra Yarra (below) has long been renowned as one of Alex Russell's best short holes, and it was recorded by golf writer Jack Dillon as being his personal favourite. The large step between the lower section of the green where the hole is cut in this photograph, and the elevated rear section, can clearly be seen.

Yarra Yarra Golf Club

subdued with the relaying of the greens over time.

It is of more than passing interest that Colt and MacKenzie's partner, Hugh Alison, designed his greens along similar lines to those of MacKenzie and Russell at Royal Melbourne, as suggested by golf historian Tom MacWood in the following excerpt from 'Golf Architecture' magazine in 2003:

C. H. ALISON.

"Greenside mounds would often encroach upon the putting surfaces. This was Alison's preferred method of creating undulations in his greens, extending and merging either natural undulations or mounds into the putting surfaces. And like many designers, his greens were oriented to one side or the other through the placement of greenside bunkers or deep hollows, rewarding those who chose the best angle of attack (occasionally the centre was the preferred approach). Another common device was the tilting of his greens sideways—an approach from the wrong side or a poorly struck one would often fall away."

Paraparaumu Beach also gives the impression that some of the intrusion from the mounds and bunkers has been diminished at some holes. The loss of bold intrusions into the greens at Royal Melbourne can be seen in a comparison of a photograph of the 12th green on the East Course in 1935 and today's green. The result is that the strategy of playing to the middle of the green and taking two putts, has less strategic reward these days. Previously, from the centre of the green there was a straightforward putt to any pin, however, 'go for the pin' and finish in the adjacent quarter of many of the greens and a three-putt was a real possibility for even the best of putters, but this applies to a somewhat lesser degree today. This attribute was more a feature of the old West Course greens than the East.

Alex Russell sometimes used swales to great effect, especially in the East Course, but at all times these flow into the fall of the land, giving the whole exercise a very natural look. With the relaying of the greens most of the swales now extend much further into the greens than before.

On some short par fours at Royal Melbourne, the back section, or even the whole of the green, falls away gently from the fairway. Examples include the 3rd West, 5th and 15th East Course. The 3rd West green is one of the most highly regarded greens on

Golf course architect C.H. Alison (left) once famously played his ball from the clubhouse roof at Woking in a match for Oxford vs Cambridge in 1904

191

Chapter 14 | GOLF DESIGN PHILOSOPHY

the West Course and its fall-away character strongly protects this relatively short par four of 324m. Australian golf course architect Harley Kruse selected this hole as his selection in the 2004 book "Favourite Holes by Design: The Architect's Choice" and he wrote:

"Getting to the nub of this great hole, it is with the short, fiendish second shot, and the "all-world" green, where this hole becomes really interesting – most players are happy to walk off with a par on their card. This especially applies at tournament time when Royal Melbourne's greens are famously firm and fast. When approaching the green, players must figure out how to best deal with a deep, long, and diagonal hollow in front of the green. It gathers-up and slews weak shots to the right – toward the small, deep greenside bunker. Two bunkers lurk alongside the left of the green, but the key to the short game on the third hole is landing the ball precisely – not quite on a dime, but not far off it – on account of the green sloping heavily from front to back. This distance-control factor is critical."

At Royal Melbourne, the approaches to the greens are a crucial aspect of the design of both courses. MacKenzie believed that mounds and hollows should help the player who has positioned the ball correctly, but disadvantage the player who is playing from the wrong position. In this connection under the heading "Approaches", Dr Martin Hawtree wrote:

"We suspect the influence of Russell who went on to develop his ideas on the East Course with his recollections of Scottish links and St Andrews. We have seen nothing like this in Yorkshire or Ireland prior to MacKenzie's visit to Australia, although MacKenzie himself was more than familiar with St Andrews."

Russell's approaches to Yarra Yarra and Lake Karrinyup greens may be more subdued, but in Paraparaumu Beach he had the perfect environment to express his ideas. What must be remembered is that at Royal Melbourne, Russell had Morcom to shape the approaches, at his other courses, he did not. Many of Morcom's hollows constructed using horse and scoop can best be described as works of art.

In all cases, Russell's greens are predicated by the site and then developed to suit the type of shot that needs to be played from a certain position. If Russell's approaches and greens show the influence of Scottish links, then again, who were the architects that would have influenced these approaches? His golf most likely started at school in Perthshire, with visits to

*The delightful modelling of the approach to the
17th green on the West Course is a prime example of
Russell's vision and Morcom's constructional genius*

local courses and ones as far away as St Andrews, and again, architects such as Tom Morris and James Braid come to mind.

While Russell no doubt would have studied the courses of several British architects prior to Dr MacKenzie's arrival in Melbourne, it is fair to say that MacKenzie's influence must have been greatest in the West Course greens, and indirectly in those of the East. It goes beyond reason that after his many discussions with MacKenzie, Russell discarded MacKenzie's wishes and philosophies for his own ideas.

There is a case for including "Mick" Morcom at this point. When MacKenzie visited Kingston Heath, the course, including all the greens, had been constructed by Morcom to Dan Soutar's design. Here MacKenzie altered the 15th and 16th holes, and developed a scheme of bunkering. MacKenzie's admiration for the quality and naturalness of the work carried out by Morcom has been well documented. The following question arises. Did MacKenzie take the practical approach that as Morcom had built excellent greens using the rolling edge approach, did he have Morcom continue with that method at Royal Melbourne, especially if

Russell had similar views to Morcom? Phillip Russell, Alex's son, described the relationship between Russell and Morcom as being one of a *"mutual admiration society."* Russell and MacKenzie obviously swapped ideas, but how much did Russell and Morcom do the same? It is one thing for Alex Russell to have ideas on how the approaches and design of greens would help create strategic holes, and another for someone to produce the results requested on the ground, and Morcom was his master craftsman for both courses at Royal Melbourne. One sees the strategic use of hollows and mounds in other Russell courses but nowhere are they as bold, or perhaps as well integrated into the entire greensite composition, as in the courses of Royal Melbourne, especially the East Course.

While the Yarra Yarra greens have a similar rolling edge, most are less prominent than those at Royal Melbourne, however the intrusion at the 11th green at Yarra Yarra is clearly a significant one. While Paraparaumu Beach greens are often set amongst natural dune mounds, the intrusions are far less dramatic than one suspects they might have been originally.

The valley before the green of the 1st East (right) is artfully shaped and the upslope is taken well into the putting surface before it begins to level off at the point where the shoulders from the two bunkers enter the green

View from behind the 3rd West green (below) looking back up the fairway. The modelling of the diagonal swale and mounds immediately in front of the green is masterful and, together with the fall-away slope in the green, form the defining features of this wonderful par four hole.

The Bunkers of MacKenzie, Russell and Morcom at Royal Melbourne

Russell believed in big eye-catching bunkers, as did MacKenzie. However, those Morcom and his son Vern produced at Kingston Heath for MacKenzie are different to those Morcom created at Royal Melbourne for Russell. Examples of these are on the 3rd, 4th, 13th and 15th holes at Kingston Heath. It would appear from courses which MacKenzie, Russell and Morcom designed outside of Royal Melbourne, that all three had a broadly similar approach to bunkering. Therefore, in an attempt to elaborate on one, in this case Russell, it is important to look at all three and note any minor variations.

In a club the size of Royal Melbourne, as also in other clubs, there would be a wide spectrum of views on the function of bunkers, and the degree of penalty that should be created by them. It is therefore appropriate to consider the philosophies of these men in regard to bunkers.

In "The Spirit of St Andrews", MacKenzie wrote:

> "Most golfers have an entirely erroneous view of the real object of hazards. The majority of them simply look upon hazards as a means of punishing a bad shot, when their real object is to make the game interesting."

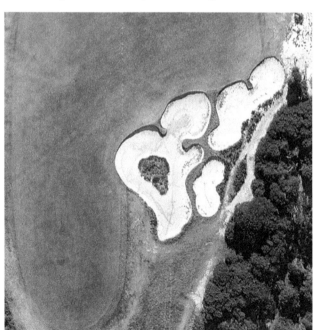

While MacKenzie talks of heroic carries, he clearly does not confine his carries only to the scratch marker. He intimates that shorter carries achieved by longer handicappers can also give great pleasure, or as he termed it, *"pleasurable excitement."* He also quoted John L. Low, one of the pioneers of the school of strategic architecture, who wrote that, *"No bunker is unfair wherever it is placed".* MacKenzie also believed that *"not one* (bunker) *should be made which has not some influence on the line of play."*

The West Course at Royal Melbourne still has some old Sandringham bunkers, which were at the sides of the fairways, and therefore were there for mostly penal reasons. In MacKenzie's Final 27-hole plan, most of these were eliminated, however, some were retained. Russell's East Course has no such bunkers. One must go over, or around, the East Course bunkers, never is it necessary to go between two of them.

The West Course features a number of carry bunkers, a design feature that Russell rarely used on the East Course. The carry bunker on the 2nd West (above) was originally a heroic carry back in 1931, today it is far less so, even though the tee was recently pushed back a further 10m, making the carry now 210m.

Aerial view of the dramatic carry bunkers (left) situated into the hill face on the 18th West. Even in 1931 these could have been carried comfortably by long-hitting golfers of the day like Alex Russell. Today these bunkers are only a bother to shorter hitters.

The spectacular approach and greenside bunkering of
the 18th on the West Course (above) were modifications
of the old bunkering from when it was the 7th hole of
the Sandringham course (see inset right)

Diagonal Bunkering

In the game's earliest times when nature's hazards were the only obstacles to be encountered on the links, it seems certain that playing across a hazard that was positioned oblique to the line of play added some extra interest to the shot. However, by the time man became more actively involved in the laying out of golf courses, this strategic feature appeared to be forgotten. Many courses planned around the turn of the last century featured bunkering laid out at right angles to the line of play, to be carried like steeplechases, eliminating any strategic possibilities. It was not until the Golden Age of golf course architecture in the 1920s and 1930s, that studious and imaginative architects, such as A.W. Tillinghast, Robert Hunter, Tom Simpson, Dr Alister MacKenzie and Australia's own Alex Russell, rediscovered such strategic principles as the oblique hazard by studying and learning from the great courses.

One of Russell's preferences was to stagger bunkers in a diagonal line across the fairway as seen in 10th East, 17th East, and 9th at Yarra Yarra. The 17th hole on the East Course is also the equivalent hole on the Composite Course and is one of the better-known holes in Australia due to its prominence in the clinches of a number of televised championships. The 10th is far less famous, but still shares one intrinsic feature that defines each hole – a cluster of yawning fairway bunkers in the second shot range, extending from the right front of each green back at a diagonal for some 60m, covering the full width of the fairway.

Sited at the easternmost edge of the course, the 10th is a 450 metre dogleg to the right. From the tee, two fairway bunkers frame the shot, with the first of the pair eating across the direct line of play, although the carry now is quite short. Once safely on the fairway, the golfer is faced with a series of alternatives; go straight for the green across the longest carry of this diagonal Sahara; try for a shorter carry of sand to the left that will leave a straightforward pitch up the length of the green; or lay up short of the hazard and be confronted by a difficult approach to the elevated green. As this hole is shorter than the 17th, the diagonal hazard here influences many more second shots as a result.

Russell built a diagonal chain of three bunkers to guard the par five 9th green at Yarra Yarra. This was constructed a few years prior to both the Royal Melbourne courses, so this is almost certainly Russell's first use of a diagonal bunker complex. By contrast with the two examples mentioned on the East Course, the diagonal complex is at the left side of the green, the low side, and runs back towards the right and out into the fairway. A further difference is that it does not cut across all the fairway as the Royal Melbourne examples do, but stops partway into the fairway, leaving a narrow band of fairway along the high side that shorter hitters can run their approach shots through.

Examples of Russell's diagonal bunkering at Royal Melbourne's 10th East (far left), 17th East (left) and Yarra Yarra's 9th hole (above)

View from behind the 17th green on Russell's East Course at Royal Melbourne showing the diagonal bunker chain that runs out into the second shot landing area. At right can be seen the tee shot for the 2nd West, with the 4th West hill bunkers in the centre distance

More on Bunkering

Dr MacKenzie often commented that *"On many courses there are too many bunkers."* The plan hanging on the Lounge Room wall in the Royal Melbourne clubhouse shows bunkers in 42 locations for the West Course. The present West Course has bunkers in 74 different locations. The term 'locations' has been used because there are places where the plan depicts one bunker but in construction this has become a complex with more than one bunker. For example, the three drive bunkers on the hill at 4th West are only shown as one bunker on the plan. Of the 74 locations, 16 would appear to be old Sandringham bunkers, which MacKenzie indicated should be removed, but have instead been retained. Applying the same concept of 'locations', Russell had around 50 'locations' on the East Course.

On the construction of bunkers, MacKenzie's position was very specific:

> *"Ordinary bunkers, as a rule, are made in quite the wrong way. The face is usually too upright and the ball gets into an unplayable position under the face. The bottom of the bank of a bunker should have a considerable slope so that the ball always rolls towards the middle. The top of a bunker may, as it usually does in nature, be made to over-hang a little so that a topped ball may be prevented from running through."*

Regarding the top overhanging, this is an aspect which has not been followed at Royal Melbourne, but is a feature of MacKenzie courses as illustrated by various photographs and is to be found in Morcom's construction of MacKenzie's bunkers at Kingston Heath. The sharp edge to the lip of the bunkers

appears to be a feature of Morcom's work. It is found in the old Sandringham bunkers, and is also in the bunkers at Yarra Bend Golf Course, which he designed.

Russell used the cut-faced bunkers at Royal Melbourne, Yarra Yarra, Lake Karrinyup and possibly at Paraparaumu Beach initially, but needed to change at the latter. The bunkers at Paraparaumu Beach now are smaller and deeper with the ball often finishing not far back from the face, but as has been mentioned earlier, soil and wind conditions necessitated a different approach. Erosion over the years has made many bunkers at all the courses much deeper with the result the slope from the face is much steeper with the ball not necessarily running back to the middle of the bunker.

There is no written philosophy by Morcom on bunkers, we only have his work. Similarly there is little by way of written word from Alex Russell, however, in his report of 30 November 1933 for Lake Karrinyup Country Club he reviewed the course he had designed in 1928 and wrote:

HOW A BUNKER SHOULD BE MADE.
One of the new hazards at Weston-super-Mare. Note how the face of the bunker is curved ; this makes upkeep easier, as the sand is not blown out.

A MacKenzie bunker at Weston-super-Mare Golf Club near Bristol in England (above)

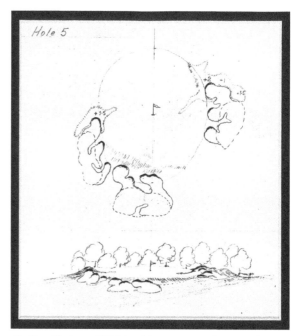

Alex Russell's plan ca1933 (above) for revisions to the greenside bunkering on the 4th hole at Lake Karrinyup in Perth. Note how he proposed that the three existing bunkers be re-cut in more dramatic shapes and all be taken in closer to the putting surface.

"Practically all bunkers are too small and too narrow. One of the most important things is to increase the area of the bunkers to make them more visible and more alarming. The mounds at the back of the bunkers are nearly all too abrupt. This makes them unnatural looking and also hard to upkeep. Bunkers should generally be large in area but shallow especially if not near a green." [Russell's underlining.]

If for some, shallow bunkers appear to lack 'penalty', it should be remembered that MacKenzie believed in match play, and was somewhat dismissive of medal play and the "card and pencil" mentality that it brought forth in many players. Therefore, being bunkered meant being disadvantaged, and a situation from which by a good shot, but a more difficult one, recovery was possible. Being bunkered though did not automatically mean loss of the hole, at best gaining a half was still possible. Furthermore, as MacKenzie pointed out, those wanting bunkers to be more severe are often the low markers who usually have little difficulty carrying over the them.

From these collected comments, it can be seen how the MacKenzie, Russell, Morcom bunkers at Royal Melbourne came to be formed the way they were. The bunkers are large, they have the scalloped edges to be found typically in MacKenzie's bunkers elsewhere, but not with the over-hanging grassy lips. The faces of the bunkers mostly return the ball to the middle of the bunker, as does the portion furthest from the green, consequently the ball does not run back close to the bunker edge furthest from the green.

The fairway bunkers were once shallower than they are today. One could take a fairway wood into the bunkers at the 2nd West until the wind and play made that bunker much deeper, as has occurred by now in most of the fairway bunkers at Royal Melbourne. The shoulders of the fairway bunkers spread out into the fairway so that the bunkers appear to have been cut in a natural ridge, and after one has passed by them, and then looks back, the bunkers are no longer visible. Indeed, when looking back, the ground into which the bunker has been set, blends so well into the fairway, that even by knowing the bunker is there, it is often difficult to judge where the bunker starts and finishes.

The greenside bunkers also blend into the surrounding ground, with the mound from a raised lip often spreading into the green, to provide the contour that gives character to the greens. Russell, in his review of Lake Karrinyup, stated that the greenside aspect of the bunkers should spread out more gently which obviously spreads the bank into the margins of the green. In no cases do the bunkers of MacKenzie or Russell

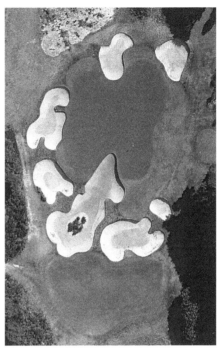

Aerial photograph of Russell's 16th green on the East Course at Royal Melbourne (above) showing the central bunker that eats considerably into the front of the green. Note the narrow opening at the front right for shorter hitters.

Alex Russell on Sand Bunkers in 1939

Russell was reported during a trip to Sydney in several newspapers across the country in 1939 as saying that sand bunkers near greens were obsolete. *"Since the advent of the sand iron and dynamiter, anyone can get consistently out of sand bunkers near greens. No particular skill is required either. To find a suitable substitute for bunkers as a punishment for shots off the line is one of the big problems of modern golf course architecture."* Russell then suggested deep thickly grassed hollows as the solution. *"Much more skill would thus be required to hit the ball near the hole than is the case now,"* he said.

This elicited a number of responses, most along the lines that bunkers were still difficult to recover from for the average golfer, with one Sydney professional noting that, *"in my opinion a golf course without bunkers would not be a golf course at all."* Fortunately for us today, clubs with Alex Russell designed courses did not take heed of his 1939 opinion.

rise up out of a flat plain like Mt Vesuvius. Where bunkers like that appear in a Russell course, one can be certain that they are not original Russell bunkers.

That there is a consistent pattern to the bunkering of MacKenzie, Russell and Morcom is shown by their work at other courses, although Morcom's bunkers at Yarra Bend are much smaller, and shallower when adjacent to a green, this is what one would expect at a public course, especially when the bunkers have hard bases due to the course's clay soils.

While Russell used a similar approach at Yarra Yarra and Lake Karrinyup, at the latter the scalloping where used, is far less dramatic, but then again Russell was not there to oversee the work. At Paraparaumu Beach in New Zealand, Russell was forced by local conditions to change his original approach.

It is perhaps of more than passing interest that most of the bunkers created by Claude Crockford, Morcom's successor as the Royal Melbourne head greenkeeper, for example at the corner of 6th West, front right of 9th West and front left of 12th East (now grassed over), resemble those of the old remaining Sandringham bunkers, examples of which are the bunkers on the right of the drive at 17th West, and those at 15th West (except the green-side bunkers). This is not altogether surprising since Crockford worked with Morcom for a short time before the latter's death, and Crockford's previous position had been Greenkeeper at Yarra Bend and had a role in its construction.

However, it should also be noted that Crockford, under Ivo Whitton's supervision, constructed the new short 7th West hole and its bunkers, and he completely refashioned the large approach bunker at 6th West. Crockford routinely restored the greenside bunkers when relaying the greens in the 1950s and 1960s, and added tongues and walk-ins to many of the larger bunkers, however, he mostly maintained the original character of those bunkers.

So, while MacKenzie, Russell, and Morcom had similar philosophies and were prepared to modify their bunkers to suit the conditions, the bunkers they created were subtly different. MacKenzie's bunkers had overhanging edges. The bunkers created by Morcom at Royal Melbourne are bolder than those at Russell courses outside Royal Melbourne, but both men preferred sharply cut tops to the faces of the bunkers. This does not mean that Russell was not influenced by MacKenzie, they clearly had similar approaches or MacKenzie would not have made Russell a partner. Rather, Russell's discussions with MacKenzie would have helped clarify his own ideas.

In a letter to Paraparaumu Russell stated:

> *"Generally speaking no green is bunkered heavily on both sides with the exception of those drive and pitch holes where some bunkering is necessary".*

This is perhaps not completely true in his design at Royal Melbourne, but it is true in that bunkers are rarely on both sides in front of the green.

MacKenzie and Russell both considered the longer marker, and that golfer's enjoyment of the game was paramount. As Robert Tyre 'Bobby' Jones pointed out:

> *"In large measure, the popularity which the game of golf will enjoy in the future depends on the quality of the courses we provide for the future. A great majority of the players, then and now, will be 'average golfers.' Our courses must be built for them as well as for the 'scratch man'."*

"In a letter received by a friend in Melbourne, Alex Russell, who is at present abroad, gives some interesting impressions of British courses. At the time of writing he had seen only the inland courses, which greatly disappointed him. They were neither as well laid out nor as well kept as the best in Victoria, he asserted."

Referee, Sydney, 25th July 1935

The great Bobby Jones (far right) as drawn by the English golfing artist Charles Ambrose.

The bunker guarding the front right of the 10th green at Paraparaumu Beach (right) is smaller and less dramatic than Russell's Melbourne bunkering but is site appropriate given the windy conditions that prevail there.

The tumbling and rumpled terrain of Paraparaumu Beach must have looked like a godsend when Alex Russell first saw the land back in 1949. The 15th green is in the foreground with the 3rd green immediately beyond.

Stanley Melbourne Bruce, Prime Minister of Australia from 1923–1929

Chapter 15

POLITICAL FLIRTATIONS

Alex Russell had strong political connections on both his side of the family and that of his wife Jess, nee Fairbairn. Thomas Russell, a cousin of Alex's grandfather, had been a Member of the Victorian State Parliament, as had Alex's father's cousin, Philip Russell of 'Carngham', while the Fairbairn family were to have four generations in the Federal Parliament.

Stanley Melbourne Bruce

Alex had become friendly with politician Stanley Melbourne Bruce who was a fellow member at Royal Melbourne Golf Club. Bruce served as Prime Minister of Australia from February 1923 to October 1929, and he appointed Russell, then 31 years old, as his Private or Confidential Secretary sometime prior to August 1923, a position he appears to have held for around 12 months. Alex travelled to Britain with Prime Minister Bruce to attend the Imperial Conference held at No.10 Downing Street in London in October 1923, as part of a large retinue of advisers. The official party travelled to England on the 'Orvieto', stopping in at Adelaide on 3rd September 1923 on their way.

'The Worker' newspaper in Brisbane listed some nine advisors who would be assisting Bruce, including a Senator and an Admiral, while *"Alex Russell is to accompany the party as Bruce's private secretary."* Mrs Stanley Bruce and Mrs Alex Russell both accompanied their husbands on the trip to England, returning to Australia in early 1924. Russell stepped down from his role in the Prime Minister's Department upon his return. While it is not known for certain whether this was paid or unpaid employment for Russell, a profile of Russell published in 'Punch' on 10 September 1925 noted that *"Russell received nothing a week from the Commonwealth, and with his customary humility he urged that this was too much and that he would do everything to reduce his salary. Anyhow, he went to England in the train of the last Prime Ministerial army to visit Downing Street, and he gave further exhibitions of tact."*

There has been speculation that Russell was appointed more as Bruce's travelling golfing partner than as his private secretary, but playing golf with the Prime Minister while he was in Britain may well have been part of Russell's unofficial job description. Russell's work for the Prime Minister was considered somewhat mysterious by political insiders and it is reported that he spent a good deal of

AUSTRALIA'S MYSTERY MAN
Bruce's Offsider Without Portfolio
REDUCTIO AD ALEX RUSSELL

THE mystery man in Australian politics to-day is undoubtedly a young gentleman named Mr. Alex Russell.

That is, if he is in Australian politics, which does not seem to be established. But this merely deepens the mystery.

If Mr. Russell is not in politics, what is he doing up at the Federal Treasury, where he has a comfortable room all to himself, and is treated with the deference due to a Minister. It is not suggested that he passes a busy day playing noughts and crosses with himself or reading the telephone book. But if politics is his business, how is it applied?

An attendant, being somewhat in doubt the other day, handed him a query in the form of a pile of official papers. Mr. Russell bade him take them away. "I am not the Prime Minister's private secretary," he remarked somewhat irritably.

Something had been gathered at all events in the process of elimination. But still there is a mystery.

Mr. Anstey, whose mind is full of unhealthy curiosity, approached the subject from another angle a few days ago, when he asked Mr. Bruce in the House, if secret and confidential communications from the Imperial Government did not come under the observation of Mr. Russell. Pressed to answer the questions directly, Mr. Bruce said that they did not. More elimination of possibilities.

Still Mr. Russell undoubtedly sets an example to Government clerks in the matter of keeping office hours. He even goes down to the House, and from the Members' Gallery studies the debates with an appearance of interest.

One gathers on inquiry that Mr. Russell is not paid for these services. In fact, money is no object to him, for he is the son of Philip Russell, a Western districts squatter, and can afford to work for nothing. Whether he has been taken on as an improver or to set an example in economy in the service, is not widely known.

It is said that Mr. Russell is a student of politics on a high and impersonal plane. This may be so. On the other hand, he may just represent so much money in the corporeal shape of a pleasant young man, in which case the Prime Minister divorced from the worldly interest of Flinders Lane, has solved the problem of making money talk, and play golf, and even accompany him to Europe.

For the Russells have booked with the party. When they get on board, it will be a case of "squatter-vous," for Mrs. Russell was Jess Fairbairn, daughter of the ex-Senator—a man of broad acres.

They are taking officially Mr. Strahan in place of Percy Deane, also Miss Thomas, a young lady secretary from the softgoods side. But no messenger. They will pick one up at Australia House.

A messenger, asked if he was making the trip, was emphatic. "It was all right with Billy," he said, "but a man could never keep up with this mob."

Capt. Russell

Russell was considered 'Australia's Mystery Man' as it seemed no-one could work out precisely what his role was for the Prime Minister

time in Canberra during this period, watching Parliament in session from the Member's Gallery and in an office in the Federal Treasury. No doubt one of his tasks was to play golf with the Prime Minister at the Canberra links.

An article in 'Smith's Weekly' on 25 August 1923 was entitled "Australia's Mystery Man", and endeavoured to find out exactly what Russell was doing for the Prime Minister. It noted that when Russell was handed a *"query in the form of a pile of official papers, Mr Russell bade him take them away. "I am not the Prime Minister's private secretary," he remarked somewhat irritably."* His role was even the subject of a question to the Prime Minister in the House of Representatives:

"Mr Anstey, whose mind is full of unhealthy curiosity, approached the subject from another angle a few days ago, when he asked Mr Bruce in the House, if secret and confidential communications from the Imperial Government did not come under the observation of Mr Russell. Pressed to answer the questions directly, Mr Bruce said that they did not. More elimination of possibilities."

The report also noted that Russell was not paid for his services, *"In fact money is no object to him, for he is the son of Philip Russell, a Western Districts squatter, and can afford to work for nothing."* Stanley Bruce later became President of Royal Melbourne Golf Club from 1930 to 1932, and was the first Australian to be elected as Captain of The Royal and Ancient Golf Club of St Andrews in 1954. His R&A Captain's coat is on display at Royal Melbourne, on loan from the National Archives in Canberra.

Alex and Jess Russell (above) photographed on the 'Orvieto' on 1 September 1923 leaving Melbourne with the Prime Minister's entourage, bound for the Imperial Conference in London. Russell was described in the newspaper as the Prime Minister's "private secretary".

Stanley Bruce opening the Canberra Golf Club's extended links in 1927 (above), and with his wife Ethel (right) at The Lodge in Canberra.

A State Seat

Alex Russell did harbour some political ambitions of his own, and in 1926 he was announced as a pre-selected candidate for the seat of Grenville in the Legislative Assembly of Victoria, on behalf of the National Federation, who were running candidates in all the seats held by the Labor Party. A relative, George Russell, had previously held Grenville, south-west of Ballarat, from 1892 to 1900. On 1 June 1926, 'Golf' magazine reported on a rumour:

> *"Is it to be Mr Alec Russell, M.L.A., or, perhaps later, The Hon. Alec Russell, M.L.A.? For Dame Rumour hath it, that the Victorian Champion is to seek parliamentary honours at the next State election. Grenville, the present seat of Arthur Hughes, Labor M.L.A., is said to be the subject of Russell's attack, so it is said. Is there any prospect of the legislation allowing us an extra day a week off to practice golf if Alec gets in?"*

Russell was active in *"conducting a vigorous canvass against the sitting Labor representative Mr A. Hughes,"* according to an article in 'The Age' on 5 August 1926. The article added that *"he has already addressed meetings in many parts of the electorate, and at an early date he will open a new branch of the A.W.N.L. (Australian Women's National League) at Rokewood. On Saturday, 14th August, he will speak at a National Federation branch formation meeting at Yendon, and on 18th he will address the annual meeting of the Federation at Smythesdale."* However, all this canvassing was to no avail, as the seat of Grenville was abolished in a redistribution later in 1926 and Russell, thankfully from the view of golf course design in Australia, was forced to put his political ambitions to one side.

The Federal Sphere

Some years later, Russell revived those ambitions. After being rejected by the Army when he attempted to enlist upon the outbreak of World War II, he decided instead to look for another sphere in which he could serve his country. Russell was a strong believer that wartime was no time for party politics and that a National Government of co-operation was needed to best see the country through the war. To that end, he decided in 1940 to stand for the Federal seat of Ballaarat in the election that was due to be held in December 1940 or January 1941 at the latest.

Following the air crash in August 1940 in which three cabinet ministers were killed, including Jim Fairbairn, the Minister

Jim Fairbairn (above right), Jess Russell's cousin, lost his life in the crash of an RAAF Boston bomber (right) in Canberra in August 1940. The accident, which saw three cabinet ministers killed, was the catalyst for the 1940 Federal Election.

for Air and Civil Aviation, cousin of Alex's wife Jess, the Prime Minister Robert Menzies decided to bring forward the General Election to 21 September 1940 rather than face three by-elections.

Russell's decision to stand for election was announced on 28 August, with 'The Argus' reporting the next day that there would be a triangular contest in Ballaarat as *"Major Alex Russell, M.C., a pastoralist and well-known sportsman, announced yesterday that he would nominate for the seat as a National Government candidate. He said that he had agreed to do so in response to representations by many influential organisations in the electorate."*

ALEX RUSSELL, Australian national golf champion, 1924, who is a candidate for Ballarat in the House of Representatives.

Alex Russell—Politician?

IN the hubbub raised by the barring of Jim Ferrier, Australian golf champion, from the United States amateur championship, the news that Henry Cotton, Britain's greatest golfer, had joined the Royal Air Force as a pilot did not receive the prominence that it deserved. Golfers have made a fine response to their country's call, and Cotton's enlistment with the R.A.F. should be a great inspiration to all young golfers. The older school of golfers is also doing its part, and it is worthy of mention that Alex. Russell, the winner of the Australian open championship in 1924, has answered the country's call for men of ability and energy to serve in the political field. Russell, who served with the rank of major in the last war, has done much for the game of golf in an administrative sphere, and many courses bear the mark of his skill as a golf architect. Knowing his capabilities, golfers will be delighted if he is successful in winning the Ballarat seat.

ELECTORS OF

BALLAARAT

VOTE:—

RUSSELL 1

Major ALEX. RUSSELL, M.C.
Pastoralist — Soldier — Sportsman.

Rise above party politics—vote for the best man for the job of winning the war—

VOTE:—

RUSSELL 1

A BIG MAN FOR A BIG JOB.

Authorised by S. C. Henderson. 45 Lydiard Street North, Ballarat. Phone 196.

A meeting of 50 *"friends and supporters of Major Alex Russell, National government candidate"* was held at Craig's Hotel in Ballarat on 6 September. An organising committee, along with a women's committee, were formed and his campaign was to be formally opened with a campaign speech at the City Hall on 10 September.

In his speech he appealed for support as a non-party candidate, believing people wanted an alternative to *"party hacks."* Russell said that the party system *"made impossible concentration of the national effort on the great objective of fighting the war to a just and assured peace."* He pledged his support to *"no party government, but I pledge it to any government whose members are appointed for their personal qualities of administration or leadership, whether their peace-time politics be Labor, U.A.P. or Country party."*

During the campaign a number of his quotes were reported by 'The Argus' in their *"Candidates are Saying"* section. Some of these included:

> *"Farmers have made the greatest sacrifice in this war. In the distribution of cost and sacrifices these people must be given preferential consideration – a levelling up process as far as they are concerned. – Major Alex Russell (Nat. Government, Ballarat)"*

> *"There can be no equality of sacrifice under a party Government, because the section which that party represents will be safeguarded. National Government is impossible unless electors give the direction by electing non-party members. – Major Alex Russell (Ind., Ballarat)"*

> *"People should have an opportunity to declare themselves for a thorough-going war effort, instead of one delineated by sectional interests, hampered by petty rivalries and compromised by vote-catching concessions. That is why I am standing as a non-party candidate committed to a national government. – Major Alex Russell (Ind., Ballarat)"*

> *"I pledge my support to no party government, but I pledge it to any government whose members are appointed for their personal qualities of administration or leadership, whether their peace-time politics be Labor, U.A.P. or Country Party. My policy is a total war effort in fact and not in theory, a national government, and true equality of whatever sacrifices must be made to preserve national existence. – Major Alex Russell (Ind., Ballarat)"*

Russell ran this campaign advertisement in 'The Argus' in Melbourne on 19 September 1940, with the slogan 'A Big Man for a Big Job.'

The day before the election, Russell gave a speech at Castlemaine, warning *"that an Australian dictatorship, whether of the extreme right or the extreme left, was the almost inevitable consequence of party politics in war time……The only safeguard was to keep power away from parties by electing non-party men."*

When the votes were tallied, Russell came a distant third in the seat, with Reginald Pollard, the Labor sitting member, re-elected very narrowly from Menzies' United Australia Party candidate. Russell's preferences were directed to the U.A.P. candidate at a ratio of about 4 to 1, indicating that most of the electors who voted for Russell had conservative leanings. Russell, for all his efforts, received just 5,749 first preference votes out of the 48,041 votes cast. Menzies' government was re-elected narrowly, relying on the support of two independents who later withdrew their support in 1941 and gave it instead to John Curtin's Labor Party.

Reg Pollard, the Labor sitting member, was re<elected in the 1940 General Election ahead of Montgomery and Alex Russell

Alethea Russell, Alex's daughter-in-law, recalls that he *"stood for Ballarat as an 'Independent' and lost. I remember my father saying that Alex couldn't work with any Committee, so he had to stand as an independent. He drove his Chrysler around Ballarat with a large banner on it."*

Australian federal election, 1940: Ballaarat				
Party	Candidate	Votes	%	±%
Labor	Reg Pollard	22,715	47.8	-2.8
United Australia	Edward Montgomery	19,089	40.1	-9.3
Independent	Alex Russell	5,749	12.1	+12.1
	Total formal votes	47,553	99.0	
	Informal votes	488	1.0	
	Turnout	48,041	96.8	

The final election results for the seat of Ballaarat (above) showed Alex Russell in a distant third place

Caricature of Alex Russell (right) that featured in 'Punch' magazine's series of 'Prominent Personalities' on 10 September 1925

Alethea Fairbairn was 13 years old at the time and her father commanded the No 1 WAGS (RAAF) in Ballarat. She would spend her school holidays in the town in a house her mother had rented.

Following his defeat in the 1940 election, Russell abandoned any further political ambitions.

Prominent Personalities
ALEX. RUSSELL

L.F.Reynolds

THE MAWALLOK HOMESTEAD FROM THE NORTH

Chapter 16

MAWALLOK & MERINOS

"The Call of a Frog – "Mawallok" was the indigenous name of the Warrapingo tribe for the area, and if repeated with correct inflection and timing – "Mah-woll-ok" – it is easy to see how these two match."

The 'Mawallok' pastoral property near Beaufort in Victoria's Western District was initially around 20,000 acres in size and grew to 28,000 acres with periodic acquisitions, but over ensuing years parcels were progressively sold off down to its present size of 5,851 acres. In the early years, the property name was spelt variously as 'Mahkwallok', 'Mahwallok' and 'Mawallock' until the spelling of the name as it is today was settled upon. The original bluestone homestead, which is now covered by a Heritage Listing, was constructed in the 1850s and extended in 1867 by Alexander Russell, while the wool shed was built in 1860. His son Philip built a new house around 1910 in the 'Arts and Craft' style and had a garden designed, at least in part, by William Guilfoyle of Melbourne Botanic Gardens fame, around the same time.

Alex Russell returned to 'Mawallok' in 1932 to live and to manage the property, and upon his father's death in 1937, Alex became the owner of 'Mawallok'. It became important for its Merino stud rams and he also established a 6-hole golf course near the lake on the property and close by the house. When sold to new owners outside the family in 1980, the Russell family had owned 'Mawallok' through four generations for a period of 133 years. One of the secrets of the property was described by Philip Russell as the 'Miracle of Mawallok', being the third-largest running spring in Victoria that flows out of volcanic rock into a deep pool, which today feeds the 4 ha lake and irrigates the lawns and gardens.

Originally, 'Mawallok' was a portion of St Enoch's run, taken up by Thomas Steel and Richard Black in 1838, only three years after the establishment of Melbourne. For nine years, Steel and Black worked the run in two sections. When the partnership was dissolved in 1847, Black retained 'St. Enoch', with Steel taking 'Mawallok'. However, Steel did not retain his share for long and sold it the same year to the firm of Russell & Co, a joint venture of Alexander Russell, his brother George Russell of 'Golf Hill', and the Rev. Dr John Lillie, of Hobart Town.

George Russell had owned a flock of sheep for many years, and when 'Mawallok' was purchased he gave them to his brother

Alexander to enable him to provide his share in the partnership. Alexander Russell managed the station, and over time he bought out the other partners, eventually becoming the sole owner. When he died in 1869 he left the property to his son Philip, who at that time was a boy of just three years. Until Philip came of age, trustees took care of the estate and for most of this time 'Mawallok' was managed by George Lewis, of Stoneleigh, a nephew of Alexander Russell, until 1887 when Philp turned 21. In 1888, Philip married Mary Gray Guthrie, and in the same year he purchased Osborne House in Geelong, overlooking Corio Bay, where they lived until 1903 when Philip travelled to Britain for treatment of his tuberculosis.

THE ENTRANCE GATES AND DRIVE TO MAWALLOK HOMESTEAD

GRAND CHAMPION RAM

The ram illustrated gained the champion ticket at Ballarat for grass-fed ram. There was a keen tussle with the champion at the recent sheepbreeders' Show in Melbourne. He was afterwards awarded the grand champion ribbon, defeating the champion fed ram. Both were bred by Mr F. Russell, of Mawallok, Beaufort.

'Mawallok' featured in the Australian Pastoral Review in 1931, with a number of photographs of the property, buildings and stock depicted. The homestead (opposite) and the entrance gates (above right) are shown here. Philip Russell bred the Grand Champion grass-fed merino ram (right) at the Ballarat Show in 1918.

The New Homestead and Gardens

On his return from Britain in 1909, Philip made 'Mawallok' his home and personally ran the estate, with assistance from a manager. Philip embarked on several projects, erecting a sizeable new two-storey house to an 'Arts and Crafts' design by Melbourne architects Klingender and Alsop. Interestingly the tender notice for the construction of the new house put out by the architects and published in 'The Argus' dates from 27 June 1908, some 18 months before the generally accepted date of 1910 for its construction. The tender notice called for the *"erection of large Two-storey Brick residence at "Mawallok," Beaufort, for Philip Russell, Esq."* From the plans of the house that survive, there was an intent to build the house with thin reinforced concrete walls, in contrast to the brick walls that were indicated in the tender notice, and it is known that architect Rodney Alsop was an early user of reinforced concrete in his structures. Perhaps a change to the construction method meant the house was re-tendered later, however, this has not been able to be established. Concrete was used in the construction of the walls of the house when it was eventually built.

Philip's wife Mary, known to the family as 'Cissie', was a keen gardener and must have been delighted with the beautiful new gardens around the homestead based in part on a plan by William Guilfoyle, the designer and director of the Melbourne Botanic Gardens. A report on 'Mawallok' in 'The Australasian' newspaper on 17 August 1912 noted that, *"The grounds have been laid out by more than one master mind, including the late Mr Guilfoyle."* As Rodney Alsop, of the architectural firm of Klingender and Alsop, was also a talented landscape architect, there is a strong likelihood that he was one of the other *"master minds"* of the grounds around the homestead. This included damming the run-off from the spring to form a lake of about 10 acres (4 ha). In 1927, a new dam was built by Sir John Monash, the soldier and engineer, which enlarged the lake to 22 acres (9 ha). Around 1935, Alex added a 6-hole golf course with its holes located around the lake. There was a long shady drive all the way to the lake, and the house and gardens now all have a Heritage Listing.

Alex's father Philip set about improving the pastures of the 3,000 acres (1,200 ha), which had basalt rocks and volcanic soil, by top-dressing and sowing with subterranean clover and English rye grass. During his absence overseas, rabbits had become a major problem. On the flatter ground the burrows could be dug out, but where the ground was stony, ploughing up the burrows

ANOTHER VIEW OF THE HOUSE

MAWALLOK, VICTORIA

A CORNER OF THE GARDEN

William Guilfoyle

A VIEW LOOKING ACROSS THE GARDEN FROM THE MAWALLOK HOMESTEAD

Views of the house and garden, (right and top) in the Australian Pastoral Review in 1931

MAWALLOK, VICTORIA

THE ROSE GARDEN, TAKEN FROM THE ROCKERY IN NOVEMBER 1930

THE PERGOLA WALK IN MAWALLOK GARDEN

RODNEY ALSOP

*Caricature of the architect
Rodney Alsop (left)*

*More views of the
'Mawallok' garden (above)*

*Architect's plan of the new
residence for Philip Russell
at 'Mawallok,' prepared
by the firm of Klingender
and Alsop of Melbourne.
At some time in the past
the plan was damaged by
having three sections cut
out of it. Whether this was
deliberate or accidental is
not known.*

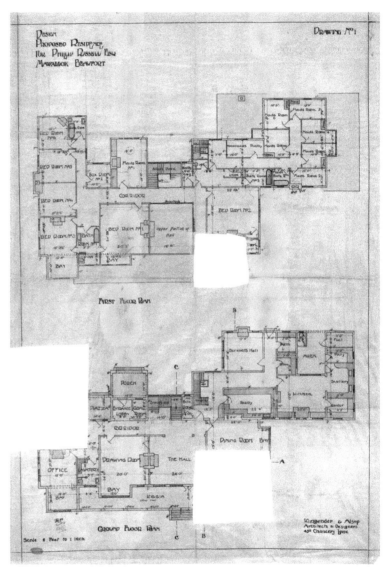

was near to impossible so the problem was largely tackled with ferrets and dogs. Philip had one man working full-time on this problem, sometimes more. In addition, where stone walls had been undermined by rabbits these needed to be pulled down and rebuilt. The extermination of the rabbit pest was an enormous task. Philip was praised for what he achieved, and when he sought permission to place swinging rabbit proof gates on two adjacent unused roads the Riponshire Council had no objections. Alex's sister Joan, in a 1909 letter to 'The Australasian' newspaper's *'Young Folk'* page, wrote about her pets and how she would walk her father's greyhound, which chased down rabbits.

Traditionally, 'Mawallok' had run sheep and cattle, but Philip, instead of following on from the previous policy of dealing mostly in fat lambs, decided to concentrate far more on sheep breeding and wool growing. In this, no doubt, his study as a veterinarian was invaluable. To the traditional Victorian Merino blood lines, he added first Tasmanian stock and then a line from the Riverina, which probably came from the legendary Peppin brothers' Riverina stud, renowned for the fineness of the wool and hardiness of their sheep.

As a result, rams, ewes and wethers from 'Mawallok' became winners of numerous prizes at shows, especially in Ballarat, where Philip and his cousin, another Philip Russell of 'Carngham', dominated the merino events. Routine reports from the sale-yards mention 'Mawallok' prices so frequently, it was almost as if this was the benchmark. If one knew what 'Mawallok' was fetching, then one could assess how much one's own sheep were likely to bring at a sale.

Philip similarly improved the quality of his cattle by careful breeding and bringing in new blood lines, again winning prizes with his shorthorns. In Melbourne, apart from being known as a wealthy grazier, he was perhaps best known as a breeder of racehorses. His horses won two Australian Cups, with horses running under his colours of orange with white sleeves and a black cap. For a while he produced some good horses but few top race winners. This changed when around 1919 he retired his stallion Berriedale, and sent his mares to the leading stallions of the time.

Philip was on the committee of the Victoria Racing Club, firstly before he went to Britain and again in 1917. He held the position until resigning not long before his death in 1937. Philip was highly regarded in the sport, yet he did not bet heavily and raced purely for the enjoyment of the sport. He also bred polo ponies, being an excellent polo player himself, and was a stalwart of the Geelong and Melbourne Polo Clubs.

MAWALLOK, VICTORIA

THREE-YEAR-OLD BULLOCKS IN SUBTERRANEAN CLOVER

MAWALLOK, VICTORIA

THE FRIESIAN STUD AT MAWALLOK

MAWALLOK, VICTORIA

THREE-YEAR-OLD WETHERS MUSTERED FOR DIPPING AT MAWALLOK

Livestock at 'Mawallok' depicted in the
Australian Pastoral Review in 1931

At Osborne House, Philip had had his own polo field, which doubled as a cricket ground. He was a decent golfer but never in the class of his son Alex.

As previously mentioned, Philip had a small zoo at Osborne House, and at 'Mawallok' again he set up a small one of native animals. The local flora and fauna of the area were encouraged and this, enhanced by the lake, meant many bird species found sanctuary at 'Mawallok'. Philip also had his own workshop with a lathe, an interest that Alex certainly inherited from his father.

In 1928, Alex Russell started spending more time at 'Mawallok', coinciding with an absence from Royal Melbourne Golf Club where he had resigned from the two-man committee overseeing construction of the West Course, due to a disagreement with the other member over a matter of principle.

His son Philip noted that, at one time or another, Alex had resigned from virtually every committee that he had served on, *"He resigned from Royal Melbourne, he resigned from the Melbourne Club, he resigned from the Barwon Heads Golf Club. Because he disagreed with them. And he was probably right."* Here was a man who stood for his principles and what he believed was right. Others likely perceived it as bloody-mindedness, but he was respected for it.

Alex's mother had died in January that year and no doubt Alex wished to help his father Philip who had just lost his wife of 40 years. Alex's increased involvement allowed Philip, with Alex's younger sister Philippa as company, to make a twelve-month long trip to Europe in 1929. In 1932, Alex Russell assumed control of the property following a disagreement with his father. Alex's son Philip recalled that the two had an argument about the readiness of the fire truck which broke down on its way to a fire a few miles from 'Mawallok':

> *"Well, then they had a row in 1932, in 1932 they moved. They were staying for Christmas at Mawallok and the fire truck didn't get to the fire. And that is when the change was made. And Big Gran as we called him, came to live in Melbourne, and Dad moved to Mawallok without hardly knowing where the front gate was. Big Gran said to my father, if you know so much about it, then you run it, and walked out."*

On 29 January 1932, 'The Age' noted in its country news section that Dick O'Neill had been appointed to run 'Mawallok,' *"Mr R. O'Neil, recently manager of Neerin Neerin Estate, is returning to Mawallok Estate as manager. Mr Philip Russell is going to Melbourne to reside, and Mr Alex. Russell will live at Mawallok."*

Dick O'Neill (left) managed the 'Mawallok' property for the Russell family for a number of years

SUCCESSFUL AT SHEEP SHOW

Studmasters of champion rams at the Ballarat Sheep Show. Messrs. R. O'Neill (left), of Mawallok, and R. Robinson, of Trawalla.

Philip was quite disparaging of his father's interest in farming, and it is clear from this, that in Philip's view, that he and Dick O'Neill as managers were largely responsible for the day-to-day running of 'Mawallok' while Alex was the owner:

> *"I've got another list of what my father was the worst at, and that was farming. And there he was, the owner of a beautiful property....and he didn't know one end of the sheep from another. He wasn't interested. He was the worst rider of a horse you have ever seen. He used to come and watch us do the lamb marking or ask who's the expert classing the sheep? He'd come over and he'd stay 5 minutes while Frank classed another few sheep and we'd class sheep all day, every day for about 4 days to improve our flock.*
>
> *He came back once with a movie camera and showed me making silage and making hay and I'd done a bit of research about this so we didn't make hay during the war, or anything like that but we got going to make it and dad showed us a film about some hay making and that sort of stuff in Scotland. Well it's a bit different from Beaufort but he wanted to be doing the same as they were in Scotland."*

The annual sale of rams at 'Mawallok' extended for a week and became a legendary business and social event in the region. Alex, like his father, had overseen a considerable increase in the carrying capacity of the estate, so that at the end of Alex's tenure it had doubled what it had been when Philip arrived, a feature that was extended further by Alex's son Philip, during his stewardship from late 1945 till 1980. Alex served on the committee of the Australian Sheep Breeders' Association from 1939 to 1958, and was president from 1950 to 1951, and despite Philip's views, others thought that he had something to offer. He also served for many years on the Ballarat Sheep Show Committee.

In 1937, Alex was the first pastoralist to take out drought insurance. The policy was issued by the Eagle Star Insurance Company, the first company in Australia to write this type of business. The period covered was August 20th to November 5th 1937. Depending on certain fixed shortages of rainfall, compared with the 'Mawallok average', the company agreed to pay up to a maximum of £1,000.

MAWALLOK, VICTORIA

THE LAKE AT THE FOOT OF THE HOMESTEAD GARDEN

ONE OF THE STUD SHORTHORN BULLS AT MAWALLOK

Charity Events at 'Mawallok'

Over the time of the Russell family's association with 'Mawallok', it was the scene of many charitable activities, of which three stand as examples. In 1902, during the severe drought that had affected the country for some years, Philip Russell did not just donate to the relief fund but offered to take 25 horses from drought-affected properties to graze at 'Mawallok', and to provide work for distressed farmers in the district. In 1917, his wife 'Cissie' Russell authorized the purchasing of Christmas presents for the children of each local married soldier on active service. 'The Argus' of 6 January 1941 reported on a charitable garden party at 'Mawallok':

> *"GARDEN PARTY AT MAWALLOK, BEAUFORT, Sunday – Sir Winston and Lady Dugan were present yesterday at a garden party held at Mawallok Station, the home of Major Alex Russell and Mrs Russell, in aid of the Beaufort branch of the Red Cross Society. The lawns and garden leading down to the lake provided an ideal setting. More than 800 people were present, and about £120 was raised. The Beaufort town band provided the musical programme. Sir Winston Dugan opened the fete and expressed appreciation of the work being done for the Red Cross throughout Australia."*

The lake at 'Mawallok' and a stud shorthorn bull (left) depicted in the Australian Pastoral Review in 1931.

Views inside the 'Mawallok' house in 1934 (above), including the bedroom where the Duke of Gloucester would be sleeping

Important Guests

Over the years many important people have stayed at 'Mawallok' as guests of the Russell family. In 1917 the Governor-General Sir Ronald Munro-Ferguson and Lady Helen Ferguson were guests. His Royal Highness the Duke of Gloucester stayed at 'Mawallok' on three occasions, the first two visits were during his 1934 tour of Australia, and again when Governor-General of Australia in 1945. His 1934 visits were found to be considerably newsworthy in newspapers of the day, even to the point of publishing photographs of the bedroom where the Duke would be sleeping. Prince Henry, Duke of Gloucester, the third of the five sons of King George V, was reported as having spent the afternoon of Monday 5 October 1934 and all day Tuesday at 'Mawallok,' where he spent his time riding and playing tennis. It was reported that the Duke was accompanied by a staff of 16. So, it was not simply a matter of accommodating the Duke and two or three of his staff, that *"with the extra servants needing beds, Mrs Russell has had to arrange for a cottage near the house to be converted into several bedrooms."* The Duke had spent the morning of 5 November 1934 in Geelong for its centenary celebrations and then motored to 'Mawallok' in the afternoon, arriving *"at about 3.30, and immediately went riding. He rode hard for two hours, and returned to the homestead before sunset."*

In December 1945, the Duke, this time accompanied by his wife the Duchess of Gloucester and their son, Prince William, *"were the guests of Colonel and Mrs Alex. Russell, at "Mawallok." They thoroughly enjoyed their visit, and were greatly refreshed by it. Prince William was delighted by picnics and boating on the lake. The Duchess rode daily with the Duke, and she and the Duke played a great deal of tennis."* Through 1949 and 1950, Philip and Alethea Russell spent a year abroad and one of the highlights was *"a weekend spent staying with the Duke and Duchess of Gloucester, whom they had previously met in Australia."*

Sir Winston Dugan, Governor of Victoria, and Lady Dugan were entertained at 'Mawallok' more than once. Lady Dugan had stayed there when visiting the Western District in her position as president of the Victorian Red Cross. Similarly, Sir Dallas Brookes, when he was the State Governor, stayed at 'Mawallok' several times and opened charitable garden fetes that the Russells had organised. When he left the property in 1980, Philip Russell recalled that every Governor of Victoria had been a guest at 'Mawallok' except the then current one.

The Duke of Gloucester, the third son of King George V (right), stayed on two occasions with the Russells at 'Mawallok', the first in 1934 and the second in 1945 when he was the Governor General of Australia. The Duke was a keen horseman (below) and rode regularly when he stayed at 'Mawallok.'

Sir Dallas Brooks, the long-serving Governor of Victoria from 1949 to 1963

Mrs. Alexander Russell, at whose lovely home, Mawallok, Beaufort (V.), the Duke of Gloucester will be a guest during his visit to Victoria.

Edwina, Lady Mountbatten stayed with the Russells at 'Mawallok' in Easter 1946 having met Lieut. Colonel Alex Russell at a temporary hospital in Ceylon, which he had been involved in setting-up. It is related in the next chapter that Lady Mountbatten, not long after the release of prisoners of war from Japanese camps, made a visit to the hospital. The Russells also stayed with Viscount and Lady Mountbatten on a trip to Britain. Another prominent guest at 'Mawallok' was the English novelist and humourist A.P. Herbert, who stayed with the Russells in 1954.

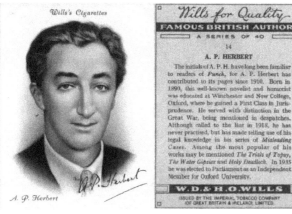

A.P. Herbert

Apart from important visitors, socially 'Mawallok' was one of the centres of Victoria's Western District "squattocracy". In March 1926, a polo tournament, held over three days at Carranballac Estate, the property of Captain and Mrs Gordon Chirnside, near Skipton, was attended by the "Who's Who" of the Western District. The following night there was a dance hosted by the Russells at 'Mawallok' where, as reported by 'The Australasian' newspaper, *"Mr and Mrs Phillip Russell entertained a large number of guests at a delightful dance at Mawallok, Beaufort. The house was decorated with masses of exquisite flowers, and dancing took place in the dining-room, while at supper-time the many guests gathered in the flower-decked billiard room. The hostess wore a lovely gown of black lace, with a gleaming hairband of silver tissue and green grapes."*

In Alex's time, when the Ballarat Golf Club held its annual tournament, the Russells often had fellow golfers stay with them – Ivo and Mrs Whitton were among those

The manager's cottage at 'Mawallok' (right)

guests in 1933 and 1934. At the 1933 tournament, Jess Russell was the winner of the women's scratch event. As important members of the establishment, the newspapers of the time did not just print notices about births, engagements, weddings, and deaths, all these events and other activities of the family were covered in some depth.

Alex's mother 'Cissie' was a keen gardener and had rose gardens at both Osborne House and 'Mawallok'. Alister Clark, a well-known breeder of roses near Bulla, north of Melbourne, who bred some 122 new rose varieties between 1912 and his death in 1949, named one after her, "Mrs Philip Russell". Unfortunately, like a great many of Clark's roses, it either became extinct or lost, and even if someone thought they had a specimen, it would be hard to prove its provenance. It was a large bush, up to 1.5 metres tall, with dark red hybrid tea blooms, which had almost black areas in places and bloomed in clusters throughout the season. It was introduced in 1927, just a few months before 'Cissie' died in January 1928.

As with any rural property, 'Mawallok' had its share of tragedies. A number of the farm workers, or their sons, went off to World War I and many did not come back. Bushfires in the country were, and still are, a constant threat, but perhaps the most devastating one for the Beaufort district, and which also involved 'Mawallok', was in February 1914 when 50,000 acres (20,000 ha) were burnt and thousands of sheep lost. Of over 100,000 sheep in the district, initially it was reported that only 6,000 were accounted for unharmed. Country roads have always carried a risk and in 1934 Alex Russell crashed his car after trying to avoid a cow, fortunately he was unhurt. Not so lucky on another occasion was a farm worker riding to 'Mawallok' on his bike.

MAWALLOK, VICTORIA

THE MANAGER'S COTTAGE

Alex's daughter Robina shared her recollections of the ram sales at Mawallok:

> *"The Ram Sales were quite a thing. At the time we had a manager who was very good at trimming the rams to hide any defaults! He was also caught by my father feeding oats to the show rams that were entered in grass-fed competitions, so they had to be withdrawn.*
>
> *The main sales went on and people came from far and near and also just to look. When the main sales were over the rams that been used by the stud were sold and local farmers turned up and then the real bargaining began. It took much longer to sell 2 rams than 10 and Dick O'Neill (the manager) really enjoyed himself! I remember seeing one bewhiskered farmer drive off with 2 rams tied sitting on the back seat looking like their owner."*

When Alex passed away in 1961 'The Pastoral Review' printed his obituary and noted that:

> *"During Colonel Russell's period of ownership the production of wool per acre was doubled and Mawallok became widely known as a "show place" in the Western District, with first class improvements and stock. The latest methods of pasture improvement and fodder conservation were employed, and it was typical of the owner's progressive outlook that Mawallok was the first Victorian property (and the second in Australia) to use a pick-up hay baler."*

When Philip took over the property from Alex he branched out into pigs and Christmas trees, and multiplied wool production five or six-fold. When he sold the property in 1980 'Mawallok' amounted to 5,805 acres (2,350 ha) with a population of 12,400 sheep, 225 cattle and 1665 pigs. And so ended the 133 year stewardship of 'Mawallok' by the Russell family, with all the improvements that this had entailed.

The logo for 'Mawallok' (above) designed by Philip Russell in 1982

The sundial at 'Mawallok' (left)

Major and Mrs Alec Russell are well known in the golf world. The sideboard shows a number of trophies that they have won.

The sideboard in the 'Mawallok' house (right) was weighed down by silverware won by Alex and Jess in their golfing careers

1937 Ballarat Show Grand Champion merino ram (left) bred at 'Mallok'

MAWALLOK'S GRAND CHAMPION MERINO RAM, stud by Major Alex Russell, Beaufort (V.)

Lieut.-Colonel Alex Russell, seated third from left, in his role as Chief Commissioner of the Australian Red Cross Field Force, with the ARC Board

WAR AGAIN

With the outbreak of World War II in September 1939, Alex Russell again volunteered for service overseas, but was rejected for three reasons: his age of 47 years, his not having been a member of the Military Reserves, and his fitness given that he weighed 15 stone (95kg) at the time. He was eventually able to join the Reserves, also called the Citizen Military Forces, and on 29 April 1940, he was commissioned as a Major in the Reserve Military Forces of the Commonwealth, by the Governor-General Baron Gowrie. Russell's World War I commission had been with the British Expeditionary Forces.

Reserve Military Forces

Russell's Mobilisation Attestation Form was signed by him on 11 July 1940, stating that he enlisted at Caulfield that day, with his unit being Headquarters Southern Command, based in Collins Street, Melbourne. He was 48 years old, married to Jess Lucy Russell, occupation Grazier, with the religious denomination of Church of England. His medical examination declared him fit for Class II service, with the note *"Defective Vision."*

Russell took extended leave without pay from the end of August 1940 to devote to his campaign to be elected to the Federal Parliament in the 1940 Election held on 21 September. After his loss in the seat of Ballaarat, he returned to his unit on 1 October 1940. In May 1941 he was detached to 'Wooloomanata', a station property near Lara owned by his wife's cousin Jim Fairbairn, where the homestead was used as a training school for Southern Command. As Fairbairn was a keen and experienced flyer, the property had an airstrip known as "Esther's Paddock" and in 1943 the Spitfires of 79th Squadron RAAF were based there for a month of forming-up before moving to New Guinea. Russell spent a month at 'Wooloomanata' before rejoining Headquarters.

'Wooloomanata' homestead near Lara, Victoria (above), where Alex Russell spent a month at the Southern Command training school in 1941

On 8 August 1941, the Central Council of the Australian Red Cross approved a motion to appoint Major Alex Russell a Member of the Australian Red Cross Society and the Deputy Commissioner to the Middle East Overseas Unit, with *"Representative (Officer Status) with the Australian Military Forces".*

The Australian Red Cross – Deputy Commissioner

His appointment as Deputy Commissioner was noted in the society's magazine called 'Notes on Services', *"to assist Colonel Cohen in the ever-growing work of the Australian Red Cross Service in the Middle East, two new appointments have been made in the persons of Major Alex Russell, M.C., of Victoria, and Mr F. E. Headlam, of Sydney. Both have now arrived in the Middle East. Major Russell was appointed Deputy-Commissioner in the Middle East and he comes next in seniority to Colonel Cohen. He is a well-known Victorian pastoralist and amateur golfer who served during the last war with the British Army, gaining distinction by winning the Military Cross. Major Russell now holds the rank of Major in the Southern Command."*

One announcement of his appointment appeared in 'The Age' on 21 August 1941 and noted that, *"Major Alex. Russell, grazier, of Mawallok, Beaufort, who is at present a staff officer at Southern Command, and who will go as depot commissioner in a voluntary capacity."* Another report noted that *"Russell will act as deputy to Colonel Harold Cohen."*

The new Assistant Commissioner was Felix E. "Peter" Headlam, like Russell, another prominent golfer and member of Royal Melbourne. He was club champion in 1925, 1932 and 1934

Newspaper article from 12 August 1941 (above) reporting on the appointments of the noted golfers Alex Russell and F.E. Headlam as Red Cross Commissioners

NOTED GOLFERS RED CROSS COMMISSIONERS

MESSRS. ALEX. RUSSELL and F. E. Headlam, well-known Australian amateur golfers, have been appointed to high posts in the Australian Red Cross Service abroad, subject to medical tests.

Mr. Russell has been appointed deputy commissioner and Mr. Headlam assistant commissioner.

Grazier and soldier, as well as golfer, Mr. Russell last year contested Ballarat seat at the Federal elections.

He won the Military Cross with the British Army in the last war, and is now a major in the Southern Command.

One of the few amateurs to win the Australian open golf championship, he is also known as an expert at designing golf courses, among his successes being Royal Melbourne and Yarra Yarra.

Mr. Headlam was formerly a member of the executive of Ford's Motors (Geelong), and went to Sydney several years ago. One of Australia's finest amateur golfers, he has been captain of the N.S.W. interstate team and has won several important titles. He served in the last war.

Mr. Alex Russell

Mr. F. E. Headlam

and a member of its dominant pennant team during the 1920s. Headlam was also club champion at Geelong Golf Club and a former executive of the Ford Motor Company in Geelong. After moving to Sydney in 1933, he represented New South Wales in the annual Interstate Series matches. Again like Russell, Headlam served in France in the Australian Artillery during World War I in the 31st Battery 8th FAB, and was wounded during action. While Headlam said that he had not been involved in the Red Cross before, he had been *"at the receiving end"* of their services during the first war.

According to newspaper reports, Russell spent time in Palestine, Egypt (Cairo), Syria and the Suez Canal in undertaking his role as Deputy Commissioner. A later article on his appointment as Chief Commissioner said that he *"was Deputy Commissioner for the Red Cross in the Middle East for a period before the 6th and 7th Divisions returned to Australia."*

One of the members (now deceased) of Royal Melbourne once spoke of meeting Alex Russell in Cairo during the war, while his son Philip recalled catching up with his father in Palestine who took him to dinner at an officer's nightclub, quite a highlight for an enlisted man.

Reserve Military Forces – Once More

Russell returned to Australia from the Middle East in 1942, and on 30 March 1942, he was 'taken on strength' back to Headquarters Southern Command, 1st Corp, with the rank of Major. On 17 April 1942 he was transferred to 'G' Branch of the 1st Military District at the Headquarters of 1st Australian Corps, and performed the duty of Camp Commandant HQ 1st Australian Corps from April 1942 to November 1942.

The A.I.F.

On 4 August 1942, Alex Russell volunteered and this time was accepted for the Australian Imperial Forces and was given the serial number VX108098. He was straight away sent to New Guinea, leaving Brisbane on 12 August on the U.S. troopship 'S.S. John Hart' bound for Port Morseby, arriving there on 20 August. A few months later Russell was sent back to Townsville by plane on 8 November 1942, and on 27 November he was appointed Assistant Director Amenities (ADA) at LHQ "A" Branch.

In December 1942, he was appointed ADA, Milne Force and on 4 December promoted to Lieutenant Colonel. At the end of April 1943, he was appointed Director of Amenities, Land

Headquarters (LHQ) in Melbourne. In June 1943 he travelled back to Port Moresby for a week, before returning to Australia.

It was while he was in New Guinea that Lt Col. Alex Russell was "Mentioned in Dispatches", for *"Gallant & Distinguished Services SWP (South West Pacific) area"*, with the award being promulgated on 23 December 1943. Russell's daughter Robina recalled that he was on General Thomas Blamey's staff while in Port Moresby, a story which Philip related:

> *"Well, he had a wonderful job at Port Moresby. He had a motor bike and he was camp commandant, something like that. He dined in the upper class tent with the brigadiers and he got up to half colonel doing it and he got a mention in dispatches. This is from Robina, my sister. He was on Tom Blamey's staff in Port Moresby and he ... Tom Blamey decided that the war was ending and we'd have to look after the fellows that had been prisoners of war and got back to Japan as prisoners. I don't know if that was the moment that Tom Blamey got rid of him from the army so he could do this job as Red Cross Commissioner."*

Lieut.-Colonel Alex Russell

The Australian Red Cross – Chief Commissioner

Admiral Louis Mountbatten, the Supreme Allied Commander of Allied Forces South East Asian Command, had warned General Blamey of the possibility of the release of a large number of Prisoners of War of the Japanese as a result of the Burma campaign in June 1945. It would appear that Blamey had anticipated this possibility, as Lionel Wigmore in the official Australian history of World War II stated that the Australians were well prepared and that the 2nd Australian Prisoners of War Reception Group, under Brigadier Lloyd, had sent contact groups to India and Ceylon well before the end of the war. Once it became clear that POWs would be sent to Ceylon, a 600-bed hospital was established there.

Blamey was one of General Monash's senior officers in World War I and the thoroughness of Monash when it came to planning ahead with detailed logistics is well documented. From his experiences in that war, Blamey would have been aware of the requirements when it came to dealing with the released POWs. No doubt Blamey, as early as October 1943, saw the importance of the role of the Australian Red Cross in this and that Alex Russell, who was on his staff and had previous senior ARC experience, would be an ideal person to be involved with this pre-planning, and with the ARC's involvement, when the time came.

With the turning of the war in 1943, Blamey asked Russell to take on the task of repatriating back to Australia those soldiers who had been prisoners of the Japanese. To take on this role Alex Russell first needed to be discharged, which occurred at Caulfield Depot on 19 October 1943. He then could actively take up the position of Chief Commissioner of the Australian Red Cross, a position he held until late 1945.

To describe his role with the Australian Red Cross, it is perhaps best to quote an extract from the 1944-45 Annual Report of the Australian Red Cross Society:

> "The Chief Commissioner, Lieutenant-Colonel Russell, paid a visit to Ceylon and the Burma front and attended a Red Cross Conference called at the request of the Supreme Commander, Admiral Lord Louis Mountbatten, with the object of co-ordinating the work of various Red Cross organisations in South East Asia. Commissioner O.B. Williams is our permanent representative.
>
> Chief Commissioner Russell inspected the various branches of work of the Australian Unit in Ceylon, and found that

> wherever he went in Ceylon, India, and even Burma, the Society's service was well known and highly praised.
>
> In the forward areas in Burma, Colonel Russell visited hospitals, convalescent depots and other medical posts.
>
> The Chief Commissioner in the course of the year carried out tours of inspection in all forward areas in the south-west Pacific area."

Russell reported back to the ARC in October 1944 that he had "travelled over 30,000 miles around the outskirts of Australia and in New Guinea in the last year and I am satisfied that the Field Force is upholding the good name of the Society to practically every sick and wounded man of the three services....During the last twelve months the number of the Red Cross field force personnel has grown from 224 to 426," so it is clear that Russell was heading up a sizable field organisation.

LT.-COL. A. RUSSELL

. . . Red Cross Field Force.

LIEUT.-COLONEL ALEX RUSSELL, M.C., has been released by Army to become Chief Commissioner of Australian Red Cross Field Force. Post is full-time job, as he must be able to proceed at any time to any place Red Cross work requires. Was for time Deputy Red Cross Commissioner, Middle East. Is well-known amateur golfer, and grazier of Victoria's Western District.

In the Australian Red Cross 'Notes on Activities Number 65', pages 3 and 4 under 'Australian Red Cross Relief in the Pacific Area', The Chairman, Dr (Sir) John Newman-Morris and Chief Commissioner Alex Russell, reported on the state of health of the released prisoners of war. Newman-Morris stated that the stories of ill-treatment and atrocities had not been exaggerated, while Russell was concerned that while this had occurred, it had not been the case in all POW camps, but was being given undue publicity.

> "The prisoners as I saw them were mostly very thin indeed," said Chief Commissioner Russell, "and must have been even thinner when they were recovered, some of them had put on one or two stone in weight. They are slow of thought, having spent the last three and a half years thinking only of food and how to get it ... In spite of all the starvation and ill-treatment, which they have suffered, they are absolutely un-daunted and were never defeated by the Japs."

> Russell's appointment as the ARC Chief Commissioner appeared in the Australian Women's Weekly on 6 November 1943

Released Australian Prisoners of War enjoying a drink in the Red Cross Hut at the Labuan Reception Camp in October 1945 (right)

The ARC had co-operated with the American Red Cross in Manila, where Russell visited in September 1945, establishing recreation huts at the reception camp there. He also toured the Morotai and Labuan reception camps on the same trip. Newman-Morris, Russell and the psychiatrist, who had been sent to the recovery centres, all commented on how very few were the psychiatric cases. Russell continued:

> *"Amongst the prisoners of war I did not find one who was anxious to return immediately to his home. They all felt that they would like to travel back on a ship after a period in the reception camp, in order that they might return to their families in a better mental and physical condition than they are now."*

Newman-Morris made a similar judgement and pointed out, *"The trip home by plane is exhausting for a man in normal health; it is altogether too much of a strain for men who have only recently been rescued from near starvation."* Both men commented on the plight of civilians in some areas as being as bad or worse that the POWs.

Alex's daughter Robina recalled her father's work with the Prisoners of War:

> *"He found this very up-setting as so many of them were so ill mentally as well as physically – no counselling in those days. While in Ceylon, Lady Mountbatten came to inspect the hospital he was setting up. She had one look at the scene, she took off her coat and with her secretary sat down between the stretchers and took down letters to the families. His (her father's) health never really came right after the war and then he had a series of strokes."*

Edwina, Lady Mountbatten, wife of Lord Louis Mountbatten, was the Chairman of the British Red Cross Society and she visited the rehabilitation hospital that Russell had helped to set up in Ceylon for the released POWs. While each country took responsibility for their own nationals, wherever possible, the overall co-ordination in South East Asia was in the hands of the British. Initially there were strong reservations about this visit as it was thought it would only disrupt what needed to be done.

However, when Lady Mountbatten took off her gloves, obtained pen and paper and started writing letters on behalf of the survivors, this proved to be a great morale booster for the men. Her interest in the ex-prisoners of war and the Australian Red Cross continued after the war had ended. In 1946, while visiting Australia, during a tour of Red Cross activities at other repatriation centres, in South East Asia, she gave unstinting praise for the role of the ARC in Ceylon and other areas.

Edwina, Lady Mountbatten (left), and (above, second from right) touring the 3rd Australian Prisoner of War Reception Camp in Manila, Philippines, with Australian Red Cross Welfare officers and nursing sisters in June 1945

Australian War Memorial

At the meeting of the National Council of the ARC in September 1945, following his return from the visit to the reception camps at Manila, Morotai and Labuan, Russell was quoted as saying that:

> *"It was great to see thousands of released prisoners laughing and talking and drinking coffee in the two recreation centres at the reception camp in Manila. Australian Red Cross personnel, with those from America and Britain, are doing wonderful work under adverse conditions. Transport is hard to obtain in Manila, and the climate is difficult to work in being very hot and rainy."* He added that *"he was agreeably surprised to find how well the majority of the prisoners were. He hoped that 80p.c. would be absolutely normal by Christmas. The prisoners were mainly subjected to general ill-treatment and to starvation, but good food and fresh clothing were already making a world of difference to them."*

Russell's work as Chief Commissioner of the Australian Red Cross must have been outstanding because he was later awarded a Knighthood of the Order of St John of Jerusalem as listed in the 'London Gazette' of 9th June 1948:

> *"The KING has been graciously pleased to sanction the following Promotions in, and Appointments to, the Venerable Order of the Hospital of St John of Jerusalem:*
>
> *As Knights. – Lieut Colonel Alex Russell, M.C."*

Although sponsors of such commendations are never known, it is quite likely that Lady Mountbatten sponsored this, as she was highly placed in, and worked much of her life, from before her marriage until her death, for the Order of St John's Ambulance Brigade, which had amalgamated with the Red Cross in Britain. In addition, this honour originated in Britain, not in Australia. Therefore, one can assume that this knighthood is an indication of the high regard by Lady Mountbatten for the work that Alex Russell was carrying out in South East Asia for the ARC.

After meeting initially in Ceylon, Russell and Lady Mountbatten must have become friends, as during the Mountbattens trip to Australia and New Zealand in April 1946, Lady Mountbatten was invited to spend Easter at 'Mawallok' and she arrived by car on Thursday evening 18 April. It was reported that she was *"spending a restful week end at Mawallok, Beaufort, as the guest of Colonel and Mrs Alex Russell. In the middle of a strenuous tour she is enjoying a good rest and a glimpse of Australian country life. Tomorrow* (Sunday) *morning she will leave for Tasmania."*

Lieut.-Colonel Alex Russell in New Guinea (right) in his role as the Chief Commissioner of the Australian Red Cross

223

Bravery tends to be associated with risking one's life, or physical injury, and Alex Russell had shown this in World War I by being awarded the Military Cross. However, there is another form of bravery, where a person goes into an area of horror, but where he must put his own feelings aside to provide the help that is needed. Alex Russell clearly had shown this type of bravery as well. Consistently pushing the horror aside takes its toll, because when the task is completed, the horror comes to the fore again, and is the substance of nightmares and what now would be termed post-traumatic stress syndrome. There is clear evidence that this Burma experience changed Alex Russell for the rest of his life.

In February 1946, Russell advised the ARC of his desire to be demobilised from the Field Force and this took place on 19 March. The certificate he received on his demobilisation noted that he had served the Society on full-time war service for 1,118 days, of which 827 days were in Australia and 291 days outside of Australia in the Middle East, Ceylon, New Guinea, Morotai and Manila. On 28 May 1946, a meeting of the National Council of the Australian Red Cross conferred Honorary Life Membership of the Society on Lieutenant Colonel Alex Russell, M.C., the Society's highest honour and a worthy tribute for his years of dedicated service.

Military Decorations

In addition to the Military Cross that he won in World War I, and the Knighthood of the Order of St John of Jerusalem, Alex Russell also was awarded the 1939-45 Star, the Defence Medal, the War Medal and the Australian Service Medal 1939-45, as well as being Mentioned in Despatches for *"Gallant & Distinguished Services SWP (South West Pacific) area,"* promulgated on 23 December 1943.

Cross of the Order of the Hospital of St. John of Jerusalem (right), awarded to Alex Russell on 9 June 1948

The Peugeot vehicle that Philip Russell Sr. drove as an ambulance during World War I in France was brought back to Australia and used as the farm and fire truck at 'Mawallok.' This photograph, taken in about 1932 or 1933, shows Alex Russell (right) and 'Bo' Fairbairn (centre) on the running board of the truck, with their children sitting on the bonnet, from left, Virginia Russell, Philip Russell, Robina Russell, Fred Fairbairn and 'Tink' Fairbairn.

Chapter 18

FAMILY LIFE

There were a number of marriages between cousins in the Russell family. The first Philip (1766-1833) married his cousin Anne Russell, and later took a second cousin Anne Carstairs as his second wife. George Russell married his cousin Euphemia Carstairs, while Alex's son Philip married his second cousin Alethea Fairbairn.

Marriage

Lieutenant Alex Russell, RGA, married Jess Lucy Fairbairn in London on Friday 14 September 1917 while on leave from the artillery training courses that he attended following his recovery from shell-fire injuries. Alex had known Jess from early childhood as she was the little sister of Gordon 'Bo' Fairbairn, his earliest and best friend, and at the wedding held at Holy Trinity Church in Sloane Street, 'Bo' was his best man.

There is a story that Alex first proposed to Jess when she was four. Alex had found a ring in a Christmas cracker and put it on Jess's finger, but there was difficulty getting the ring off and Alex later recalled that her finger became infected as a result. Fortunately, this incident was forgiven in time for the actual wedding. It is also known that Alex had been writing Jess romantic letters from since his time at Geelong Grammar in 1911.

The wedding notice, published in 'The Times' of London on 8 September 1917, indicated that the wedding ceremony would commence at 1pm and that *"all friends would be very welcome at the church."* Jess was described as the *"eldest daughter of Mr and Mrs F. W. Fairbairn, of Logan Downs, Queensland, and Sydney House, Farnham Common, Bucks...."* Fred Fairbairn had been the Australian Red Cross Commissioner in Europe, based in London for the first few years of the war.

'The Australasian' reported the day before the wedding that it would, *"be a very quiet affair. No invitations have been issued, but friends will probably go to greet the young people."* It also added that her parents were now living at Farnham Common. The marriage records show that Alex's residence at the time of marriage was 136 Sloane Street in London, possibly where his parents had been staying when they were in London. Witnesses were Lena Fairbairn, Jean Fairbairn and Ethel Norman Johnson, as neither the groom's nor the bride's parents were in England at the time of the wedding, suggesting perhaps that it had been quite quickly arranged to fit in with Alex's leave.

R.G.A. OFFICER MARRIED

Alex and Jess's wedding featured prominently in the 'Daily Mirror' newspaper in London on 15th September 1917, despite the misspelling of her surname

Lieutenant Alex Russell, R.G.A., and his bride (Miss Jess Rainbairn) after their return from Holy Trinity, Sloane-street, yesterday.

One report stated that the bride was given away by Mrs George Chirnside and following the ceremony the reception was held at her house in Park Lane, while another suggested she was given away by her uncle Steven Fairbairn and that the bride's maternal aunt, Mrs Clive Robertson, gave the wedding tea which was held at Mrs Chirnside's flat. This report referred to Jess as a *"dark-eyed bride"* who was to *"wear a beautiful wedding gown of Georgette made by "Lucille," who is also supplying a confection for her sister who is to be bridesmaid."*

The newly-weds enjoyed a two-stage honeymoon, and *"the first part of the honeymoon was to be spent at Mr and Mrs Norman Holme Johnson's house at St George's Hill, Weybridge, Mrs Johnson being a sister of Mrs Philip Russell, and aunt of the bridegroom. Later Lieut. and Mrs Russell propose going on to Lyndhurst, in the New Forest."*

Jess stayed in England after the honeymoon with her younger sister Jean, likely at their parents' home in Farnham Common, while Alex went to Lydd in Kent to complete his training courses and thence back to France on 20 November 1917. Alex's parents, along with his younger sisters Jean and Philippa, accompanied by a nurse for Philippa who was quite sickly, had sailed back to Australia from England in December 1916, prior to the wedding and arrived in Melbourne in January 1917. Once Alex was demobilised following the Armistice, he and Jess stayed in England for a few months until leaving for Australia, arriving back in Melbourne on 20 February 1919 aboard the 'S.S. Orsova.' The 'Riponshire Advocate' on 1 March 1919 reported upon the couple's return and suggested they would stay in Melbourne for a period before visiting 'Mawallok'.

Alex and Jess's first child Philip was born in September 1919 not long after their return from England and 'Table Talk' reported on the arrival in their social pages the week after the birth, writing that *"the stork paid a visit to Major and Mrs Alex Russell last week at South Yarra, and left them a son and heir, and incidentally turned two or our smartest matrons into grandmothers.....There has been great preparation for the advent of this infant, the first grandchild to further link up two of our best known families...."* Soon after the birth of Philip, the couple's first daughter Virginia came along the following year, and after a gap of nearly a decade, their second daughter Robina was born in 1929.

1923 photograph in 'The Home' magazine showing Jess Russell with her two young children, Philip and Virginia

Jess Lucy Russell (nee Fairbairn)

Jess Russell 1895 – 1983

Jess Lucy Fairbairn was born in Clermont, Queensland on 8 April 1895 to Frederick and Rhoda Fairbairn at their Logan Downs property. Fred Fairbairn owned property in the Western District of Victoria and in Geelong, and when Jess was growing up, her family spent time in both Queensland and Victoria.

She was educated at Toorak College in Melbourne and travelled with her family to England prior to World War I. After returning to Australia, she made her debut at a ball in Melbourne given by her parents to celebrate the construction of their newly built Logan House, on Toorak Road at South Yarra, in November 1914. She returned to England shortly after and became a Voluntary Aid Detachment nurse before joining the RAF as a driver later in the war.

Jess Russell was an accomplished golfer. She was runner-up three times in the Australian Ladies Amateur Championship (1927, 1930, 1932) but unfortunately fell just short of victory each time. Jess won the Australian Ladies Foursomes Championship twice, in 1926 and 1927, and represented Victoria six times. She was a member of the Australian 'Tasman Cup' Team in 1933, and at Royal Melbourne her name is commemorated by the "Jess Russell Foursomes Championship Cup" presented by Philip Russell in 1983 in memory of his mother.

In 1927, Jess set a course record of 78 at Barwon Heads, where the Russells were also members, which stood for 22 years. In 1930, when she was runner-up to Susie Tolhurst in the Australian Women's Amateur, Alex was also runner-up in the men's national title to Harry Hattersley, and this was the first time that a husband and wife had both made their respective national finals.

Jess was a very social person and society arrangements were important to her. In the immediate post-war years after returning from England as a married woman, Jess and her sister Jean were the prime movers in setting up and running a series of dances known as "Dazzle Balls" for their fancy dress and exotic outfits that were worn. At the 1920 Dazzle Ball Jess wore a costume described as *"Chinese in design, the clinging trousers and bodice being all in one, with jumper of gold tissue embroidered in multi colour. The Pagoda Headdress, also of tissue, dangled with many coloured silk pom-poms."* Alex, who was the treasurer for the 1920 ball, got into the fancy dress spirit too, *"Major Alec Russell was an Arab chief."* Tickets were one guinea

Thrilling Battle in Australian Women's Golf Championship

One of the closest contests in the history of Australian Women's golf took place last week at Commonwealth when Miss S. Tolhurst and Mrs Alex. Russell met in the 36-hole final of the Championship. Above: Two views of the course, and Miss Tolhurst (inset) with the trophy.

Mrs Alex. Russell, runner-up in the exciting struggle for the Women's Australian championship, won by Miss S. Tolhurst.

Jess Russell (above and above right) made the final of the Australian Women's Amateur Championship held at the Commonwealth Golf Club in 1930 but lost to Susie Tolhurst. The same year Alex lost the men's final to Harry Hattersley.

The swing of Jess Russell, shown at impact (right), displays a wonderful extension through the ball in this 1925 photograph

Mrs. Alex. Russell in action. Note ball leaving the club.

Mr Alex Russell demonstrates a chip shot, with Mrs Russell an interested onlooker.

At the races (right) – Jess Russell loved going to the races and she is seen here with Alex at the 1922 Melbourne Cup in this photograph published in 'The Home' magazine

OFF TO LUNCH.

Left to right: Mr. Lauchlan Mackinnon (son of Sir Lauchlan Mackinnon), Mrs. Alec Russell (formerly Miss Jess Fairbairn), Mrs. Lauchlan Mackinnon (who is the daughter of the late Mr. James Law, proprietor of the *Scotsman*, Edinburgh), Major Alec Russell, Mrs. Russell Clarke (whose husband is the son of the late Sir William Clarke).

(21 shillings) each and any profits after expenses were donated to the Children's Hospital.

She was also a very keen race-goer, and went to the races every opportunity she could. She was well-known for her many charitable works and was prominent in her service at the Air Force Canteen at Air Force House in Melbourne during World War II. She also aided the Victorian Missions to Seamen. With prisoners of war being repatriated home in late 1945, Jess proposed that returned servicemen and their wives might come to stay at 'Mawallok' for a short holiday, a fortnight per couple was suggested, and she and Alex had furnished a cottage on the property for their guests. Alex and Jess also hosted a number of fetes and garden parties at 'Mawallok', a number of which were to raise funds for various causes, including one in December 1952 that was opened by the Governor of Victoria, Sir Dallas Brookes, to raise funds for a new hall for the Beaufort Girl Guides and Boy Scouts.

Her daughter Robina recalled that:

> "'Jet' as her grandchildren and many others called her, was born in Queensland. When she was about 12 she, 'Bo' and Jean were seen riding past the men's quarters naked and Grandfather realised it was time they were tamed. So they were packed up and off to the U.K. and sent to Heathfield (very posh and had Princesses and Lady this and that). The girls there thought she was going to be black.
>
> The Fairbairn family seemed to go back and forth from Australia a lot and so did the Russells. I have a newspaper cutting of her coming-out-ball in Melbourne – the Russells were there too. As she was very pretty and vivacious I guess she was the Belle of the Ball. She and Dad had very good senses of humour and scored off each other. One amusing story was her telling a cousin that to get out of a deep bunker you waited for your partner to go to the other side of the green and you make a lot of noise and throw a handful of sand and the ball on the green at the same time. My brother said he had seen her do it while playing against Dad. Having known each other all their lives they were best friends and both playing good golf they could travel anywhere and play.
>
> She loved people and young people particularly. When the Polio scare was on in the 30's she told all her city friends to send their children up to us in the country, they would be safer. Perhaps she hadn't realised it was going to be 6 months! Dad disappeared to the club for peace and quiet for

Jess Russell serving young airmen in the canteen at Air Force House in Melbourne in 1943 (left). Jess was a prominent member of the volunteer committee that ran Force House, which was open 24 hours a day to serve RAAF personnel

long periods. I can still see one teenager saying "I haven't got a table napkin" so she tore hers in half.

> She loved entertaining. One lunch before one of the garden parties I remember had The Governor, his wife, The Bishop of Ballarat, Peter Thomson, his caddy, 2 models from Myers – whom she sat in between the Governor and the Bishop – and got away with it!! Mind you there was always STAFF. She always had someone to help and had a way of keeping them."

Robina also recalled that her mother was full of fun and always exaggerated her stories and was never one to let the facts get in the way of a good story. She was an active participant in practical jokes and was certainly "a character." She also noted that Alex and Jess were devoted to each other.

Her grandson William Keddell, Robina's son, recalled that:

"Grandma was a great larger-than-life character and a famous and much-loved exaggerator. Nothing was not possible in her eyes. She always came for Christmas and summer holidays with us in New Zealand. She could be famously regal. She hated small-minded bigots and could cut them down to size in an instant.

She gave a party for me once in Melbourne when I was 19 because I was headed to Western Australia to find work so she invited the head of Western Mining to give me a job and a few other friends – almost all males. Everyone enjoyed that her stories were not necessarily truthful......Reputedly she died laughing at one of her own jokes.

When I travelled with her once to Alice Springs and Darwin there were always all sorts of people who came up to us because they remembered her fondly from the War when she ran a hostel of sorts for soldiers. All her grandchildren called her 'Jet'."

Her father Frederick Fairbairn had been captain of the Geelong Golf Club (1899, 1905 to 1906) and club champion in 1910. Her mother Rhoda was an accomplished golfer and was Ladies' president of Geelong Golf Club for a number of years, as was Alex's mother 'Cissie'. Frederick's eldest brother (Sir) George Fairbairn was president of Royal Melbourne from 1904 to 1906, and was said to be the first Australian pastoralist to have owned a million sheep.

Jess Russell's cousin, the Hon. James Valentine "Jim" Fairbairn, Minister of Air and Civil Aviation, who was tragically killed in a plane crash in Canberra in 1940, was also the president of Royal Melbourne Golf Club at the time. Part of the Canberra Airport, the Fairbairn Airbase, is named in his honour. The Fairbairns were an athletic family and the family name was well-known in rowing circles. The Fairbairn Challenge Cup is still awarded to the 'Head of the River' crew at the annual regatta for Victorian private schools, and was first presented by Jess's uncle Charles Fairbairn (1858-1925) in 1911. There is also the Fairbairn Cup competed for at Cambridge University which honours Stephen Fairbairn, youngest brother of Frederick and Charles. Stephen was regarded as the

Jess's father Fred Fairbairn and her brother Gordon, better known as 'Bo,' were both Geelong Grammar School students

Geelong Grammar School Archives

Father and Son
F. W. Fairbairn, Captain of Cricket Eleven, 1883 and 1884.
G. A. Fairbairn, Captain of Cricket Eleven, 1909 and 1910.

outstanding coach of all time in England, and originator of the Fairbairn style of rowing.

Gordon 'Bo' Fairbairn, Jess's brother and Alex's best friend, played cricket for Cambridge and Middlesex as a spin bowler and a middle-order batsman, and during World War I was gassed while on active service and later recuperated in Egypt. Alex Russell was at Cambridge with both 'Bo' and Osborne Fairbairn, Jess's cousin, and some years later Osborne's daughter, Alethea, married Alex's son Philip in 1946, further linking the Russell and Fairbairn families together.

Alex and Jess Russell liked to argue, according to son Philip, and an article from 'The Sunday Mail' newspaper in Adelaide from August 1932 depicted Jess's feisty attitude with her husband:

"Mrs Alex Russell, who is in Adelaide for the women's national golf championships at Kooyonga, told this week how her golf-famous husband made a mistake about her ability at the royal and ancient game. Mrs Russell is probably the finest woman golfer in Australia who has never held a big title. When she was thinking of going to Melbourne from

the western district of Victoria to compete in the Victorian women's championship, her husband tried to dissuade her. "There are only eight to qualify," he said. "The chances are that as you are short of practice at Royal Melbourne you won't be one of them." But Mrs Russell entered and qualified easily. That night Alex Russell received the following telegram from his wife:- "Qualified third. Comb that out of your beard.""

While they were two of the finest golfers Victoria ever produced, arguably the best husband and wife ahead of Sloan Morpeth and his wife Susie Tolhurst, Alex and Jess generally steered clear of partnering in mixed foursomes for that obvious reason, however, they did play together in a number of events with some success. Their son Philip later recalled an occasion when they did play mixed foursomes together. Alex had hit the ball into a greenside bunker and as Jess was getting ready to play her shot, Alex said to her caddy, *"Dynamite her please caddy,"* showing little confidence that she could get out of the bunker safely. Jess overheard this remark and deliberately thinned her ball, hitting it as far out as she could over the green. Over to you now husband!

Having left the management of 'Mawallok' to their son Philip, Jess and Alex moved to a flat at Walsh Street in South Yarra in 1960, and after Alex's death the following year, she lived out the remainder of her energetic and full life at Walsh Street with friends and family until her death on 14 September 1983, aged 88.

The HOME, October 2nd, 1934.

Best friends (above) – Alex Russell and 'Bo' Fairbairn

Alex and Jess (left) with her cousin Jim Fairbairn

A glamorous Jess Russell graced the Society Pages in a number of newspapers and magazines over the years – this photograph (right) was from October 1934 in the lead up to the visit to 'Mawallok' by the Duke of Gloucester

Above: Mrs. Alex Russell, with Mr. Alex Russell, of Mawallok, Beaufort, Victoria, will entertain the Duke of Gloucester at her country home.

An invitation to a ball at Buckingham Palace (right) was a highlight of the Russells' trip to England in 1935

Miss L. Baynes, Mrs. A. Russell, Mr. A. Russell and Mr. G. A. Fairbairn resting in front of the club house after their round.

Alex and Jess photographed with Jess's brother 'Bo' Fairbairn (left) at a Mixed Foursomes event held at Metropolitan GC in September 1926. Alex and Jess tied for the best gross score with a 79, while 'Bo' and his partner, Miss Baynes, shot 84 off the stick.

Jess at the Flemington races in 1926 with her cousin Osborne Fairbairn's wife (right), whose daughter Alethea later married Alex and Jess's son Philip in 1946

Mrs. Osborne Fairbairn and Mrs. Alec Russell at Flemington

Alex and Jess on board the 'Orvieto' on their way to England and the Imperial Conference in 1923 (below)

Alex and Jess at the races in July 1936 (above) with Mrs Kenneth Mackinnon

Alex Russell (standing) and Jess (seated far right) at a social gathering in 1921 at Werribee Park (left)

Philip Russell 1919 – 2009

Philip Russell, like his father and grandfather before him, was educated at Geelong Grammar and had a distinguished military career during World War II. He initially enlisted in the infantry at the age of 20, some nineteen hours after war was declared, but soon after decided upon a shift into the artillery, which Alex was able to arrange through his military connections. Philip served in eleven countries, including Greece, Crete, and Egypt, primarily as a forward observation officer.

He had refused a commission initially in 1940, but accepted one in 1942. From 1943 to 1945 he undertook intelligence operations, often behind Japanese lines, in New Guinea, and was recommended for a Military Cross on three occasions. He finished the war patrolling behind the Japanese lines in Bougainville and came home three stone (19 kg) lighter than when he left the country at the start of the war.

In private life Philip restored 'Mawallok' and its famed Merino stud to its pre-war state and went on to greatly improve the property's yield, serving as its manager for 34 years. Philip and his wife Alethea (nee Fairbairn) had 4 children: Alexander (Sandy), Ian, Susan and Caroline. He was president of the Victorian division of the Liberal Party and a Life Governor of the Australian Sheep Breeders' Association.

He travelled widely and was in demand as a lecturer, while the latter part of his life after selling 'Mawallok' was spent at Ocean Grove, and then at Barwon Heads. Philip was an accomplished artist, a talent he had shown while still at school. He understood art and had a good eye for quality art and undertook several exhibitions of his own work. He was a generous benefactor of the Geelong Art Gallery and became that institution's second only life member. Philip passed away in 2009, aged 89.

Philip Russell

ALETHEA FAIRBAIRN **PHILIP RUSSELL**
Victorian squatting families united

Philip and Alethea's engagement announcement in 1946 (above) and at the Melbourne Cup in November 1953 (right), as seen by the Australian Women's Weekly

GREY TOPPER. Mr. Philip Russell was among the many male punters who wore toppers. His wife wore a shell hat, feather-trimmed, to match her smart shantung suit.

Virginia Fairbairn Russell (Simpson) 1920 – 1962

Virginia was educated at the Clyde Girl's Grammar School at Woodend and then went on to finishing school in Paris, spending 18 months at Madame Boussier's establishment. She spent a year in England in 1939 and during World War II she worked in the Red Cross POW department in Melbourne, a job her father no doubt arranged for her. In 1947 she married Derek Simpson, the brother of her friend Audrey, and moved to Adelaide to live with him. She raised three daughters: Serena (Watson), Victoria (Seekamp) and Fiona (Dowling).

Virginia enjoyed both golf and tennis and loved playing bridge, and was an associate member at Royal Melbourne for a period, winning a handicap competition in 1941 off a handicap of 26. Jess often went to Adelaide to visit Virginia and the grandchildren, and in turn they often stayed at 'Mawallok'. Virginia was never very strong physically according to her younger sister and she passed away on 27 August 1962, aged 42, after a battle with Muscular Dystrophy, with her children aged 12, 9 and 7 years.

Virginia Russell

Robina Russell (Keddell, later Westenra) 1929 -

Robina was born in 1929, nine years after her elder sister Virginia and she recalls that her birth *"was a mistake and I was always blamed for spoiling the chances of my mother not winning the Ladies Golf championships that year!"* She was educated at Toorak College, like her mother, and after taking a two-year Horticulture course at Burnley College in Melbourne, travelled to Africa where she married Peter Keddell.

The couple emigrated to New Zealand where they farmed a property and raised three sons, William, Philip and Stephen. After a divorce from her first husband, Robina later married Gerald Westenra and she still lives in New Zealand. Her interests include gardening, perhaps a legacy from growing up with the 'Mawallok' garden, as well as art, music and history. She has volunteered with Riding-for-Disabled for 25 years and currently volunteers with Meals-on-Wheels in her home town of Tauranga.

Left to Right: Miss Robina Russell, Mrs. Philip Russell and Mrs. Alex. Russell, photographed at the cocktail party given by Mr. and Mrs. Alex. Russell at Menzies' Hotel yesterday.

Robina, Alethea and Jess featured in the Society Pages in March 1950

Robina Russell with her son Philip at 'Mawallok'

Two Australian Open champions together – the 1924 champion Alex Russell congratulates Norman Von Nida on his victory in the 1953 Australian Open held over the Russell designed East Course at Royal Melbourne

Bruce Howard – State Library of Victoria

Chapter 19

RUSSELL THE GOLF ADMINISTRATOR

Contribution to the Royal Melbourne Golf Club

Alex Russell's contribution to Royal Melbourne was far greater than just his involvement with Dr MacKenzie in creating the West Course, and designing the East Course on his own. The magnitude of these twin achievements tends to overshadow his many other significant contributions to the club's development.

In 1929, the members rejected the proposed new clubhouse on the hill, which was to cost an estimated £60,000, as being too expensive, and set a financial limit of £40,000. A new clubhouse plan was produced but its cost still exceeded the £40,000. When the proposal for the new clubhouse had been rejected a second time, many of the Council felt the need to resign. This led to an Extraordinary General Meeting being held on 12 August 1929 to change the club's constitution, and a new ballot for office bearers and councillors was held on 28 September. Alex Russell was elected to Council with the greatest number of votes.

He was immediately appointed to both the Green committee and the Tennis committee, and was to serve for over 25 years on the Green committee, most of the time as Chairman. He made many decisions about top-dressing, poisoning of weeds and, no doubt in conjunction with greenkeeper Claude Crockford, devised a plan to drain the area of 7th, 8th, 11th and 12th holes of the East Course in 1937. He investigated the possibility of a fairway watering system, and supported the search for bore water.

Alex Russell continued his research into grasses. As MacKenzie had been an agent for the seed company Sutton & Sons of Reading, Sutton's Mix, a combination of fescue and South German bent, was used on the greens on both courses at Royal Melbourne. Morcom had used a mixture of Kentucky Bluegrass and Creeping Bentgrass as early as 1918. With the respect these two men had for each other, it is quite likely that the club's research into turf grasses was undertaken by Russell and Morcom together. Russell was the club's representative at the Victorian Golf Associations' Greenkeeping Research Group for many years. When a Golf Club Organisation meeting was arranged in 1931, both Russell and Morcom represented the club. Appreciation of Russell's actions at the Board of the Greenkeeping Research Group was recorded.

While it is usually the captain's role to deal with matters concerning the club's professional, Russell's name appears in the minutes on several occasions in relation to this. Russell also recommended on more than one occasion an increase in wages for Claude Crockford, Morcom's replacement as Head Greenkeeper, and his staff.

In 1939, Russell took on a significant role in the running of the Australian Championships held at Royal Melbourne's West Course, with golf writer Jack Dillon later noting that *"his organisation of the 1939 Australian championship meeting set an all-time efficiency standard for such an occasion."* Russell had other responsibilities out on the course in that event too. The former Australian Open champion Jim Ferrier, writing in the 'Sydney Morning Herald' about the championship, noted that, *"during play so far, I have not yet discovered a flat putt over four feet. The holes are usually placed on slopes, as the greens have no flat surfaces. This morning, A. Russell, the well-known golf architect, who is a member of the club, went around with the greenkeeper marking out where the holes are to be placed during the championship."* Alex Russell, in his usual thorough manner, was leaving nothing to chance.

When in 1940, Mr Ryan replaced Mr Lewis as Secretary of Royal Melbourne, the names of those proposing and seconding motions were rarely included in the Council minutes. The motions that Alex Russell had been involved with sponsoring are interesting in that several were involved with the playing rights of women and their rights. It appeared that he was supportive of women and their rights. Russell was also a supporter of the Victorian Ladies' Golf Union in their requests for the use of a course, as he was of requests from the Royal Melbourne Associates. He also spoke about the times when women were to be allowed on the course which included playing on weekends, and stated that the Associates' playing rights should be expressed in more concise form.

In his communications to other clubs where he had designed the course, he placed an emphasis on the need for women's tees, which was part of his belief that people of all standards should be able to enjoy their

golf and have a course of appropriate length and difficulty, an approach similarly commented upon by Dr MacKenzie. Jess Russell told one female member, an 'associate' in those days, that the women's tees on the West Course had been an after-thought. Some of the placements tend to confirm this, however, this is not true of the East, or at those courses that Russell designed on his own. It is pertinent to repeat prominent women's golf administrator Mrs Gatehouse's comments about the Yarra Yarra course:

> *"During all the years I have been making scratch scores, this is the first course I have ever been on where the ladies tees have been out in the correct spots without having to be altered in any way."*

World War II interrupted Russell's role at Royal Melbourne from August 1941 to early 1946. Before enlisting he had suggested that head greenkeeper, Claude Crockford, might wish to close one course as a method of saving money and to reduce the stress on Crockford's greatly reduced ground staff. Crockford preferred to maintain both courses with a staff of four elderly men. Apparently he felt that if he let one course 'go' it would be very difficult to bring it back to good condition again. Russell also sensibly suggested that the Victorian championship and club championship not be played during the war.

Soon after his return from war duties, Russell and Crockford presented a report on the courses, and a three-year plan of works and improvements was developed to bring the courses back to good order, while the report also pointed out that additional staff would be required. In 1946, Sandringham City Council proposed a plan that included acquiring the club's land north of Cheltenham Road which contained the West Course holes from 13 to 16. Russell stressed the importance of acquiring all the blocks where the practice fairway now exists, so that if the club did lose the land over the road, it would have land on which to build some replacement holes. While this threat of acquisition was satisfactorily resolved, Russell still pressed for the security that the blocks along Cheltenham Road would provide, in the event of a later acquisition, and that the failure to purchase any one property, would doom the four-hole fall-back plan. All blocks were successfully purchased by 1955. The club's Council also examined the potential of purchasing land further out of the city and in 1947 Russell inspected potential land at Dingley.

In the late 1940s a problem had emerged with errant golf balls going into houses along the Ardoyne Street boundary of the West Course. Rapidly growing eucalypt trees were planted and the 11th West was played from a temporary tee. To compensate for the loss of yardage, the 12th West was extended by Alex Russell in 1950 to a par five with a new green to the left rear of the old green.

A further threat to the course was the ever-increasing Federal Land Tax and Municipal Rates, which would have made the financial burden prohibitive for the club to remain where it was. In October 1951, Russell suggested that the club should, once more, explore the possibility of purchasing land further from the CBD. Then there arose the threat of a railway line from Moorabbin to Ricketts Point passing through the course just near the clubhouse. Thanks to what started as a Private Members Bill in the Victorian Parliament, but was taken over by the Hamer Government after negotiations with the Labor Opposition, the *"Cultural and Recreational Lands Act"* was passed. This protected clubs from prohibitive rates, or being compulsorily acquired without a specific act of Parliament. While this threat existed, a committee which included Alex Russell had been searching for suitable sites if relocation was needed. Fortunately, it was not.

Claude Crockford, Royal Melbourne's long-serving head greenkeeper, worked closely with Alex Russell during Russell's time on the club's Council

In 1953, the club undertook discussions with the Frankston Golf Club that was experiencing financial difficulties. Russell inspected the club's 250 acre (100 ha) site which was home to their 9-hole course and pronounced that it was suitable for expansion to 18 holes. Royal Melbourne made an offer to Frankston to purchase their land but it was rejected. That same year Russell was noted as an *"important personality"* at Royal Melbourne when the club successfully hosted the Australian Open over his East Course.

Alex Russell continued to make minor changes to both the courses until 1955 when he failed to gain re-election to Council. Following this he was rarely seen at Royal Melbourne, preferring to play his golf at Barwon Heads and the country courses in the Western District such as Beaufort and Gala.

Contribution to the Barwon Heads Golf Club

Alex Russell served on the committee at Barwon Heads for a number of years, was the captain from 1946 to 1949 and president from 1950 to 1952. In his time at Barwon Heads he won the Services Cup in 1937. Although details are sketchy, Russell was involved in some course alterations undertaken through this period. His wife Jess was also a member, first joining in 1926 until resigning her membership in 1976.

Turf Research

Alex Russell developed a keen interest in golf course turf and its maintenance, doubly important in his twin roles as the chairman of Royal Melbourne's greens committee and as a consulting golf course architect to a number of golf clubs. There are many references within the Royal Melbourne minutes to Russell's activities regarding turf research, including:

> 24th November 1929. *Experimental Plots*
>
> *"The action of Mr Russell and Mr Blewett in forming experimental plots on 3rd, 4th, 15th and 16th was approved."* [The numbering of the holes would be the Sandringham holes]
>
> 16th June 1930. *Annual General Meeting, Annual Report of Council.*
>
> *"Members are greatly indebted to Mr Alex Russell for the time and attention he has given in the laying-out of the 'MacKenzie' [West] and 'Cheltenham' [East] courses, beside research work in the direction of improving our fairways and greens."* An appreciation of M. A. Morcom follows.

> 28th November 1935. Correspondence.
>
> *"The Board of Greenkeeper's Research. Received. Appreciation of Mr Russell's action to be recorded."*

Alex Russell was also the Royal Melbourne representative on the VGA Greenkeepers' Research Committee and attended a number of meetings through the 1930s, including some with Claude Crockford.

ALEX RUSSELL

At Lake Karrinyup in Western Australia, Russell oversaw trials of a number of turf varieties for both fairways and greens and he also made a suggestion in 1928 about how to put nutrients into the fairway soil by planting *"a cover crop of peas, vetch, etc. at the beginning of the wet season. This crop should be turned in when sufficiently grown and after further manuring couch grass should be ploughed in or planted by hand. This cover crop should put considerable necessary humus into the ground helping to build up a firmer turf and to conserve moisture."* In his 1933 report to the club he discussed the use of heavier soil for topdressing the greens *"to encourage the fescue at the expense of the couch,"* and suggested the use of a combination of Sulphate of Ammonia and Sulphate of Iron as fertilizer, instead of straight Sulphate of Ammonia, while *"once a year a complete manure containing some lime might be used."* Similarly at Riversdale, Russell gave advice on turf establishment and maintenance, and oversaw the test plots.

At 'Mawallok,' in order to increase the carrying capacity of the land, the pasture needed to be improved and Russell researched and selected the best grasses for the pastures. 'The Australasian' featured 'Mawallok' in its 'Famous Pastoral Properties' on 7 December 1940 and noted that *"the improvement in pasture by scientific means has been invaluable. About 1,500 acres has been improved with rye grass and clover, and in 1939 500 tons of ensilage, and 500 tons of pressed clover hay were put away."*

Victorian Golf Association

Alex Russell was selected as captain and manager of the 1930 Victorian team to represent the state in the Kirk-Windeyer Cup competition played in New Zealand. 'Golf' magazine in its 2 June 1930 edition noted that:

> *"Members of Victoria's Kirk-Windeyer Cup team are unanimous in their praise of Alex. Russell as manager and captain of the team. They went out of their way to express their appreciation of the fine way in which he looked after his charges on the trip, and of the manner in which he fostered the team spirit. Mrs Russell, too, came in for her share of praise. The players appreciated greatly all that she did in helping to make their trip an enjoyable and memorable one."*

Russell served on a VGA committee in 1934 organised to formulate the basis for a state-wide system of handicapping. Other prominent members of the committee included Ivo Whitton, A.W. Jackson, Mick Ryan and Sloan Morpeth.

Russell could see flaws in the existing pennant match system and in 1930 he made a suggestion for a grading system for pennant golf that was eventually adopted by the VGA. He proposed a series of grades, with groups of four teams in each grade. Matches could readily be played on a home and away basis, and at the end of each season the top team in that grade would be promoted into the next highest grade, while the last team in the higher grade would be relegated into the next grade down. This system of promotion and relegation is still used in most pennant series played across Australia.

Russell also acted as referee for some important matches. In July 1925 he officiated in the final of the Sun-Herald £500 Tournament at Royal Melbourne between Tom Howard and Bill Spicer. In 1939 he was the referee for the final match in 'The Australasian' Challenge Shield foursomes held at Royal Melbourne's East Course on a stormy day, *"there was casual water everywhere, and on this point Alex Russell had to give decisions. Disguised in a sou'-wester and waterproof overalls, he controlled play with the assistance of Arthur Le Fevre to the satisfaction of all concerned. "When I was asked to act as referee," he said, "I studied the weather chart before I accepted, but I am afraid I could not have read it accurately, or I should never have taken on the job."* During the match the Kingston Heath and Victorian amateur Mick Ryan called a penalty on himself when the ball moved after he had addressed a 20-foot putt on the

THE VICTORIAN TEAM WHICH PLAYED NEW ZEALAND FOR THE RIGHT TO CHALLENGE NEW SOUTH WALES FOR THE KIRK-WINDEYER CUP
From left: A. Russell, A. A. Hancock, F. L. Bulte, M. J. Ryan (Amateur Champion of Australia)

Alex Russell was the captain and manager of the Victorian team to New Zealand in 1930

11th green. No-one else saw the ball move, and Russell later remarked, *"That ball probably moved about a thousandth of an inch, but Ryan had no doubt about what was right. Some people seem to think that unless a ball moves at least three inches there is no need to take note of it."*

On 16 March 2016, Alex Russell was inducted into the Victorian Golfing Industry's *'Hall of Fame'* in acknowledgement of his service to golf in Victoria, a long-overdue recognition of his many contributions to the game.

Australian Golf Union

For a number of years there had been dissatisfaction on the part of competitors with how the Australian Championship meetings were scheduled and conducted by the Australian Golf Union. In the December 1925 issue of 'Golf' magazine, an article on this subject was published by a writer using the pen name of "All Square". The 'Referee' newspaper in Sydney summarised the article in a brief column and revealed the writer's identity:

> *"In the December issue of "Golf" "All Square" has written a sane article embracing all important problems, and how they may be solved. He deals with the fact that the past meeting was unnecessarily too long, and that course congestion could be avoided by eliminating the many who have not even a stray dog's chance to win.*
>
> *"All Square" is Alex Russell, an Open champion, and as the programme for the coming season is about to be drawn up it would add interest to the meeting in general if the "powers that be" gave his programme the big consideration which is due to it."*

It is not known if the AGU gave his suggestions any credence, but it shows that Russell was willing to put his time and energy into improving the way that golf championships were run. Unfortunately, this is the only article by "All Square" that the authors have been able to find.

Alex Russell was for a time one of Royal Melbourne's delegates on the Council of the AGU and attended a number of their annual meetings, including the 1930 meeting at The Metropolitan Golf Club and the following year's meeting held at The Australian Golf Club in Sydney during the Australian Championships in late August. Royal Melbourne had applied to the AGU to have their new West Course rated as a

THE REFEREE, Mr. Alex Russell.

Alex Russell (left), in his wet-weather gear, refereed the final of the Australasian Shield Foursomes in the rain on his East Course at Royal Melbourne in 1939
State Library of Victoria

championship one and at this meeting *"Messrs. A. Russell, C. Lane, and D. Turner, sen., were appointed to inspect and report at next annual meeting."* The course was duly rated. Russell was also appointed to a sub-committee, along with Ivo Whitton and J. Hunter of Queensland, to *"be delegated to go into the question of establishing a national system of handicapping."*

Russell and Ivo Whitton were asked by the AGU to visit Perth and report on the suitability of their courses to host the Australian Championships in the near future. They visited Perth in September 1948 in the capacity of an official AGU sub-committee, and after an inspection of the courses it was apparent the only one potentially suitable was Lake Karrinyup, and that was only after a number of suggested alterations to the course that the pair proposed. While the contents of their report back to the AGU is not known, Russell made it clear to the club that they would need to undertake some modifications if they were to be successful. He wrote to Lake Karrinyup shortly after, setting out the work he recommended, with the club implementing it all promptly and going on to successfully host the championships in 1952.

GOLF CHAMPIONS IN OLD BOYS' CONTEST

Russell with his friend and rival Ivo Whitton

TWO NOTED VICTORIAN GOLFERS, Alex Russell (left) and Ivo Whitton, at Metropolitan today for the Old Public Schoolboys' golf. They attended Wesley and Melbourne Grammar respectively.

Alex Russell skiing at
Mount Buller in 1932

Chapter 20

ALEX RUSSELL THE MAN

Describing a person's character more than 50 years after their death is difficult. There are now very few people alive today who knew him at all, and only one of these, his daughter Robina, can say she knew him well. Fortunately, his son Philip gave some recorded interviews about his father, including one with the authors prior to his death in 2009, and these give a very personal insight from a son into his father. However, one thing that is beyond dispute is that Alex Russell was a highly intelligent and creative man.

People likely saw Alex Russell in different ways. Some found him aloof, and given his propensity to not tolerate fools gladly, and with his high intelligence, would have found him intimidating as well. Accordingly, they may have chosen not to like him. He was a man who initially withheld his counsel, however, when he did speak, he spoke his mind and was mostly listened to, but he could sometimes appear aggressive when he felt strongly about a point. Russell's son, Philip, said that he could at times be taciturn and pompous, recalling that:

> "Alex Russell was a brilliant athlete: never used his engineering degree: had a very clear brain: modest of his many achievements: underneath he was a shy gentleman: did not find it easy to communicate with everyone, but had many friends."

He also described his father as being *"always right"* and that he *"was always having a row with someone. Very stubborn if he had a point of view."* According to his daughter-in-law Alethea Russell, Alex *"and his wife always fought, they loved fighting,"* to which his son Philip added that *"Dad loved fighting the most, Mum always gave in in the end."*

Alex was not a good letter-writer, only writing once to his son and that was on the occasion of his 21st birthday. In all the times Alex visited the school for committee meetings of the Old Geelong Grammarians while Philip was a student, he never took the time to say hello to his son when he was there. He did though leave a 36-hole event at Barwon Heads one day so that he could go and watch Philip in his school sports day.

His daughter Robina thinks that basically her father was shy, despite his outward confidence. He had a good sense of humour, with quick and witty responses, and the evidence suggests that

it was a rather dry sense of humour. She wrote that *"people found him dour but his friends and family knew him to have a very quick wit and sense of humour."* Her descriptions of some family incidents indicate a man with significant warmth, while Philip described him as *"a very kind man."* Robina stressed his absolute belief in fairness, and gave as an example that of a man who was sacked without any explanation from a firm her father was associated with. When Russell heard about this he sought out the man and explained all the reasons for his dismissal to him. To his way of thinking that was only fair. Russell's belief in fairness also surfaces in his golf courses where lesser players and women are shown due consideration.

Robina wrote of her father:

> "Alex Russell was a very able man in many spheres. He had a clear logical brain. He excelled at any sport and was also a good shot. As a father he was old-fashioned in today's world and left our upbringing more to his wife. He had a very funny dry sense of humour and was very kind but had a temper which was better avoided. My early memories of him were accompanying him opening gates as we went around the property and also his expertise of beautifully made bows and arrows which got lost very easily."

Alex Russell chose his close friends carefully and was very loyal to those he did choose, just as they were to him. He was widely respected for his many gifts including leadership, involving him in a wide variety of committees. He was made a Life Member of Royal Melbourne, Yarra Yarra and Royal Adelaide for his services to these golf clubs and to golf in general, and was a Life Member of the Red Cross Society for his outstanding services to that organisation during World War II. Similarly, when Russell first stood for Council at Royal Melbourne in 1928 following the resignation of the majority of Council members over the clubhouse issue, he polled the most votes of any candidate, and remained a member of Council from 1928 to 1955, a period of 27 years. He became Private or Confidential Secretary to Stanley Bruce for around 12 months when Bruce was Prime Minister of Australia in 1923-24. From the press articles of the time, of which the authors have seen more than 400 where his name is mentioned, he comes through in a very positive light as a person. Alex Russell may have appeared aloof but overall the impression is that here was a man widely respected, and generally liked by others. If this was not true, he would not have held as many important positions as he did.

Alex's father, Philip, was three when his father, Alexander, died. At 12 years of age Philip was sent to Edinburgh to be educated, and it is likely that he never had a true father figure. Alex saw his own father as authoritarian and someone to be avoided, so it would appear Alex may also have lacked a proper father/son relationship. Alex's own son, Philip, was 12 when they moved to 'Mawallok' and was a boarder at Geelong Grammar School from 1930 to 1938. He was 20 when Alex went to war again, from which they both returned different men. Alex, in turn, appears to have had difficulty forming a sound relationship with his own son, however, his relationship with his daughter Robina appears to have been a better one.

Russell the Sportsman

Alex Russell excelled at any sport in which he participated, and these were many and varied. The first mention of his formal involvement in sport is in cricket at Trinity College at Glenalmond in Scotland, when he represented the school in the under-14 team in May 1905. His father Philip was a keen cricketer who had put together an Osborne House team of local cricketers, known as "The Nondescripts", who played at the private cricket ground that he had established at Osborne House. It is very likely that Alex and his best friend 'Bo' Fairbairn both learnt the game there. Fairbairn was captain of the Geelong Grammar School's cricket team in 1910, a role that Russell held in the latter part of the following year. Both were slow bowlers and batsmen, with 'Bo' Fairbairn being good enough to play county cricket in England after the war. Russell also played Australian Rules football in the school's First XVIII team, but was described by his son Philip as not being that good a footballer. Alex was a member of the school shooting team as shooting was long an interest of his. It ran in the family too, with his father Philip, 'Big Gran' as his grandson Philip called him, and his son both keen shooters and excellent marksmen.

Alex was also a good tennis player, winning the Freshman's Championship at Cambridge and some years later Norman (later Sir Norman) Brookes, a Wimbledon Champion and Australian Davis Cup representative, stated that Russell could have been a Davis Cup calibre player had he chosen tennis ahead of golf. His son Phillip later recalled that his father had a very good second serve and that he beat him at table tennis once but that it was the only time he ever beat his father at any sport. Russell also excelled at other racquet sports including

squash and Royal Tennis played at the Royal Melbourne Tennis Club's court in Exhibition Street, Melbourne.

'Golf' magazine wrote of *"Russell's Versatility"* in its 10 August 1925 issue, noting that:

> *"Alec Russell, Open Champion of Australia, can do more than play golf. A few years ago he had the makings of a first-rate cricketer. Even better was his attempt at tennis, and no less an authority than Norman Brookes assures us that had he persevered with the game Russell might have become one*

Australian tennis champion Norman Brookes, twice winner of the Wimbledon singles championship, was a keen and talented golfer and a member at Royal Melbourne. He knew Russell well and believed that he could have been one of the best tennis players in Australia if he had not chosen golf.

of the finest wielders of the racket in this country. Poor eyesight proved the drawback to both of these games, and it was only when the Open Champion was fitted up with his present well-known pair of "Harold Lloyd's" that he was able to do anything good at golf."

At Cambridge, Russell won a Half Blue for billiards by representing Cambridge against Oxford, and it was reported that after an important round of golf he would often play billiards to unwind and "keep his eye in." Russell played some competitive billiards in Victoria, and in 1927 was reported as playing for the first time in the qualifying rounds of the Victorian Amateur Billiards Championship. The reporter noted of Russell's play that he was doing well in his match *"but was far too impatient; many of his opportunities were lost owing to his hard striking,"* and he eventually lost. Philip recalled that his father won the billiards championship at the Melbourne Club where Alex was a member. A few years earlier Russell donated a *"fine rosewood billiard table"* to the Barwon Heads Golf Club.

Robina recalls that her father once claimed *"the world's longest drive from outside the Melbourne Club three blocks to outside Henry Bucks menswear. It got tracked in the tram line! (at 2am)."* Alex was a long-time member of the Melbourne Club, joining on 4 July 1919 and remaining a member until his death in 1961. Club records show that he was a regular participant in billiards tournaments until 1951. His first appearance came in the tournament "Leura June 1924", with a handicap of "75 behind", when he proceeded as far as the Semi-Final. He performed similarly in the following year and by August 1926 his handicap was recorded as "owes 90". In 1930 he reached the Final, playing against the Hon. W.L.R. Clarke. The winner is not named, but Clarke is recorded as "rec. 70, 232"; Russell "250." The first prize trophy for this Handicap Billiards Tournament was valued at £21, the second prize at £7. At the 1931 tournament, Russell's handicap appeared as "owes 100". The results are not regularly recorded thereafter until 1945, when Russell (owes 100, 192) met and lost to R.C.M. Kimpton (250). Russell continued to enter tournaments, not passing beyond the heats, until 1950.

In 1946 the Melbourne Club secretary asked Norman Barrett and Alex Russell to suggest improvements to the billiard rooms. Their reply included suggestions they had received in a report from Walter Lindrum, the Australian billiards champion. The club's history book, "Number 36 Collins Street" by Ronald McNicoll, contains one reference to Russell and his friend Alan Ritchie getting into some trouble with the committee, *"More and more members such as A.B. Ritchie and Alex Russell, incurred the Committee's displeasure by buying drinks for non-resident members or strangers out of permitted hours, thereby endangering the club's licence".*

Russell was an enthusiastic skier and noted in his war diary in November 1915, that a snowfall had reminded him that he would have been getting ready to go to St Moritz in eastern Switzerland at that time of the year. His sister Joan had written about a family holiday at St Moritz in 1909, a trip that the young Alex no doubt participated in, and it would appear that he visited St Moritz quite regularly when in England. Alex was also photographed as a young man standing proudly in front of the sign for the Cresta Run, the great toboggan run at St Moritz, with tobogganing one of his favoured winter pursuits there.

He was also an early participant in snow and skiing activities in Australia at Mt Buller in the Victorian Alps. In the late 1920s, Russell, Alan Ritchie and the Austrian, Helmut Koffler, who built the first chalet at Mt Buller in 1929, were involved in establishing the first ski run at Mt Buller, according to Russell's son Philip, who later recalled:

> *"Helmet Koffler would help with the breakfast wash up then he'd grease up the skis....in those days you had to wax the bottom of your skis to make it slidier, you know. You ran into the shed and picked up your skis and Dad spent some time ... and then Helmet Koffler suddenly gave us half an hour's start and he was at the top of the Buller run, before we were, but we were lousy skiers but Dad was pretty good. I wouldn't say he was a champion but he and Alan Richie, who wouldn't be a champion either, but they built the thing and encouraged a lot of people to go there."*

Philip also noted that his father and 'Bo' Fairbairn once went cross-country skiing across Norway during their stay at Cambridge University, while the time Alex spent in Scotland as a boy with the ghillie Bathgate led to a lifelong interest in fishing and shooting.

The Austrian skier Helmut Koffler built the first chalet at Mount Buller and was involved with Alex Russell and Alan Ritchie in establishing the first ski run there

H. KOFLER,

Alex Russell enjoyed many forms of winter sports, tobogganing on the Cresta Run at St. Moritz (left), cross-country skiing (right) and making a snow camp at Mount Buller (below)

Jess's cousin Jim Fairbairn got Alex interested in flying in the 1930s and the two men embarked on a number of flying trips together. In 1931, the 'Referee' newspaper in Sydney noted that, *"The famous Russell family of golfers has been badly bitten by the aviation bug. Mr and Mrs Alex Russell spent a recent week-end in the Western District, where Jim Fairbairn, brother of Mrs Russell* [cousin], *took them on several sky trips. And now, according to "Alex," they won't be happy until they possess a Moth of their own,"* However, there is no record that the Russells went so far as to purchase their own plane. The interest in aviation lasted for some years, as Fairbairn and Russell flew to Mildura and Broken Hill in June 1937, however, their plans to continue into the Northern Territory as far as Alice Springs and Tennant Creek had to be abandoned due to engine trouble, and the pair returned by way of Adelaide. In February 1939, it was announced that Jim Fairbairn *"who is a former war pilot, and has owned and flown aeroplanes for several years, has planned another long flight for next winter. Accompanied by Major Alex. Russell, he will fly his De Havilland Dragonfly, "The Spirit of Flinders," through Central Australia, Darwin, to Bali, Java and Singapore, to investigate trade, defence, and air mail facilities."* However, it appears that due to Fairbairn's other commitments, this flight with Russell never took place.

Alex Russell the fisherman (above) and Jim Fairbairn the pilot and politician (right)

Some of Alex's other passions included crossword puzzles, especially those from 'The Times', as well as wireless radio and mechanical tinkering. He made his own radio in the 1920s and had a special room for it added to his house 'Raith' at Sandringham. Philip recalled that his father built a ramp into the house at 'Mawallok' so that he could roll the lawnmower up onto the workbench where he was constantly tinkering with it. He had a lathe too, possibly the same one his father had at 'Mawallok' and Philip recalled that *"anything that broke down, he fixed it. He was very, very mechanical."* Alethea Russell noted that at Cambridge her father Osborne Fairbairn, 'Bo' Fairbairn and Alex Russell all *"used to have motorbikes and they had 5 minutes to pull each other's motorbikes to pieces and then they swapped....they had to put yours back together, and the one that was last paid for lunch."*

Jim Fairbairn's de Havilland Moth VH-UMU (top) in which he took Alex Russell on a number of flights during the 1930s. Fairbairn later updated to a new de Havilland Dragonfly that he purchased in England and flew back to Australia. Fairbairn is pictured standing with his new plane (above).

Showing his artistic side, Alex made a number of table mats for a garden fete held at 'Mawallok' in November 1952, with the 'Argus' noting that he had *"produced vast quantities of table mats, with attractive prints as decorations,"* and had been *"a one-man working bee"* leading up to the fete.

One story that Philip related about his father concerned his driving, of a car and not a golf ball. When Alex was pulled over by the police one evening for running a red light, in order to get off, Alex told the policeman that he had the Governors of Western Australia and South Australia in the back seat, to which the policeman replied *"I suppose you have the Governor of Victoria in the front?"* Alex's response was blithely, *"As a matter of fact I do."*

Russell certainly did have his share of interesting motor-car incidents over the years. In June 1930 he was charged with driving his car at a *"speed dangerous to the public"* on St Kilda Road at Prahran and he and his solicitor mounted a defence to the charge that Russell's speed on that road of 45 miles per hour was not dangerous as there was little traffic. The Clerk of Courts threw a spanner into the works by producing a map of Prahran that showed that no part of St Kilda Road was within the Municipality of Prahran and so the case was dismissed.

In August 1934, his car was damaged when he tried to avoid colliding with a stray cow on the Western Highway when returning to 'Mawallok' from Ballarat. While Russell was said to be uninjured, the report neglected to mention the fate of the cow. In 1936, Russell was fined £2 on a charge of having overtaken three cars on the wrong side of the Geelong to Melbourne road. The police stated that Russell passed three cars travelling in the same direction on their left. Russell's solicitor told the court that the traffic was congested *"and Russell had an opportunity to get clear by passing other cars on the wrong side. He felt that by doing so he had relieved the congestion"*, at least for himself.

Russell was also an active 'old boy' of Geelong Grammar School and was on the OGG Committee for a number of years. He served as president in 1936.

Alex's health deteriorated through the late 1950s and he formally relinquished the running of 'Mawallok' to his son Phillip who had been effectively the property manager since the end of World War II. Alex and Jess then moved back to Melbourne to live. Shortly before his death he was admitted to the Heidelberg Repatriation General Hospital as Jess could no longer cope with nursing him at their South Yarra flat in Walsh Street.

Unfortunately, their daughter Virginia was seriously ill in Adelaide at the same time and likely to die soon from Muscular Dystrophy. Jess was visiting Alex each day at the hospital and she was eventually persuaded to go over to Adelaide to see her daughter, but sadly, while she was visiting Virginia, Alex passed away. Virginia succumbed a few months after her father, which must have been a wrenching time for Jess, losing her husband and daughter so close together.

Alex Russell died on 22 November 1961, aged 69, following a series of strokes spread over some years, with the first one coming in 1950. The cause of death on his death certificate was listed as *"hypertensive cerebrovascular disease."* He was cremated at the Springvale Crematorium after a private family service at the Toorak Presbyterian Church at 10.20am on 24 November, a private man to the end. Russell's estate was later sworn for probate at £223,068. Jess lived until she was 88, passing away in 1983.

A young Alex Russell (above)

The Toorak Presbyterian Church (left) where Alex Russell's private family funeral service was held on 24 November 1961

Alex Russell's Legacy

From an international perspective, Russell may not have gained the recognition that he deserved as a golf course architect. By all accounts, playing the role of understudy to Dr Alister MacKenzie did not bother him. Curiously, MacKenzie failed to mention Alex Russell at all in his book "The Spirit of St Andrews," but neither does he mention the Royal Melbourne Golf Club, nor any of his many other contributions to golf courses around Australia, apart from commenting that there was magnificent sand dune country in Adelaide and Sydney and that the Melbourne courses reminded him of Sunningdale. Nevertheless, it is fair to postulate that if it were not for MacKenzie's visit to Australia in 1926, Russell may never have gained any acclaim as a golf course architect. Prior to this he was famed for his ability with club and ball, not with pencil and sketchpad.

Without doubt, Alex Russell was a champion golfer, but champions rarely leave anything but a transitory legacy to their sport. In Russell's case, that legacy is classical golf course architecture, influenced by the master, Dr MacKenzie, which will be enduring and enjoyed by generations of golfers to come.

Victorian golf writer Jack Dillon knew Alex Russell well and penned these words about the man in 1954:

> *"Few have contributed as much to Australian golf as Alex Russell. He was our **ONLY** fully qualified links architect. He had the clearest, most incisive, and most informed mind I have encountered in golf. He approached all problems of turf and ground as a scientist. The East Course of RMGC is a monument to his ability. His organisation of the 1939 Australian Championship meeting set an all-time efficiency standard for such an occasion."*

Alex Russell was a man who was much more than a career golf course architect. He gave great service to his country in times of war, fine service to the community by his involvement on numerous committees and charities, and wonderful service to the game of golf in Australia through the many golf courses he designed and as an administrator of the game.

Alex Russell

1892 - 1961

ACKNOWLEDGEMENTS

Firstly the authors would like to express our gratitude to the late Paul Rak, former CEO of the Royal Melbourne Golf Club. It was his support and encouragement to collect all the articles and essays by both authors, both short and long, as well as their presentations on the subject of Alex Russell, into book form. This became the final impulse to start on the book they had both hoped to write one day. While a great deal of the information in this book was obtained from publicly accessible sources, obviously much could only be acquired with considerable assistance from others. Naturally, this book could not have been written without detailed information, photographs and other memorabilia that were generously provided by members of the Russell family: Philip Russell (Alex's son), Robina Westenra (Alex's daughter), Alethea Russell (Philip's wife), Caroline Russell and William Keddell (grandchildren). Further help came from Michael Collins-Persse and Geoffrey Laurenson providing details of Alex's time at Geelong Grammar School, Mrs Elaine Mundill for assistance on his schooling at Trinity College, Glenalmond, and Liam Tarry of the 'London Gazette' for exact details of Alex Russell's gazetted awards. Mark Guiniven from Paraparaumu Beach undertook a good deal of research into Alex Russell's life in the early stages of the project. Unfortunately, he was unable to continue that work, but we are grateful for the invaluable contribution Mark was able to make.

Considerable help was provided by the historians at a number of Russell designed golf clubs: Leo Barber at Paraparaumu Beach, Alex Cleave at Lake Karrinyup, Susan Harrison and Moira Drew at Royal Melbourne, with Moira also helping with information relating to Alex Russell's work with the Australian Red Cross, Graeme McEachran at Cottesloe, Ian Rowell at Riversdale, Peter Swan, Tony Hirst and Tim Groves at Yarra Yarra, and Syd Thomson at Portsea. Brendan Moloney provided much of the story about Russell's role at Peninsula Golf Club, while members of the Phillip Island and District Historical Society kindly gave of their time, taking the authors to the site where the Summerland course had existed and providing much helpful information, including an original plan of the course drawn by Russell in 1929.

Cecily Close provided details about Alex Russell's time at the Melbourne Club and his excellence in billiards there. Leon Rowbell (Leon Old Golf Collection) provided images and information about Russell from his extensive personal archives, while John Lovell assisted with research into Russell's life in the early days of this project. The National Library of Australia's Trove website provided access to a searchable database of old newspapers and journals, without which this book would be far less complete. Special thanks are due to Helen Coutts-Green for her contributions and eagle-eyed proof-reading of the manuscript.

Our publisher, Graeme Ryan of Ryan Publishing, has our thanks for his support and editing skills, and for providing the means by which it has been possible to bring this project to reality. The authors wish to thank The Royal Melbourne Golf Club, Riversdale Golf Club, Yarra Yarra Golf Club, Lake Karrinyup Country Club and Paraparaumu Beach Golf Club for their financial support. This book would not have been possible without it. And finally, the work of the late Hedley Ham provided the core of research and our promise to him to one day publish this book has been a constant driver in this achievement.

Hedley Ham

PICTURE CREDITS

Australian War Memorial
27 (top), 35, 37 (main), 222 (top & middle)

British Newspaper Archive
65 (bottom), 66 (left), 191, 200 (right), 225

Cottesloe Golf Club
175,

Neil Crafter
vii, 5, 33, 40 (left), 58, 60, 62, 71, 74, 87, 91 (top), 104, 105, 113, 114, 127, 128 (right), 171, 198 (left), 236

Geelong Grammar School Archives
19 (top), 20, 21, 229

Glenalmond College
18 (middle)

John Green
83, 93, 129 (main), 188, 189, 192, 193, 194 (right), 195 (main), 197

Mark Guiniven
144

David Ham
250

Bruce Howard
234

Imperial War Museum
24, 30

Lake Karrinyup Country Club
65 (top), 131, 134, 135, 136, 137, 141, 142 (right, left), 143, 174, 176 (left), 198 (right)

Leon Old Golf Collection
42 (top), 53 (bottom), 55 (right), 125, 161

National Archives of Australia
181, 182, 183

National Library of Australia – Trove Newspaper Archive
48 (left), 53 (top), 75, 80 (inset), 109 (bottom), 111 (bottom left), 123 (bottom), 130, 132, 133, 139, 160 (bottom), 169, 170 (top left), 172 (top), 173, 176 (right), 203, 205 (right), 206, 207 (top left), 209 (bottom), 213, 214 (right), 215 (bottom right), 217 (bottom left & right), 221, 232 (bottom), 233 (left & top right), 243

Paraparaumu Beach Golf Club
145, 146 (bottom), 148, 149, 150, 151, 152, 154, 186, 200 (bottom), 201

Phillip Island & District Historical Society
117, 118, 120 (top), 121, 122, 123 (top), 124, 126

Portsea Golf Club
166, 167, 168

Riversdale Golf Club
110

Royal Adelaide Golf Club
184

The Royal Melbourne Golf Club
42 (bottom), 45 (bottom), 57 (top), 59, 63, 66 (right), 68, 69, 70, 72, 77, 78, 79 (bottom), 80 (main), 84, 86, 87 (inset), 88, 89, 90 (right), 91 (main & bottom), 92, 156, 170 (right & bottom), 187, 190 (top), 195 (inset)

Caroline Russell
34

Philip Russell
i, viii, ix, 4, 6, 7 (top), 8, 9, 10, 11, 12, 16 (top), 17 (bottom), 18 (bottom), 19

(bottom), 22 (top), 23, 25, 27, 28, 29, 32, 37 (inset), 38, 43 (left), 44, 47, 49, 50, 51, 54, 55 (left), 56, 64, 66 (middle), 73, 81, 82, 147 (top), 165, 208, 209 (top), 178 (right), 210, 211, 212, 214 (left), 216 (bottom), 218, 219 (right), 220, 226 (top), 227 (main), 230 (top & bottom left), 231 (top right), 238, 239 (bottom), 240, 244, 245 (left), 246 (right), 247 (main), 249, 253

Sandringham Historical Society
57 (right)

State Library of New South Wales
46 (left), 102 (bottom), 179 (left)

State Library of Victoria
1, 3, 7 (bottom), 13, 14, 40 (right), 41, 42 (middle), 43 (right), 45, 46 (right), 52, 57 (left), 67 (right), 79 (top), 90 (left), 94, 95, 97, 106 (left), 108, 11 (top), 112, 115, 116, 119, 120 (left), 128 (left), 129 (top), 142 (middle), 158, 159, 160 (top), 172 (bottom), 177, 185, 202, 204, 207 (right), 211 (bottom left), 215 (main), 226 (bottom), 227, 228 (top), 230 (bottom right), 231, 237, 239 (top), 242, 247 (left), 257

Robina Westenra
iv, 164, 217 (top left), 223 (top), 224, 228 (bottom), 232 (top), 233 (bottom right)

Yarra Yarra Golf Club
96, 99, 101, 102 (top), 103, 106 (right), 107, 109 (top), 190 (main)

BIBLIOGRAPHY

Allen, Richard and **Johnson**, Joseph. *The Royal Melbourne Golf Club: 125 Years 1891-2016*. Melbourne: The Royal Melbourne Golf Club, 2016.

Arnold, John and **Johnson**, Joseph. *Riversdale Golf Club 1892-1992: A Centenary History*. Melbourne: Riversdale Golf Club, 1992.

Barker, Keith. *Lake Karrinyup – As it was in the Beginning*. Perth: Barker, 1969

Barnaby, J.W. *A History of Royal Melbourne*. Melbourne: The Royal Melbourne Golf Club in Association with the Macmillan Company of Australia, 1972.

Bates, Weston. *Heads You Win: A History of the Barwon Heads Golf Club*. Barwon Heads: Barwon Heads Golf Club, 2007.

Brown, P. L. (editor). *The Narrative of George Russell of Golf Hill with Russelliana and Selected Papers*. London: Oxford University Press, 1935.

Colt, H.S. and **Alison**, C.H. *Some Essays on Golf-Course Architecture*. London: Country Life, 1920.

Cornish, Geoffrey and Whitten, Ronald. *The Golf Course*. Sydney: William Collins Pty. Ltd., 1981.

Cornish, Geoffrey and Whitten, Ronald. *The Architects of Golf*. New York: Harper Collins Publishers, 1993.

Crafter, Neil and **Green**, John. *MacKenzie's Plan for Royal Melbourne: Discovery of the Doctor's own Sketch Plan*. Golf Architecture magazine, Issue 9. Adelaide: The Society of Australian Golf Course Architects, 2006.

Crafter, Neil. *The Good Doctor's Prescriptions: Dr MacKenzie's Australian Writings from 1926*. Golf Architecture magazine, Issue 8. Adelaide: The Society of Australian Golf Course Architects, 2005.

Crockford, Claude. *The Complete Golf Course Turf and Design*. Melbourne: Thomson Wolveridge & Associates, 1993.

Cudmore, Michael. *The Royal Adelaide Golf Club 1892-1992*. Adelaide: The Royal Adelaide Golf Club, 1992

Doak, Tom; **Scott**, James; **Haddock**, Ray. *The Life and Work of Dr Alister MacKenzie*. Chelsea, Michigan: Sleeping Bear Press, 2001.

Gatliff, Ian. *Pastures to Pars: A View Over 75 Years – The History of The Croydon Golf Club*. Croydon: Croydon Golf Club, 2000.

Green, John. *MacKenzie, Russell and Morcom: The West Course at Royal Melbourne*. Golf Architecture magazine, Issue 7. Adelaide: The Society of Australian Golf Course Architects, 2004.

Green, John. *The Royal Melbourne Golf Club: History of the Courses*. Glen Waverly, Victoria. Full Swing Golf Publications, 2011.

Hawtree, Fred. *Colt & Co.; Golf Course Architects*. Oxford: Cambuc Archive, 1991.

Hawtree, Martin. *Strategic Review of the Royal Melbourne Golf Courses*. Woodstock, England. Hawtree Ltd. 2003 (unpublished review for The Royal Melbourne Golf Club.)

Hirst, Anthony and **Crafter**, Neil. *Great Australian Golf Course Architects: Alex Russell*. Golf Architecture magazine, Issue 6. Adelaide: The Society of Australian Golf Course Architects, 2003

Hornabrook, John. *Golden Years of New Zealand Golf*. Christchurch: Whitcombe & Tombs, 1967.

Hunter, Robert. *The Links*. New York, London: Charles Scribner's Sons, 1926.

Hurdzan, C.B. *A History of The Keysborough Golf Club (Originally Albert Park Golf Club) 1899-1990*. Melbourne: Keysborough Golf Inc., 1991.

Innes, David. *The Story of Golf in New South Wales 1851-1987*. Sydney: New South Wales Golf Association, 1988.

Johnson, Joseph. *The Royal Melbourne Golf Club. A Centenary History*. Melbourne: The Royal Melbourne Golf Club, 1998.

Johnson, Joseph. *From Eyrie to Eagles. The History of the Yarra Yarra Golf Club*. Melbourne: The Yarra Yarra Golf Club, 1998.

Long, Gordon. *The History of the Geelong Golf Club 1992-1992, 100th Anniversary*. Geelong: Geelong Golf Club, 1992.

MacKenzie, Alister. *The Spirit of St Andrews.* Chelsea, Michigan: Sleeping Bear Press, 1995.

MacKenzie, Alister. *Golf Course Architecture*. London: Simpkin, Marshall, Hamilton, Kent & Co., 1920.

McNicoll, Ronald. *Number 36 Collins Street: Melbourne Club 1838-1988.* Sydney: Allen & Unwin, 1988.

Ramsay, Tom. *Twenty-five Great Australian Golf Courses and How to Play Them.* Sydney: Rigby Publishing Limited, 1981.

Roberts, Phil. *Golf at the Arch: A Centenary History of The Ballarat Golf Club 1895-1995*. Ballarat: Ballarat Golf Club Inc., 1995.

Scarth, John. *A Round Forever*. Perth: J. Scarth, 2000.

Thomson, Syd; **Powell**, Pauline; **Crockett**, Cheryl. *Within a Bull's Roar – Portsea Golf Club The First 75 Years.* Portsea: Portsea Golf Club, 2001.

Wallace, Jim. *Golf at the Links; Paraparaumu Beach Golf Club Inc.* Paraparaumu, N.Z.: Paraparaumu Beach Golf Club Jubilee Committee, 1999.

White, Michael. *Lake Karrinyup Country Club – 1928-1988*. Sydney: Lester-Townsend Publishing Pty Ltd, 1988.

Caricatures by Wells depicting the main protagonists in the 1924 Australian Open. Unfortunately Wells had the scores wrong, substituting the three round scores instead of the final 72-hole scores.

INDEX

Milton Keynes UK
Ingram Content Group UK Ltd.
UKHW052143091224
452112UK00005B/23